Data Structures
and
Program Design

PRENTICE-HALL SOFTWARE SERIES
Brian W. Kernighan, adviser

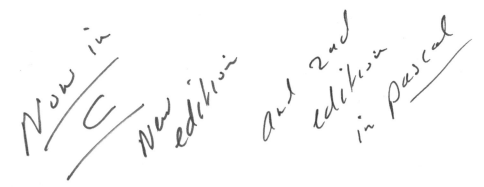

Data Structures and Program Design

ROBERT L. KRUSE

St. Mary's University
Halifax, Nova Scotia

PRENTICE-HALL, INC., ENGLEWOOD CLIFFS, NEW JERSEY 07632

Library of Congress Cataloging in Publication Data

Kruse, Robert Leroy, (date)
   Data structures and program design.

   (Prentice-Hall software series)
   Includes bibliographical references and index.
   1. Electronic digital computers—Programming.
2. Data structures (Computer science) 3. PASCAL
(Computer program language) I. Title. II. Series.
QA76.6.K77 1983   001.64'2   83-13839
ISBN 0-13-196253-1

Editorial/production supervision: *Lynn Frankel*
Cover design: *Photo Plus Art (Celine A. Brandes)*
Manufacturing buyer: *Gordon Osbourne*
Art production: *Toni Sterling*

© 1984 by Prentice-Hall, Inc., Englewood Cliffs, New Jersey 07632

Printed in the United States of America

10 9 8 7 6 5 4 3

ISBN 0-13-196253-1

Prentice-Hall International, Inc., *London*
Prentice-Hall of Australia Pty. Ltd., *Sydney*
Editora Prentice-Hall do Brasil, Ltda., *Rio de Janeiro*
Prentice-Hall of Canada, Inc., *Toronto*
Prentice Hall of India Pte. Ltd., *New Delhi*
Prentice Hall of Japan, Inc., *Tokyo*
Prentice Hall of Southeast Asia Pte. Ltd., *Singapore*
Whitehall Books Ltd., *Wellington, New Zealand*

for my mother
Esther Kruse

Contents

Preface

An apprentice carpenter may want only a hammer and a saw, but a master craftsman employs many precision tools. Computer programming likewise requires sophisticated tools to cope with the complexity of real applications, and only practice with these tools will build skill in their use. This book treats structured problem-solving, elementary data structures, and the comparative study of algorithms as fundamental tools of program design. Several case studies of substantial size are worked out in detail, to show how all the tools are used together to build complete programs.

Many of the algorithms and data structures studied here possess an intrinsic elegance, a simplicity that cloaks the range and power of their applicability. Before long the student discovers that vast improvements can be made over the naive methods usually used in introductory courses. And yet this elegance of method is tempered with uncertainty. The student soon finds that it can be far from obvious which of several approaches will prove best in particular applications. Hence comes an early opportunity to introduce truly difficult problems of both intrinsic interest and practical importance, and to exhibit the applicability of combinatorial mathematics to algorithm analysis.

The goal of programming is the construction of complete, functioning programs. Many students, however, find difficulty in translating abstract ideas into practice. This book, therefore, takes special care in the formulation of ideas into algorithms, and in the refinement of algorithms into concrete programs which can be applied to practical problems. The selection of data structures, similarly, is carefully separated from the selection of methods for their representation in storage.

I believe in progressing from the concrete to the abstract, in the careful development of motivating examples, followed by the presentation of ideas in a more general form. At an early stage of their careers most students need reinforcement from seeing the immediate application of the ideas that they study, and require the practice of writing and running programs which illustrate each important concept that they learn. The exercises, therefore, constitute an indispensable part of this book. Many of these are immediate applications of the topic under study, often requesting that programs be written and run, so that algorithms may be tested and compared. Some are larger projects, and a few are suitable for use by a group of several students working together.

Synopsis.

By working through the first large project (Conway's game of Life), Chapter 1 expounds principles of top-down refinement, program design, review and testing, principles that the student will see demonstrated and is expected to follow throughout the sequel. Review of the problem then leads to a second algorithm for its solution, an algorithm that shows why care must be taken in the choice of data structures, and illustrates a substantial trade-off between space and time requirements. This project also provides an opportunity for the student to review the syntax of Pascal, the programming language used throughout the book.

Chapter 2 begins the study of data structures with stacks, queues, and other lists, in both contiguous and linked representations. Pascal provides excellent facilities to ease the problems of implementing data structures within a program, and Pascal procedures are used constantly to illustrate the processing of each new structure. A major goal of Chapter 2 is that the student should be able to draw a clear distinction between an abstract data structure and the ways in which it can be represented concretely, so that in designing programs he can choose both the data structures and their representations more wisely.*

Chapter 3, on information retrieval, discusses selected algorithms for searching, table lookup, and hash-table access. Chapter 4 continues with the study of several sorting methods. The algorithms in these two chapters are chosen to illustrate the interplay among data structures, their representation in storage, and the methods required for their use. The text highlights the crucial choices to be made regarding best use of space, time, and programming effort.

These choices require that we find analytical methods to assess algorithms, and producing such analyses is a battle for which combinatorial mathematics must provide the arsenal. At an elementary level we can expect the student neither to be well armed nor to possess the mathematical maturity needed to hone his skills to perfection. My goal, therefore, is only to help the student recognize the importance of such skills, and glad for later chances to study mathematics. Appendix A presents some necessary mathematics. Most of the topics in the appendix will be familiar to the well-prepared student, but are included to help with common deficiencies. The final two sections of Appendix A, on Fibonacci and Catalan numbers, are more advanced, are not needed for any vital purpose in the text, but are included to encourage combinatorial interest in the more mathematically inclined.

Binary trees are surely among the most elegant of data structures. Their study,

* The pronouns "he", "his" and "him" are used to include both sexes without prejudice.

which begins in Chapter 5, ties together concepts from lists, searching and sorting. At the same time, binary trees provide a natural example of recursively defined data structures, and therewith afford an excellent opportunity for the student to become more comfortable with recursive algorithms.

Chapter 9 completes the study of data structures by collecting several further applications of trees as data structures. The chapter begins by continuing the study of balanced binary search trees begun in Chapter 5, culminating in the development of algorithms for processing AVL trees. The second section applies a contiguous representation of binary trees to the development of heapsort and the study of priority queues. The second half of the chapter is devoted to multiway trees. Lexicographic trees lead to algorithms for processing tries; and B-trees are studied as an important class of multiway search trees. The presentations of the four major topics of Chapter 9 are independent from each other, and any of these sections may be studied at any time after the completion of Chapter 5.

Chapters 6 and 8 are large case studies, worked out in detail. Chapter 6 develops a program to produce a word list or index of a text, thereby illustrating the top-down design and refinement of data structures together with algorithms, and demonstrating non-trivial applications of hash tables and of binary search trees. The resulting program (nearly 1000 lines in Pascal) also illustrates techniques for processing of textual information and files.

The case study in Chapter 8 examines the Polish notation in considerable detail, exploring the interplay of recursion, trees and stacks as vehicles for problem solving and algorithm development. Some of the questions addressed can serve as an informal introduction to compiler design. Again, the algorithms are fully developed within a functioning Pascal program. This program accepts as input an expression in ordinary (infix) form, translates the expression into postfix form, and evaluates the expression for specified values of the variable(s).

Recursion is a powerful tool, but one that is often misunderstood and sometimes used improperly. Some textbooks treat it as an afterthought, applying it only to trivial examples and apologizing for its alleged expense. Others give little regard to its pitfalls. I have therefore essayed to provide as balanced a treatment as possible. Whenever recursion is the natural approach it is used without hesitation. When non-recursive methods are equally transparent, they are preferred. Chapter 7 (which is sufficiently independent to be studied earlier if desired) studies recursion in some depth. It includes examples illustrating a broad range of applications, an exposition of the implementation of recursion, and guidelines for deciding whether recursion is or is not an appropriate method to follow.

Removal of recursion is a topic that, I hope, the programmer may soon no longer need to study. But at present much important work must be done in contexts (like FORTRAN or COBOL) disallowing recursion. Methods for manual recursion removal are therefore required, and are collected for reference as Appendix B. Some instructors will wish to include the study of threaded binary trees with Chapter 5; this section is therefore written so that it can be read independently of the remainder of

Appendix B.

Appendix C, finally, includes the standard diagrams and tables describing Pascal syntax, as well as further information to help with programming problems.

Course Structure.

The prerequisite for this book is a first course in programming, with experience using the elementary features of Pascal. Chapter 1 includes a brief discussion of records, and Chapter 2 a thorough study of pointer types, in case students have not previously met these topics. Several aspects of file processing are covered in Chapter 6. A good knowledge of high school mathematics will suffice for almost all the algorithm analyses, but further (perhaps concurrent) preparation in discrete mathematics will prove valuable.

This book includes all the topics of Course CS2 (*Computer Programming II*) from ACM *Curriculum '78*, with additional emphasis on data structures, so that it is also suitable for a version of Course CS7 (*Data Structures and Algorithm Analysis*) that emphasizes program design, with implementations and applications of data structures.

This book also covers most of the topics specified for Course IS2 (*Program, Data, and File Structures*) from the ACM recommendations for information systems curricula [*Communications of the ACM* 25 (1982), 781–805]. With additional content on data structures (and less emphasis on files), the book shares the objectives of Course IS2 [*op. cit.,* p. 793]:

1. To continue the development of discipline in program design, in style and expression, and in debugging and testing, especially for larger programs.
2. To introduce algorithmic analysis.
3. To introduce basic aspects of string processing, recursion, and simple data structures.
4. To introduce concepts and techniques of structuring data on bulk storage devices.
5. To provide experience in the use of bulk storage devices.
6. To provide the foundation for applications of data structures and file processing techniques.
7. To provide the technical foundation for structured systems design.

A one-term course based on Course CS2 from *Curriculum '78* should include most of Chapters 1–4, omitting the more detailed algorithm analyses. Additional topics may be chosen from Chapter 5 (binary trees), Chapter 7 (recursion), or the large case studies (Chapters 6 and 8), according to the interests of students and instructor.

An elementary data-structures course should consider Chapter 1 briefly (to look at the questions of data-structuring and time-space tradeoffs), emphasize Chapters 2, 3, 5, and 9, and select other topics as time permits.

A more advanced course in Data Structures and Algorithm Analysis (ACM course CS7) should begin with a brief review of Chapters 1–4, placing special emphasis on the analysis of algorithms and criteria for their selection under various conditions. The remaining chapters will then provide a solid core of material on data structures, algorithm design, and applications.

A two-term course can cover almost all the contents of this book, thereby attaining a satisfying integration of many of the topics from both of ACM courses CS2 and CS7. Students need time and practice to understand general methods. By combining the study of various data structures and algorithms with their implementation in projects of realistic size, an integrated course can build a solid foundation on which later, more theoretical courses can be built. Even if it is not covered in its entirety, this book will provide enough depth to enable interested students to continue using it as a reference in later work. It is important in any case to assign major programming projects, and to allow adequate time for completion of these projects.

Acknowledgments.

The writing, rewriting, and production of this book have been an arduous task, but one that has been made easier by the help of other people. My mother, first of all, gave me the patient understanding and love without which the work could not have been completed. Family and friends have spoken words of encouragement; colleagues have given valuable suggestions and advice; and students have shown the enthusiasm and joy of discovery that make the effort worthwhile.

Several reviewers have helped, by questions and comments, to clarify the aims and exposition of the book. BRIAN W. KERNIGHAN was particularly helpful in reading several versions of the manuscript, and providing many careful, detailed comments.

Preliminary versions of the manuscript have been used by several classes, with different levels of preparation, at St. Mary's University, the University of Alberta, and (by T. B. MCLEAN and his students) at Georgia Southern College. Student reaction has led to many improvements in the exposition. H. O'CONNELL and B. LEE were especially helpful in pointing out misprints and obscurities.

Computer facilities for the production of this book have been provided by St. Mary's University, the University of Alberta, and Dalhousie University. The Computing Science Department at Alberta extended generous hospitality to me during a sabbatical leave in 1982.

The programs in this book have been extracted from the text and tested by computer, many under several different compilers on different systems. The book was typeset at the University of Alberta, as an experiment in combining an automated typesetting system with fine tuning under manual control.

ROBERT L. KRUSE

Data Structures
and
Program Design

Chapter 1

Programming Principles

This chapter summarizes important principles of good pro-
gramming, especially as applied to large projects, and illustrates
methods for discovering effective algorithms. In the process we
exhibit questions in program design that we shall address in later
chapters, and review many of the special features of the language
Pascal by using them to write programs.

1.1 Introduction.

The greatest difficulties of writing large computer programs are not in deciding what the goals of the program should be, nor even in finding methods that can be used to reach these goals. The president of a business might say, "Let's get a computer to keep track of all our inventory information, accounting records, and personnel files, and let it tell us when inventories need to be re-ordered, when budget lines are overspent, and let it handle the payroll." With enough time and effort a staff of systems analysts and programmers might be able to determine how various staff members are now doing these tasks, and write programs to do the work in the same way.

This approach, however, is almost certain to be a disastrous failure. While inter-viewing employees, the systems analysts will find some tasks that can be put on the computer easily, and will proceed to do so. Then, as they move other work to the computer, they will find that it depends on the first tasks, but the output from these, unfortunately, is not quite in the proper form. Hence they need more programming to convert the data from the form given for one task, to the form needed for another. The programming project begins to resemble a patchwork quilt. Some of the pieces are stronger, some weaker. Some of the pieces are carefully sewn onto the adjacent ones, some barely tacked together. If the programmers are lucky, their creation may hold together well enough to do most of the routine work most of the time. But if any change must be made, it will have unpredictable consequences throughout the system. Later, a new request will come along, or an unexpected problem, perhaps even an emergency, and the programmers' efforts will prove as effective as using a patchwork quilt as a safety net for people jumping from a tall building.

The main purpose of this book is to describe programming methods and tools that will prove effective for projects of realistic size, programs much larger than those ordinarily used to illustrate features of elementary programming. Since a piecemeal approach to large problems is doomed to fail, we must first of all adopt a consistent, unified, and logical approach, and must be careful to observe important principles of program design, principles that are sometimes ignored in writing small programs, but whose neglect will prove disastrous for large projects.

The first major hurdle in attacking a large problem is deciding exactly what the problem is. It is necessary to translate vague goals, contradictory requests, and perhaps unstated desires into a precisely formulated project which can be programmed. And the methods or divisions of work which people have previously used are not necessarily the best for use in a machine. Hence our approach must be to determine overall goals, but precise ones, and then slowly divide the work into smaller problems until they become of manageable size.

The maxim that many programmers observe, "First make your program work, then make it pretty," may be effective for small programs, but not for large ones. Each part of a large program must be well organized, clearly written, and thoroughly understood, or else its structure will have been forgotten, and it can no longer be tied to the other parts of the project at some much later time, perhaps by another programmer. Hence we do not separate style from other parts of program design, but from the beginning we must be careful to form good habits.

Even with very large projects, difficulties usually arise not from inability to find a solution, but rather that there can be so many different methods and algorithms that might work that it can be hard to decide which is best, which may lead to programming difficulties, or which may be hopelessly inefficient. The greatest room for variability in algorithm design is generally in the way in which the data of the program are stored:

▶ how they are arranged in relation to each other,

▶ which data are kept in memory,

▶ which are calculated when needed,

▶ which are kept in files, and how the files are arranged.

A second goal of this book, therefore, is to present several elegant, yet fundamentally simple ideas for the organization of data, and several powerful algorithms for important tasks within data processing, such as sorting and searching.

When there are several different ways to organize data and devise algorithms, then it becomes important to develop criteria to recommend a choice. Hence we devote attention to analyzing the behavior of algorithms under various conditions.

The difficulty of debugging a program goes up much faster than its size. That is, if one program is twice the size of another, then it will likely not take twice as long to debug, but perhaps four times as long. Many very large programs (such as operating systems) are put into use still containing bugs that the programmers have despaired of finding, because the difficulties seem insurmountable. Sometimes projects that have consumed years of effort must be discarded because it is impossible to discover why they will not work. If we do not wish such a fate for our projects, then we must use methods that will

> ▶ reduce the number of bugs, making it easier to spot those that remain,

> ▶ enable us to verify in advance that our algorithms are correct, and

> ▶ provide us with ways to test our programs so that we can be reasonably confident that they will not misbehave.

Development of such methods is another of our goals, but one that cannot yet be fully within our grasp.

Informal surveys show that, once a large and important program is fully debugged and in use, then only about half of the programming effort that will be invested altogether in the project will have been completed. *Maintenance* of programs, that is, modifications needed to meet new requests and new operating environments, takes, on average, about half of the programming investment. For this reason, it is essential that a large project be written to make it as easy to understand and modify as possible.

The programming language Pascal has several features that make it the most appropriate choice to express the algorithms we shall develop. Pascal has been carefully designed to facilitate the discipline of writing carefully structured programs, with requirements implementing principles of program design. It contains relatively few features, in comparison with most high-level languages, so that it can be mastered quickly, and yet it contains powerful features for handling data which ease the translation from general algorithms to specific programs.

Several sections of this chapter mention some features of Pascal informally as they appear while we write programs. For the precise details of Pascal grammar, consult Appendix C.

1.2 The Game of Life.

If I may take the liberty to abuse an old proverb,

One concrete problem is worth a thousand unapplied abstractions.

Throughout this chapter we shall concentrate on one case study which, while not large by realistic standards, illustrates both the methods of program design and the pitfalls that we should learn to avoid. Sometimes the example motivates general principles; sometimes the general discussion comes first; always it is with the view of discovering general methods that will prove their value in a range of practical applications. In later chapters we shall employ similar methods for much larger projects.

The example we shall use is the game called *Life,* which was introduced by the British mathematician J. H. CONWAY in 1970.

1.2.1 Rules for the game of Life.

The setup of the game (which is really a simulation, not a game with players) is that of an unbounded rectangular grid in which each cell can either be occupied by an organism or not. Which cells are alive changes from generation to generation according to the number of neighboring cells which are alive, as follows:

1. The neighbors of a given cell are the eight cells that touch it vertically, horizontally, or diagonally.

2. If a cell is alive but either has no neighboring cells alive or only one alive, then in the next generation the cell dies of loneliness.

3. If a cell is alive and has four or more neighboring cells also alive, then in the next generation the cell dies of overcrowding.

4. A living cell with either two or three living neighbors remains alive in the next generation.

5. If a cell is dead, then in the next generation it will become alive if it has exactly three neighboring cells, no more or fewer, that are already alive. All other dead cells remain dead in the next generation.

6. All births and deaths take place at exactly the same time, so that dying cells can help to give birth to another, but cannot prevent the death of others by reducing overcrowding, nor can cells being born either preserve or kill cells living in the previous generation.

1.2.2 Examples.

As a first example, notice that the community

will die out in one generation. On the other hand, the community

will never change, and the two communities

                          and

continue to alternate from generation to generation.

It is a surprising fact that from very simple initial configurations quite complicated progressions of Life communities can develop over many generations, and it is generally not obvious what will happen as generations progress. Some very small initial configurations will grow into large communities; others will slowly die out; many will reach a state where they do not change, or where they go through a repeating pattern every few generations.

Not long after its invention MARTIN GARDNER discussed the Life game in his column in *Scientific American*, and, from that time on, it has fascinated many people, so that there has even been a quarterly journal devoted to related topics. It makes an ideal display for home microcomputers.

Our first goal, of course, is to write a program that will show how an initial community will change from generation to generation.

1.2.3 The solution.

At most a few minutes' thought will show that the solution to the Life problem is so simple that it would be a good exercise in a beginning programming class who had just learned about arrays. All we have to do is to set up a large rectangular array whose entries correspond to the Life cells, and will be marked with the status of the cell, either alive or dead. To determine what happens from one generation to the next, we then need only count the number of living neighbors of each cell and apply the rules. Since, however, we shall be using loops to go through the array, we must be careful not to violate rule 6 by allowing changes made earlier to affect the count of neighbors for cells studied later. The easiest way to avoid this pitfall is to set up a second array that will represent the community at the next generation, and, after it has been completely calculated, then make the generation change by copying it to the original array.

Next let us rewrite this method as the steps of an informal algorithm.

Initialize an array called **map** to contain the initial configuration of live cells.
Determine how many generations the game should run.
Repeat the following steps for the number of generations desired:
    For each cell in the array do the following:
        Count the number of live neighbors of the cell. If the count is 0, 1, 4, 5, 6, 7, or 8 then set the corresponding cell in another array called **newmap** to be dead; if the count is 3 then set the corresponding cell to be alive; and if the count is 2 then set the corresponding cell to be the same as the cell in array **map**.
    Copy the array **newmap** into the array **map**.
    Print the array **map** for the user.

1.2.4 Life: The main program.

The preceding outline of an algorithm for the game of Life translates into the following Pascal program.

```
program Life(input, output);
{Simulation of Conway's game of Life on a bounded grid.}
{Version 1.}
const
  maxrow = 50;                    {maximum number of rows allowed}
  maxcol = 80;                    {maximum number of columns allowed}
type
  row = 1..maxrow;
  col = 1..maxcol;
  status = (dead, alive);
  grid = array[row, col] of status;
var
  map,
  newmap: grid;
  i :  row;
  j :  col;
  generation,
  lastgeneration: integer;

{The declarations of the procedures and functions will go here.}

begin
  Initialize;
  generation := 0;
  WriteMap;
  for generation := 1 to lastgeneration do
  begin
    for i := 1 to maxrow do for j := 1 to maxcol do
      case NeighborCount(i,j) of
        0,1:       newmap[i,j] := dead;
        2:             newmap[i,j] := map[i,j];
        3:         newmap[i,j] := alive;
        4,5,6,7,8: newmap[i,j] := dead
      end;
    map := newmap;
    WriteMap
  end                                    {processing one generation}
end.
```

In this program we still must write the procedures Initialize and WriteMap, that will do the input and output, as well as the function NeighborCount(i,j), that will count the number of cells neighboring the one in i,j which are occupied in the array map. The action of the program Life is entirely straightforward. First we read in the initial situation to establish the first configuration of occupied cells and to determine the number of generations that the simulation will run. Then we commence a loop with one pass through for each generation. Within this loop we first have a nested pair of loops on i and j that will run over all entries in the array **map**. The body of these nested loops consists of the one special statement **case** $\cdots$ **end**, which is a multi-way selection statement. In the present application the function NeighborCount(i,j) will return one of the values 0, 1, $\cdots$, 8, and for each of these cases we can take a separate action, or, as in our program, some of the cases may lead to the same action. You should check that the action prescribed in each case corresponds correctly to the rules 2, 3, 4 and 5 of Section 1.2.1. Finally, after using the nested loops and case statement to set up the array **newmap**, the assignment statement

$$\text{map} := \text{newmap}$$

copies it into array **map**, and the procedure WriteMap will write out the result.

Exercises

1. Calculate what will happen to each of the following communities over the course of at least 10 generations.

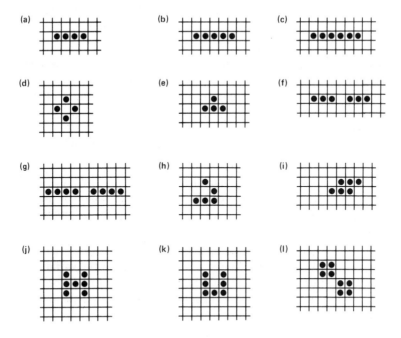

2. Look up and read all the *Scientific American* columns on the Life game.

1.3 Programming style.

Before we turn to writing the subprograms for the Life game, let us pause to consider several principles that we should be careful to employ in programming.

1.3.1 Names.

In the story of creation (Genesis 2:19), God brought all the animals to Adam to see what names he would give them. According to an old Jewish tradition, it was only when Adam had named an animal that it sprang to life. This story brings an important moral to computer programming: Even if data and algorithms exist before, it is only when they are given meaningful names that their places in the program can be properly recognized and appreciated, that they first acquire a life of their own.

For a program to work properly, it is of the utmost importance to know exactly what each variable represents, and to know exactly what each subprogram does. A section to explain the variables and subprograms should therefore always be included, and their names should be chosen with care so as to identify their meanings clearly and succinctly. Doing this is not always an easy task, but it is important enough to be singled out as our first programming precept:

Programming Precept

Always name your variables and subprograms
with the greatest care, and explain them thoroughly.

Pascal goes far toward enforcing this precept by requiring a section to declare variables, and allows an even more extensive use of names than most languages. Constants used different places can be given names, and so can different data types, a feature that allows the compiler to catch errors that might otherwise be difficult to spot.

The careful choice of names can go a long way in clarifying a program and in helping to avoid misprints and common errors. Some guidelines are as follows:

1. Give special care to the choice of names for procedures, functions, constants, and all global variables and types used in different parts of the program. These names should be meaningful and should suggest clearly the purpose of the subprogram, variable, and the like.

2. Keep the names simple for variables used only briefly and locally. A single letter is often a good choice for the variable controlling a **for** loop, but would be a poor choice for a procedure or for a variable used three or four times in widely separated parts of the program.

3. Use common prefixes or suffixes to associate names of the same general category. The files used in a program, for example, might be called

InputFile TransactionFile TotalFile OutFile RejectFile.

4. Avoid deliberate misspellings and meaningless suffixes to obtain different names. Of all the names

   > index   indx   ndex   indexx   index2   index3

   only one (the first) should be used. When you are tempted to introduce multiple names of this sort, take it as a sign that you should think harder and devise names which better describe the intended use.

5. Avoid choosing cute names whose meaning has little or nothing to do with the problem. The statements

   > **while** TV **in** hock **do** study;
   > **if not** sleepy **then** play **else** nap;

   may be funny but they are bad programming!

6. Avoid choosing names that are close to each other in spelling or otherwise easy to confuse.

7. Be careful in the use of the letter 'l' (small ell), 'O' (capital oh) and '0' (zero). Within words or numbers these usually can be recognized from the context, and cause no problem, but 'l' and 'O' should never be used alone as names. Consider the examples:

   > l := 1;   x := 1;   x := l;   x := O

1.3.2 Documentation and format.

Most students initially regard documentation as a chore that must be endured, after a program is finished, to ensure that the marker and instructor can read it, so that no credit will be lost for obscurity. The author of a small program indeed can keep all the details in his head, and so needs documentation only to explain the program to someone else. With large programs (and with small ones after some months have elapsed) it becomes impossible to remember how every detail relates to every other, and therefore to write large programs it is essential that appropriate documentation be prepared along with each small part of the program. A good habit is to prepare documentation as the program is being written, and an even better one, as we shall see later, is to prepare part of the documentation before starting to write the program.

Not all documentation is appropriate. Almost as common as programs with little documentation or only cryptic comments are programs with verbose documentation that adds little to understanding the program. Hence our second programming precept:

Programming Precept

Keep your documentation concise but descriptive.

The style of documentation, as with all writing styles, is highly personal, and many different styles can prove effective. There are, nonetheless, some commonly accepted guidelines that should be respected.

1. Place a prologue at the beginning of each subprogram including:
   - (a) Identification (programmer's name, date, version number);
   - (b) Statement of the purpose of the subprogram and method used;
   - (c) What changes the subprogram makes and what data it uses;
   - (d) Reference to further documentation external to the program.

2. When each variable, constant, or type is declared, explain what it is and how it is used. Better still, make this information evident from the name.

3. Introduce each significant section (paragraph) of the program with a comment stating briefly its purpose or action.

4. Indicate the end of each significant section if it is not otherwise obvious.

5. Avoid comments that parrot what the code does, such as

   count := count + 1;   {Increase counter by 1}

   or that are meaningless jargon, such as

   {horse string length into correctitude}

   (This example was taken directly from a systems program).

6. Explain any statement that employs a trick or whose meaning is unclear. Better still, avoid such statements.

7. The code itself should explain *how* the program works. The documentation should explain *why* it works and *what* it does.

8. Whenever a program is modified, be sure that the documentation is correspondingly modified.

Spaces, blank lines, and indentation in a program are an important form of documentation. They make the program easy to read, allow you to tell at a glance which parts of the program relate to each other, where the major breaks occur, and precisely which statements are contained in each loop or each alternative of a conditional statement. There are many systems (some automated) for indentation and spacing, all with the goal of making it easier to determine the structure of the program.

It is therefore important that you should settle on some reasonable rules for spacing and indentation, and use your rules consistently in all programs you write, since consistency is essential if the system is to be useful in reading programs. Many professional programming groups decide on a uniform system, and insist that all the programs they write conform. Some classes or student programming teams do likewise. In this way, it becomes much easier for one programmer to read and understand the work of another.

Programming Precept

The reading time for programs is much more than the writing time.
Make reading easy to do.

1.3.3 Refinement and modularity.

Computers do not solve problems; people do. Usually the most important part of the process is dividing the problem into smaller problems that can be understood in more detail. If these are still too difficult, then they are subdivided again, and so on. In any large organization the top management cannot worry about every detail of every activity; the top managers must concentrate on general goals and problems, and delegate specific responsibilities and problems to their subordinates. Again, the middle-level managers cannot do everything: they must subdivide the work and send it to other people. So it is with computer programming. Even when a project is small enough that one person can take it from start to finish, it is most important to divide the work, starting with an overall understanding of the problem, dividing it into subproblems, and attacking each of these in turn without worrying about the others.

Let us restate this principle with a classic proverb:

Programming Precept

Don't lose sight of the forest for its trees.

This principle, called **top-down refinement**, is the real key to writing large programs that work. The principle implies the postponement of detailed consideration, but not the postponement of precision and rigor. It does not mean that the main program becomes some vague entity whose task can hardly be described. On the contrary, the main program will send almost all the work out to various subprograms (procedures and functions), and as we write the main program (which we should do first) we decide exactly how the work will be divided among them. Then, as we later work on a particular subprogram, we shall know before starting exactly what it is expected to do.

It is often not easy to decide exactly how to divide the work into subprograms, and sometimes a decision once made must later be modified. Even so, two guidelines can help in deciding how to divide the work.

Programming Precept

Each subprogram should do only one task, but do it well.

That is, we should be able to describe the purpose of a subprogram succinctly. If you find yourself writing a long paragraph to specify the task of a subprogram, then either you are giving too much detail (that is, you are writing the subprogram before it is time to do so) or you should rethink the division of work. The subprogram itself will undoubtedly contain many details, but they should not appear until the next stage of refinement.

Programming Precept

Each subprogram should hide something.

A middle-level manager in a large company does not pass on everything he receives from his departments to his superior; he summarizes, collates and weeds out the information, handles many requests himself, and only sends on what is needed at the upper levels. Similarly, he does not transmit everything he learns from higher management to his subordinates. He transmits to each person only what he needs to do his job. The subprograms we write should do likewise.

While these principles of top-down design may seem almost self-evident, the only way to learn them thoroughly is by practice. Hence throughout this book we shall be careful to apply them to the large programs that we write, and in a moment it will be appropriate to return to our first example project.

Exercises

1. The following statement is designed to check the relative sizes of three integers:

```
if x < z then if x < y then c := 1 else if y < z then c := 2 else
  c := 3 else if x < y then if x < z then c := 4 else if z < x then
  c := 5 else c := 6 else if z < x then if z < y then c := 7 else
  c := 8 else c := 9;
```

   (a)   Rewrite this statement in a form that is easier to read.
   (b)   Find any cases that can never occur, or any redundant checks.
   (c)   Write a simpler, shorter statement that accomplishes the same thing.

2. The following Pascal function calculates the cube root of a real number (by the Newton approximation), using the fact that, if y is one approximation to the cube root of x, then

$$z = \frac{2y + (x/y^2)}{3}$$

   is a closer approximation.

```
function Fcn( stuff: real): real;
var  April, Tim, Tiny, Shadow, Tom, Tam, Square: real;  flag:
        Boolean;
begin Tim := stuff; Tam := stuff; Tiny := 0.00001;
if stuff <> 0 then repeat Shadow := Tim + Tim;
```

```
Square := Tim * Tim;
Tom := (Shadow + stuff / Square);
April := Tom / 3;
if April * April * April − Tam > −Tiny then if April*April*April−Tam
     < Tiny then flag := true else flag := false else flag := false;
if flag = false then Tim := April else Tim := Tam until flag = true;
if stuff = 0 then Fcn := stuff else Fcn := April end;
```

Rewrite this function with meaningful variable names, without the extra variables that contribute nothing to the understanding, with a better layout, and without the redundant and useless statements.

3. The *mean* of a sequence of real numbers is their sum divided by the count of numbers in the sequence. The *variance* of the sequence is the mean of the squares of all numbers in the sequence, minus the square of the mean of the numbers in the sequence. The *standard deviation* is the square root of the variance. Write a well-structured Pascal function to calculate the standard deviation of a sequence of n numbers, where n is a constant, and the numbers are in an array indexed from 1 to n, which is a parameter to the function. Use, then write, subsidiary functions to calculate the mean and variance.

1.4 Coding, testing and further refinement.

The three processes in the title above go hand-in-hand, and must be done together. Yet it is important to keep them separate in our thinking, since each requires its own approach and method. *Coding* is the process of writing an algorithm in the correct syntax (grammar) of a computer language like Pascal, and *testing* is the process of running the program on sample data chosen to find errors if they are present. For further refinement we turn to the subprograms not yet written and repeat these steps.

1.4.1 Stubs.

After coding the main program, most programmers will wish to complete the writing and coding of the subprograms as soon as possible, to see if the whole project will work. For a project as small as the Life game this approach may work, but for larger projects writing and coding all the subprograms will be such a large job that, by the time it is complete, many of the details of the main program and subprograms that were written early will have been forgotten. In fact, different people may be writing different subprograms, and some of those who started the project may have left it before all subprograms are written. It is much easier to understand and debug a program when it is fresh in your mind. Hence for larger projects it is much more efficient to debug and test each subprogram as soon as it is written than it is to wait until the project has been completely coded.

Even for smaller projects there are good reasons for debugging subprograms one at a time. We might, for example, be unsure of some point of Pascal grammar that will appear in several places through the program. If we can compile each subprogram separately, then we shall quickly learn to avoid errors in grammar in later sub-programs. As a second example, suppose that we have decided that the major steps of the program should be done in a certain order. If we test the main program as soon as it is written then we may find that sometimes the major steps are done in the wrong order. We can then quickly correct the problem, doing so more easily than if we waited until the major steps were perhaps obscured by the many details contained in each of them.

To compile the program correctly, there must be something in the place of each subprogram that is used, and hence we must put in short, dummy subprograms, called *stubs.* The simplest stubs are those that do nothing at all:

procedure Initialize; **begin end;**

procedure WriteMap; **begin end;**

function NeighborCount(i: row; j: col): integer; **begin end;**

Even with these stubs we can at least compile the program and make sure that the declarations of types and variables are syntactically correct. When we execute the program, however, we find that some variables are used without initialization, and hence, to avoid these errors, we can add code to procedure Initialize. Hence the stub can slowly grow and be refined into the final form of the subprogram.

For a small project like the Life game, we can simply write each subprogram in turn, substitute it for its stub, and observe the effect on program execution.

1.4.2 Counting neighbors.

Let us now refine our program further. The function that counts neighbors of the cell in i,j is straightforward. We need only be careful, when i,j is near a boundary, that we look only at legitimate positions in the array. To do so, we introduce four variables for the lower and upper limits of the loops, and make sure that they remain within range. Since the loops will incorrectly consider that the cell in position i,j is a neighbor of itself, we must make a correction after completing the loops.

```
function NeighborCount(i:row; j:col): integer;
var
  x,                                        {loop index for row}
  xlow, xhigh: row;                         {limits for row loop}
  y,                                        {loop index for column}
  ylow, yhigh: col;                         {limits for column loop}
  count: integer;                           {counter of occupied neighbors}
begin
  if i = 1 then
    xlow := 1
  else
    xlow := i - 1;
```

```
      if i= maxrow then
        xhigh := i
      else
        xhigh := i + 1;
      if j = 1 then
        ylow := 1
      else
        ylow := j − 1;
      if j = maxcol then
        yhigh := j
      else
        yhigh := j + 1;
      count := 0;
      for x := xlow to xhigh do
        for y := ylow to yhigh do
          if map[x,y] = alive then
            count := count + 1;
      if map[i,j] = alive then
        count := count − 1;
      NeighborCount := count
    end;
```

1.4.3 Input and Output.

It now remains only to write the procedures Initialize and WriteMap that do the input and output. In computer programs designed to be used by many people, the procedures performing input and output are often the longest. Input to the program must be fully checked to be certain that it is valid and consistent, and errors in input must be processed in ways to avoid catastrophic failure or production of ridiculous results. The output must be carefully organized and formatted, with considerable thought to what should or should not be printed, and with provision of various alternatives to suit differing circumstances. The programming tools needed to design comprehensive input and output procedures, unfortunately, still differ considerably from one computer system to another, and in any case are more concerned with the details of the language and the problem at hand than with general ideas. It is therefore impossible to include as much error checking as we would wish, working only within the provisions of standard Pascal. When the programs are implemented in a particular system, additional error checking can usually be included.

Programming Precept

Keep your input and output as separate modules,
so they can be changed easily,
and can be custom-tailored to your computing system.

1. Pascal conventions.

Both input and output files in Pascal are abstractions of magnetic tapes, with operations done strictly sequentially. Pascal also sets up buffers that sometimes interact peculiarly with input or output on the terminal. When execution of a program begins, a standard Pascal system will immediately obtain the first datum from each file specified for input (placing the datum in the "file window"). This means that it is impossible in standard Pascal to write a prompting message to an interactive terminal before the program requests the first input from the terminal. Since this situation is clearly unacceptable, various solutions to this problem have been implemented in different systems, and there is no universal method to accomplish interactive input and output in Pascal.

In this book we shall use one set of conventions, one that works properly on some, but not all, systems. The reference manuals for your Pascal system should discuss input-output conventions, and from these manuals you can determine what changes will be required to run the programs in this book on your computer.

We shall use the standard procedures **read**, to obtain input data, and **readln** which completes reading one line of input and requests the next. We also use the standard procedure **eof** which takes on Boolean values, being true if and only if an end-of-file mark has been encountered. Throughout this book, when we are accepting input from the terminal, we shall check for end-of-file *after* we read, but *before* we attempt to use the data that has supposedly just been read. In this way, the user can give the end-of-file symbol instead of the data, and the program should react properly. On the other hand, when (later in the book—not in this chapter) we read data from files rather than the terminal, then (in accordance with standard Pascal's use of buffers) we must check for end-of-file *before* attempting to read the data.

Loops for reading and processing data will therefore have the general forms below.

Interactive version:

```
Read(data);
while not eof do
begin
   Readln(moredata);
   Process;
   Read(data)
end;
```

Non-interactive version:

```
while not eof(F) do
begin
   Read(F, data);
   Readln(F, moredata);
   Process
end;
```

In the interactive version it is necessary to attempt reading data both before the loop begins and at the end of the loop, so that the end-of-file condition will be properly set immediately before it is checked. In the non-interactive version, the end-of-file condition is determined from the buffer before the data are explicitly read.

2. Initialization.

The tasks that procedure Initialize must accomplish are, first, to set the number of generations that the simulation will run, and, second, to set the map to its initial configuration. The first task is simple. To initialize the map, we could consider each possible coordinate pair separately, and request the user to indicate whether the cell is to be occupied or not. This method would require the user to type in

$$\text{maxrow} \times \text{maxcol} = 50 \times 80 = 4000$$

entries, which is prohibitive. Hence, instead, we input only those coordinate pairs corresponding to initially occupied cells.

```
procedure Initialize;
var
  x,y:     integer;                              {coordinates of cell}
begin
  Writeln('This program is a simulation of the game of Life.');
  Writeln('Enter the number of generations to run.');
  Readln(lastgeneration);
  if lastgeneration <= 0 then
    writeln('No output: run of 0 generations');
  for x:=1 to maxrow do
    for y :=1 to maxcol do
      map[x,y] := dead;
  Writeln('On each line give a pair of coordinates for a living cell.');
  Writeln('Terminate the list with the end-of-file symbol.');
  Readln(x,y);

  while not eof do
  begin
    if (x >= 1) and (x <= maxrow) and (y >= 1) and
       (y <= maxcol) then
      map[x,y] := alive
    else
      writeln('Values are not within range.');
    Readln(x,y)
  end                                     {loop processing pair x,y}
end;                                                   {procedure}
```

For the output procedure WriteMap we adopt the simple method of writing out the entire array at each generation, with occupied cells denoted by * and empty cells by blanks.

```
procedure WriteMap;
const
  full = '*';
  empty = ' ';
var
  x: row;
  y: col;
begin
  Page;                                {commence a new page of output}
  Writeln('The map at generation', generation:5, ' is below:');
  for x := 1 to maxrow do
  begin
    for y := 1 to maxcol do
      if map[x,y] = alive then
        Write(full)
      else
        Write(empty);
    Writeln
  end                                  {processing row x}
end;                                   {procedure}
```

At this point, we have all subprograms for the Life simulation. It is time to pause and check that it works.

1.4.4 Drivers.

For small projects, each subprogram is usually inserted in its proper place as soon as it is written, and the resulting program can then be debugged and tested as far as possible. For large projects, however, compilation of the entire project can overwhelm that of a new subprogram being debugged, and it can be difficult to tell, looking only at the way the whole program runs, whether a particular subprogram is working correctly or not. Even in small projects the output of one subprogram may be used by another in ways that do not immediately reveal whether the information transmitted is correct.

One way to debug and test a single subprogram is to write a short auxiliary program whose purpose is to provide the necessary input for the subprogram, call it, and evaluate the result. Such an auxiliary program is called a ***driver*** for the subprogram. By using drivers, each subprogram can be isolated and studied by itself, and thereby bugs can often be spotted quickly.

As an example, let us write drivers for the subprograms of the Life project. First we consider the function NeighborCount. In the main program its output is used, but has not been directly displayed for our inspection, so we should have little confidence that it is correct. To test NeighborCount we shall supply it with the array map, call it for each entry of the array, and write out the results. The resulting driver hence uses procedure Initialize to set up the array, and bears some resemblance to the original main program.

```
program DriveNeighborCount(input, output);
{Declarations of constants, types and variables may be taken from the
main program.}
begin
  Initialize;
  for i := 1 to maxrow do
  begin
    for j := 1 to maxcol do
      Write(NeighborCount(i,j):3);
    Writeln
  end
end.
```

Sometimes two subprograms can be used to check each other. The easiest way, for example, to check procedures Initialize and WriteMap is to use a driver whose declarations are those of the main program, and whose action part is:

begin Initialize; WriteMap **end.**

Both procedures can be tested by running this driver and making sure that the configuration printed is the same as that given as input.

1.4.5 Principles of program testing.

So far we have said nothing about the choice of data to be used to test programs and subprograms. This choice, of course, depends intimately on the project under development, so we can make only some general remarks. First we should note:

Programming Precept

The quality of test data is more important than the quantity.

Many sample runs that do the same calculations in the same cases provide no more effective a test than one run. It is possible that other cases remain that have never been tested even after many sample runs. For any program of substantial complexity it is impossible to perform exhaustive tests, yet the careful choice of test data can provide substantial confidence in the program. Everyone, for example, has great confidence that the typical computer can add two floating-point numbers correctly, but this confidence is certainly not based on testing the computer by having it add all possible floating-point numbers and checking the results. If a double-precision floating-point number takes 64 bits, then there are 2^{128} distinct pairs of numbers which could be added. This number is astronomically large: all computers manufactured to date have performed altogether but a tiny fraction of this number of additions. Our confidence that computers add correctly is based on tests of each component separately; that is, by checking that each of the 64 digits is added correctly, and that carrying from one place to another is done correctly.

There are at least three general philosophies that are used in the choice of test data.

1. The black-box method.

Most users of a large program are not interested in the details of its functioning; they only wish to obtain answers. That is, they wish to treat the program as a black box; hence the name of this method. Similarly, test data should be chosen according to the specifications of the problem, without regard to the internal details of the program, to check that the program operates correctly. At a minimum the test data should be selected in the following ways:

1. *Easy values.* The program should be debugged with data that are easy to check. More than one student who tried a program only for complicated data, and thought it worked properly, has been embarrassed when the instructor tried a trivial example.

2. *Typical, realistic values.* Always try a program on data chosen to represent how the program will be used. These data should be sufficiently simple so that the results can be checked by hand.

3. *Extreme values.* Many programs err at the limits of their range of applications. It is very easy for counters or dimensions to be off by one.

4. *Illegal values.* "Garbage in, garbage out" is an old saying in computer circles that should not be respected. When a good program has garbage coming in, then its output should at least be a sensible error message. It is preferable that the program should provide some indication of the likely errors in input, and perform any calculations that remain possible after disregarding the erroneous input.

2. The glass-box method.

The second approach to choosing test data begins with the observation that a program can hardly be regarded as thoroughly tested if there are some parts of its code that, in fact, have never been executed. In the *glass-box* method of testing, the logical structure of the program is examined, and for each alternative that may occur, test data are devised that will lead to that alternative. Thus care is taken to choose data to check each possibility in each **case** statement, each clause of every **if** statement, and the termination condition of each loop.

For a large program the glass-box approach is clearly not practicable, but for a single small module it is an excellent debugging and testing method. In a well-designed program each module will involve few loops and alternatives. Hence only a few well-chosen test cases will suffice to test each module on its own.

In glass-box testing the advantages of modular program design become evident. Let us consider a typical example of a project involving 50 subprograms, each of which can involve 5 different cases or alternatives. If we were to test the whole program as one, we would need 5^{50} test cases to be sure that each alternative was tested. Each module separately requires only 5 (easier) test cases, for a total of $5 \times 50 = 250$. Hence a problem of impossible size has been reduced to one that, for a large program, is of quite modest size.

Before you conclude that glass-box testing is always the preferable method, we should comment that, in practice, black-box testing is usually more effective in uncovering errors. Perhaps one reason is that the most subtle programming errors often occur, not within a subprogram, but in the interface between subprograms, in misunderstanding of the exact conditions and standards of information interchange between subprograms. It would therefore appear that a reasonable testing philosophy for a large project would be to apply glass-box methods to each small module as it is written, and to use black-box test data for larger sections of the program when they are complete.

3. The ticking-box method.

To conclude this section let us mention one further philosophy of program testing, a philosophy that is, unfortunately, quite widely used. This might be called the *ticking-box* method. It consists of doing no testing at all after the project is fairly well debugged, but instead turning it over to the customer for trial and acceptance. The result, of course, is a time bomb.

Exercises

1. Enter the program of this section on your computer and make sure that it works correctly.

2. Test the program with the examples worked by hand in Section 1.2.

3. Run the program with several initial configurations, including the following:

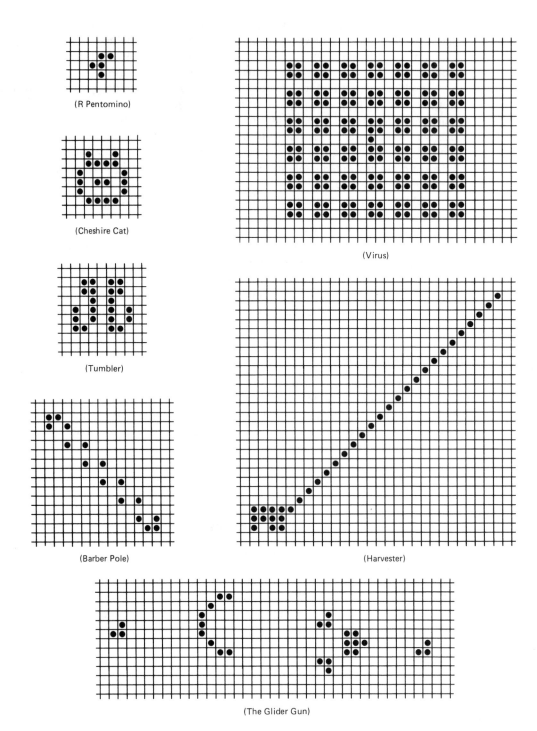

(R Pentomino)

(Cheshire Cat)

(Virus)

(Tumbler)

(Barber Pole)

(Harvester)

(The Glider Gun)

1.5 Maintenance of the program.

Now that we have a functioning program for the Life simulation, and have had opportunity to run it with various configurations to check its correctness, it is time to ask ourselves what additional features or other changes might be desirable, how much work it would be to implement them, and whether it would be worthwhile.

If you have run the Life program on a small computer or on a busy time-sharing system then you will likely have found two major problems. First, the method for input of the initial configuration is poor. It is unnatural for a person to calculate and type in the numerical coordinates of each living cell. The form of input should instead reflect the same visual imagery as the way the map is printed. Second, you may have found the program's speed somewhat disappointing. There can be a noticeable pause between printing one generation and starting to print the next.

Our next goal is to improve our program so that it will run really efficiently on a microcomputer. The problem of improving the form of input is addressed as an exercise; the text discusses the problem of improving the speed.

1.5.1 Review of the program.

We must first find out where the program is spending most of its computation time. If we examine the program, we can first note that the trouble cannot be in the procedure Initialize, since this is done only once, before the main loop is started. Within the loop that counts generations, we have a pair of nested loops that, together, will iterate

$$\mathsf{maxrow} \times \mathsf{maxcol} = 50 \times 80 = 4000$$

times. Hence program lines within these loops will contribute substantially to the time used.

The first thing done within the loops is to invoke the function NeighborCount(i,j). The function itself includes a pair of nested loops (Note that we are now nested to a total depth of 5), which usually do their inner statement 9 times. The function also does 7 statements outside the loops, for a total (usually) of 16.

Within the nested loops of the main program, besides the call to the function, there are only the comparison to find which case to do and the appropriate assignment statement; that is, there are only 2 statements additional to the 16 in the function. Outside the nested loops there is the assignment of arrays map := newmap, which, in copying 4000 entries, is about equivalent to 1 more statement within the loops. There is also a call to the procedure WriteMap, some variation of which is needed in any case so that we can see what the program is doing. Our primary concern is with the computation, however, so let us for now not worry about the time that WriteMap may need. We thus see that for each generation the computation involves about

$$4000 \times 19 = 76{,}000$$

statements, of which about $4000 \times 16 = 64,000$ are done in the function. On a small microcomputer or a tiny share of a busy time-sharing system each statement can easily require 100 to 500 microseconds for execution, so the time to calculate a generation may easily range as high as 40 seconds, a delay that most users will find unacceptable.

Since by far the greatest amount of time is used in the function calculating the number of occupied neighbors of a cell, we should concentrate our attention on doing this job more efficiently. Before starting to develop some ideas, however, let us pause momentarily to pontificate:

Programming Precept

Most programs spend 90% of their time doing 10% of their instructions.
Find this 10%, and concentrate your efforts for efficiency there.

It takes much practice and experience to decide what is important and what may be neglected in analyzing algorithms for efficiency, but it is a skill that you should carefully develop to enable you to choose alternative methods or to concentrate your programming efforts where they will do the most good.

1.5.2 Alternatives.

How can we reduce the amount of work needed to keep track of the number of occupied neighbors of each Life cell? Is it necessary for us to calculate the number of neighbors of every cell at every generation? Clearly not, if we use some way (such as an array) to remember the number of neighbors, and if this number does not change from one generation to the next. If you have spent some time experimenting with the Life program, then you will certainly have noticed that in many interesting configurations the number of occupied cells at any time is far below the total number of positions available. Out of 4000 positions, typically fewer than 100 are occupied. Our program is spending much of its time laboriously calculating the obvious facts that cells isolated from the living cells indeed have no occupied neighbors and will not become occupied. If we can prevent or substantially reduce such useless calculation we will obtain a much better program.

As a first approach, let us consider trying to limit the calculations to cells in a limited area around those that are occupied. If this occupied area (which we would have to define precisely) is roughly rectangular, then we can implement this scheme easily by replacing the limits in the loops by other variables that would bound the occupied area. But this scheme would be very inefficient if the occupied area were shaped like a large ring, or, indeed, if there were only two small occupied areas in opposite corners of a very large rectangle. To try to carry out this plan for occupied areas not at all rectangular in shape would probably require us to do so many comparisons, as well as the loops, as to obviate any saving of time.

Let us back up for a moment. If we can now decide to keep an array to remember the number of occupied neighbors of each cell, then the only counts in the array that will change from generation to generation will be those that correspond to immediate neighbors of cells that die or are born. We can substantially improve the running time of our program if we convert the function NeighborCount into an array, and add appropriate statements to update the array while we are doing the changes from one generation to the next embodied in the **case** statement, or, if we prefer (what is perhaps conceptually easier), while we are copying newmap into map we can note where the births and deaths have occurred and at that time update the array.

To emphasize that we are now using an array instead of the function NeighborCount, we shall change the name and write numbernbrs for the array.

The method we have now developed still involves scanning at least once through the full array map at every generation, which likely means much useless work. By being slightly more careful, we can avoid the need ever to look at unoccupied areas. As a cell is born or dies it changes the value of numbernbrs for each of its immediate neighbors. While making these changes, we can note when we find a cell whose count becomes such that it will be born or die in the next generation. Thus we should set up two lists that will contain the cells that, so to speak, are moribund or are expecting in the coming generation. In this way, once we have finished making the changes of the current generation and printing the map, we will have waiting for us complete lists of all the births and deaths to occur in the coming generation. It should now be clear that we really need two lists for births and two for deaths, one each for the changes being made now (which lists are depleted as we proceed) and one list each (which are being added to) containing the changes for the next generation. When the changes on the current lists are complete, we print the map, copy the coming lists to the current ones, and go on to the next generation.

Exercises

1. Rewrite the procedure Initialize so that it accepts the occupied positions in some symbolic form, such as a sequence of blanks and X's in appropriate rows, rather than requiring the occupied positions to be entered as numerical coordinate pairs.

2. On a slow-speed terminal writing out the entire map at every generation will be quite slow. If you have access to a video terminal for which the cursor can be controlled by the program, rewrite the procedure WriteMap so that it updates the map instead of completely rewriting it at each generation.

3. One idea for changing the program to save some of the **if** statements in the function NeighborCount is to add two extra rows and columns to the arrays map and newmap, by changing their dimensions to

$$[0..maxrow + 1, 0..maxcol + 1].$$

Entries in the extra rows and columns would always be dead, so that the loops in NeighborCount could always run their full range from $i - 1$ to $i + 1$ and $j - 1$ to $j + 1$. How would this change affect the count of statements executed in NeighborCount?

1.6 A second version of Life.

1.6.1 Pascal records.

Before writing down the revised Life program that follows this scheme, we should make some decisions about what variables we shall need and the ways in which we shall represent the lists and arrays. In doing so we shall use an important feature of Pascal that aids greatly in displaying the logical connections between different pieces of data, the Pascal category of types called *records*.

Any list really has two distinct parts associated with it. First is a variable that gives the number of items on the list. Second is an array that contains the items on the list. In most languages the programmer must carry the counter variable and the array separately (and doing so is a frequent source of trouble for beginners). Sometimes tricks are used, such as establishing the array to have indices commencing at 0, and using entry 0 as the counter.

The type declaration

record · · · **end**

in Pascal establishes a type consisting of several *fields* (also called *components*), each of which is itself of some (arbitrarily defined) type. In our case, we may define a type called list with declarations such as the following:

```
const maxlist = 200;                        {maximum size of lists}
type list = record
           count: 0..maxlist;
           entry: array[1 .. maxlist] of entrytype
                                        {defined elsewhere}
       end;
```

The four lists that we wish to have are now variables of type list, declared as usual:

```
var die, live, nextdie, nextlive: list;
```

Individual parts of a Pascal record variable are referenced by giving first the name of the variable, then a period '.', then the name of the part as declared in the type statement for the record. Thus the counters of entries in our four lists are denoted

| die.count | nextdie.count |
| live.count | nextlive.count |

The kth entry in list live is denoted live.entry[k].

The entries in our lists will be coordinate pairs [x,y], and there is no reason why we should not think of these pairs as a single record, by defining:

```
type coord = record
            x: row;
            y: col
        end;
```

To obtain the x coordinate of entry k of the list **nextdie** we thus write:

$$\text{nextdie.entry[k].x}$$

Although, as you can see, this notation is entirely logical, it can become a bit cumbersome, so Pascal allows the special statement

with　　recordvariable　　**do** · · · .

In the block under control of the **with** statement the record variable indicated has a special status, so that its various fields can be accessed by giving only their names, without having to repeat the name of the record variable each time.

We note that, for example, the list **nextdie** can be processed with statements such as

```
with nextdie do
  for k := 1 to count do
    with entry[k] do
      {Calculations with coordinates need specify only x or y to
      denote nextdie.entry[k].x or nextdie.entry[k].y};
```

As one further example, we can write a short procedure that will add an entry x to the end of a list L.

```
procedure Add( var L: list;  x: coord);
begin
  with L do
    if count = maxlist then
      Overflow {A separate procedure is needed to handle overflow.}
    else begin
      count := count + 1;
      entry[count] := x
    end
end;
```

1.6.2 The main program.

With these programming tools we are now ready to write our new program for the Life game. The declarations of constants, types and variables closely follow the preceding discussion.

```
program Life2(Input, Output);
{Simulation of Conway's game of Life on a bounded grid}
{Version 2}
```

```
const
  maxrow  = 50;
  maxcol  = 80;
  maxlist = 200;
type
  row = 1..maxrow;
  col = 1..maxcol;
  coord = record
              x: row;
              y: col
          end;
  list = record
              count: 0..maxlist;
              entry: array[1..maxlist] of coord
          end;
  status  = (alive, dead);

var
  map:        array[row,col] of status;
  numbernbrs: array[row,col] of integer;
  live, die,
  nextlive, nextdie: list;
  generation, lastgeneration: integer;

{Declarations of procedures to be inserted here}

begin
  Initialize;
  generation := 0;
  WriteMap;
  for generation := 1 to lastgeneration do
  begin
    Vivify;
    Kill;
    WriteMap;
    AddNeighbors;
    SubtractNeighbors;
    CopyLive;
    CopyDie
  end                                   {processing one generation}
end.                                               {program}
```

Most of the action of the program is postponed to various procedures. At each generation we first go through the list of cells waiting in lists live and die in order to update the array map. This work is done in the procedures Vivify (which means *make alive*) and Kill. After writing the revised configuration, we update the count of neighbors for each cell that has been born or has died, using the procedures AddNeighbors and SubtractNeighbors. As part of the same procedures, when the neighbor count reaches an appropriate value, a cell is added to the list nextlive or nextdie, to indicate that it will be born or die in the coming generation. Finally we must copy the lists for the coming generation into the current ones.

1.6.3 Refinement; subprograms.

Much of the work of our program will be done in the procedures AddNeighbors and SubtractNeighbors. We shall develop the first of these, leaving the second as an exercise. The procedure AddNeighbors will go through the list live, and for each entry will find its immediate neighbors (as done in the original function NeighborCount), will increase the count in numbernbrs for each of these, and must put some of these on the lists nextlive and nextdie. To determine which, let us denote by n the updated count for one of the neighbors, and consider cases.

1. It is impossible that $n = 0$, since we have just increased n by 1.

2. If $n = 1$ or $n = 2$ then the cell is already dead and it should remain dead in the next generation. We need do nothing.

3. If $n = 3$ then a previously live cell still lives; a previously dead cell must be added to the list nextlive.

4. If $n = 4$ then a previously live cell dies; add it to nextdie. If the cell is dead, it remains so.

5. If $n > 4$ then the cell is already dead (or is already on list nextdie) and stays there.

One subtle problem arises with this procedure. When the neighbor count for a dead cell reaches 3, we add it to the list nextlive; but it may well be that later in procedure AddNeighbors its neighbor count will again be increased (beyond 3) so that it should not be vivified in the next generation after all. Similarly, when the neighbor count for a live cell reaches 4, we add it to nextdie, but the procedure SubtractNeighbors may well reduce its neighbor count below 4, so that it should be removed from nextdie. Thus the final determination of lists nextlive and nextdie cannot be made until the array numbernbrs has been fully updated, but yet as we proceed we must tentatively add entries to the lists.

It turns out that, if we postpone solution of this problem, it becomes much easier. In the procedures AddNeighbors and SubtractNeighbors we add cells to nextlive and nextdie without worrying whether they will later be removed. Then when we copy nextlive and nextdie to lists live and die, we can check that the neighbor counts are correct (in live, for example, only dead cells with a neighbor count of exactly 3 should appear), and delete the erroneous entries with no difficulty.

After doing this, however, an even more subtle error remains. It is possible that the same cell may appear in list nextlive (or nextdie) more than once. A dead cell, for example, may initially have a count of 2, which when increased, adds the cell to nextlive. Its count may then be increased further, and in SubtractNeighbors decreased one or more times, perhaps ending at 3, so that SubtractNeighbors again adds it to nextlive. Then, when neighbor counts are updated in the next generation, this birth will incorrectly contribute 2 rather than 1 to the neighbor counts. We could solve this problem by searching the lists for duplicates before copying them, but to do so would be slow, and we can again solve the problem more easily by postponing it. When, in the next generation, we wish to vivify a cell, we shall first check whether it is already alive. If so, then we know that its entry is a duplicate of one earlier on list live. While we are postponing work, we might as well also postpone checking the neighbor counts: the copying procedures will now do nothing but copy lists, and all the checking is done in Vivify and Kill.

Programming Precept

Sometimes postponing problems simplifies their solution.

We can now embody all the preceding decisions into our procedures. The final versions of the copying procedures are trivial, and would normally be written directly into the main program. The first of these is:

```
procedure CopyLive;
var  k:    1..maxlist;
begin
  for k := 1 to nextlive.count do
    live.entry[k] := nextlive.entry[k];
  live.count := nextlive.count;
  nextlive.count := 0
end;
```

The procedure that both checks the list for spurious entries and vivifies the ones that remain is:

```
procedure Vivify;
var
  k:  1..maxlist;                               {used to traverse list Live}
begin
  k := 1;
  with live do
    while k <= count do with entry[k] do
    if (map[x,y] = dead) and (numbernbrs[x,y] = 3)
```

```
    then begin                                  {Make cell alive}
       map[x,y] := alive;
       k := k+1
    end
    else begin                                  {Delete entry k from the list.}
       entry[k] := entry[count];
       count := count — 1
    end
end;
```

The procedure for adding to neighbor counts is:

```
procedure AddNeighbors;
var
   i,                              {loop index for row of neighbor loops}
   ilow, ihigh: row;                              {row loop limits}
   j,                                           {column loop index}
   jlow, jhigh: col;                            {column loop limits}
   k:          0..maxlist;                      {used to traverse list}
   nbr:        coord;                       {record form of a neighbor}

begin
with live do
   for k := 1 to count do with entry[k] do
   begin
      if x = 1   then ilow := 1   else ilow := x — 1;
      if x = maxrow then ihigh := maxrow else ihigh := x + 1;
      if y = 1   then jlow := 1   else jlow := y — 1;
      if y = maxcol then jhigh := maxcol else jhigh := y + 1;

      for i := ilow to ihigh do for j := jlow to jhigh do
         if (i <> x) or (j <> y) then              {skip cell c itself}
         begin
            nbr.x := i;  nbr.y := j;          {Set up coordinate record}
            numbernbrs[i,j] := numbernbrs[i,j] + 1;
            case numbernbrs[i,j] of
               0:    Writeln('Impossible case in AddNeighbors.');
               1,2:;                              {No action needed}
               3:    if map[i,j] = dead then Add(nextlive,nbr);
               4:    if map[i,j] = alive then Add(nextdie, nbr);
               5,6,7,8:;                              {No change}
            end                                  {case statement}
         end                              {processing one neighbor}
   end                              {processing one entry from live}
end;                                             {procedure}
```

The procedures CopyDie, Kill and SubtractNeighbors are similar in form to the preceding : they will be left as exercises, as will the procedure Initialize, even though this must be substantially changed from the previous program to initialize the various lists and arrays. The procedure WriteMap can be used almost as before, but much more efficient versions are possible, using the availability of the lists live and die. The procedure Add appears in Section 1.6.1.

1.6.4 Verification of algorithms.

The fact that there were subtle errors in our initial attempts to organize the above procedures should alert us to the possible presence of further errors, or at least to the necessity of exercising more care to be sure that our algorithms are correct.

1. Possible problems.

By postponing the checking of neighbor counts we were able to avoid difficulties both with the problems of duplicate and of erroneous entries. But, for example, is it still possible that the same cell might erroneously be included in both lists nextlive and nextdie? If so, then it would first be vivified and then killed immediately in the following generation (clearly an illegal happening). The answer to this question is no, since the main program calls both procedures Vivify and Kill before either procedure AddNeighbors or SubtractNeighbors. Thus the cell keeps the same status (alive or dead) from the end of procedure Kill until the next generation, and the procedures AddNeighbors and SubtractNeighbors check that only dead cells are added to nextlive, and only living cells to nextdie.

How can we be sure that there are not more subtle questions of this sort, some of which might not be so easy to answer? The only way we can really be confident is to *prove* that our program does the right action in each case.

2. The main loop.

The difficulty with our program is that what happens in one generation might affect the next generation in some unexpected way. Therefore we focus our attention on the large loop in the main program. At the beginning of the loop it is the contents of lists live and die that determine everything that comes after. Let us therefore summarize what we know about these lists from our previous study.

> *At the beginning of the main loop, list* live *contains only dead cells, and list* die *contains only living cells, but the lists may contain duplicate entries, or spurious entries whose neighbor counts are wrong. The lists* nextlive *and* nextdie *are empty.*

At the very start of the program it is one task of procedure Initialize to ensure that the lists live and die are set up properly, so that the preceding statements are correct at the start of the first generation. What we must prove, then, is that if the statements are true at the start of any one generation, then after the seven procedure calls within the loop, they will again be true for the next generation.

3. Mathematical induction.

At this point, you should note that what we are really doing is using the method of ***mathematical induction*** to establish that the program is correct. In this method of proof, we begin by establishing the result for an initial case. Next we prove the result for a later case, say case n, by using the result for earlier cases (those between the initial case and case $n - 1$).

For our program, verification of the initial case amounts to a verification that Initialize works properly. For the second part of the proof, let us examine the actions in the main loop, assuming that the statements are correct at its beginning. Procedure Vivify uses only list live and carefully checks each entry before it vivifies a cell, removing erroneous and duplicate entries from list live as it goes. Hence at the conclusion of Vivify, list live contains only those cells that were properly vivified, and no duplicates. Procedure Kill similarly cleans up list die. Since the two lists originally had no cells in common, and none has been added to either list, no cells have been improperly both vivified and killed. Next, procedure WriteMap is called, but does not change the lists. Procedure AddNeighbors works only from list live and puts only dead cells on list nextlive, and only living ones on list nextdie. Similarly, procedure SubtractNeighbors keeps the dead and living cells properly separated. Together these two procedures add all the cells whose status should change in the next generation to the lists, but may add duplicate or spurious entries. Finally, the two copying procedures set up lists live and die and empty lists nextlive and nextdie, as required to show that all conditions in our statements are again true at the beginning of the next generation. The logic of our program is therefore correct.

4. Loop invariants.

Statements such as those we have used to do the preceding proof are called ***loop invariants.*** The purpose of a loop invariant is to capture the essence of the dynamic process. It is not always easy to find loop invariants that will lead to a proof that a program is correct, but it is a very useful exercise. Attempting to find invariants sometimes leads to simplifications in design of the algorithm, which make its correctness more obvious. Our goal should always be to make our algorithms so straightforward and clear that their logic is obviously correct, and the use of loop invariants can help in this process.

Programming Precept

Keep your algorithms as simple as you can.

Algorithm verification is a subject under active research, in which many important questions remain to be answered. Correctness proofs have not yet been supplied for a large number of important algorithms which are in constant use. Sometimes exceptional cases appear that cause an algorithm to misbehave; correctness proofs would provide a consistent means to delineate these exceptions and provide for their processing.

1.6.5 Analysis and comparison.

Let us now see about how much more quickly the program Life2 should run than the previous version. As we did before, let us ignore the time needed for input and output in the main program, and look only at the statements inside the principal loop counting generations. Since all the work of Life2 is done within procedures, we must analyze each in turn. Each of the procedures does most of its work within a loop that runs through the entries of one of the lists live, die, nextlive or nextdie. Thus the key improvement of Life2 over the original program is that the amount of computation is no longer proportional to the size of the grid, but to the number of changes being made. For a typical configuration there might be about 100 occupied cells, with likely no more than 50 dying or being born in a single generation. With these assumptions we see that each statement within the inner loops will be executed about 50 times. In Vivify there are 3 statements within the loop, in CopyLive only 1. Within the loop of AddNeighbors there are first 4 **if** statements, then 2 statements each done 9 times, and the **case** statement done 8 times, for a total count of 30. The counts for Kill, CopyDie and SubtractNeighbors are similar; thus we obtain for each generation about

$$50 \times (3+1+30+3+1+30) \quad = \quad 3400$$

statements. The number of statements executed outside the loops is insignificant (it is less than 10), so 3400 is a reasonable estimate of the statement count for each generation.

Our first version of the Life program had a count of 76,000 statements per generation. Thus our revised program should run as much as 20 times faster. This constitutes a substantial improvement, particularly in view of the fact that when program Life2 slows down, it is because many changes are being made, and not because it is repeating the same predictable calculations.

From another point of view, however, our second program is not as good as the first. This point of view is that of storage requirements. The first program used very little memory (apart from that for the instructions) except for the two arrays map and newmap. These arrays have entries which, in assuming only the two values alive and dead, can be packed in so that each entry takes only a single bit. In a typical computer with word size of 32 or 16 bits the two arrays need then occupy no more than 250 or 500 words, respectively. On the other hand, program Life2 requires, along with the space for its instructions, space for one such array, plus 4000 words for the array numbernbrs and 401 words for each of its four lists, giving a total of more than 5700 words.

We have just seen the first of many examples illustrating the substantial trade-offs that can occur between time and space in computer algorithms. Which to choose depends on the available equipment. If the storage space is available and otherwise unused it is obviously preferable to use the algorithm requiring more space and less time. If not, then time may have to be sacrificed. Finally, for an important problem, by far the best approach may be to sit back and rethink the whole problem: you will have learned much from your first efforts and may very well be able to find another approach that will save both time and space.

Programming Precept

Consider time and space trade-offs in deciding on your algorithm.

Programming Precept

Never be afraid to start over.
Next time it may be both shorter and easier.

Exercises

1. Write the procedure Kill.

2. Write the procedure SubtractNeighbors.

3. Write the procedure Initialize. Be sure to include sections to initialize the lists live and die and the array numbernbrs.

4. Write a version of the procedure WriteMap to run on a video terminal that takes advantage of the lists live and die to update the map rather than completely rewriting it at each generation.

5. Run the complete program Life2 and compare timings with those of Life1.

6. We could save the time needed to copy lists if we did two generations instead of one inside the main loop. We would pass the names of which of the lists to use to all the procedures, and in writing the instructions for the second generation we would simply swap the pairs of lists. How many statements, approximately, would be saved per generation? Do you think this change is worth implementing? If so, do it.

7. Note that there is some inefficiency in the program Life2 in having procedures AddNeighbors and SubtractNeighbors called once from the main program, since these procedures must loop through the lists live and die just as Vivify and Kill already do. It would be faster if these procedures were written to update the neighbors of only one cell, and were called from Vivify and Kill whenever a cell was vivified or killed.

    (a) Will the program work correctly if these changes are made?
    (b) If not, what further changes will make it work?
    (c) With your revised program, find the proper loop invariants and verify that your algorithm is correct.

1.7 Conclusions and Preview.

This chapter has surveyed a great deal of ground, but mainly from a bird's-eye view. Some themes we shall treat in much greater depth in later chapters; others must be postponed to more advanced courses; still others are best learned by practice.

1.7.1 The game of Life.

We are not yet finished with the game of Life, although we next shall turn to other topics. Our direction will be to find algorithms that do not require us to keep a large rectangular grid in memory. Some methods may come to mind soon, but these may require doing searching, which can be quite slow. As we develop more sophisticated data storage techniques, such as linked lists and hash tables, we shall return to the Life program to see how they may help.

For the moment, however, let me make only one observation, one that you may well have already made, and, if so, one that has likely been bothering you. What we have done throughout this chapter has been, in fact, incorrect, in that we have not been solving the Life game as it was originally described in Section 1.2. The rules make no mention of the boundaries of the grid containing the cells. In our programs, when a moving colony gets sufficiently close to a boundary, then room for neighbors disappears, and the colony will be distorted by the very presence of the boundary. That is not supposed to be.

It is of course true that in any computer simulation there are absolute bounds on the values that may appear, but certainly our use of a 50 by 80 grid is highly restrictive and arbitrary. Writing a more realistic program must be one of our goals when we return to this problem. But on a first try, restrictions are often reasonable. Nevertheless:

Programming Precept

Be sure you understand your problem completely.
If you must change its terms, explain exactly what you have done.

When we started in Section 1.2, we did nothing of the sort, but plunged right in with an approach leaving much to be desired. Almost every programmer learns this experience the hard way, and can sympathize with the following:

Programming Precept

Act in haste and repent at leisure.
Program in haste and debug forever.

The same thought can be expressed somewhat more positively:

Programming Precept

Starting afresh is usually easier than patching an old program.

A good rule of thumb is that, if more than ten percent of a program must be modified, then it is time to rewrite the program completely. With repeated patches to a large program, the number of bugs tends to remain constant. That is, the patches become so complicated that each new patch tends to introduce as many new errors as it corrects.

1.7.2 Program Design.

A major goal of this book is to evaluate algorithms that purport to solve a problem. Amongst the many criteria by which we can judge a program, the following are some of the most important:

1. Does it solve the problem as requested, according to the given specifications?

2. Does it work correctly under all conditions?

3. Does it include clear and sufficient information for its user, in the form of instructions and documentation?

4. Is it logically and clearly written, with short modules and subprograms as appropriate to do logical tasks?

5. Does it make efficient use of time and of space?

Some of these criteria will be closely studied for the programs we write. Others will not be mentioned explicitly, but not because of any lack of importance. These criteria, rather, can be met automatically if sufficient thought and effort are invested in every stage of program design. I hope that the examples we study will reveal such care.

The steps needed to meet these criteria in program design may be summarized as follows.

1. Specify the problem precisely and completely. Be sure to include all necessary user interface in the specification.

2. Design the algorithm, using the tools of data structures and of other algorithms whose function is already known.

3. Verify that the algorithm is correct, or make it so simple that its correctness is self-evident.

4. Analyze the algorithm to determine its requirements and make sure that it meets the specifications.

5. Code the algorithm into the appropriate programming language.

6. Test and evaluate the program on carefully chosen test data.

7. Repeat the above steps as needed for additional subprograms until the program is fully refined and functional.

Most sections in this book conclude with a few exercises, and among these will often be found suggestions to program and run algorithms discussed earlier. These exercises play an essential role in checking the validity of everything that is written.

1.7.3 Pascal.

In this chapter we have had a whirlwind tour of many features of Pascal. No attempt has been made to present an orderly or complete description of Pascal features. A concise summary of Pascal appears in Appendix C, to which you should refer with questions of Pascal grammar or construction. The Pascal textbooks listed at the end of this chapter provide many more examples and a full discussion of each feature.

By far the most powerful feature of Pascal is the flexibility and strength of its data types. We have hardly scratched the surface in uncovering these resources. As occasion arises we shall use the other Pascal tools in making data types: files, sets, and the pointer types that we shall introduce in the next chapter and use frequently thereafter. Variant records, where a **case** statement appears within the definition of a record type, are powerful. The ability to combine the type definitions in flexible ways (files of records, records containing arrays, arrays of records, etc.) gives almost endless ways to organize our data structures.

1.8 References for further study.

1.8.1 Pascal.

The programming language Pascal was devised by NIKLAUS WIRTH, who first published its description in 1971. The standard reference manual for Pascal, which also includes a succinct tutorial on the language, is:

> K. JENSEN and N. WIRTH, *PASCAL User Manual and Report,* second edition, Springer-Verlag, Berlin, Heidelberg, New York, 1974.

Several textbooks provide a more leisurely description of Pascal, with many examples and applications. Some books designed for introductory courses, however, omit important "advanced" features of Pascal that will be used constantly in this book. Be sure that any textbook you select covers the full vocabulary of standard Pascal. The following are some, but by no means all, of the books that are suitable.

> W. FINDLAY and D. A. WATT, *Pascal, An Introduction to Methodical Programming,* second edition, Computer Science Press, Rockville, Md., 1981.

> PETER GROGONO, *Programming in Pascal,* revised edition, Addison-Wesley, Reading, Mass., 1980.

> JIM WELSH and JOHN ELDER, *Introduction to Pascal,* second edition, Prentice-Hall, Englewood Cliffs, N.J., 1982.

> WILLIAM B. JONES, *Programming Concepts, a second course (with examples in Pascal),* Prentice-Hall, Englewood Cliffs, N.J., 1982.

The last book provides helpful information on input-output and other features whose implementations are often not standard.

1.8.2 Programming principles.

Three books that contain many helpful hints on programming style and correctness, as well as examples of good and bad practices, are:

> BRIAN KERNIGHAN and P. J. PLAUGER, *The Elements of Programming Style*, second edition, McGraw-Hill, New York, 1978.

> HENRY F. LEDGARD, PAUL A. NAGIN, and JOHN F. HUERAS, *Pascal with Style: Programming Proverbs,* Hayden Book Company, Rochelle Park, N.J., 1979.

> DENNIE VAN TASSEL, *Program Style, Design, Efficiency, Debugging, and Testing*, second edition, Prentice-Hall, Englewood Cliffs, N.J., 1978, 323 pages.

EDSGAR W. DIJKSTRA pioneered the movement known as structured programming, which insists on taking a carefully organized top-down approach to the design and writing of programs, when in 1968 he caused some consternation by publishing a letter entitled "Goto Statement Considered Harmful" in the *Communications of the ACM* (volume 11). DIJKSTRA has since published several papers and books that are most instructive in programming method. Two books of special interest are:

> O. J. DAHL, E. W. DIJKSTRA, and C. A. R. HOARE, *Structured Programming,* Academic Press, London and New York,1972.

> E. W. DIJKSTRA, *A Discipline of Programming,* Prentice-Hall, Englewood Cliffs, N.J., 1976.

Keeping programs so simple in design that they can be proved to be correct is not easy, but is very important. C. A. R. HOARE (who invented the quicksort algorithm that we shall study in Chapter 4) writes: "There are two ways of constructing a software design: One way is to make it so simple that there are obviously no deficiencies, and the other way is to make it so complicated that there are no obvious deficiencies. The first method is far more difficult." This quotation is from the 1980 Turing Award Lecture: "The emperor's old clothes", *Communications of the ACM,* 24 (1981), 75–83.

A careful discussion of structured programming and correctness proofs, with many readable examples, is:

> R. C. LINGER, H. D. MILLS, and B. I. WITT, *Structured Programming: Theory and Practice,* Addison-Wesley, Reading, Mass., 1979.

A study of proof rules for Pascal programs, with applications to structured program design, is:

> SUAD ALAGIC and MICHAEL A. ARBIB, *The Design of Well-Structured and Correct Programs,* Springer-Verlag, Berlin, Heidelberg, New York,1978.

A non-technical discussion of many advantages of structured programming is:

> C. L. McGowan and J. R. Kelly, *Top-Down Structured Programming Techniques,* Petrocelli/Charter, New York, 1975.

This book contains the development of a PL/1 program for the Life game using the same method as our first program Life1.

1.8.3 The game of Life.

The prominent British mathematician J. H. Conway has made many original contributions to subjects as diverse as the theory of finite simple groups, logic, and combinatorics. He devised the game of Life by starting with previous, technical studies of cellular automata, and devising reproduction rules that would make it difficult for a configuration to grow without bound, but for which many configurations would go through interesting progressions. The popularity of the game skyrocketed when it was discussed in:

> Martin Gardner, "Mathematical Games" (regular column), *Scientific American,* vol. 223, no. 4 (October 1970), 120–123; vol. 224, no. 2 (February 1971), 112–117.

The examples at the end of sections 1.2 and 1.4 are taken from these columns. More serious mathematical studies of the subject are:

> Arthur W. Burks, editor, *Essays on Cellular Automata,* University of Illinois Press, Urbana, Ill.,1970.

> E. F. Codd, *Cellular Automata,* Academic Press, New York, 1968.

A quarterly journal, entitled *Lifeline,* has even been published to keep the real devotees up to date on current developments in Life and related topics.

Chapter 2

Lists

This chapter introduces the study of data structures, by studying the representation of lists, both in contiguous storage and as linked lists with dynamic memory allocation.

2.1 Static and dynamic structures.

Soon after the introduction of loops and arrays, every elementary programming class attempts some programming exercise like the following:

Read an integer n, which will be at most 25, then read a list of n numbers, and then print the list in reverse order.

This little exercise will probably cause difficulty for some students. Most will realize that they need to use an array, but some will attempt to set up the array to have *n* entries, and will be confused by the error message resulting from attempting to use a variable rather than a constant to declare the size of the array. Other students will say, "I could solve the problem if I knew that there were 25 numbers, but I don't see how to handle fewer." Or, "Tell me before I write the program how large *n* is, and then I can do it."

The difficulties of these students come not from stupidity, but from thinking logically. In a beginning course there is sometimes not enough distinction drawn between two quite different concepts. First is the concept of a *list* of *n* numbers, a list whose size is variable, that is, a list for which numbers can be inserted or deleted, so that, if $n = 3$, then the list contains only 3 numbers, and if $n = 19$, then it contains 19 numbers. Second is the programming feature called an *array* or a vector, which contains a constant number of positions, that is, whose size is fixed when the program is compiled. The two concepts are, of course, related in that a list of variable size can be represented in a computer as occupying part of an array of fixed size, with some of the entries in the array remaining unused.

In this chapter we shall see that there are ways other than using arrays to keep a list of variable size within computer memory, and therefore the careful programmer needs to make a conscious decision about how the list will be represented. The need for careful decision making about how to store data, in fact, extends back even further in the process of program design. We shall soon see that there is more than one kind of list (*stacks* and *queues* are the first two kinds we study), and therefore the programmer must first decide what kind of list (or what other conceptual structure) is needed for the data, and then must decide how the conceptual structure will be represented in computer memory. By keeping these decisions separate, we shall be able both to simplify the programming process and to avoid some of the pitfalls that attend premature decisions.

2.2 Lists in contiguous representation.

In section 1.6.1 we discussed the representation of lists inside Pascal arrays. We set up a record type, so that we could keep track both of the array and of the variable that counts entries in the list, together in one structure. In this section we shall continue with similar notation. The word ***contiguous,*** which appears in the section title, means *next to each other.* Hence ***contiguous representation*** means our ordinary method of storage within arrays, with the elements of the list in adjacent positions.

2.2.1 Stacks in contiguous representation.

The easiest kind of list to use is called a ***stack*** (see Figure 2.1), which is defined formally as a list in which all insertions and deletions are made at one end, called the ***top*** of the stack. A helpful analogy is to think of a stack of trays or of plates sitting on the counter in a busy cafeteria. Throughout the lunch hour, customers take trays off the top of the stack, and employees place returned trays back on top of the stack. The tray most recently put on the stack is the first one taken off. The bottom tray is the first one put on, and the last one to be used.

Sometimes this picture is described with plates or trays on a spring-loaded device so that the top of the stack stays near the same height. This imagery is poor, and should be avoided. If we were to implement a computer stack in this way, it would mean moving every item in the stack whenever one item was inserted or deleted. This would be costly. It is far better to think of the stack as resting on a firm counter or floor, so that only the top item is moved when it is added or deleted. The spring-loaded imagery, however, has contributed a pair of colorful words that are firmly embedded in computer jargon, and which we shall use. When we add an item to a stack we say that we ***push*** it onto the stack, and when we remove an item we say that we ***pop*** it from the stack. From the same analogy, the term ***push-down list*** (or ***store***) is used synonymously with stack, but we shall not employ this term.

As one important application of stacks, consider what happens within the computer system when subprograms are called. The system (or program) must remember the place where the call was made, so that it can return there after the subprogram is complete. It must also remember all the local variables, CPU registers, and the like, so that information will not be lost while the subprogram is working. We can think of all this information as one large record, a temporary storage area for each subprogram.

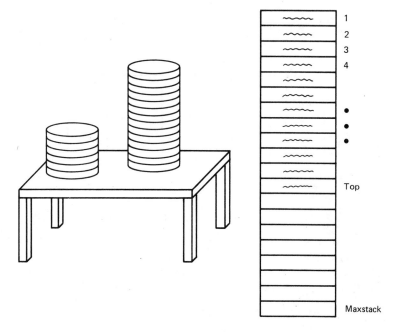

Figure 2.1. Stacks

Suppose now that we have three subprograms called *A, B* and *C*, and suppose that *A* invokes *B* and *B* invokes *C*. Then *B* will not have finished its work until *C* has finished and returned. Similarly *A* is the first to start work, but it is the last to be finished, not until sometime after *B* has finished and returned. Thus the sequence by which subprogram activity proceeds is summed up as the property *Last in, first out.* If we consider the machine's task of assigning temporary storage areas for use by subprograms, then these areas would be allocated in a list with this same property, that is, in a stack (see Figure 2.2). Hence yet one more name sometimes used for stacks is **LIFO lists,** based on the acronym for this property.

To implement a stack in a computer we need to set up an array that will hold the items in the stack, and a counter to indicate how many items there are. In Pascal we can make declarations such as the following, where **maxstack** is a constant giving the maximum size allowed for stacks, and item is a data type that depends on the application, ranging from a single number to a large block of storage.

```
type  stack = record
                 top:  0 .. maxstack;
                 entry: array[1 .. maxstack] of item
              end;
```

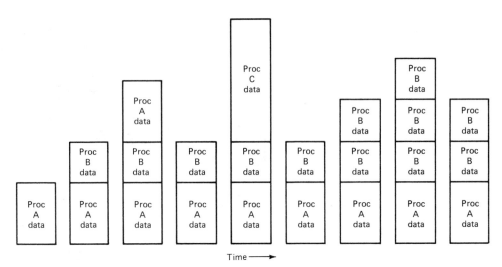

Time ⟶

Figure 2.2 Stack frames for subprogram calls

Addition and deletion are then implemented as follows. We must be careful of the
extreme cases: We might attempt to pop an item from an empty stack, or to push an
item onto a full stack. Thus we include the Boolean variables **underflow** and **overflow** to
indicate the occurrence of such events.

```
procedure Push(x: item; var S: stack; var overflow: Boolean);
begin
with S do
  if top = maxstack then
      overflow := true
  else begin
      overflow := false;
          top := top + 1;
      entry[top] := x
  end
end;
procedure Pop(var x: item; var S: stack; var underflow: Boolean);
begin
with S do
  if top = 0 then
      underflow := true
  else begin
      underflow := false;
          x := entry[top];
          top := top - 1
  end
end;
```

The substance of these procedures is so simple that often they are written in line when they are needed in a program, rather than as separate procedures. Often, moreover, the stack counter is kept as a simple variable, and the entries as an array, rather than combining the counter and the entries within a record structure. There is one important advantage, however, to using a record type to represent stacks and separate procedures to push and pop them. It may well happen that, after we start work on a large project, we realize that another way of representing our stacks in storage will prove better than the method we had used. If the instructions have been written out every time a stack is pushed or popped, then every occurrence will need to be changed. If we have used records and procedures, then only the definition of the record type and of the procedures must be altered. A second advantage is that the very appearance of the words *Push* and *Pop* will immediately alert a person reading the program to what is being done, whereas the instructions themselves might be slightly more obscure.

2.2.2 Queues in contiguous representation.

In ordinary English a queue is defined as a waiting line, like a line of people waiting to purchase tickets, where the first person in line is the first person served. For computer applications we similarly define a ***queue*** to be a list in which all additions to the list are made at one end, and all deletions from the list are made at the other end. Queues are also called ***first-in-first-out lists***, or ***FIFO*** for short.

Applications of queues are, if anything, even more common than applications of stacks, since in performing tasks by computer, as in all parts of life, it is so often necessary to wait one's turn before having access to something. Within a computer system there may be queues of tasks waiting for the line printer, for access to disk storage, or even, in a time-sharing system, for use of the CPU. Within a single program there may be multiple requests to be kept in a queue, or one task may create other tasks, which must be done in turn by keeping them in a queue.

The item in a queue ready to be served, that is, the first item that will be removed from the queue, we call the ***head*** of the queue (or, sometimes, the ***front*** of the queue). Similarly, the last item in the queue, that is, the one most recently added, we call the ***tail*** (or the ***rear***) of the queue.

As we did for stacks, we can easily create a queue in computer storage by setting up an ordinary contiguous array to hold the items. Now, however, we must keep track of both the head and the tail of the queue. One method would be to keep the head of the queue always in the first location of the array. Then an item could be added to the queue simply by increasing the counter showing the tail, in exactly the same way as we added an item to a stack. To delete an item from the queue, however, would be very expensive indeed, since after the first item was removed all the remaining items would need to be moved one position up the queue to fill in the vacancy. With a long queue this process would be prohibitively slow. Although this method of storage closely models a queue of people waiting to be served, it is a poor choice for use in computers.

For efficient processing of queues we shall therefore need two pointers, so that we can keep track of both the head and the tail of the queue without moving any items. To add an item to the queue, we simply increase the tail by one and put the item in that position. To remove an item, we take it from the position at the head, and then increase the head by one. This method, however, still has a major defect. Both the head and tail pointers are increased but never decreased. Even if there are never more than two items in the queue, an unbounded amount of storage will be needed for the queue if the sequence of operations is:

Add, Add, Delete, Add, Delete, Add, Delete, $\cdots$.

The problem is that, as the queue moves down the array, the storage space at the beginning of the array is discarded and never used again. Perhaps the queue can be likened to a snake crawling through storage. Sometimes the snake is longer, sometimes shorter, but if it always keeps crawling in a straight line, then it will soon reach the end of the storage space.

Note, however, that for applications where the queue is regularly emptied (such as when a series of requests is allowed to build up to a certain point, and then a task is initiated that clears all the requests before returning), then at a time when the queue is empty the head and tail can both be reset to the beginning of the array, and the simple scheme of using two pointers and straight-line storage becomes a very efficient storage method.

In concept we can overcome the inefficient use of space simply by thinking of the array as a circle rather than a straight line. In this way as items are added and removed from the queue the head will continually chase the tail around the array, so that the snake can keep crawling indefinitely but stay in a confined circuit (see Figure 2.3). At different times the queue will occupy different parts of the array, but we never need worry about running out of space unless the array is fully occupied, in which case we truly have overflow.

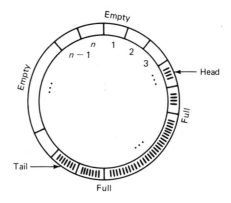

Figure 2.3. Queue in circular storage

To force the circular array into our usual image of straight-line storage is not difficult. We think of numbering the entries around the circle from 1 to n and use the same-numbered entries of the straight-line array. Then moving the pointers is just the same as doing modular arithmetic: when we increase the pointer past n we start over again at 1.

Perhaps a good human analogy of this situation is that of a priest serving communion to people kneeling at the front of a church. The communicants do not move until the priest comes by and serves them. When the priest reaches the end of the row, he returns to the beginning and starts again, since by this time a new row of people have come forward.

Before writing formal algorithms to add to and delete from a queue, let us consider the boundary conditions, that is, the indicators that a queue is empty or full. If there is exactly one entry in the queue, then the head pointer will equal the tail pointer. When this one entry is removed, the head will be increased by 1, so that an empty queue is indicated when the tail is one position before the head. Now suppose that the queue is nearly full. Then the tail will have moved well away from the head, all the way around the circle, and when the array is full the tail will be exactly one position behind the head. Thus we have another difficulty: the head and tail pointers are in exactly the same relative positions for an empty queue and for a full queue! There is no way, by looking at the pointers alone, to tell a full queue from an empty one.

There are three essentially different ways to resolve this problem. One is to insist on leaving one empty position in the array (this method will be treated as an exercise). A second is to introduce a new Boolean variable, that will be used when the tail comes just before the head to indicate whether the queue is full or not (a Boolean variable to check emptiness would be just as good). A variation of this method is to keep a counter of the number of items in the queue. The third method is to set one or both of the pointers to some value(s) that would otherwise never occur in order to indicate an empty (or full) queue. If, for example, the array entries are indexed from 1 to n, then an empty queue could be indicated by setting the tail pointer to 0.

To summarize the discussion of queues, we can now write formal algorithms for the latter two methods. Specific example programs and applications are postponed until we develop other data structures. We take the queue as stored in an array indexed with the range

1..maxqueue

and containing entries of a type called item. The integer variables head and tail will point to appropriate positions in the array. The Boolean variables overflow and under-flow will indicate the corresponding conditions.

First we take the method in which a Boolean variable full will indicate whether the queue is full. Hence the record declaration for a queue takes the form

```
queue = record
              head,
              tail: 0..maxqueue;
              entry: array[1..maxqueue] of item;
              full: Boolean
          end;
```

The queue should be initialized to be empty by setting

```
head := 1;  tail := 0;  full := false
```

for each record of type queue.

```
procedure AddQueue(x: item; var Q: queue; var overflow: Boolean);
begin
with Q do
  if full then
    overflow := true
  else begin
    overflow := false;
    if tail = maxqueue then
      tail := 1
    else
      tail := tail + 1;
    entry[tail] := x;
    if (tail = head − 1) or ((head = 1) and (tail = maxqueue))
      then full := true
  end
end;

procedure DeleteQueue(var x: item; var Q: queue; var underflow:
                                                     Boolean);
begin
with Q do
  if (not full) and ((tail = head − 1) or
            ((head = 1) and (tail = maxqueue)))
  then underflow := true
  else begin
    underflow := false;
    x : = entry[head];
    full : = false;
    if head = maxqueue then head := 1
                        else head : = head + 1
  end
end;
```

For the method that relies on special values for the pointers, we need only make a few changes in the previous declarations. The record field full is dropped from the declaration of type queue. We shall use the condition

$$\text{tail} = 0 \quad \text{and} \quad \text{head} = 1$$

to indicate an empty queue. The procedures then become:

```
procedure AddQueue(x: item; var Q: queue; var overflow: Boolean);
begin
with Q do
  if ((head = tail + 1) and (tail > 0)) or
    ((tail = maxqueue) and (head = 1)) then
    overflow : = true
  else begin
    overflow : = false;
    if tail = maxqueue then tail : = 1
                       else tail : = tail + 1;
    entry[tail]: = x
  end
end;
```

```
procedure DeleteQueue(var x: item; var Q: queue; var underflow:
                                                    Boolean);

begin
with Q do
  if tail = 0 then                         {Q is already empty}
    underflow : = true
  else begin
    underflow : = false;
    x : = entry[head];
    if head = tail then                    {Q is now empty}
    begin
      tail : = 0;
      head : = 1
    end
    else if head = maxqueue then
      head : = 1
    else
      head : = head + 1
  end
end;
```

2.2.3 Other lists in contiguous representation.

The fact that all additions and deletions are made at the ends makes the operations on stacks and queues relatively simple, but we can certainly imagine applications where changes must be made in the middle of the list. It might be necessary, for example, to add a name to a list that is kept in alphabetical order. With applications like this one, it will be necessary (with the list in contiguous representation) to move all the later items one position to make room for the new item. The algorithms for doing such operations are not difficult to write, and are left as exercises. The time required to run the algorithms, however, can become large because of the need to move items.

Sometimes other devices can be used to avoid the need to move items. In the lists live and die that we set up for the Life game, it made no difference in what order the entries were in the lists, and so when we needed to delete an item from the list, we could fill its hole simply by moving the last item from the list and reducing the count of items on the list by 1. Procedure Vivify thus had the form:

```
procedure Vivify;
i : = 1;
while i <= count do begin
  if entry[i] is OK then
  begin
    process entry[i];
    i : = i + 1
  end
  else begin
    entry[i] : = entry[count];
    count : = count − 1
  end
end.
```

Exercises

1. Sometimes a program requires two stacks containing the same kind of items. If these are assigned to separate arrays, then one stack might overflow while there was considerable unused space in the other. A neat way to avoid this problem is to put all the space in one array, and let one stack grow from one end of the array and the other stack start at the other end and grow in the opposite direction, toward the first stack. In this way, if one stack turns out to be large and the other small, then they will still both fit, and there will be no overflow until all the space is actually used. Call the two stacks A and B, and write procedures PushA, PushB, PopA and PopB to handle them. Be sure to check for overflow and underflow.

2. Write a non-recursive program that will read an integer and print all its prime divisors in descending order. For example, with the integer 2100 the output should be

7   5   5   3   2   2.

[*Hint:* The smallest divisor greater than 1 of any integer is guaranteed to be a prime. You should not use any arrays other than one stack.]

3. A stack may be regarded as a railway switching network like the one in Figure 2.4. Cars numbered 1, 2, ..., n are on the line at the left, and it is desired to rearrange (permute) the cars as they leave on the right hand track. A car that is on the spur (stack) can be left there or sent on its way down the right track, but can never be sent back to the incoming track. For example, if $n = 3$, and we have the cars 1 2 3 on the left track, then 3 first goes to the spur. We could then send 2 to the spur, then on its way to the right, then send 3 on the way, then 1, obtaining the new order 1 3 2.

   (a) For $n = 3$, find all possible permutations that can be obtained.
   (b) Same, for $n = 4$.
   (c) Same, for $n = 5$.
   (d) [*Challenging*] For general n, find how many permutations can be obtained by using this stack.

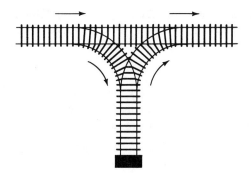

Figure 2.4. Switching network for stack permutations

4. Suppose you are a financier and purchase 100 shares of stock in Company X in each of January, April and September, and sell 100 shares in each of June and November. The prices per share in these months were

Jan	Apr	Jun	Sep	Nov
$10	$30	$20	$50	$30

   Determine the total amount of your capital gain or loss using (1) FIFO accounting and (2) LIFO accounting [that is, assuming that you keep your stock certificates in (1) a queue or (2) a stack]. The 100 shares you still own at the end of the year do not enter the calculation.

5. Implement the simpler representation of queues where it can be assumed that the queue can be emptied when necessary. Write a procedure AddQueue that will add

an item if there is room, and if not will call another procedure that will empty the queue. While writing this second procedure, you may assume the existence of an auxiliary procedure Service(x: item) that will process a single item that you have just removed from the queue.

6. Use the availability of the procedures in the text to write other procedures that will

   (a) Empty one stack onto the top of another stack.
   (b) Move all the items from a queue onto a stack.
   (c) Start with a queue and an empty stack, and use the stack to reverse the order of all the items in the queue.

7. Rewrite the first set of procedures AddQueue and DeleteQueue from the text, using an integer counter of items in the queue instead of the Boolean variable full.

8. The Boolean variable in the implementation of a queue can also be eliminated if we are willing to leave one unused entry in the array. Thus we can consider that the array is full when the tail is two positions before the head; when the tail is one position before, it will always indicate an empty queue. Rewrite the procedures to implement this scheme.

The word *deque* (pronounced either "deck" or "DQ") is a shortened form of *double-ended queue*, and denotes a list in which items can be added or deleted from either end, but no changes can be made elsewhere in the list.

9. Is it more appropriate to think of a deque as stored in a linear array or in a circular array?

10. Write the four algorithms needed to add an item to each end of a deque and to delete an item from each end of the deque.

11. Note from Figure 2.4 that a stack can be represented pictorially as a spur track on a straight railway line. A queue can be represented simply as a straight track. Devise and draw a railway switching network that will represent a deque. The network should have only one entrance and one exit.

12. Suppose that data items numbered 1, 2, 3, 4, 5, 6 come in the input stream in this order. By using (1) a queue and (2) a deque, which of the following re-arrangements can be obtained in the output order?

    (a) 1 2 3 4 5 6   (b) 2 4 3 6 5 1   (c) 1 5 2 4 3 6
    (d) 4 2 1 3 5 6   (e) 1 2 6 4 5 3   (f) 5 2 6 3 4 1

13. A *scroll* is a data structure intermediate to a deque and a queue. In a scroll all additions to the list are at its end, but deletions can be made either at the end or at the beginning. Answer the preceding four questions in the case of a scroll rather than a deque.

14. Suppose that we think of dividing a deque in half by fixing some position in the middle of it. Then the left and right halves of the deque are each a stack. Thus a

deque can be simulated by two stacks. Write algorithms that will add to and delete from each end of the deque considered in this way. When one of the two stacks is empty and the other one not, and an attempt is made to pop the empty stack, you will need to move items (equivalent to changing the place where the deque was broken in half) before the request can be satisfied. Compare your algorithms with those of Exercise 10 in regard to

    (a) clarity;
    (b) ease of composition;
    (c) storage use;
    (d) time used for typical accesses;
    (e) time used when items must be moved.

15. Consider the contiguous representation of general lists introduced in Section 1.6.1, and use the same record structure for the following algorithms. Your algorithms should not alter the relative order of the entries not deliberately changed.

    (a) Write an algorithm that deletes the last entry of a list.
    (b) Write an algorithm that deletes the first entry of a list.
    (c) Write an algorithm that deletes the entry in position k of a list.
    (d) Write an algorithm that reverses the order of the entries in a list.
    (e) Write an algorithm that inserts a new item after the entry in position k of a list.
    (f) Write an algorithm that splits a list into two other lists, so that the entries that were in odd-numbered positions are now in one list (in the same relative order as before) and those from even-numbered positions are in the other new list.

2.3 Dynamic memory allocation and pointers.

2.3.1 The problem of overflow.

In the examples we have studied so far, we have assumed that all items of data are kept within some kind of array, defined and dimensioned before the program is executed. When writing a program we have had to decide on the maximum amount of memory that would be needed for our arrays, and set this aside in the declarations. If we run the program on a small sample, then much of this space will never be used. If we decide to run the program on a large set of data, then we may exhaust the space set aside and encounter overflow, even when the computer memory itself is not fully used, simply because our original bounds on the array were too small.

Even if we are careful to declare our arrays large enough to use up all the available memory, we can still encounter overflow, since one array may reach its limit while a great deal of unused space remains in others. Since different runs of the same program may cause different lists to grow or shrink, it may be impossible to tell before the program actually executes which lists will overflow.

We now exhibit a way to keep lists and other data structures in memory without using arrays, whereby we can avoid these difficulties.

2.3.2 Pointers.

The idea we use is that of a pointer. We have been discussing pointers informally for some time, with examples such as those used to find the head and tail of a queue. We are now in a position to make a formal definition. A ***pointer*** (also called a ***link***) is defined to be a variable that gives the location of some other variable, such as some piece of data. Thus a stack pointer gives the location of the item on the top of the stack, and queue pointers give the locations of the head and tail of the queue.

With all our data kept within limited arrays, the pointers we have used have always referred to locations relative to the beginning of the array. Moreover, with entries stored contiguously (next to each other), we have needed pointers only to locate the ends of lists, not to locate entries in the middle, since we could simply count to find them. But if we rely completely on pointers to locate the items of interest, then the actual locations of the items (within arrays or otherwise) need not concern us. We can therefore adopt a more general point of view, and use pointers to locate all items of interest. Then we need not keep the items themselves within limited arrays, but may allow them to be scattered throughout the computer memory, wherever the system happens to place them.

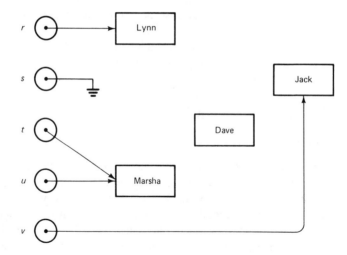

Figure 2.5. Pointers to records

As you can see from Figure 2.5, the use of pointers is quite flexible: two pointers can refer to the same record, or a pointer can refer to no record at all. We denote this latter situation within diagrams by the electrical 'ground' symbol, as shown for pointer *s*. Care must be exercised when using pointers, moreover, to be sure that, when they are moved, no record is lost. In the diagram, the record "Dave" is lost, with no pointer referring to it, and therefore there is no way to find it.

2.3.3 Dynamic memory allocation.

As well as preventing unnecessary overflow problems, the use of pointers has great advantages in a multiprogramming (time-sharing) environment. If we use arrays to reserve in advance the maximum amount of memory that our program might need, then this memory is assigned to us and will be unavailable for other users. If it is necessary to page our job out of memory, then time may be lost as unused memory is copied to and from a disk. Instead of using arrays to hold all our items, we can begin very small, with space only for the program instructions and simple variables, and whenever we need space for an additional item we can request the system for the needed memory. Similarly, when an item is no longer needed, its space can be returned to the system which can then assign it to another user. In this way a program can start small and grow only as necessary, so that when it is small it can run more efficiently, and when necessary it can grow to the limits of the computer system. The process that assigns and reassigns memory in this way is called *dynamic memory allocation*.

Even with only one user this dynamic control of memory can prove useful. During one part of a task a large amount of memory may be needed for some purpose, which can later be released, and then allocated again for another purpose, perhaps now containing data of a completely different type than before.

2.3.4 Pointers and dynamic memory in Pascal

Most newer programming languages (including Pascal) provide powerful facilities for processing pointers, and standard procedures for requesting additional memory and for releasing memory during program execution. In many of our programs from now on we shall employ these facilities and thereby dispense with the artificial restrictions that the use of arrays and contiguous storage has imposed.

Variables that can be used during execution of a Pascal program come in two varieties. *Static variables* are those that are declared and named, as usual, while writing the program. Space for them exists as long as the program in which they are declared is running. *Dynamic variables* are created (and perhaps destroyed) during program execution. Since dynamic variables do not exist while the program is compiled, but only when it is run, they cannot be assigned names while it is being written. The only way to access dynamic variables is by using pointers. On the other hand, a dynamic variable, when it is created, does contain data and must have a type like any other variable. Thus we can talk about creating a new dynamic variable of type x and setting a pointer to point to it, or of moving a pointer from one dynamic variable of type x to another, or of returning a dynamic variable of type x to the system.

Pascal sets stringent rules for the use of pointer variables. Each pointer is *bound* to the type of variable to which it points, and the same pointer can never be used to point (at different times) to variables of different types. Similarly, pointer variables cannot be used to point to static variables. Static variables are referenced only by using their names—just as we have always done—and if we wish to use pointers to refer to positions within arrays, then as before we do so with variables (like counters) of the same type that indexes the array.

Pascal uses an upward arrow or caret ($\uparrow$ or $\wedge$) to denote the word *pointer*. (These two symbols are usually different representations of the same character.) When these symbols are not available, the symbol @ is used instead. We declare a pointer type that is bound to a type xxx with a declaration such as

type pointer = $\uparrow$xxx.

As we can with any other type, we can now declare variables that have type **pointer**, and these variables point to dynamic variables of type xxx.

When more than one type of dynamic variable is in use, we can name the pointer type to reflect the type of dynamic variables, with declarations such as

type pointxxx = $\uparrow$xxx;
pointyyy = $\uparrow$yyy;

A pointer to dynamic variables of type xxx is then simply declared as a variable of type **pointxxx**. The words *link* and *reference* are also frequently used for pointer types. The type xxx to which a pointer refers can be arbitrary, but in most applications it will usually be a record.

The creation and destruction of dynamic variables is done with standard procedures in Pascal. If **p** has been declared as a pointer to type xxx, then the call

new(p)

creates a new dynamic variable of type xxx and assigns its location to the pointer **p**. Similarly, the call

dispose(p)

returns the space used by the variable of type xxx to the system (*warning:* some Pascal systems will lose the space and never reuse it). After the procedure **dispose(p)** is called, the pointer variable **p** is undefined, and so cannot be used until it is assigned a new value.

One additional feature should be mentioned. Sometimes a pointer **p** has no variable at which it is currently pointing. This situation can be established by the assignment

p := **nil**

and subsequently checked by a condition such as

if p $<>$ **nil then** $\cdots$.

In diagrams we use the electrical ground symbol

for **nil** pointers. Unless **p** is immediately reassigned after a call **dispose(p)**, then it is wise to set **p** := **nil,** to be sure that **p** is not used with an undefined value. Figure 2.6 illustrates these actions.

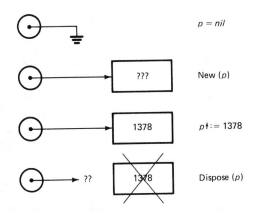

$p = nil$

New (p)

$p\uparrow := 1378$

Dispose (p)

Figure 2.6. Assigning and disposing of dynamic variables

2.3.5 Actions with pointers.

Upward arrows ($\uparrow$) to denote *pointer* appear not only in the declarations of a Pascal program, but also in the action part. But here the arrow appears not to the left of a type, but to the right of a pointer variable. Thus p$\uparrow$ denotes the variable to which p points. At first this notation may appear slightly confusing, but its logic will become clear if you remember that $\uparrow$ means *points*. Thus the declaration

p: ↑xxx

is read "p points to xxx" and p$\uparrow$ is read "what p points to." Again the words *link* and *reference* are often used in this connection. The action of taking p$\uparrow$ is sometimes called "dereferencing the pointer p."

Notice the similarity between this notation and that used in Pascal for a *file window*. If F is a file, then F$\uparrow$ denotes the one entry of the file that is currently accessible to the program. In other words, F$\uparrow$ is the position within the file to which the program currently points, just as p$\uparrow$ is the position within memory to which the pointer p currently points.

The only use of variables of type $\uparrow$xxx is to find the location of variables of type xxx. Thus pointer variables can participate in assignment statements, can be checked for equality, and (as parameters) can appear in calls to subprograms, but they can appear nowhere else. The programmer is not allowed to do arithmetic with pointers, since they are addresses, not numbers with intrinsic meaning. Reading or writing the values of pointers is also not allowed, since they are addresses assigned while the program is running, may differ from one run of the program to the next, and their values (as addresses in the computer memory) are implementation features with which the programmer should not be directly concerned. (Some Pascal systems do allow pointer values to be written out for debugging purposes, so that the programmer can check that appropriate equalities hold and appropriate pointer assignments have been made.)

Note that the preceding restrictions on using pointers do not apply to the dynamic variables to which the pointers refer. If **p** is a pointer, then **p↑** is not usually a pointer (although it is legal for pointers to point to pointers), but a variable of some other type **xxx**, and therefore **p↑** can be used in any legitimate way for type **xxx**.

In regard to assignment statements, it is important to remember the difference between **p := q** and **p↑ := q↑**, both of which are legal (provided that **p** and **q** are bound to the same type), but which have quite different effects. The first statement makes **p** point to the same object to which **q** points, but does not change the value of either that object, or of the other object that was formerly **p↑**. The latter object will be lost unless there is some other pointer variable that still refers to it. The second statement, **p↑ := q↑**, on the contrary, copies the value of the object **q↑** into the object **p↑**, so that we now have two objects with the same value, with **p** and **q** pointing to the two separate copies. Finally, the two assignment statements **p := q↑** and **p↑ := q** have mixed types and are illegal (except in the rare case that the **p** and **q** point to pointers of their same type!). See Figure 2.7.

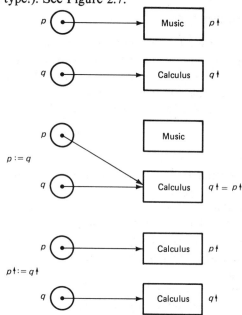

Figure 2.7. Assignment of pointer variables

Exercises

These exercises are based on the following declarations, where we assume that the type item has been previously declared in the program.

```
type    pointer = ↑item;
var     p, q, r:    pointer;
        x, y, z:    item;
```

1. For each of the following statements, either describe its effect, or state why it is illegal.

   (a) new(p)   (f) r : = **nil**   (k) dispose(r)
   (b) new(q↑)   (g) z : = p↑   (l) x : = new(p)
   (c) new(x)   (h) p : = ↑x   (m) q↑ : = **nil**
   (d) p : = r   (i) dispose(y)   (n) p↑ : = x↑
   (e) q : = y   (j) dispose(p↑)   (o) z : = **nil**

2. Write a Pascal procedure to interchange pointers **p** and **q**, so that after the procedure is performed **p** will point to the item to which **q** formerly pointed, and vice versa.

3. Write a Pascal procedure that makes **p** point to the same item to which **q** points, and disposes of the item to which **p** formerly pointed.

4. Write a Pascal procedure that creates a new variable with **p** pointing to it, and with contents the same as those of the item to which **q** points.

2.4 Linked lists.

With these tools of pointers and pointer types we can now study a new way to represent lists. The items in the list will all be dynamic variables; hence a separate pointer is needed to locate each item. Putting these pointers in some static structure like an array would negate several benefits of dynamic memory; hence instead we let each item in our list point to the next. This idea is illustrated in Figure 2.8.

As you can see, a linked list is simple in concept. It uses the same idea as a children's treasure hunt, where each clue that is found tells where to find the next one. Or consider friends passing a popular cassette around. Fred has it, and has promised to give it to Jackie. Carol asks Jackie if she can borrow it, and then will next share it with Tom. And so it goes. With some practice in their use, you will find that linked lists are just as easy to work with as contiguous lists. The methods differ greatly, however, so we shall illustrate the use of linked lists by writing several short procedures. Others appear as exercises.

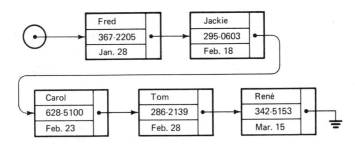

Figure 2.8. A linked list

2.4.1 Algorithms for simply linked lists.

To write the procedures we shall first need a formal declaration of the structure of a node within a linked list:

```
pointer = ↑node;
node  = record
                {In this part should be inserted all the information
                            fields that are part of the record};
                next: pointer      {link to next node in the list}
     end;
```

This notation will be standard for the rest of the chapter.

By use of the pointer field **next** we can get from any node in the linked list to the next one, and thereby can work our way through the list, once we have started. We must now, however, address a small problem that never arises with static variables and arrays: How do we find the beginning of the list? One method is to insist that the first node in the list be a static variable, even though all the remaining nodes are dynamically allocated. In this way the first node will have a unique name to which we can refer. Although we shall sometimes use this method, it has the disadvantage that the first node is treated differently from all the others, a fact that can superficially complicate the algorithms. Even when the list is empty the space for one node is still reserved, so sometimes it is difficult to tell an empty list from one with a single node.

Usually we shall employ another method that avoids these problems. The *header* for a linked list is a simple pointer variable that locates the beginning of the list. Usually the header will be a static variable, and by using its value we can arrive at the first (dynamic) node of the list. The header is also sometimes called the *base* or the *anchor* of the list. These terms are quite descriptive of providing a variable that ties down the beginning of the list, but since they are not so widely used we shall generally employ the term "header".

Finding the end of a linked list is a much easier task. Since each node contains a pointer to the next, the pointer field of the last node of the list has nowhere to point, so we give it the special value **nil.** In this way we know that we are at the end of the list if and only if the node we are using has a **nil** pointer to the next. Here we have one small advantage of linked lists over a contiguous representation: there is no need to keep an explicit counter of the number of nodes in the list.

When execution of the program starts, we shall wish to initialize the linked list to be empty; with a header pointer this is now easy. The header is a static variable, so it exists when the program begins, and to set its value to indicate that its list is empty we need only the assignment

header := **nil;**

To illustrate the kind of actions we can perform with linked lists, let us consider for a moment the problem of editing text. Suppose that each node holds one word plus the link to the next node. The sentence "Stacks are lists" appears as in part (a) of

Figure 2.9. If we add the word "simple" we obtain the list in part (b). Next we decide to change "lists" to "structures" and insert "but important data" to obtain part (c), and finally decide to delete "simple but", and so arrive at the list shown in part (d).

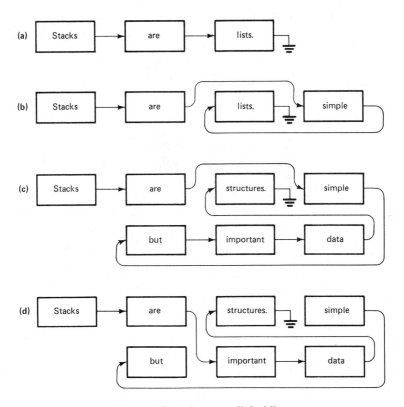

Figure 2.9. Actions on a linked list

2.4.2 Linked stacks.

A stack is the simplest kind of list, since all additions and deletions are made at the same end. Hence it is appropriate for us to begin with algorithms to manipulate linked stacks.

The first question to settle regarding linked stacks is to determine which end of the linked list will be used for additions and deletions. At first glance it may appear that (as for contiguous lists) it might be easier to add an item at the end of the list, but this representation makes popping the stack difficult: there is no quick way to find the node immediately before a given node in a linked list, since the links stored in the list give only one-way directions. Thus, after we remove the last element, to find the new element at the end of the list it might be necessary to trace all the way from the head of the list. To pop our linked stack it is better to make all additions and deletions at the beginning of the list. Since the header points to the first node of the list, which will be the top of the stack, we shall denote by top the header for our linked stack.

Let us start with an empty stack, which now means

$$\text{top} = \textbf{nil}$$

and add the first node. We shall assume that this node already exists, with a variable p that points to it. Pushing it onto the stack involves the instructions

$$\text{top} := \text{p}; \ \text{p↑.next} := \textbf{nil}$$

As we continue, let us suppose that we already have the stack, and that we wish to push a node p↑ onto it. To insert p↑ at the beginning of the list requires adjusting the links as shown in Figure 2.10. We thus obtain the following procedure.

procedure Push(p: pointer; **var** top: pointer);
{Push the node p↑ onto the stack beginning with top↑.}
begin
p↑.next : = top;   {New node points to former top of stack.}
top := p   {Set the top to the new node.}
end;

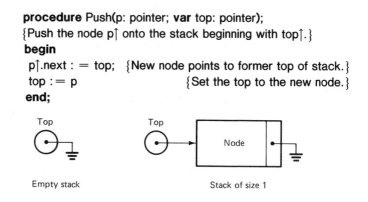

Empty stack   Stack of size 1

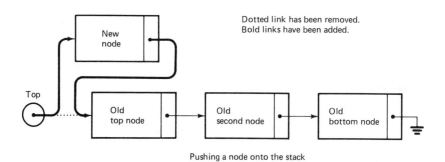

Pushing a node onto the stack

Figure 2.10. Operations on a linked stack

Note that this procedure works just as well to add the first node to an empty stack as to add another node to a non-empty stack.

It is just as easy to pop the top node from the stack:

procedure Pop(**var** p, top: pointer);
                    {Pops the node p↑ from the stack beginning at top↑}

```
begin
if top = nil then Stackempty(top)
else begin
  p := top;                              {Pop the top node.}
  top := p↑.next                  {Move the top down the list.}
end
end;
```

Note that the principal instructions for popping the linked stack are exactly the reverse of those for pushing a node onto the stack. In popping the stack it is necessary to check the stack for emptiness, but in pushing it there is no need to check for overflow, since the procedure itself does not call for any additional memory. The extra memory for the new node is already assigned to p↑. Finally, you should note that both parameters in the procedure that pops the stack are called by reference, but in pushing p↑ onto the stack only top need be called by reference. The formal reason, of course, is that in procedure Pop both the variables top and p are changed, while in procedure Push the variable p is not changed. The point of possible confusion, however, is that, even if parameter p is only a local copy of some actual parameter, the local copy p and the actual parameter both point to the same node p↑, and so procedure Push is quite capable of making changes in the actual node p↑ whether its parameter p is called by value or by reference.

2.4.3 The available-space list.

In standard Pascal, the way to acquire memory and create a new node is to use the procedure new(p), and the way to return memory to the operating system is to use the procedure dispose(p). On some systems, however, the procedure dispose(p) either does nothing (in which case the node p↑ becomes "lost" to the program and will never be reused), or the procedure is inefficient. If our program is one that continually sets up new nodes and disposes of others, then we shall often find it necessary to write our own procedures to keep track of nodes that are no longer needed, and to reuse the space when new nodes are later required.

Since our nodes come from a linked structure, we can take the nodes that are no longer needed and link them together as a list. The order in which they might be reused makes no difference since they are indistinguishable as empty blocks of memory, so we might as well put them in a linked stack, since its operations are particularly easy. Thus we need only one variable

var availnode: pointer

which we use to point to the top node on the space-available stack. When we wish to acquire a new node, we should first attempt to pop the stack of nodes that are no longer in use, and only if the stack is empty do we need to go to the computer system by using the procedure new(p). Since at the start of the main program no nodes have been acquired from the system, the program should include at its beginning the statement

availnode := **nil**;

and the following procedure should be used in place of **new(p)**.

```
procedure NewNode(var p: pointer);
begin
  if availnode = nil then new(p)
  else begin p : = availnode;
  availnode : = p↑.next
  end
end;
```

The procedure replacing **dispose(p)** pushes p↑ onto the stack.

```
procedure DisposeNode( p: pointer);
begin
  if p = nil then
    Error                                {Attempt to dispose of nothing}
  else begin
    p↑.next : = availnode;
    availnode : = p
  end
end;
```

2.4.4 Linked queues.

In contiguous storage, queues were significantly harder to handle than stacks, because it was necessary to treat straight-line storage as though it were arranged in a circle, and the extreme cases of full queues and empty queues could cause difficulties. It is for queues that linked storage really comes into its own. Linked queues (Figure 2.11) are just as easy to handle as linked stacks. We need only keep two pointers, **head** and **tail**, that will point respectively to the beginning and the end of the queue. To add a node p↑ to the queue we need only write:

```
procedure AddQueue(p: pointer; var  head, tail: pointer);
begin
  if tail = nil then
  begin
    head := p;
    tail := p
  end
  else begin
    tail↑.next: = p;
    tail: = p
  end;
  p↑.next: = nil
end;
```

and to remove p↑ from the head of the queue we write:

```
procedure DeleteQueue(var p, head, tail: pointer; var underflow: Boolean);
begin
  if head = nil then
    underflow : = true
  else begin
    underflow : = false;
    p : = head;
    head : = head↑.next ;
    if head = nil  then tail : = nil;
  end
end;
```

If you compare these algorithms with those needed to manipulate contiguous queues, you will see what a triumph linked lists have won.

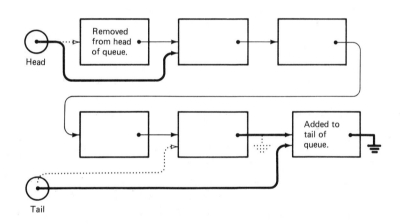

Figure 2.11. Operations on a linked queue

2.4.5 Other lists.

Let us continue to develop some familiarity with linked lists by looking at lists in which accesses are made other than at the ends and by writing sample instructions for several common tasks. The first of these is *list traversal*, which means to move through the list, visiting each node in turn. What we mean by *visiting* each node depends entirely on the application; it might mean printing out some information, or doing some task that depends on the data in the node. Thus we leave the task unspecified and use a call to a procedure named Visit(p). To traverse the list we shall again need an auxiliary pointer p, that will start at the first node on the list and move from node to node. We need a loop to accomplish this movement, and since we wish to allow the possibility of an empty list (for which the loop will not iterate at all), the correct form will be a **while** loop. The termination condition is when p points off the end of the list, whereupon we have p = **nil**. We therefore have:

```
procedure Traverse(header : pointer);              {first node of list}
var  p : pointer;
begin
  p : = header;                                    {p starts at the first node}
  while p <> nil do begin
   Visit(p);
   p : = p↑.next;                                  {move p one node down the list}
  end
end;
```

Next let us consider the problem of inserting a new node into our list, but not necessarily at the beginning. If p is a pointer and we wish to insert the new node *after* p↑, then the method used for adding to a queue works with little change:

```
procedure InsertAfter(p, q: pointer);
                           {Insert node q↑ after node p↑ in linked list.}
begin
  if (p = nil) or (q = nil ) then
   Error                                           {external procedure}
  else begin
   q↑.next : = p↑.next;
   p↑.next : = q
  end
end;
```

Suppose, however, that p points to a node in the middle of the list, and we wish to insert a new node *before* p↑. We now have a difficulty, since the link that must be changed is the one coming into p↑, and there is no way to find this link from p and q, since we cannot move backward through the list. One way to find the link entering p↑ is to start at the head of the list and traverse it to the desired point, but this method is poor, since its running time is proportional to the length of the list up to p↑, which we do not know in advance. A second method, the details of which are left as an exercise, is to use a small trick. First insert the node q↑ after p↑ instead of before p↑. Then, by copying appropriate information fields between records, swap the information in p↑ and q↑ so that the information in q↑ comes before that in p↑. This method, while likely better than the first, may be slow if the information fields are large, and will be dangerous if not fatal if there are other variables elsewhere in the program that point to either of the two nodes that were swapped.

Hence we shall consider yet a third method to solve the problem of inserting q↑ before p↑, a method requiring slightly more bookkeeping, but one that moves only pointers, never the information in the nodes, and whose running time does not depend on the length of the list. What we do is to propose keeping a second pointer variable throughout all our processing of the list. This second pointer r will move in lock step with p, with r↑ always kept exactly one node before p↑. Inserting the new node q↑ before p↑ is now easy, since it is only inserting q↑ after r↑, and then updating r by setting r := q. Inserting the new node before the first node of the list (in which case the trailing pointer r is undefined) is now a special case, but an easy one similar to adding a node to a linked stack. This process is illustrated in Figure 2.12, which leads to the following algorithm.

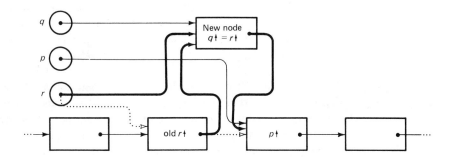

Figure 2.12. Insertion into a linked list with two pointers

```
procedure InsertBetween(q: pointer; var header, r, p: pointer);
{Inserts q↑ into list starting at header↑, between the nodes r↑ and p↑,
which will be maintained as adjacent.}
begin
    if p = header then                    {q↑ is to be inserted first in the list}
    begin
      q↑.next : = p;
      r : = q;                            {r was previously undefined}
      header : = q                        {q↑ is now at head of the list}
    end
    else begin
      q↑.next : = p;
      r↑.next : = q;
      r : = q
    end
end;
```

With the second pointer, however, other operations can become slightly more difficult. When we traverse the list, for example, we must be more careful to get things started correctly. When p points to the head of the list, then r is necessarily undefined. Thus the first step of traversal must be considered separately. The details are left as an exercise.

2.4.6 Comparison of representations.

Now that we have seen several algorithms for manipulating linked lists, let us pause to assess some relative advantages of linked and of contiguous representation.

The foremost advantage of linked storage is flexibility. Overflow is no problem until the computer memory is actually exhausted. Especially when the individual records are quite large, it may be difficult to determine the amount of contiguous static storage that might be needed, while keeping enough free for other needs. With dynamic allocation there is no need to attempt such decisions in advance.

Changes, especially insertions and deletions, can be made in the middle of a linked list much more easily than in the middle of a contiguous list. Even queues are easier to handle in linked storage. If the records are large, then it is much quicker to change the values of a few pointers than to copy the records themselves from one location to another.

The first drawback of linked lists is that the links themselves take space, space that might otherwise be needed for additional data. In most systems a pointer requires the same amount of storage (one word) as an integer. Thus a list of integers will require double the space in linked storage that it would require in contiguous storage. On the other hand, in many practical applications the nodes in the list are quite large, with data fields taking hundreds of words altogether. If each node contains 100 words of data, then using linked storage will increase the memory requirement by only one percent, an insignificant amount.

A second drawback of linked lists is that they are not suited to random access. With contiguous storage the program can refer to any position within a list as quickly as to any other position. With a linked list it may be necessary to trace down a long path to reach the desired node.

Finally, access to a node in linked storage may take slightly more computer time, since it is necessary first to obtain the pointer and then go to the address. This consideration, however, is usually of no importance. Similarly, you may find at first that writing algorithms to manipulate linked lists takes a bit more programming effort, but with practice this discrepancy will decrease.

In summary, therefore, we can conclude that contiguous storage is generally preferable when the records are individually very small, when few additions or deletions need to be made in the middle of a list, and when random access is important. Linked storage proves superior when the records are large, and flexibility is needed in adding, deleting, and rearranging the nodes.

2.4.7 Programming hints.

To close this section, we include several suggestions for programming with linked lists, as well as some pitfalls to avoid.

1. Draw "before" and "after" diagrams of the appropriate part of the linked list, showing the relevant pointers and the way in which they should be changed.

2. To determine in what order values should be placed in the pointer fields to implement the various changes, it is usually better first to assign the values to previously undefined pointers, then to those with value **nil,** and finally to the remaining pointers. When one pointer variable has been copied to another, the first is free to be reassigned to its new location.

3. Be sure that no links are left undefined at the conclusion of your algorithm, either as links in new nodes that have never been assigned, or links in old nodes that have become dangling, that is, that point to nodes that are no longer used. Such links should either be reassigned to nodes still in use or set to the value **nil.**

4. Always verify that your algorithm works correctly for an empty list and for a list with only one node.

5. Never use constructions such as p↑.next↑.next, even though they are syntactically correct. A single variable should involve only a single pointer reference. Constructions with repeated references usually indicate that the algorithm can be improved by rethinking what pointer variables should be declared in the algorithm, introducing new ones if necessary, so that no variable includes more than one pointer reference (↑).

6. It is possible that two (or more) different pointer variables can point to the same node. Since this node can thereby be accessed under two different names, it is called an *alias variable.* The node can be changed using one name and later used with the other name, perhaps without realizing that it has been changed. One pointer can be changed to another node, and the second left dangling. Alias variables are therefore dangerous and should be avoided as much as possible. Be sure you clearly understand whenever you must have two pointers that refer to the same node, and remember that changing one reference requires changing the other.

Exercises

1. Brief review questions.

    (a) When deleting an item from a linked stack or queue, we checked for underflow, but when adding an item, we did not check for overflow. Why?

    (b) Why is the parameter **p** in procedure **NewNode** called by reference, but called by value in procedure **DisposeNode**?

    (c) What would happen if the two assignment statements in procedure **InsertAfter** were interchanged?

    (d) Write a Pascal function that counts the number of nodes in a linked list.

2. Write a procedure that will concatenate two linked lists. The procedure should have two parameters, pointers to the beginning of the lists, and the procedure should link the end of the first list to the beginning of the second.

3. Write a procedure that will split a list in two. The procedure will use two pointers as parameters; **p** will point to the beginning of the list, and **q** to the node at which it should be split, so that all nodes before q↑ are in the first list, and all nodes after q↑ are in the second list. Is it easier to put q↑ into the first list after splitting, or into the second?

4. Write instructions that will insert a node before the node p↑ of a linked list by the following method. First insert the new node after p↑, then copy the information fields of p↑ into the new node, and then put the new information fields into p↑. Do you need to make a special case when p↑ is the first node of the list?

5. Modify the instructions to traverse a linked list, so that it will keep two pointers p and r in lock step, with r↑ always moving one node behind p↑ (that is, r↑ is one node closer to the head of the list).

6. Write instructions to delete the node p↑ from a linked list, assuming a pointer r to the node before p↑.

7. Write instructions to delete the node p↑ from somewhere in the middle of a linked list without keeping the second pointer in lock step. You will need to copy information fields from one node to another. Will your procedure work when p↑ is the first or the last node in the list? If not, what changes are needed?

8. Write instructions that will reverse a linked list while traversing it only once. At the conclusion, each node should point to the node that was previously its predecessor; the header should point to the node that was formerly at the end, and the node that was formerly first should have a **nil** link.

9. Write an algorithm that will split a linked list into two linked lists, so that successive nodes go to different lists (the first, third, and all odd-numbered nodes to the first list, and the second, fourth, and even-numbered nodes to the second).

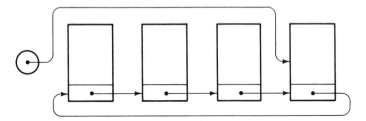

Figure 2.13. A circularly linked list with tail pointer

A *circularly linked list* (see Figure 2.13) is one in which the node at the end of the list, instead of having a **nil** pointer, points back to the node at the head of the list. We then need only one pointer tail both to add to and delete from either end of the list, since we know that tail↑.next points back to the head of the list. For each of the following exercises, assume that the list is specified by a tail pointer and ensure that your algorithm leaves the appropriate pointer(s) pointing to the tails of the appropriate list(s) on conclusion.

10. Write algorithms to add to and to delete from a queue stored as a circularly linked list.

11. Write an algorithm to traverse a circularly linked list, visiting each node. First do the case where only a single pointer moves through the list, and then describe the changes necessary to traverse the list with two pointers moving in lock step, one immediately behind the other.

12. Write an algorithm to delete a node from a circularly linked list.

13. Write an algorithm that will concatenate two circularly linked lists, producing a circularly linked list.

14. Write an algorithm that will split a circularly linked list into two circularly linked lists.

15. Devise an algorithm that will return all the nodes of a circularly linked list to the stack of available (unused) nodes, such that the running time of your algorithm does not depend on the number of nodes being returned.

16. Recall that a *deque* is a list in which additions or deletions can be made at either end, but not in the middle of the list. With a deque stored as a circularly linked list, write algorithms to add an item to either end of the deque, and to delete an item from either end.

17. A *doubly linked list* (see Figure 2.14) is a linked list in which each node contains two links, one to the next node in the list, and one to the preceding node. It is thus possible to move either direction through the list while keeping only one pointer. Write algorithms as follows:

    (a) Add a node after p↑.
    (b) Add a node before p↑.
    (c) Delete node p↑.
    (d) Traverse the list.

18. A doubly linked list can be made circular by setting the values of links in the first and last nodes appropriately. Discuss the advantages and disadvantages of a circular doubly linked list in doing the various list operations.

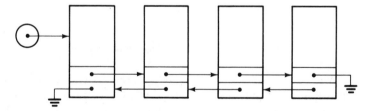

Figure 2.14. Doubly linked list with header

2.5 Polynomial arithmetic.

2.5.1 Definitions.

The usual way in which people calculate with polynomials is by taking a sum of terms, each of which consists of a coefficient and an exponent. In a computer we can similarly represent a polynomial as a list of pairs of coefficients and exponents, with rules for adding and multiplying two such sequences.

2.5.2 Computer representation.

Should we use contiguous or linked lists? If we know in advance a bound on the degree of the polynomials that can occur and if polynomials with many non-zero terms are likely, then we should probably do better with contiguous lists. But if we do not know a bound on the degree, or if polynomials with only a few non-zero terms are likely to appear, then we shall find linked storage preferable. To illustrate the use of linked lists, we adopt the latter representation, as illustrated in Figure 2.15.

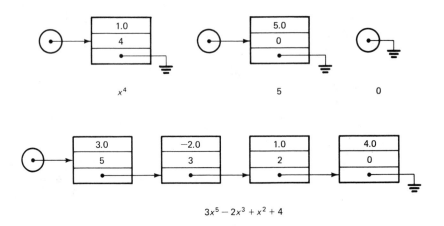

Figure 2.15. Polynomial as a linked list

We shall consider that each node represents one term of a polynomial, and we shall keep track of only the non-zero terms. Hence each node will be a record containing both the coefficient and the exponent of the variable. We shall also require, as usual for linked lists, a pointer to the next term of the polynomial. To refer to polynomials we shall always use header variables for the lists; hence it is sensible to use the pointer type polynomial for the headers. Moreover, the remaining terms after any given term are again a (smaller) polynomial, so the field next again naturally has type polynomial. As Pascal declarations we thus obtain:

```
type
    polynomial = ↑term;
         term = record
                      coef: real;
                      exp: integer;
                      next: polynomial
               end;
```

We have not yet indicated the order of storing the terms of the polynomial. If we allow them to be stored in any order, then it might be difficult to recognize that

$$x^5 + x^2 - 3 \quad \text{and} \quad -3 + x^5 + x^2 \quad \text{and} \quad x^2 - 3 + x^5$$

all represent the same polynomial. Hence we adopt the usual convention that the terms of every polynomial are stored in the order of decreasing exponent within the linked list, and we further assume that no two terms have the same exponent, and that no term has a 0 coefficient.

2.5.3 Addition of polynomials.

This ordering of the terms of polynomials simplifies their addition, and is, as well, the ordering that people normally use. To add two polynomials we need only scan through them once each. If we find terms with the same exponent in the two polynomials, then we add the coefficients; otherwise we copy the term with larger exponent into the sum and go on. When we reach the end of one of the polynomials, then any remaining part of the other is copied to the sum. We must also be careful not to include terms with 0 coefficient in the sum.

Since we are using header nodes of the pointer type **polynomial** to locate polynomials, we can write the algorithm to add polynomials as a function. This function will thus create a new polynomial; the original summands are left unchanged.

At several places in the algorithm we must create a new term and place it at the end of the sum; for convenience we do so in a separate procedure called **MakeTerm**, with the coefficient and exponent as calling parameters. The pointer **last** will always refer to the last term of the sum, and will be updated by the auxiliary procedure **MakeTerm**, which we write first.

```
procedure MakeTerm( coef: real; exp: integer);
{Creates a term with given coefficient and exponent, and attaches it
after the term pointed to by variable 'last'. Procedure assigns the
function name 'Add' to first term created.}
var
    t : polynomial;                          {used to create new term.}
begin
    New(t);
    t↑.coef : = coef;
    t↑.exp : = exp;
    t↑.next : = nil;
```

```
      if last = nil then                    {Is this the first term created?}
        Add : = t                           {Done for first term only, with empty list}
      else
        last↑.next : = t;        {If this is not first term, attach to end of list.}
      last : = t
    end;
```

We shall use this procedure whenever we make a new term in the addition function.

```
    function Add( p, q: polynomial): polynomial;
    var
      last : polynomial;                    {pointer to the last term of sum}
      c : real;                             {coefficient of a tentative term}
    {Declaration of procedure MakeTerm to be inserted here}
    begin                                   {Function Add(p,q)}
      last : = nil;                         {Initially sum is empty}
      Add : = nil;
      while (p <> nil) and (q <> nil) do
        if p↑.exp = q↑.exp then
        begin                               {Add terms with equal exponents}
          c : = p↑.coef + q↑.coef;
          if c <> 0 then                    {Forget a new term with 0 coefficient}
            MakeTerm(c, p↑.exp);
          p : = p↑.next;
          q : = q↑.next
        end
        else if p↑.exp > q↑.exp then
        with p↑ do begin                    {Copy from p, since p has larger exp.}
          MakeTerm( coef, exp);
          p : = next
        end else
        with q↑ do begin                    {Copy from q, since q has larger exp.}
          MakeTerm( coef, exp);
          q : = next
        end;
              {At this point, one of the two summands has been exhausted.
              At most one of the following copying loops will be executed.}
      while p <> nil do
      with p↑ do begin
        MakeTerm( coef, exp);
        p : = next
      end;
      while q <> nil do
      with q↑ do begin
        MakeTerm( coef, exp);
        q : = next
      end
    end;                                    {Function Add}
```

2.5.4 Group project.

Other operations on polynomials can be programmed as functions or procedures of the same general nature as our function for addition. Some of these are easy: subtraction is almost identical with addition; multiplying a polynomial by a scalar produces an algorithm that is even simpler than addition.

Production of a coherent package of algorithms for manipulating polynomials makes an interesting group project. Different members of the group can write functions or procedures for different operations. Some of these are indicated as exercises below, but you may wish to include additional features as well. Any additional features should be planned carefully to be sure that they can be implemented in a reasonable time, without disrupting other parts of the program.

After deciding on the division of work among its members, the most important decisions of the group relate to the exact ways in which the procedures and functions should communicate with each other, and especially with the calling program. If, for example, you use the addition function in the text as a guideline, then you will find that several of the functions need procedures like **MakeTerm**, but differing very slightly from each other. If you follow the method outlined in Exercise 1 of this section, then you will find that all the functions can use the same version of **MakeTerm**. There may be other changes you wish to make. Be certain that the precise details are spelled out clearly and completely for all members of the group.

Next, you will find that it is too much to hope that all members of the group will complete their work at the same time, or that all parts of the project can be combined and debugged together. You will therefore need to use program stubs and drivers (see Section 1.4) to debug and test the various parts of the project. One member of the group might take special responsibility for these. In any case, you will find it very effective for different members to read and help debug and test each other's subprograms.

Finally, there are the responsibilities of making sure that all members of the group complete their work on time, of keeping track of the progress of various aspects of the project, of making sure that no subprograms are integrated into the project before they are thoroughly debugged and tested, and then of combining all the work into the finished product.

Exercises

1. Every time a new term is created, procedure **MakeTerm** must check whether or not it is the first term of the new polynomial. Implement the following changes that will eliminate the need for this check, and thereby speed up the algorithm.

    (a) At the beginning of function **Add**, create a new term (leave its coefficient and exponent fields undefined), and set both **last** and another pointer (which we might call **head**) to it. This first term will be an artificial header that will never be used.

    (b) Simplify procedure **MakeTerm**, using the fact that **last** is never **nil**.

    (c) At the end of function **Add**, set the function name to the first real term (which is **head↑.next**) and dispose of the artificial term.

2. Write an algorithm that will input a sequence of coefficients and exponents from the user, and form them into a linked polynomial as described in this section.

3. Write a function that will subtract two polynomials.

4. Write a function that will compute the derivative of a polynomial.

5. Write a function that will multiply a polynomial by a monomial (that is, by a polynomial consisting of a single term).

6. Use the function of Exercise 5, together with the function that adds polynomials, to write a function that multiplies two polynomials.

7. Write a function that, given a polynomial and a real number, evaluates the polynomial at that number.

8. [Requires some knowledge of numerical methods] Write a procedure that will determine all real roots of a polynomial (given as a linked list).

9. Same as Exercise 8, but find all complex roots and multiplicities.

10. Write a procedure that will print a polynomial as a sequence of coefficients and exponents, arranged attractively.

11. Write a procedure that will print a polynomial as a product of linear factors, arranged attractively. [Use the procedure of Exercise 9 to find the roots.]

12. Write a procedure that will divide one polynomial by another. The result of the procedure will be two new polynomials, the quotient and the remainder, where the remainder, if not 0, has degree strictly less than that of the divisor.

13. Write a procedure that erases (disposes of) a polynomial.

14. Find what changes are needed in Exercise 13 and in the other procedures and functions so as to reuse space for terms on systems where the standard procedure **dispose(   )** does not work efficiently.

15. If polynomials are stored as circularly linked lists instead of simply linked lists, then a polynomial can be erased more quickly. What changes are needed to the addition function (and other subprograms) to implement circularly linked lists?

16. [Larger project] Write an interactive system that will allow a user to set up several polynomials, call the preceding functions and procedures to perform various operations as desired, and print out the results as desired. You will need to decide how to assign names to the various polynomials and how the user is to specify what operations are to be done with which polynomials.

17. Consider generalizing the project of Exercise 16 to polynomials in several variables. Fixing the number of variables to be some small number will be much easier than allowing an arbitrary number of variables to be specified when the user runs the program.

2.6 Linked lists in arrays.

Several of the older but widely-used computer languages, such as FORTRAN, COBOL and BASIC, do not provide facilities for dynamic storage allocation or pointers. Even when implemented in these languages, however, there are many applications for which the methods of linked lists are preferable to those of contiguous lists; applications where, for example, the ease of changing a pointer rather than copying a large record proves advantageous. This section shows how to represent linked lists using only simple integer variables and arrays.

The idea is simple: we begin with a large array (or several arrays to hold different parts of a record), and regard the array as our allocation of unused space. We then set up our own procedures to keep track of which parts of the array are unused, and to link entries of the array together in the desired order. The one feature that we must lose in this method is the dynamic allocation of storage, since we must decide in advance how much space to allocate to each array. All the remaining advantages of linked lists, such as flexibility in rearranging large records or ease in making insertions or deletions anywhere in the list, will still apply, and linked lists still prove a valuable method.

The representation of linked lists within arrays even proves valuable in languages like Pascal that do provide pointer types and dynamic memory allocation. The applications for which arrays may prove preferable are those where the number of items in a list is known in advance, where the links are frequently rearranged, but relatively few additions or deletions are made, or applications where the same data are sometimes best treated as a linked list, and other times as a contiguous list.

The main goal of this section, however, is to demonstrate the use of linked lists in contexts without pointer types, and to emphasize this goal we shall write the algorithms of this section in FORTRAN. Since FORTRAN does not provide for record types, it is necessary to treat each component of a record as a separate variable. We shall then need several arrays to represent a linked list. A particular record might be regarded as in position k (where k is some index), and then the array entry name(k) might be the corresponding name, address(k) the corresponding address entry from another array, info(k) further information, and next(k) will be the link to the next record in the linked list.

In this representation, pointers become indices relative to the start of arrays, and links of a list are stored in an array, each entry of which shows where, within the array, the next entry of the list is stored.

For the sake of programming in FORTRAN we shall use two arrays, info(   ) to hold the information in the nodes and next(   ) to give the link to the next node. Since these arrays must be accessible to all the subroutines, we shall assume that they are in a common block, and are indexed from 1 to some bound, which, to be definite, we take as 100. The choice of this bound is, of course, arbitrary, and in an application it would be replaced by an appropriate number. Since we begin the indices with 1, we can make another arbitrary choice and represent **nil** pointers by the index 0.

With these conventions, let us see what the representation will produce on a sample list of fourteen names. The result is shown in Figure 2.16, with the names linked in alphabetical order.

Index	Info	Next
1	Tim	5
2	Dot	3
3	Eva	7
4	Roy	1
5	Tom	0
6	Kim	13
7	Guy	14
8	Amy	10
9	Jon	12
10	Ann	2
11	Jim	9
12	Kay	6
13	Ron	4
14	Jan	11
15	• • •	?
100	• • •	?

Figure 2.16. Linked list of names in arrays

You should take a moment to trace through this table, drawing an arrow from each name to its successor in alphabetical order, and observing the corresponding indices entered in the table Next( ).

To obtain the flavor of representing linked lists in arrays, let us rewrite several of the algorithms of this chapter with this representation.

Our first task should be to set up a list of available space, and write subroutines to obtain a new node and to return a node to available space. For these purposes we need an integer variable avail that will give the index of the top of the available-space stack. If this stack is empty (which will be represented by avail = 0) then we will need to obtain a new node. Thus we shall keep another integer variable lastused that will count the total number of positions within our arrays that have been used to hold list entries. When lastused exceeds 100 (the bound we have assumed for array size) then we will have overflow. Since these two variables are used by different subprograms, we shall assume that they are in the common block with link( ) and info( ). When the main program starts, both variables avail and lastnode should be initialized to 0.

We now have enough information to rewrite the procedures NewNode and DisposeNode for linked lists in arrays:

```
      Subroutine NewNode(p)
C     p will be index of the new node returned by the subroutine.
      Integer p, avail, lastnode
      Common avail, lastnode, next(100), info(100)
      If (avail .ne. 0) then
```

```
      p = avail
      avail = next(avail)
   Else if (lastnode .lt. 100) then
      lastnode = lastnode + 1
      p = lastnode
   Else
      Call overflow
   Endif
   Return
   End

   Subroutine DisposeNode(p)
C  Returns node with index p to available space.
   Integer p, avail
   Common avail, lastnode, next(100), info(100)
   If (p .eq. 0) Return
   next(p) = avail
   avail   = p
   Return
   End
```

The translation of other procedures so as to manipulate linked lists represented within arrays proceeds in much the same way, and the details can safely be left as exercises. To provide further models, however, let us write translations of the procedures to traverse a list, and to add a node after a given one in a list.

```
   Subroutine Traverse(head)
C  Traverses the linked list that begins at index head.
   Integer head, p, avail
   Common avail, lastnode, next(100), info(100)
   p = head
   While (p .ne. 0)
      Call Visit(p)
      p = next(p)
   Endwhile
   Return
   End

   Subroutine AddAfter(p, q)
C  Adds node with index q to linked list, after node at p.
   Integer p, q, next, avail
   Common avail, lastnode, next(100), info(100)
   If (p .eq. 0 .or. q .eq. 0) Call Error
   next(q) = next(p)
   next(p) = q
   Return
   End
```

Exercises

1. Write a FORTRAN function that counts the number of nodes in a linked list represented in an array.

2. Write a FORTRAN subroutine that will concatenate two linked lists. The subroutine should have two parameters, pointers to the beginning of the lists, and the subroutine should link the end of the first list to the beginning of the second.

3. Write a FORTRAN subroutine that will split a list in two. The subroutine will use two pointers as parameters; p will point to the beginning of the list and q to the node at which it should be split. Is it easier to require that q initially point to the node that will be last in the first list after splitting, or to the node that will be first in the second list?

4. Write instructions that will reverse a linked list within an array while traversing it only once. At the conclusion, each node should point to the node that was previously its predecessor; the header should point to the node that was formerly at the end, and the node that was formerly first should have a 0 link.

2.7 General definitions and specific representations.

Suppose that in deciphering a long and poorly documented program you found the following sets of instructions.

$$\text{xxt}\uparrow.\text{xlnk} := \text{w}; \quad \text{w}\uparrow.\text{xlnk} := \textbf{nil}; \quad \text{xxt} := \text{w};$$

and

```
if ((xxh = xxt + 1) and (xxt > 0)) or ((xxt = mxx) and (xxh = 1))
  then overflow
  else begin
    xxt := xxt + 1;
    if xxt > mxx then xxt := 1;
    xx[xxt] := wi
  end;
```

In isolation it may not be clear what either of these sections of code is intended to do, and without further explanation it would probably take some minutes to realize that in fact they have essentially the same function! Both segments are intended to add an item to the end of a queue, the first queue in a linked representation, and the second queue in contiguous storage.

Researchers working in different subjects frequently have ideas that are fundamentally similar but are developed for different purposes and expressed in different language. Often years will pass before anyone realizes the similarity of the work, but when the observation is made, insight from one subject can help with the other. In computer science, even so, the same basic idea often appears in quite different disguises that obscure the similarity. But if we can discover and emphasize the similarities, then we may be able to generalize the ideas and obtain easier ways to meet the requirements of many applications.

When we first introduced stacks and queues, we considered them only as they are represented in contiguous storage; and yet when we studied linked stacks and queues there was little difficulty in recognizing the same underlying logical structure. Which of the two representations is better depends very much on the application. Sometimes the third way, where a linked list is represented inside an array, is superior to both of the others. Perhaps in some special application a very unusual representation that we have not considered at all will prove even better. Over the next several years there may well be developments both in computer hardware and software that will produce ways to represent stacks and queues that are preferable to any of the methods we have studied. No such development, however, will change the basic concept of a stack or a queue, nor what computational tasks can, or cannot, be done by using stacks or queues.

Although we have been careful to devise a correct definition of each new structure as we have first studied it, sometimes these definitions have depended on the representation in computer memory. To achieve greater generality in what follows, we should now pause to see how best to separate the underlying logical structures from their concrete realizations, in the hope that we can thereby be able to make intelligent choices concerning both the data structures we need and the way to represent them.

The first such definition we can give is that of a *sequential list*. What the entries in the list will be depends on the application; for the moment we can simply call the entries *nodes*. A node might be a single number, or a large and complicated record. A sequential list is then either empty or is a finite ordered n-tuple

$$(a_1, \ a_2, \ a_3, \ \cdots \ , \ a_n)$$

where the a_i, $1 \leq i \leq n$, are nodes.

Next we would like to define stacks and queues, but if you consider the definitions, you will realize that there will be nothing regarding organizing the nodes to distinguish these structures from a sequential list. The only difference concerns the rules by which changes or accesses can be made to the list. Hence, before turning to these other structures, we should complete the definition of a sequential list by specifying what operations can be done with a sequential list. These include:

1. Find the length of (number of nodes in) the sequential list.

2. Retrieve any node from the sequential list.

3. Store a new node replacing the node at any given position in the list.

4. Insert a new node into the list at any position, thereby increasing the index number of all following nodes by 1.

5. Delete any node from the list, thereby decreasing the index number of all following nodes by 1.

It is now easy to see what changes are needed to define stacks and queues.

A *stack* is defined in the same way as a sequential list, except that the operations are restricted to:

1. Determine if the stack is empty or not.

2. Retrieve the last node from the stack, if it is not empty.

3. Insert a new node after the last node of the stack.

4. Delete the last node of the stack, if it is not empty.

A *queue* is defined in the same way as a sequential list, except that the operations are restricted to:

1. Determine if the queue is empty or not.

2. Retrieve the first node in the queue, if it is not empty.

3. Insert a new node after the last node in the queue.

4. Delete the first node in the queue, if it is not empty.

The important principle that appears in the preceding definitions is that there must always be two parts appearing in the definition of a data structure: first is a description of the way in which the data are related to each other; and second is a list of the operations that can be performed within the data structure.

Note that in the definitions we have never mentioned the way to represent the list, but have buried the details in the undefined word "*n*-tuple" used to set up a sequential list. The definition of this term in mathematics usually starts with a single entry ($n = 1$) and adjoins additional entries by induction. We can do the same with nodes, but we have left unspecified how to adjoin a new node. We could use links to adjoin the new node to the previous list, thereby obtaining a linked sequential list, or we could put the new node at the next address in memory beyond the end of the previous list, thereby obtaining a contiguous sequential list. In either case, the nodes are regarded logically as being in a straight row like the numbers 1, 2, 3, · · · , and this is what we mean by *sequential.*

From now on we shall draw a careful distinction between the word *sequential* and the word *contiguous,* which we take to mean that the nodes have adjacent addresses in memory. Hence, as we have already done, we can contrast the linked and contiguous representations of sequential lists or other data structures.

The way in which an underlying structure is represented can have substantial effects on program development and on the capabilities and usefulness of the result. Sometimes these effects can be subtle. The underlying mathematical concept of a real number, for example, is usually (but not always) represented by a computer as a floating-point number with a certain degree of precision, and the inherent limitations in this representation often produce difficulties with round-off error. Drawing a clear separation between the logical structure of our data and its representation in computer memory will help us in designing programs. Our first step is to recognize the logical connections among the data, and then to embody these connections in a logical data structure. Later we can consider our data structures and decide what is the best way to represent them for efficiency of programming and execution. By separating these decisions they both become easier, and we avoid the pitfalls that attend premature commitment.

Exercises

1. Some of the operations allowed on sequential lists will be easier with contiguous representation, and some will be easier with linked representation. Which will be which, and why?

2. Give formal definitions of the terms *deque* and *scroll*, using the definitions given for stack and queue as models.

2.8 References for further study.

The one major reference for this chapter, and the foremost one for the next several chapters as well, is the encyclopaedic work:

DONALD E. KNUTH, *The Art of Computer Programming*, Addison-Wesley, Reading, Mass.

Three volumes have appeared to date:

> *1. Fundamental Algorithms*, second edition, 1973, 634 pages.
> *2. Seminumerical Algorithms*, second edition, 1980, 700 pages.
> *3. Sorting and Searching,* 1973, 722 pages.

In the sequel, references to this series of books will be given only by the name 'KNUTH', together with volume and page numbers.

With the exception of Pascal features and dynamic memory allocation, the contents of the current chapter form the subject of KNUTH, volume 1, pages 228–295, where almost all topics are studied in more depth. The algorithms are written both in English and in an assembler language, in which KNUTH calculates detailed counts of operations to compare various algorithms. Without the availability of the pointer types from Pascal, the programs become more complicated.

Contiguous stacks and queues occupy pages 234–251, and linked lists pages 251–272. Our algorithm for polynomial addition is taken from KNUTH, pages 272–276, except that KNUTH uses a circularly linked list. Pages 279–295 are devoted to the study of queues as applied to the simulation of an elevator.

For additional details regarding the implementation of pointer types in Pascal, the best reference is the Pascal manual for your system. Several implementations of Pascal either do not use the standard procedures **new** and **dispose,** or provide alternate methods that may be superior. Since the details of these methods depend on the system, we cannot provide more information here.

Chapter 3

Information Retrieval

This chapter studies four important methods for retrieving information from a list: sequential search, binary search, table lookup, and methods for using hash tables. One of our major purposes is to compare various algorithms, to see which are preferable under different conditions. To do this we shall develop more sophisticated tools, such as comparison trees, which help to analyze the performance of algorithms. The chapter concludes by returning to the Life game, to obtain a program without the previous constraints.

3.1 Searching: Introduction and Notation.

Information retrieval is one of the most important applications of computers. We are given a name, and asked for an associated telephone listing. We are given an account number, and asked for the transactions occurring in that account. We are given an employee name or number, and asked for the personnel records of the employee.

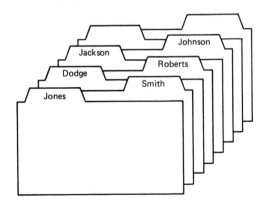

Figure 3.1. Records and their keys

In these examples and a host of others we are given one piece of information, which we shall call a *key*, and asked to find a record that contains other information associated with the key. A rule which, for simplicity, we adopt throughout this chapter is that, given a key, there should be only one record with that key. On the other hand, it is quite possible that, given a key, there is no record at all that has that key.

Searching for keys to locate records is often the most time-consuming action in a program, and therefore the way the records are arranged and the choice of method used for searching can make a substantial difference in the program's performance. The searching problem falls naturally into two cases. If there are many records, perhaps each one quite large, then it will be necessary to store the records in files on disk or tape, external to the computer memory. In the other case, the records to be searched are kept within the computer memory. These cases are called *external* and *internal* searching, respectively. In this chapter we consider only internal searching.

To write our programs in Pascal, we establish some notation. What we have called records will indeed be Pascal records, and the Pascal type that these records have we shall name either as item or as node. One of the fields (or components) of each item will be denoted key and have a type called keytype. We thus assume that the program will have declarations of the form:

```
type  keytype  =  ···;
      item  =  record
                  ···                          {various components};
              key: keytype;
                  ···                          {more components}
          end;
```

Typical declarations for the key type are:

```
keytype = real;
keytype = integer;
keytype = packed array[1..8] of char.
```

The items will always be considered to be in a list, but at different times we shall consider both algorithms for the case of a linked list and of a contiguous list (stored within an array). In the latter case, we shall take the list as indexed from 1 to n, and stored in an array L[   ]. In both cases we shall always denote by n the number of entries in the list. For simplicity we shall assume that $n > 0$.

The key for which we are searching through the list will always be denoted by x, and will be called the *target* of the search.

3.2 Sequential search.

Beyond doubt the simplest way to do a search is to begin at one end of the list and scan down it until the desired key is found or the other end is reached. This is our first method.

3.2.1 Contiguous version.

In the case when the list is in a contiguous array L, with index type index, we obtain the following procedure. The index p at the conclusion gives the location of the target x, or is 0 if the search was unsuccessful.

```
procedure SequentialSearch(var p: index; x: keytype);
{Contiguous version. Uses array L indexed from 1 to n.}
begin
  p : = 1;
  while (x <> L[p].key) and (p < n) do
    p : = p + 1;
  if x <> L[p].key then
    p : = 0;                           {search is unsuccessful}
end;
```

The **while** loop in this procedure keeps moving through the list as long as the target key x has not been found. It is tempting to replace the condition p < n by p <= n, in the hope of avoiding the comparison of keys outside the loop. Doing this, however, could make the final attempt at iteration look in the possibly nonexistent position L[n + 1], which might be an error. Thus we postpone checking x against the final item in L until after the loop. In any case, some such comparison is required in Pascal, since we cannot tell which of the two conditions terminated the **while** loop.

3.2.2 Linked version.

A version of sequential search for linked lists is equally easy. Here we take p as a pointer that initially points to the first node of the list, and at the conclusion will point to the target x, or will be **nil** if the search was unsuccessful.

```
procedure SequentialSearch( var p: pointer; x: keytype);
{Version for linked lists. Pointer p is used for both input and output.}
begin
  if p <> nil then
  begin
    while (p↑.next <> nil) and (x <> p↑.key) do
      p : = p↑.next;
    if x <> p↑.key then
      p : = nil
  end
end;
```

3.2.3 Comparison of keys versus running time.

As you can see, the basic method of sequential search is exactly the same for both the contiguous and linked versions, even though the mechanics differ. In fact, the target is compared to exactly the same keys in the nodes (or items) of the list in either version. Although the running times of the two versions may differ a little, in both of them all the actions go in lock step with comparison of keys. Hence, if we wish to estimate how long sequential search is likely to require, or if we wish to compare it with some other method, then knowing the number of comparisons of keys that it makes will give us the most useful information, information actually more useful than the total running time, which is too much dependent on whether we have the contiguous or linked version, or what particular machine is being used.

3.2.4 Analysis of sequential search.

Short as sequential search is, when we start to count comparisons of keys we run into difficulties because we do not know how many times the loop will be iterated. We have no way to know in advance whether or not the search will be successful. If it is, we do not know if the target will be the first key on the list, the last, or somewhere between. Thus, to obtain useful information, we must do several analyses.

Fortunately, these are all easy. If the search is unsuccessful, then the target will have been compared to all items in the list, for a total of n comparisons of keys, where n is the length of the list. For a successful search, if the target is in position k, then it will have been compared with the first k keys in the list, for a total of exactly k comparisons. Thus the best time for a successful search is 1 comparison, and the worst is n comparisons.

We have obtained very detailed information about the timing of sequential search, information that is really too detailed for most uses, in that we generally will not know exactly where in a list a particular key may appear. Instead, it will generally be much more helpful if we can determine the *average* behavior of an algorithm. But what do we mean by average? One reasonable assumption, the one that we shall make, is to take each possibility once and average the results.

Note, however, that this assumption may be very far from the actual situation. Not all English words, for example, appear equally often in a typical essay. The telephone operator receives far more requests for the number of a large business than for that of an average family. The Pascal compiler encounters the key words **if, begin** and **end** far more often than the key words **label, downto** and **packed**.

There are a great many interesting, but exceedingly difficult, problems associated with analyzing algorithms where the input is chosen according to some statistical distribution. These problems, however, would take us too far afield to be considered here.

Under the assumption of equal likelihood, we can find the average number of key comparisons done in a successful sequential search. We simply add the number needed for all the successful searches, and divide by n, the number of items in the list. The result is

$$\frac{1+2+3+\ \cdots\ +n}{n}.$$

The first formula established in Appendix A is

$$1+2+3+\ \cdots\ +n\ =\ \tfrac{1}{2}n(n+1).$$

Hence the average number of key comparisons done by sequential search in the successful case is

$$\frac{n(n+1)}{2n}\ =\ \tfrac{1}{2}(n+1).$$

At the moment, we have nothing with which to compare this number, so it is time to consider another method.

Exercises

1. One good check for any algorithm is to see what it does in extreme cases. Determine what both versions of sequential search do when

   (a) There is only one item in the list.
   (b) The list is empty.

2. If we can assume that the keys in the list have been arranged in order (e.g., numerical or alphabetical order), then we can terminate unsuccessful searches more quickly. If the smallest keys come first, then we can terminate the search as soon as a key greater than or equal to the target key has been found. If we assume that it is equally likely that a target key not in the list is in any one of the $n+1$ intervals (before the first key, between a pair of keys, or after the last key), then what is the average number of comparisons for unsuccessful search in this version?

3. Write a program to check the contiguous version of sequential search. You should set up an array to hold the list, and put keys in it. An appropriate choice for the keys would be the integers from 1 to n. Modify the sequential search procedure so that it keeps a counter of the number of key comparisons that it makes. Find out how many comparisons are done in an unsuccessful search (for a key not in the list). Also call the procedure to search once for each key that is in the list, and thereby calculate the average number of comparisons made for a successful search. Run your program for representative values of n, such as $n = 10$, $n = 100$, $n = 1000$.

4. Do Exercise 3 for a linked list instead of a contiguous list.

At each iteration, sequential search checks two inequalities, one a comparison of keys to see if the target x has been found, and the other a comparison of indices to see if the bound n has been reached. A good way to speed up the algorithm by eliminating the second comparison is to make sure that eventually key x will be found, by increasing the size of the list, and adding an extra item at the end with key x. Such an item placed in a list to ensure that a process terminates is called a ***sentinel***. When the loop terminates, the search will have been successful if x was found among the first n entries, and unsuccessful if the final dummy item was the one found.

5. Write a Pascal procedure that embodies this idea in the contiguous version of sequential search.

6. Find the number of comparisons of keys done by your procedure written in Exercise 5 for

   (a) unsuccessful search.
   (b) best successful search.
   (c) worst successful search.
   (d) average successful search.

7. In the linked version of sequential search, suppose that (as we have assumed) we are given a pointer only to the start of the list. Explain why adding a sentinel to the list is not a particularly helpful idea. What extra information would make it worthwhile?

8. Take the program written in Exercise 3 to check the contiguous version of sequential search, and insert the version that uses a sentinel. Also insert instructions (system dependent) for obtaining the CPU time used. For various values of n, determine whether the version with or without sentinel is faster. Find the crossover point between the two versions, if there is one. That is, at what point is the extra time needed to insert a sentinel at the end of the list the same as the time needed for extra comparisons of indices in the version without sentinel?

3.3 Binary search.

Sequential search is easy to write and efficient for short lists, but a disaster for long ones. Imagine trying to find the name "Thomas Z. Smith" in the Toronto telephone book by reading one name at a time starting at the front of the book! To find any item in a long list there are far more efficient methods. One of the best is first to compare the item with one in the center of the list and then restrict our attention to only the first or second half of the list, depending on whether the item comes before or after the central one. In this way, at each step we reduce the length of the list to be searched by half. In only twenty comparisons this method will locate any requested name in a list of about a million names.

The method we are discussing is called ***binary search***. This approach requires that the items in the list be of a scalar or other type that can be regarded as totally ordered, and that the list already be completely in order. We shall assume that the keys can be compared under the operations '$<$' and '$>$' (for example, that they are numbers), but the algorithms can easily be extended to care for words or other character strings as keys.

Binary search is not good for linked lists, since it requires jumping back and forth from one end of the list to the middle, an action easy within an array, but slow for a linked list. Hence this section studies only contiguous lists.

Several slightly different algorithms for binary search can be written.

3.3.1 The forgetful version.

Perhaps the simplest algorithm is to forget the possibility that the target key x might be found quickly, and continue, whether x has been found or not, to subdivide the list until what remains has length 1. Our first program proceeds in this way. We shall use three indices in the program: top and bottom will bracket the part of the list that may contain x, and mid will be the midpoint of this reduced list.

```
procedure Binary1( var p: index; x: keytype);
{Forgetful version. At conclusion, p gives the index of target x,  or p =
0 if search is unsuccessful.}
var
  top,
  bottom,
  mid : index;
begin
  top : = n;
  bottom : = 1;
  while top > bottom do
  begin
    mid : = (top + bottom) div 2;
    if x > L[mid].key then bottom := mid+1 else top : = mid
  end;
  if x = L[top].key then
    p : = top
  else
    p : = 0
end;
```

Note that the **if** statement that divides the list in half is not symmetrical, in that the condition tested puts the midpoint into the lower of the two intervals at each iteration. On the other hand, integer division of positive integers always truncates downward. It is only these two facts together that ensure that the loop always terminates. Let us determine what occurs toward the end of the search. The loop will iterate only as long as top > bottom. But this condition implies that when mid is calculated we always have

$$\text{bottom} \le \text{mid} < \text{top}$$

since integer division truncates downward. Next, the **if** statement reduces the size of the interval from top − bottom either to top − (mid + 1) or to mid − bottom, both of which, by the inequality, are strictly less than top − bottom. Thus at each iteration the size of the interval strictly decreases, so the algorithm will eventually terminate.

3.3.2 Recognizing equality.

Although Binary1 is about the simplest form of binary search, it will often make unnecessary iterations because it fails to recognize that it has found the target x before continuing to iterate. Thus the time may be better with the following variation, which checks at each stage to see if it has found x.

```
procedure Binary2( var p: index; x: keytype);
{Version that recognizes discovery of target x.   Index p is location of x
if found, otherwise p = 0.}
var
  top,
  bottom,
  mid:        integer;       {mid will be index of x when it is found in L.}
begin
  top : = n;
  bottom : = 1;
  repeat
    mid : = (top + bottom) div 2;
    if x < L[mid].key then top := mid − 1 else bottom := mid + 1
  until (x = L[mid].key) or (top < bottom);
  if x = L[mid].key then
    p : = mid
  else
    p : = 0
end;
```

As you can see, the loop in this program has been rearranged from the use of a **while** statement to the use of a **repeat** ··· **until** statement. In this way the target x can be checked against the key at mid without having to give a separate calculation of mid before starting the loop, so the program is slightly shorter.

Proving that the loop in Binary2 terminates is easier than the proof for Binary1. In Binary2 the form of the **if** statement within the loop guarantees that the length of the interval is reduced by more than half at each iteration. To see that the termination condition top < bottom is required rather than top = bottom, suppose that the length reaches 2, that is, top = bottom + 1. Then, at the next iteration, the loop assigns mid : = bottom, and the **then** clause of the **if** statement (if it occurs) will set top to bottom − 1. Thus the termination condition given is the correct one.

Which of these two versions of binary search will be the faster? Clearly, Binary2 will be faster if we are fortunate to find x near the beginning of the search. But each iteration of Binary2 requires two comparisons, whereas Binary1 requires only one. Is it possible that, if many iterations are needed, then Binary1 may be faster? To answer this question, we shall develop a new method in the next section.

Exercises

1. Write a program to test Binary1, following the general instructions given for the similar exercise concerning sequential search in the last section. You should check both successful and unsuccessful searches for selected values of n. If your system can provide a measure of elapsed CPU time, you should also obtain timings for your procedure.

2. Write a program to test Binary2, as in Exercise 1.

3. Rewrite Binary2 to use **while** $\cdots$ **do** $\cdots$ in place of **repeat** $\cdots$ **until** $\cdots$ You should be able to make it run slightly faster in the process.

4. It is redundant to keep three pointers in binary search: bottom, mid, and top, since mid is guaranteed to be halfway between. Modify the binary search algorithm (either or both versions) so that it keeps only two pointers, mid and the distance from mid to bottom or top. Run both your version and one of the versions in the text to see which is faster.

5. On most computers addition is faster than division. Use the following idea to make a new version of binary search that does no division. First use addition to construct an auxiliary table of the powers of 2 that are less than n, and then, by adding and subtracting appropriate entries from this table, reduce the bounds of the interval being searched.

6. Suppose that L_1 and L_2 are lists containing n_1 and n_2 integers, respectively, and both lists are already sorted into numerical order. Use binary search to find the median of the n_1+n_2 integers in the combined lists.

3.4 Comparison trees.

The *comparison tree* (also called *decision tree* or *search tree*) of an algorithm is obtained by tracing through the action of the algorithm, representing each comparison by a *vertex* of the tree (which we draw as a circle). Inside the circle we put the index of the key against which we are comparing the target key x. *Branches* (lines) drawn down from the circle represent the possible outcomes of the comparison and are labeled accordingly. When the algorithm terminates, we put either F (for failure) or the index where x is found at the end of the appropriate branch, which we call a *leaf*, and draw as a square. Leaves are also sometimes called ***end-vertices*** or ***external vertices*** of the tree. Obviously, then, the other vertices can be called the ***internal vertices*** of the tree.

The comparison tree for sequential search is especially simple; it is drawn in Figure 3.2.

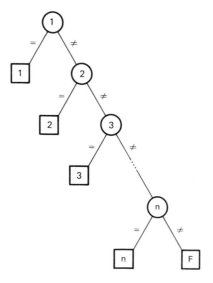

Figure 3.2. Comparison tree for sequential search

The number of comparisons done by an algorithm in a particular search is the number of circular nodes traversed in going from the top of the tree (which is called its ***root***) down the appropriate path to a leaf. The number of branches traversed to reach a vertex from the root is called the ***level*** of the vertex. Thus the root itself has level 0, the vertices immediately below it have level 1, etc. The largest level that occurs is called the ***height*** of the tree. As is traditional, we shall now mix our metaphors by thinking of family trees, and call the vertices immediately below a vertex v the ***children*** of v, and the vertex immediately above v the ***parent*** of v.

3.4.1 Analysis for $n = 10$.

That sequential search on average does far more comparisons than binary search is obvious from comparing the shape of its tree with those of Binary1 and Binary2, which for $n = 10$ are drawn in Figures 3.3 and 3.4, respectively. Sequential search has a long, narrow tree, which means many comparisons, whereas the trees for binary search are much wider and shorter.

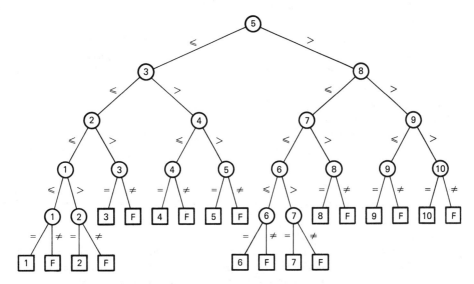

Figure 3.3. Comparison tree for Binary 1, $n = 10$

In Binary2 we combine two comparisons to obtain one three-way comparison for each pass through the loop. Thus the drawing is more compact, but remember that two comparisons are really done for each of the vertices shown. In Binary2, moreover, the final comparison done after the loop finishes is only a repetition of a comparison done in the **until** clause; hence it is not shown on the diagram, whereas the final comparison in Binary1 produces new information and is shown in the diagram for Binary1. Drawing the tree this way, moreover, means that every vertex that is not a leaf terminates some successful search, and the leaves correspond to unsuccessful searches.

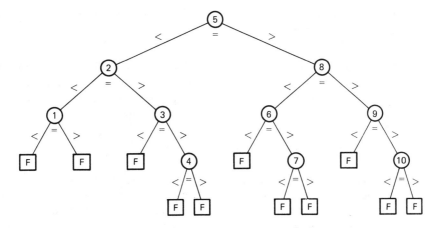

Figure 3.4. Comparison tree for Binary2, $n = 10$

It is this last way of drawing comparison trees that will be our standard way in the future.

From the trees it is easy to read off how many comparisons will be done when $n = 10$. In the worst case it is simply one more than the height of the tree; in fact, in every case it is the number of circular vertices lying between the root and the vertex that terminates the search.

In Binary1 every search terminates at a leaf; to obtain the average number of comparisons for both successful and unsuccessful searches, we need what is called the ***external path length*** of the tree: the sum of the number of branches traversed in going from the root once to every leaf in the tree. For the tree in Figure 3.3, the external path length is

$$4 \times 5 + 6 \times 4 + 4 \times 5 + 6 \times 4 \ = \ 88.$$

Half of the leaves correspond to successful searches, and half to unsuccessful. Hence the average number of comparisons needed for either a successful or unsuccessful search by Binary1 is $44/10 \ = \ 4.4$, when $n = 10$.

In the tree as it is drawn for Binary2, all the leaves correspond to unsuccessful searches; hence the external path length leads to the number of comparisons for an unsuccessful search. For successful searches, we need the ***internal path length***, which is defined to be the sum, over all vertices that are not leaves, of the number of branches from the root to the vertex. For the tree in Figure 3.4 the internal path length is

$$0+1+2+2+3+1+2+3+2+3 \ = \ 19.$$

Recall that Binary2 does two comparisons for each non-leaf, and note that the number of these circular vertices traversed is one more than the number of branches (for each of the $n = 10$ vertices), so we obtain the average number of comparisons for a successful search to be

$$2 \times \left(\frac{19}{10} + 1 \right) = \ 5.8.$$

For an unsuccessful search by Binary2 we need the external path length of the tree in Figure 3.4. This is

$$5 \times 3 + 6 \times 4 \ = \ 39.$$

We shall assume for unsuccessful searches that the $n+1$ intervals (less than the first key, between a pair of successive keys, or greater than the largest) are all equally likely; for the diagram we therefore assume that any of the 11 failure leaves are equally likely. Thus the average number of comparisons for an unsuccessful search is

$$\frac{2 \times 39}{11} \ \approx \ 7.1.$$

Hence, for $n = 10$, Binary1 does slightly fewer comparisons in each case. To be fair, however, we should note that the two comparisons done by Binary2 at each circular vertex are closely related (the same keys are being compared), so an optimizing compiler may not do as much work as two full comparisons, in which case, in fact, Binary2 may be a slightly better choice when $n = 10$.

3.4.2 Generalization.

What happens when n is larger than 10? For longer lists, it may be impossible to draw the complete comparison tree, but from the examples with $n = 10$ we can make some observations that will always be true.

1. 2-trees.

Let us define a *2-tree* as a tree in which every vertex except the leaves has exactly 2 children. Both versions of comparison trees that we have drawn fit this definition, and are 2-trees. We can make several observations about 2-trees that will provide information about the behavior of binary search methods for all values of n.

Other terms for 2-tree are **strictly binary tree** and **extended binary tree**, but we shall not use these terms, because they are too easily confused with the term "binary tree" which (when introduced in Chapter 5) has a somewhat different meaning.

In a 2-tree the number of vertices on any level can be no more than twice the number on the level above, since each vertex has either 0 or 2 children (depending on whether it is a leaf or not). Since there is one vertex on level 0 (the root) the number of vertices on level t is at most 2^t for all $t \geq 0$. We thus have the facts:

LEMMA 3.1. *The number of vertices on each level of a 2-tree is at most twice the number on the level immediately above.*

LEMMA 3.2. *In a 2-tree, the number of vertices on level t is at most 2^t for $t \geq 0$.*

2. Analysis of Binary1.

For Binary1 both successful and unsuccessful searches terminate at leaves; there are thus $2n$ leaves, and they are on at most two adjacent levels. The height (number of levels below root) is the maximum number of key comparisons that the algorithm does, and is at most one more than the average number. By Lemma 3.2, the height is also the smallest integer t such that $2^t \geq 2n$. Take logarithms with base 2. (For a review of properties of logarithms, see Appendix A.) We obtain that the number of comparisons of keys done by Binary1 in searching a list of n items is approximately

$$\lg n + 1.$$

As can be seen from the tree, the number of comparisons is essentially independent of whether the search is successful or not.

3. Notation.

The notation for base 2 logarithms just used will be standard. In analyzing algorithms we shall also sometimes need natural logarithms (taken with base $e = 2.71828...$). We shall denote a natural logarithm by ln. We shall rarely need logarithms to any other base. We thus summarize:

Convention

Unless stated otherwise, all logarithms are taken with base 2.
The symbol

lg

denotes a logarithm with base 2, and the symbol

ln

denotes a natural logarithm.
When the base for logarithms is not specified
(or is not important), then the symbol

log

will be used.

After we take logarithms, we frequently need to move either up or down to the next integer. To specify this action, we define the *floor* of a real number x to be the largest integer less than or equal to x, and the *ceiling* of x to be the smallest integer greater than or equal to x. We denote the floor of x by $\lfloor x \rfloor$ and the ceiling of x by $\lceil x \rceil$.

4. Analysis of Binary2.

To count the comparisons made by Binary2 for a general value of n for an unsuccessful search, we must essentially find the external path length of its comparison tree. This tree is again full at the top, with all its leaves on at most two adjacent levels at the bottom. There is one node at the root, two immediately below the root, four on level 2, and so on. By Lemma 3.2 there are 2^t vertices on each level, until the last level is reached, which may have fewer. The following formula from Appendix A then adds the number of vertices from the root through level m:

$$1 + 2 + 4 + \cdots + 2^{m-1} \ = \ 2^m - 1.$$

This formula tells us that the bottom level of the comparison tree will come out full when $n = 2^m - 1$ for some m. For other values of n, our results will be approximate, but not off by more than one comparison. Taking (base 2) logarithms, we obtain that $m = \lg(n+1)$. This value is the distance from the root to the leaves, and is also the number of double comparisons done in an unsuccessful search.

5. The path length theorem.

To calculate the average number for a successful search, we first obtain an interesting and important relationship that holds for any 2-tree.

THEOREM 3.3.   *Denote the external path length of a 2-tree by E, the internal path length by I, and let q be the number of vertices that are not leaves. Then*

$$E \ = \ I + 2q.$$

To prove the theorem we use the method of mathematical induction. If the tree contains only its root, and no other vertices, then $E = I = q = 0$, and the first case of the theorem is trivially correct. Now take a larger tree, and let v be some vertex that is not a leaf, but for which both the children of v are leaves. Let k be the number of branches on the path from the root to v. Now let us delete the two children of v from the 2-tree. Since v is not a leaf but its children are, the number of non-leaves goes down from q to $q-1$. The internal path length I is reduced by the distance to v, that is, to $I-k$. The distance to each child of v is $k+1$, so the external path length is reduced from E to $E-2(k+1)$, but v is now a leaf, so its distance, k, must be added, giving a new external path length of

$$E-2(k+1)+k \;=\; E-k-2.$$

Since the new tree has fewer vertices than the old one, by induction hypothesis we know that

$$E-k-2 \;=\; (I-k)+2(q-1).$$

Rearrangement of this equation gives the desired result.

6. Binary 2, successful search.

In the comparison tree of **Binary2** the distance to the leaves is $\lg(n+1)$, as we have seen. The number of leaves is $n+1$, so the external path length is about

$$(n+1)\lg(n+1).$$

The theorem then shows that the internal path length is about

$$(n+1)\lg(n+1)-2n.$$

To obtain the average number of comparisons done in a successful search we must first divide by n (the number of non-leaves), and then add 1 and double, since two comparisons were done at each circular node. The result is approximately

$$2\lg n - 2.$$

3.4.3 Comparison of methods.

Note the similarities and differences in the formulae for the two versions of binary search. In both cases the times are proportional to $\lg n$, except for small constant terms, and the coefficients of $\lg n$ are, in both cases, the number of comparisons inside the loop. The fact that the loop in **Binary2** can terminate quickly contributes disappointingly little to improving its speed; it does not reduce the coefficient of $\lg n$ at all, but only reduces the constant term from $+1$ to -2. A moment's examination of the comparison trees will show why. More than half the vertices occur at the bottom level, and so their loops cannot terminate early. More than half the remaining ones could terminate only one iteration early. Thus, for large n, the number of vertices relatively high in the tree, say in the top half of the levels, is negligible in comparison with the number at the bottom level.

With the smaller coefficient of lg n, Binary1 will probably run faster when n is sufficiently large, but with the smaller constant term, Binary2 may run faster when n is small. But for such a small value of n, the overhead in setting up binary search, and the extra programming effort, probably make it a more expensive method to use than sequential search. Thus we arrive at the conclusion, quite contrary to what we would intuitively conclude, that Binary2 is probably not worth the effort, since for large problems Binary1 is likely better, and for small problems, SequentialSearch. To be fair, however, with some computers and optimizing compilers the two comparisons needed in Binary2 will not take double the time of the one in Binary1, so it may be that Binary2 proves the better choice.

Our object in doing analysis of algorithms is to help us decide which may be better under appropriate circumstances. Disregarding the preceding provisos, we have now been able to make such a decision, and have available to us information that might otherwise not be obvious.

3.4.4 A general relationship.

Before leaving this section, let us use Theorem 3.3 to obtain a relationship between the average number of key comparisons for successful and for unsuccessful searches, a relationship that holds for any searching method for which the comparison tree can be drawn as we did for Binary2. If I and E are the internal and external path lengths of the tree, respectively, and n is the number of items in the list, so that n is also the number of non-leaves in the tree, then we know that the average number of circular nodes passed through in a successful search is

$$ S \;=\; \frac{I}{n} + 1 $$

and the average number for an unsuccessful search is

$$ U \;=\; \frac{E}{n+1}. $$

By Theorem 3.3, $E = I + 2n$. We can therefore conclude that:

> THEOREM 3.4.   *Under the above conditions, the average numbers of key comparisons done in successful and unsuccessful searches are related by*
>
> $$ S \;=\; \left(1 + \frac{1}{n}\right)U - 1. $$

In other words, the average number of comparisons for a successful search is almost exactly the same as that for an unsuccessful search. Knowing that an item is in the list is very little help in finding it, if you are searching by means of comparisons of keys.

Exercises

1. Draw the comparison trees for Binary1 and Binary2 when

    (a) $n = 5$
    (b) $n = 7$
    (c) $n = 8$
    (d) $n = 13$.

    Calculate the external and internal path lengths for each of these trees, and verify that the conclusion of Theorem 3.3 holds.

2. Sequential search has less overhead than binary search, and so may run faster for small n. Find the break-even point (for each of the binary search procedures), in terms of the formulae for the number of comparisons done in the average successful search.

3. We have ignored the time needed to initialize the search procedures and to complete index calculations. For this reason, sequential search will be the better method for values of n somewhat larger than your answer to Exercise 2. Compare the results of your test programs written for sequential search and binary search (both versions) in previous exercises, to determine the cross-over point on your computer.

4. Suppose that you have a list of 10,000 names in alphabetical order in an array, and you must frequently look for various names. It turns out that 20% of the names account for 80% of the table lookups. Instead of doing a binary search over all 10,000 names every time, consider the possibility of splitting the table into two, a high-frequency table of 2000 names, and a low-frequency table of the remaining 8000 names. To look up a name, you will first use binary search on the high-frequency table, and 80% of the time you will not need to go on to the second stage, where you use binary search on the low frequency table. Is this scheme worth the effort? Justify your answer by finding the number of comparisons done for the average search, both in the new scheme and in a binary search of a single table of 10,000 names.

5. Write a program that will do a "hybrid" search, using binary search (your choice of the two algorithms or some variation) for large lists, and switching to sequential search when the list is sufficiently reduced. (Because of different overhead, the best switch-over point is not necessarily the same as your answer to Exercise 2.)

6. If you modified binary search so that it divided the list not essentially in half at each pass, but instead into two pieces of sizes about ⅓ and ⅔ of the remaining list, then what would be the approximate effect on its average count of comparisons?

7. Write a "ternary" search algorithm that examines the key ⅓ of the way through the list, and if the target key x is greater, then examines the key ⅔ of the way through, and thus in any case at each pass reduces the length of the list by a factor of 3. Compare the count of comparisons of your algorithm with binary search.

8. Run Binary1 and Binary2, searching once for each key present, in order to find which is faster on your computer for values of n about equal to:

   (a) $n = 10$.
   (b) $n = 300$.
   (c) $n = 900$.

3.5 Lower Bounds.

We know that for an ordered contiguous list, binary search is much faster than sequential search. It is only natural to ask if we can find another method that is much faster than binary search. By being clever we may be able to reduce the work done in each iteration by a bit, and thereby speed up the algorithm. One method, called *Fibonacci search*, even manages to replace the division inside the loop by certain subtractions (with no auxiliary table needed), which on some computers will produce a little improvement. But the reason why binary search is so much faster than sequential search is not that there are fewer steps within its loop (there are actually more), but that the loop is iterated fewer times, about lg n times instead of n times, and as the number n increases, the value of lg n grows much more slowly than the value of n. Figure 3.5 graphs the number of comparisons done by sequential and binary search, $\frac{1}{2}(n+1)$ and lg $n+1$, respectively.

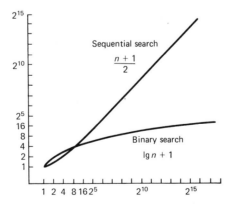

Figure 3.5. Sequential vs. binary search (logarithmic scale)

Let us now ask whether any search method can find its target using fewer comparisons of keys than binary search. We shall see that the answer is no, providing we stay within the class of algorithms that rely only on comparisons of keys to determine where to look.

To be definite, let us establish some conventions. Let us think of comparisons of keys as done in the fashion of **Binary2**, where each comparison might find the target, in which case the algorithm terminates, or otherwise produces at most two branches. Let us take an arbitrary search algorithm that works by such comparisons of keys, and imagine drawing its comparison tree for some value of n. The tree will then look something like Figure 3.4, except that possibly some of the branches will be missing, or there may be more at the bottom. The labels may be quite different (which means that the actual comparisons of keys differ), but that need not concern us, since we wish only to count comparisons of keys, which means to determine path lengths in the tree. In particular, the height of the tree is the largest number of comparisons of keys needed, which gives a worst-case count for the algorithm.

If the height of the arbitrary tree is m, then by Lemma 3.2 the total number of interior vertices (all but the leaves) is at most

$$1 + 2 + 4 + \cdots + 2^{m-1} \;=\; 2^m - 1.$$

On the other hand, the algorithm must be able successfully to find all n of the keys in its list, and it cannot find more than one key in one comparison (although some comparisons of keys may not locate any key), and so the number of comparisons of keys, hence of interior vertices, is at least n. We have therefore shown that

$$n \;\leq\; \textit{number of interior vertices} \;\leq\; 2^m - 1,$$

which, by taking logarithms, becomes $m \geq \lg(n+1)$. Since m must be an integer, this value moves up to the ceiling,

$$m \;\geq\; \lceil \lg(n+1) \rceil.$$

We thus have a lower bound on the height of an arbitrary comparison tree. From Section 3.4.2, however, we know that the comparison tree for **Binary2** has exactly this height. Therefore we have established:

> **THEOREM 3.5.** *Any search algorithm that uses only comparisons of keys will, in its worst case for a successful search of n keys, make at least $\lceil \lg(n+1) \rceil$ comparisons of keys. Binary search achieves this best possible bound.*

A similar result provides a lower bound for the *average* number S of comparisons done by any search using key comparisons. The proof is outlined in the exercises. The exact result is:

$$S \;\geq\; k + 1 - \frac{2^{k+1} - k - 2}{n},$$

where $k = \lfloor \lg n \rfloor$. For all practical purposes, however, we can simplify this result by noting that $2^k \leq n < 2^{k+1}$, and hence the quotient in the above expression is always less than 2 (and is never very much less than 1). We can therefore obtain the less precise bound that $S > k - 1$. We restate this fact for future reference.

> THEOREM 3.6. *Any search algorithm that relies only on comparisons of keys must, on average, make more than* $\lfloor \lg n \rfloor - 1$ *comparisons of keys to find a key in a list of n keys.*

Hence there is very little difference between the worst-case bound and the average-case bound. By Theorem 3.4, moreover, it does not much matter whether the search is successful or not, in determining the bound in these theorems.

Just because we have found the preceding bounds does not imply that no algorithm can run faster than binary search, only those that rely only on comparisons of keys. To take a simple example, suppose that our keys are the integers from 1 to n themselves. If we know that the target key x is an integer in this range, then we would never perform a search algorithm to locate its item; we would simply store the items in a list indexed from 1 to n, and immediately look in index x to find the desired item.

This idea can be extended to obtain another method, called **interpolation search**. We assume that the keys are either numerical or are information, such as words, that can be readily encoded as numbers. The method also assumes that the keys in the list are uniformly distributed; that is, the probability of a key being in a particular range equals its probability of being in any other range of the same length. To find the target key x, interpolation search then estimates, according to the magnitude of the number x relative to the first and last entries of the list, about where x would be in the list, and looks there. It then reduces the size of the list according as x is less than or greater than the key examined. It can be shown that on average, with uniformly distributed keys, interpolation search will take about $\lg \lg n$ comparisons of keys, which, for large n, is considerably fewer than binary search requires.

Finally, we should repeat that, even for search by comparisons, our assumption that requests for all keys are equally likely may be far from correct. If one or two keys are much more likely than the others, then even sequential search, if it looks for those keys first, may be better than any other method.

The importance of search, or, more generally, information retrieval, is so fundamental that much of data structures is devoted to its methods, and in later chapters we shall return to these problems again and again.

Exercises

1. Suppose that T is a 2-tree for which the external (and therefore also the internal) path length is minimal amongst all 2-trees with the same number of leaves and other vertices. Show that all the leaves must be on the same level or two adjacent levels. [*Hint*: Suppose instead that there is a leaf high in the tree. Take a pair of leaves at the bottom, both children of the same vertex, and move them up to become children of the leaf high in the tree.]

2. Let T be a 2-tree in which all the leaves are on the same level or two adjacent levels. Suppose that T has n internal vertices, and let $k = \lfloor \lg n \rfloor$. Show that the external path length of T is $(n+1)(k+2) - 2^{k+1}$.

3. Prove the exact version of Theorem 3.6 by using the results of Exercises 1 and 2.

4. Write a program to do interpolation search, and run it on the same sets of data used to test the binary search programs. See the references at the end of the chapter for suggestions and program analysis.

3.6 Table lookup and arrays.

3.6.1 Breaking the lg n barrier.

In the last section we showed that, by use of key comparisons alone, it is impossible to complete a search of n items in fewer than lg n comparisons (on average). But this result speaks only of searching by key comparisons. If we can use some other method, then we may be able to arrange our table so that we can locate a given item even more quickly.

In fact, we commonly do so. If we have 500 different records, with an index between 1 and 500 assigned to each, then we would never think of using sequential or binary search to locate a record. We would simply store the records in an array of size 500, and use the index n to locate the record of item n by ordinary table lookup.

Both table lookup and searching share the same essential purpose, that of information retrieval. We begin with a key (which may be complicated or simply an index) and wish to find the location of the item (if any) with that key. In other words, both table lookup and our searching algorithms provide *functions* from the set of keys to locations in a list or array. The functions are in fact one-to-one from the set of keys that actually occur to the set of locations that actually occur, since we assume that each item has only one key, and there is only one item with a given key.

In this section we study ways to represent and access arrays in contiguous storage, beginning with ordinary rectangular arrays, and then considering arrays with restricted location of non-zero entries, such as triangular matrices. We then turn to more general problems, with the purpose of introducing and motivating the use of access tables for information retrieval.

We shall see that, depending on the shape of the array, several steps may be needed to retrieve an entry, but, even so, the time required is only a small constant (that is, it does not depend on the size of the table), and thus table lookup can be more efficient than other searching methods.

3.6.2 Rectangular arrays.

Because of the importance of rectangular arrays, almost all high-level languages provide convenient and efficient means to store and access them, so that generally the programmer need not worry about the details. Nonetheless, computer storage is fundamentally arranged in a contiguous sequence (that is, in a straight line with each entry next to another), so for every access to a rectangular array the machine must do some work to convert the location within a rectangle to a position along a line. Let us take a slightly closer look at this process.

Perhaps the most natural way to read a rectangular array is to read the entries of the first row from left to right, then the entries of the second row, and so on until the last row has been read. This is also the order in which most compilers store a rectangular array, and is called *row-major ordering* (see Figure 3.6). For example, if the rows of an array are numbered from 1 to 2 and the columns are numbered from 1 to 3, then the order of indices with which the entries are stored in row-major ordering is

$$[1,1] \quad [1,2] \quad [1,3] \quad [2,1] \quad [2,2] \quad [2,3].$$

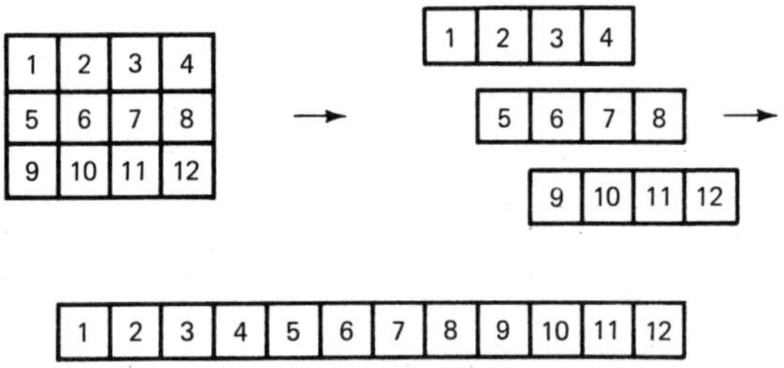

Figure 3.6. Sequential representation of a rectangular array

Standard FORTRAN instead uses *column-major ordering*, in which the entries of the first column come first, and so on. The previous example in column-major ordering is

$$[1,1] \quad [2,1] \quad [1,2] \quad [2,2] \quad [1,3] \quad [2,3].$$

In the general problem, the compiler must be able to start with an index $[i, j]$ and calculate where the corresponding entry of the array will be. We shall derive a formula for this calculation. For simplicity we shall use only row-major ordering, and suppose that the rows are numbered from 0 to $m-1$ and the columns from 0 to $n-1$. The general case is treated as an exercise. Altogether, the array will have mn entries, as must its contiguous sequential representation. We number the entries in the sequential array from 0 to $mn-1$. To obtain the formula calculating the position where $[i, j]$ goes, we first consider some special cases. Clearly $[0,0]$ goes to position 0, and, in fact, the entire first row is easy: $[0,j]$ goes to position j. The first entry of the second row, $[1,0]$, comes after $[0, n-1]$, and thus goes into position n. Continuing, we see that $[1,j]$ goes to position $n+j$. Entries of the next row will have two full rows, that is, $2n$ entries, preceding them. It is now easy to see that the desired formula is:

Entry $[i, j]$ *goes to position* $in+j$.

A formula of this kind, that gives the sequential location of an array entry, is called an *index function*.

The index function for rectangular arrays is certainly not difficult to calculate, and the compilers of most high-level languages will simply write into the machine-language program the necessary steps for each reference to a rectangular array. On small machines, however, multiplication can be quite slow, so a slightly different method can be used to eliminate the multiplications.

This method is to keep an auxiliary vector, a part of the multiplication table for n. The vector will contain the values

$$0, \quad n, \quad 2n, \quad 3n, \quad \cdots, \quad (m-1)n.$$

Note that this vector is much smaller (usually) than the rectangular array, so that it can be kept permanently without losing too much space. Its entries then need be calculated only once (and note that they can be calculated using only addition). For all later references to the rectangular array, the compiler can find the position of $[i, j]$ by taking the entry in position i of the auxiliary table, adding j, and going to the resulting position(see Figure 3.7).

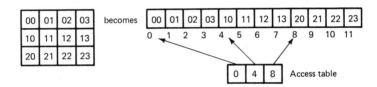

Figure 3.7. Access table for a rectangular array

This auxiliary table provides our first example of an ***access table***. In general, an access table is an auxiliary array used to find data stored elsewhere. The terms ***access vector*** and ***dope vector*** (the latter especially when additional information is included) are also used. The remaining parts of this section show several applications of access tables.

3.6.3 Triangular arrays.

Information that is naturally regarded as a rectangular array may sometimes not require every position in the rectangle for its representation. Often some of the positions within the rectangular matrix will be required to be 0. Several such examples are shown in Figure 3.8. At other times, some of the entries can easily be determined from others, as in the cases of symmetric and skew-symmetric matrices.

Let us consider the representation of a lower triangular matrix shown in Figure 3.8. Such a matrix can be defined formally as a square array for which the entry is 0 in every position where the column index is greater than the row index. We can avoid storing all the 0's by mapping the triangular matrix into a sequential array as shown in Figure 3.9.

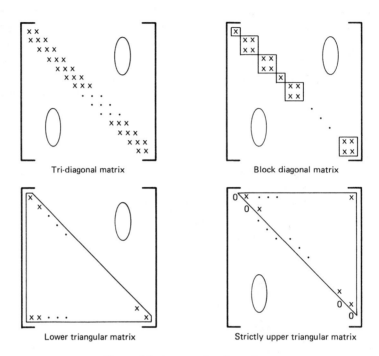

Figure 3.8. Arrays of various shapes

To construct the index function that describes this mapping, we again make the slight simplification of assuming that the rows and the columns are numbered starting with 0. To find the position where $[i, j]$ goes, we now need to find where row number i starts, and then to locate column j we need only add j to the starting point of row i. If the entries of the sequential array are also numbered starting with 0, then the index

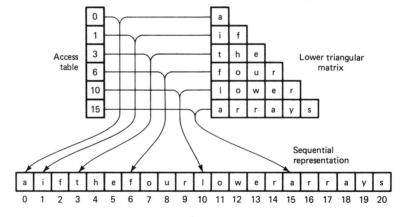

Figure 3.9. Sequential representation of a triangular matrix

of the starting point will be the same as the number of entries that precede row *i*. Clearly, there are 0 entries before row 0, and only the one entry of row 0 precedes row 1. For row 2, there are $1+2 = 3$ preceding entries, and in general we see that preceding row *i* there are exactly

$$1+2+ \cdots +i = \tfrac{1}{2}i(i+1)$$

entries. Hence the desired function is that entry $[i, j]$ of the triangular matrix corresponds to entry

$$\tfrac{1}{2}i(i+1)+j$$

of the sequential array.

As we did for rectangular arrays, we can again avoid all multiplications and divisions by setting up an access table whose entries correspond to the row indices of the triangular matrix. Position *i* of the access table will permanently contain the value $\tfrac{1}{2}i(i+1)$. The access table will be calculated only once at the start of the program, and then used repeatedly at each reference to the triangular array. Note that even the initial calculation of this access table requires no multiplication or division, but only addition to calculate its entries in the order

$$0, \quad 1, \quad 1+2, \quad (1+2)+3, \quad \cdots .$$

3.6.4 Jagged arrays.

In both of the preceding examples we have considered a rectangular array as made up from its rows. In ordinary rectangular arrays all the rows have the same length; in triangular arrays the length of each row can be found from a simple function of its index. We now consider the case of jagged arrays such as the one in Figure 3.10, where there is no predictable relation between the position of a row and its length.

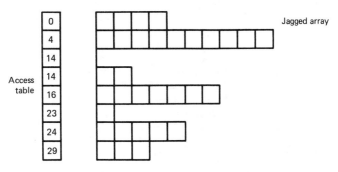

Figure 3.10. Access table for jagged array

It is clear from the diagram that, even though we are not able to give an *a priori* function to map the jagged array into sequential storage, the use of an access table remains as easy as in the previous examples, and elements of the jagged array can be referenced just as quickly. To set up the access table, we must construct the jagged array in its natural order, beginning with its first row. Entry 0 of the access table is, as before, the start of the sequential array. After each row of the jagged array has been constructed, the index of the first unused position of the sequential storage should then be entered as the next entry in the access table, and used to start constructing the next row of the jagged array.

3.6.5 Inverted arrays.

We conclude this section with an example that illustrates the usefulness of setting up more than one access table referring to records within a single storage area.

Consider the problem faced by the telephone company in accessing the records of its customers. To publish the telephone book the records must be sorted alphabetically by the name of the subscriber. But to process long-distance charges the accounts must be sorted by telephone number. To do routine maintenance the company also needs to have its subscribers sorted by address, so that a repairman may be able to work on several lines with one trip. Conceivably, the telephone company could keep three (or more) sets of its records, one sorted by name, one by number, and one by address. This way, however, would not only be very wasteful of storage space, but would introduce endless headaches if one set of records were updated but another was not, and erroneous and unpredictable information might be used.

By using access tables we can avoid the multiple sets of records, and we can still find the records by any of the three keys almost as quickly as if they were fully sorted by that key. For the names we set up one access table. The first entry in this table is the position where the records of the subscriber whose name is first in alphabetical order are stored, the second entry gives the location of the second (in alphabetical order) subscriber's records, and so on. In a second access table the first entry is the location of the subscriber's records whose telephone number happens to be smallest in

Index	Name	Address	Phone
1	Hill, Thomas M.	High Towers	2829478
2	Baker, John M.	17 King St.	2884285
3	Roberts, L. B.	53 Ash St.	4372296
4	King, Barbara	High Towers	2863386
5	Hill, Thomas M.	39 King St.	2495723
6	Byers, Carolyn	118 Maple Dr.	4394231
7	Moody, C. L.	High Towers	2822214

Access Tables		
Name	Address	Phone
2	3	5
6	1	7
1	4	1
5	7	4
4	2	2
7	5	3
3	6	6

Figure 3.11. Multi-key access tables: an inverted array

numerical order. In yet a third access table the entries give the locations of the records sorted lexicographically by address. Notice that in this method all the fields that are treated as keys are processed in the same way. There is no particular reason why the records themselves need to be sorted according to one key rather than another, or, in fact, why they need to be sorted at all. The records themselves can be kept in an arbitrary order—say the order in which they were first entered into the system. It also makes no difference whether the records are in an array, with entries in the access tables being indices of the array, or whether the records are in dynamic storage, with the access tables holding pointers to individual records. In any case, it is the access tables which are used for information retrieval, and, as ordinary sequential arrays, they may be used for table lookup, or binary search, or any other purpose for which contiguous storage is appropriate.

The implementation of this scheme for a small number of accounts is shown in Figure 3.11.

Exercises

1. What is the index function for a two dimensional rectangular array with bounds

$$\textbf{array}[0..m-1, \quad 0..n-1]$$

   under column-major ordering?

2. Give the index function, with row-major ordering, for a two dimensional array with arbitrary bounds

$$\textbf{array}[r..s, \quad t..u].$$

3. Find the index function, with the generalization of row-major ordering, for an array with d dimensions and arbitrary bounds for each dimension.

4. The ***main diagonal*** of a square matrix consists of the entries for which the row and column indices are equal. A ***diagonal matrix*** is a square matrix in which all entries not on the main diagonal are 0. Describe a way to store a diagonal matrix without using space for entries that are necessarily 0, and give the corresponding index function.

5. A ***tri-diagonal matrix*** is a square matrix in which all entries are 0 except possibly those on the main diagonal and on the diagonals immediately above and below it. That is, T is a tri-diagonal matrix means that $T[i, j] = 0$ unless $|i-j| \leq 1$.

   (a) Devise a space-efficient storage scheme for tri-diagonal matrices, and give the corresponding index function.

   (b) The ***transpose*** of a matrix is the matrix obtained by interchanging its rows with the corresponding columns. That is, matrix B is the transpose of matrix A means that $B[j, i] = A[i, j]$ for all (allowable) indices i and j. Write a procedure that transposes a tri-diagonal matrix using the storage scheme devised in part (a).

6. Implement the method described in the text that uses an access table to store a lower triangular matrix, as applied in the following exercises.

   (a) Write a procedure that will read the entries of a lower triangular matrix from the terminal.

   (b) Write a procedure that will print a lower triangular matrix at the terminal.

   (c) Suppose that a lower triangular matrix is a table of distances between cities, as often appears on a road map. Write a procedure that will check the triangle rule: The distance from city A to city C is never more than the distance from A to city B, plus the distance from B to C.

   (d) An ***upper triangular matrix*** is one in which all entries below the main diagonal are 0. Describe the modifications necessary to use the access-table method to store an upper triangular matrix.

   (e) The transpose of a lower triangular matrix will be an upper triangular matrix. Write a procedure that will transpose a lower triangular matrix, using access tables to refer to both matrices.

3.7 Hashing.

3.7.1 Sparse tables.

1. Index functions.

We can continue to exploit table lookup even in situations where the key is no longer an index that can be used directly, as in array indexing. What we can do is to set up a one-to-one correspondence between the keys by which we wish to retrieve information and indices that we can use to access an array. The index function that we produce may be somewhat more complicated than those of the previous section, since it may need to convert the key from, say, alphabetic information to an integer, but in principle it can still be done. The only difficulty arises when the number of possible keys exceeds the amount of space available for our table. If, for example, our keys are alphabetical words of eight letters, then there are $26^8 \approx 2 \times 10^{11}$ possible keys, a number much greater than the number of positions that will be available in high-speed memory. In practice, however, only a small fraction of these keys will actually occur. That is, the table is *sparse*. Conceptually, we can regard it as indexed by a very large set, but with relatively few positions actually occupied. In Pascal, for example, we might think in terms of conceptual declarations such as

$$\textbf{type} \ \cdots \ = \text{sparse table [keytype] } \textbf{of} \text{ item.}$$

Even though it may not be possible to implement a declaration such as this, it is often helpful in problem solving to begin with such a picture, and only slowly tie down the details of how it is put into practice.

2. Hash tables

The idea of a **hash table** (such as that shown in Figure 3.12) is to allow many of the different possible keys that might occur to be mapped to the same location in an array under the action of the index function. Then there will be a possibility that two records will want to be in the same place, but if the number of keys that actually occur is small relative to the size of the array, then this possibility will cause little loss of time. Even when most entries in the array are occupied, hash methods can be an effective means of information retrieval. We begin with a **hash function** that takes a key and maps it to some index in the array. This function will generally map several different keys to the same index. If the desired record is in the location given by the index, then our problem is solved; otherwise we must use some method to resolve the **collision** that may have occurred between two records wanting to go to the same location. There are thus two questions we must answer to use hashing. First, we must find good hash functions, and, second, we must determine how to resolve collisions.

do	record		in	end		const
		var			function	
of	case	array		packed		mod
	program		until		else	
if		label		then		file
with	to		div		and	type
	begin			not		
downto			set		while	or
nil		for	repeat		goto	procedure

Figure 3.12. A hash table

Before approaching these questions, let us pause to outline informally the steps needed to use hashing.

3. Algorithm outlines

First, an array must be declared that will hold the hash table. With ordinary arrays the keys used to locate entries are usually the indices, so there is no need to keep them within the array itself; but for a hash array, several possible keys will correspond to the same index, so one field within each record in the array must be reserved for the key itself.

Next, all locations in the array must be initialized to show that they are empty. How this is done depends on the application; often it is accomplished by setting the key fields to some value that is guaranteed never to occur as an actual key. With alphanumeric keys, for example, a key consisting of all blanks might represent an empty position.

To insert a record into the hash table, the hash function for the key is first calculated. If the corresponding location is empty, then the record can be inserted, else if the keys are equal then insertion of the new record would not be allowed, and in the remaining case (a record with a different key is in the location) it becomes necessary to resolve the collision.

To retrieve the record with a given key is entirely similar. First the hash function for the key is computed. If the desired record is in the corresponding location, then the retrieval has succeeded; otherwise while the location is non-empty and not all locations have been examined, follow the same steps used for collision resolution. If an empty position is found, or all locations have been considered, then no record with the given key is in the table, and the search is unsuccessful.

3.7.2 Choosing a hash function.

The two principal criteria in selecting a hash function are that it should be easy and quick to compute, and that it should achieve an even distribution of the keys that actually occur across the range of indices. If we know in advance exactly what keys will occur, then it is possible to construct hash functions that will be very efficient, but generally we do not know in advance what keys will occur. Therefore, the usual way is for the hash function to take the key, chop it up, mix the pieces together in various ways, and thereby obtain an index that (like the pseudo-random numbers generated by computer) will be uniformly distributed over the range of indices.

It is from this process that the word "hash" comes, since the process converts the key into something that bears little resemblance to the key itself. At the same time, it is hoped that any patterns or regularities that may occur in the keys will be destroyed, so that the results will be randomly distributed.

Even though the term "hash" is very descriptive, in some books the more technical terms *scatter-storage* or *key-transformation* are used in its place.

We shall consider three methods that can be put together in various ways to build a hash function.

1. Truncation

Ignore part of the key, and use the remaining part directly as the index (considering non-numeric fields as their numerical codes). If the keys, for example, are eight-digit integers and the hash table has 1000 locations, then the first, second and fifth digits from the right might make the hash function, so that 62538194 maps to 394. Truncation is a very fast method, but often fails to distribute the keys evenly through the table.

2. Folding

Partition the key into several parts and combine the parts in a convenient way (often using addition or multiplication) to obtain the index. For example, an eight-digit integer can be divided into groups of 3, 3, and 2 digits, the groups added together, and truncated if necessary to be in the proper range of indices. Hence 62538194 maps to $625+381+94 = 1100$, which is truncated to 100. Since all information in the key can affect the value of the function, folding often achieves a better spread of indices than truncation by itself.

3. Modular arithmetic

Convert the key to an integer (using the preceding devices as desired), divide by the size of the index range, and take the remainder as the result. This amounts to using the Pascal operator **mod**. The spread achieved by taking a remainder depends very much on the modulus (in this case, the size of the hash array). If the modulus is a power of a small integer like 2 or 10, then many keys tend to map to the same index, while other indices remain unused. The best choice for modulus is a prime number, which usually has the effect of spreading the keys quite uniformly. (We shall see later that a prime modulus also improves an important method for collision resolution.) Hence, rather than choosing a hash table size of 1000, it is better to choose either 997 or 1009. Taking the remainder is usually the best way to conclude calculating the hash function, since it can achieve a good spread at the same time that it ensures that the result is in the proper range. About the only reservation is that, on a tiny machine with no hardware division, the calculation can be slow, so other methods should be considered.

4. Pascal example

As a simple example, let us write a hash function in Pascal for transforming a key consisting of eight alphanumeric characters into an integer in the range

$$0 .. \text{hashsize} - 1.$$

That is, we shall begin with the type

type keytype = **array**[1..8] **of** char;

We can then write one simple hash function as follows:

```
function Hash(x: keytype): integer;
var
  i :  1..8;
  h :  integer;
begin
  h : = 0;
  for i : = 1 to 8 do
    h : = h + ord(x[i]);
  Hash : = h mod hashsize
end;
```

We have simply added the integer codes corresponding to each of the eight characters. There is no reason to believe that this method will be better (or worse), however, than any number of others. We could, for example, subtract some of the codes, multiply them in pairs, or ignore every other character. Sometimes an application will suggest that one hash function is better than another; sometimes it requires experimentation to settle on a good one.

3.7.3 Collision resolution with open addressing.

1. Linear probing.

The simplest method to resolve a collision is to start with the hash address (the location where the collision occurred) and do a sequential search for the desired key or an empty location. Hence this method searches in a straight line, and is therefore called *linear probing*. The table should be considered circular, so that when the last location is reached, the search proceeds to the first location of the table.

2. Clustering.

The major drawback of linear probing is that, as the table becomes about half full, there is a tendency toward *clustering*; that is, records start to appear in long strings of adjacent positions, with gaps between the strings. Thus the sequential searches needed to find an empty position become longer and longer. For consider the example in Figure 3.13, where the occupied positions are crossed off. Suppose that there are n locations in the array, and that the hash function chooses any of them with equal probability $1/n$. Begin with a fairly uniform spread, as shown in the top diagram. If a new insertion hashes to location b, then it will go there, but if it hashes to location a (which is full) then it will also go into b. Thus the probability that b will be filled has doubled to $2/n$. At the next stage, an attempted insertion into any of locations $a, b, c,$ or d will end up in d, so the probability of filling d is $4/n$. After this, e has probability $5/n$ of being filled, and so the most likely occurrence is to make the string beginning at location a longer and longer.

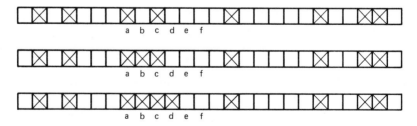

Figure 3.13. Clustering in a Hash Table

The problem of clustering is thus one of instability; if a few keys happen randomly to be near each other, then it becomes more and more likely that other keys will join them, and the distribution will become progressively more unbalanced.

3. Increment functions.

If we are to avoid the problem of clustering, then we must use some more sophisticated way to select the sequence of locations to check when a collision occurs. There are many ways to do so. One, called **rehashing**, uses a second hash function to obtain the second position to consider. If this is filled, then some other method is needed to get the third position, and so on. But if we have a fairly good spread from the first hash function, then little is to be gained by an independent second hash function. We will do just as well to find a more sophisticated way of determining the distance to move from the first hash position, and apply this method, whatever the first hash location is. Hence we wish to design an increment function that can depend on the key, or on the number of probes already made, and that will avoid clustering.

4. Quadratic probing.

If there is a collision at hash address h, this method probes the table at locations $h+1, h+4, h+9, \cdots$, that is, at locations $h+i^2 \pmod{\textsf{hashsize}}$ for $i = 1, 2, \cdots$. That is, the increment function is i^2.

This method substantially reduces clustering, but it is not obvious that it will probe all locations in the table, and in fact it does not. If hashsize is a power of 2, then few positions are probed. Suppose that hashsize is a prime. If we reach the same location at probe i and at probe j, then

$$h+i^2 \;\equiv\; h+j^2 \pmod{\textsf{hashsize}}$$

so that

$$(i-j)(i+j) \;\equiv\; 0 \pmod{\textsf{hashsize}}.$$

Since hashsize is a prime, it must divide one factor. It divides $i-j$ only when j differs from i by a multiple of hashsize, so at least hashsize probes have been made. Hashsize divides $i+j$, however, when $j = \textsf{hashsize}-i$, so the total number of distinct positions that will be probed is exactly

$$(\textsf{hashsize} + 1) \textbf{ div } 2.$$

It is customary to take overflow as occurring when this number of positions has been probed, and the results are quite satisfactory.

Note that quadratic probing can be accomplished without doing multiplications: After the first probe at position x, the increment is set to 1. At each successive probe, the increment is increased by 1 after it has been added to the previous location. Hence probe i will look in position

$$x+1+2+ \cdots +(i-1) \;=\; x+\tfrac{1}{2}(i-1)i.$$

5. Key-dependent increments.

Rather than having the increment depend on the number of probes already made, we can let it be some simple function of the key itself. For example, we could truncate the key to a single character and use its code as the increment. In Pascal, we might write

$$\text{increment} := \text{ord}(k[1]).$$

A good approach, when the remainder after division is taken as the hash function, is to let the increment depend on the quotient of the same division. An optimizing compiler should specify the division only once, so the calculation will be fast and the results generally satisfactory.

In this method the increment, once determined, remains constant. If hashsize is a prime, it follows that the probes will step through all the entries of the array before any repetitions. Hence overflow will not be indicated until the array is completely full.

6. Random probing.

A final method is to use a pseudo-random number generator to obtain the increment. The generator used should be one that always generates the same sequence provided it starts with the same seed. The seed, then, can be specified as some function of the key. This method is excellent in avoiding clustering, but is likely to be slower than the others.

7. Pascal algorithms.

To conclude the discussion of open addressing, we continue to study the Pascal example already introduced, which used alphanumeric keys of the type

type keytype = **array**[1..8] **of** char.

We set up the hash table with the declarations

```
const hashsize = 997    {a prime number of appropriate size};
      hashmax  = 996                        { = hashsize − 1};
var  H: array[0..hashmax] of item            {hash table};
```

The hash table must be initialized by defining a special key called blankword, that consists of eight blanks, and setting the key field of each item in H to blankword.

We shall use the hash function already written, and since we shall keep a counter c to ensure against overflow, for simplicity we use quadratic probing, employing c to determine the increment.

With these conventions, let us write a procedure to insert a record r, with key r.key, into the hash table H.

```
procedure Insert(r: item);
var
  c: integer;                          {counter to be sure that table is not full}
  p: integer;                          {position currently probed in H}
begin
  p := Hash(r.key);
  c := 0;
  while (H[p].key <> blankword)        {location empty?}
    and (H[p].key <> r.key)            {target key found?}
    and (c < (hashsize + 1) div 2) do  {overflow?}
    begin
      c := c + 1;
      p := p + c;
      if p > hashmax then p := p mod hashsize
    end;
  if H[p].key = blankword then
    H[p]:= r                           {Insert new item r}
  else if H[p].key = r.key then
    Error                              {Same key cannot appear twice}
  else  Overflow                       {Counter has reached its limit}
end;
```

A procedure to retrieve the record (if any) with a given key will have a similar form, and is left as an exercise.

8. Deletions.

Up to now we have said nothing about deleting items from a hash table. At first glance, it may appear to be an easy task, requiring only marking the deleted location with the special key indicating that it is empty. This method will not work. The reason is that an empty location is used as the signal to stop the search for a target key. Suppose that, before the deletion, there had been a collision or two, and that some item whose hash address is the now-deleted position is actually stored elsewhere in the table. If we now try to retrieve that item, then the now-empty position will stop the search, and it is impossible to find the item, even though it is still in the table.

One method to remedy this difficulty is to invent another special key, to be placed in any deleted position. This special key would indicate that this position is free to receive an insertion when desired, but that it should not be used to terminate the search for some other item in the table. Using this second special key will, however, make the algorithms somewhat more complicated and a bit slower. With the methods we have so far studied for hash tables, deletions are indeed awkward and should be avoided as much as possible.

3.7.4 Collision resolution by chaining.

Up to now we have implicitly assumed that we are using only contiguous storage while working with hash tables. Contiguous storage for the hash table itself is, in fact, the natural choice, since we wish to be able to refer quickly to random positions in the table, and linked storage is not suited to random access. There is, however, no reason why linked storage should not be used for the records themselves. We can take the hash table itself as an array of pointers to the records, that is, as an array of list headers.

It is traditional to refer to the linked lists from the hash table as *chains*, and call this method collision resolution by *chaining*. An example appears in Figure 3.14.

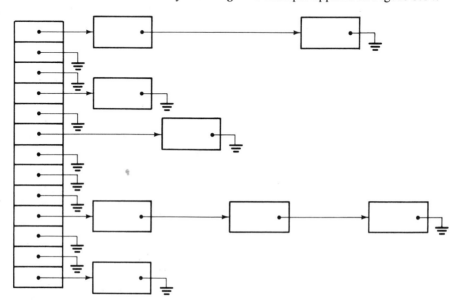

Figure 3.14. A chained hash table

1. Advantages of linked storage.

There are several advantages to this point of view. The first, and the most important when the records themselves are quite large, is that considerable space may be saved. Since the hash table is a contiguous array, enough space must be set aside at compilation time to avoid overflow. If the records themselves are in the hash table, then if there are many empty positions (as is desirable to help avoid the cost of collisions), then these will consume considerable space that might be needed elsewhere. If, on the other hand, the hash table contains only pointers to the records, pointers that require only one word each, then the size of the hash table may be reduced by a large factor (essentially by a factor equal to the size of the records), and will become small relative to the space available for the records or for other uses.

The second major advantage of keeping only pointers in the hash table is that it allows simple and efficient collision handling. We need only add a link field to each record, and organize all the records with a single hash address as a linked list. With a good hash function few keys will give the same hash address, so the linked lists will be short and can be searched quickly. Clustering is no problem at all, because keys with distinct hash addresses always go to distinct lists.

A third advantage is that it is no longer necessary that the size of the hash table exceed the number of records. If there are more records than entries in the table, it means only that some of the linked lists are now sure to have more than one record. Even if there are several times more records than the size of the table, the average length of the linked lists will remain small.

Finally, deletion becomes an easy and efficient task in a chained hash table. Deletion proceeds in exactly the same way as deletion from a simple linked list.

2. Disadvantage of linked storage.

These advantages of chained hash tables are indeed powerful. Lest you believe that chaining is always superior to open addressing, let us point out one important disadvantage: All of the links require space. If the records are large, then this space is negligible in comparison with that needed for the records themselves, but if the records are small, then it is not.

Suppose, for example, that the links take one word each, and that the items themselves take only one word (which is the key alone). Such applications are quite common, where we use the hash table only to answer some yes-no question about the key. Suppose that we use chaining, and make the hash table itself quite small, with the same number n of entries as the number of items. Then we shall use $3n$ words of storage altogether: n for the hash table, n for the keys, and n for the links to find the next item (if any) on each chain. Since the hash table will be nearly full, there will be many collisions, and some of the chains will have several items. Hence searching will be a bit slow. Suppose, on the other hand, that we use open addressing. The same $3n$ words of storage put entirely into the hash table will mean that it will be only one third full, and therefore there will be relatively few collisions, and the search for any given item will be faster.

3. Pascal algorithms.

A chained hash table in Pascal takes declarations like:

```
type   pointer  =  ↑item;
var    H: array [0 .. hashmax] of pointer;
```

The record type called item now needs an additional field, called next, that points to the next item on a linked list.

The code needed to initialize the hash table is:

```
for i := 0 to hashmax do H[i] := nil;
```

We can even use previously written procedures to use the hash table. The hash function itself is no different from that used with open addressing; for data retrieval we can use the procedure SequentialSearch (linked version) from Section 3.2; and for insertion we can use the procedure Push for linked stacks from Section 2.4. These are so simple, however, that instead we write them into our procedures.

For access and retrieval we obtain:

```
procedure Retrieve(x: keytype; var p: pointer);
{Finds item with key x in hash table  and returns with p pointing to that
                        item, or p = nil if retrieval was unsuccessful.}
var
   finished:     Boolean;          {determines when search has finished}
begin
   p := H[Hash(x)];               {p points to head of list containing x}
   finished := false;
   repeat
     if p = nil then
        finished := true           {Search concludes unsuccessfully.}
     else if p↑.key = x then
        finished := true              {Search concludes successfully.}
     else
        p := p↑.next
   until finished
end;
```

Our procedure for inserting a new entry will assume that the key does not appear already; otherwise only the most recent insertion with a given key will be retrievable.

```
procedure Insert(p: pointer);
{Inserts item p↑ into chained hash table, assuming no other item with key
                        p↑.key is in the table.}
var
   i:   integer;                        {used for index in hash table}
begin
   i          := Hash(p↑.key);
   p↑.next    := H[i];
   H[i]       := p
end;
```

As you can see, both of these procedures are significantly simpler than the versions for open addressing, since collision resolution is not a problem.

3.7.5 Analysis of hashing.

1. The birthday surprise.

The likelihood of collisions in hashing relates to the well-known mathematical diversion: How many randomly chosen people need to be in a room before it becomes likely that two people will have the same birthday (month and day)? Since (apart from leap years) there are 365 possible birthdays, most people guess that the answer will be in the hundreds, but in fact the answer is only 24 people.

We can determine the probabilities for this question by answering its opposite: With m randomly chosen people in a room, what is the probability that no two have the same birthday? Start with any person, and check his birthday off on a calendar. The probability that a second person has a different birthday is $364/365$. Check it off. The probability that a third person has a different birthday is now $363/365$. Continuing this way, we see that if the first $m-1$ people have different birthdays, then the probability that person m has a different birthday is $(365-m+1)/365$. Since the birthdays of different people are independent, the probabilities multiply, and we obtain that the probability that m people all have different birthdays is

$$\frac{364}{365} \times \frac{363}{365} \times \frac{362}{365} \times \cdots \times \frac{365-m+1}{365}.$$

This expression becomes less than 0.5 whenever $m \geq 24$.

In regard to hashing, the birthday surprise tells us that with any problem of reasonable size, we are almost certain to have some collisions. Our approach, therefore, should not be only to try to minimize the number of collisions, but also to handle those that occur as expeditiously as possible.

2. Counting probes.

As with other methods of information retrieval, we would like to know how many comparisons of keys occur on average during both successful and unsuccessful attempts to locate a given target key. We shall use the word ***probe*** for looking at one item and comparing its key with the target.

The number of probes we need clearly depends on how full the table is. Therefore (as for searching methods), we let n be the number of items in the table, and we let t (which is the same as hashsize) be the number of positions in the array. The ***load factor*** of the table is $\lambda = n/t$. Thus $\lambda = 0$ signifies an empty table, and $\lambda = 0.5$ a table that is half full. For open addressing, λ can never exceed 1, but for chaining there is no limit on the size of λ. We consider chaining and open addressing separately.

3. Analysis of chaining.

With a chained hash table we go directly to one of the linked lists before doing any probes. Suppose that the chain that will contain the target (if it is present) has k items.

If the search is unsuccessful, then the target will be compared with all k of the corresponding keys. Since the items are distributed uniformly over all t lists (equal probability of appearing on any list), the expected number of items on the one being searched is $\lambda = n/t$. Hence the average number of probes for an unsuccessful search is λ.

Now suppose that the search is successful. From the analysis of sequential search we know that the average number of comparisons is $\frac{1}{2}(k+1)$, where k is the length of the chain containing the target. But the expected length of this chain is no longer λ, since we know in advance that it must contain at least one item (the target). The $n-1$ items other than the target are distributed uniformly over all t chains; hence the expected number on the chain with the target is $1+(n-1)/t$. Except for tables of trivially small size, we may approximate $(n-1)/t$ by $n/t = \lambda$. Hence the average number of probes for a successful search is very nearly

$$\tfrac{1}{2}(k+1) \ \approx \ \tfrac{1}{2}(1+\lambda+1) \ = \ 1+\tfrac{1}{2}\lambda.$$

4. Analysis of open addressing.

For our analysis of the number of probes done in open addressing, let us first ignore the problem of clustering by assuming that not only are the first probes random, but after a collision the next probe will be random over all remaining positions of the table. In fact, let us assume that the table is so large that all the probes can be regarded as independent events.

Let us first study an unsuccessful search. The probability that the first probe hits an occupied cell is λ, the load factor. The probability that a probe hits an empty cell is $1-\lambda$. The probability that the unsuccessful search terminates in exactly two probes is therefore $\lambda(1-\lambda)$, and, similarly, the probability that exactly k probes are made in an unsuccessful search is $\lambda^{k-1}(1-\lambda)$. The expected number $U(\lambda)$ of probes in an unsuccessful search is therefore

$$U(\lambda) \ = \ \sum_{k=1}^{\infty} k\lambda^{k-1}(1-\lambda).$$

This sum is evaluated in Appendix A; we obtain thereby

$$U(\lambda) \ = \ \frac{1}{(1-\lambda)^2}(1-\lambda) \ = \ \frac{1}{1-\lambda}.$$

To count the probes needed for a successful search, we note that the number needed will be exactly one more than the number of probes in the unsuccessful search made before inserting the item. Now let us consider the table as beginning empty, with each item added one at a time. As these items are inserted, the load factor grows slowly from 0 to its final value, λ. It is reasonable for us to approximate this step-by-step growth by continuous growth, and replace a sum with an integral. We conclude that the average number of probes in a successful search is approximately

$$S(\lambda) \ = \ \frac{1}{\lambda}\int_0^{\lambda} U(\mu)d\mu \ = \ \frac{1}{\lambda}\ln\frac{1}{1-\lambda}.$$

Similar calculations may be done for open addressing with linear probing, where it is no longer reasonable to assume that successive probes are independent. The details, however, are rather more complicated, so we present only the results. For the complete derivation, consult the references at the end of the chapter. For linear probing the average number of probes for an unsuccessful search increases to

$$\frac{1}{2}\left[1 + \frac{1}{(1-\lambda)^2}\right]$$

and for a successful search the number becomes

$$\frac{1}{2}\left[1 + \frac{1}{1-\lambda}\right].$$

5. Comparisons.

Figure 3.15 gives the values of the above expressions for different values of the load factor.

Load factor	0.10	0.50	0.80	0.90	0.99	2.00
Successful search						
Chaining	1.05	1.25	1.40	1.45	1.50	2.00
Open, random probes	1.05	1.4	2.0	2.6	4.6	—
linear probes	1.06	1.5	3.0	5.5	50.5	—
Unsuccessful search						
Chaining	0.10	0.50	0.80	0.90	0.99	2.00
Open, random probes	1.1	2.0	5.0	10.0	100.	—
linear probes	1.12	2.5	13.	50.	5000.	—

Figure 3.15. Theoretical comparison of hashing methods

We can draw several conclusions from this table. First, it is clear that chaining consistently requires fewer probes than open addressing. On the other hand, traversal of the linked lists is usually slower than sequential access, which can reduce the advantage, especially if key comparisons can be done quickly. Chaining comes into its own when the records are large and comparison of keys takes significant time. Chaining is also especially advantageous when unsuccessful searches are common, since with chaining an empty list or very short list may be found, so that often no key comparisons at all need be done to show that a search is unsuccessful.

With open addressing and successful searches, the simpler method of linear probing is not significantly slower than more sophisticated methods, at least until the table is almost completely full. For unsuccessful searches, however, clustering quickly causes linear probing to degenerate into a long sequential search. We might conclude, therefore, that if searches are quite likely to be successful, and the load factor is moderate, then linear probing is quite satisfactory, but in other circumstances another method should be used.

It is important to remember that the computations giving Figure 3.15 are only approximate, and also that in practice nothing is completely random, so that we can always expect some differences between the theoretical results and actual computations. For sake of comparison, therefore, Figure 3.16 gives the results of one empirical study, using 900 keys that are pseudo-random numbers between 0 and 1.

Load factor	0.1	0.5	0.8	0.9	0.99	2.0
Successful search						
Chaining	1.04	1.2	1.4	1.4	1.5	2.0
Open, quadratic probes	1.04	1.5	2.1	2.7	5.2	—
linear probes	1.05	1.6	3.4	6.2	21.3	—
Unsuccessful search						
Chaining	0.11	0.53	0.78	0.90	0.99	2.04
Open, quadratic probes	1.13	2.2	5.2	11.9	126.	—
linear probes	1.13	2.7	15.4	59.8	430.	—

Figure 3.16. Empirical comparison of hashing methods

In comparison with other methods of information retrieval, the important thing to note about all these numbers is that they depend only on the load factor, not on the absolute number of items in the table. Retrieval from a hash table with 20,000 items in 40,000 possible positions is no slower, on average, than retrieval from a table with 20 items in 40 possible positions. With sequential search, a list 1000 times the size will take 1000 times as long to search. With binary search this ratio is reduced to 10 (more precisely, to lg 1000), but still the time needed increases with the size, which it does not with hashing.

Finally, we should emphasize the importance of devising a good hash function, one that executes quickly and maximizes the spread of the keys. With a poor hash function, hashing can degenerate to the performance of sequential search.

Exercises

1. Write a Pascal procedure to retrieve an item from a hash table with open addressing and (a) linear probing; (b) quadratic probing.

2. Devise a simple, easy to calculate hash function for mapping three-letter words to integers between 0 and $n-1$, inclusive. Find the values of your function on the words

   PAL LAP PAM MAP PAT PET SET SAT TAT BAT

   for $n = 11, 13, 17, 19$. Try for as few collisions as possible.

3. If individual records are small, then open addressing requires less total memory for a given load factor; but for large records, chaining requires less space altogether, since the hash table itself can be smaller while maintaining the same

load factor. Find the break-even point for storage use as a function of the load factor.

4. Figures 3.15 and 3.16 are somewhat distorted in favor of chaining, because no account is taken of the space needed for links (see part 2 of Section 3.7.4). Produce tables like Figure 3.15, where the load factors are calculated for the case of chaining, and for open addressing the space required by links is added to the hash table, thereby reducing the load factor.

   (a) Given n items in the linked storage connected to a chained hash table, with k words per item (plus 1 more for the link), and with load factor λ, find the total amount of storage that will be used, including links.
   (b) If this same amount of storage is used in a hash table with open addressing and n items of k words each, find the resulting load factor. This is the load factor to use in computing the revised tables.
   (c) Produce one table for the case $k = 1$.
   (d) Produce another table for the case $k = 5$.
   (e) What will the table look like when each item takes 100 words?

5. One reason why the answer to the birthday problem is surprising is that it differs from the answers to apparently related questions. For the following, suppose that there are n people in the room, and disregard leap years.

   (a) What is the probability that someone in the room will have a birthday on a random date drawn from a hat?
   (b) What is the probability that at least two people in the room will have that same random birthday?
   (c) If we choose one person and find his birthday, what is the probability that someone else in the room will share the birthday?

6. Produce a table like Figure 3.16 for your computer by writing and running test programs to implement the various kinds of hash tables and load factors.

7. Another method for resolving collisions with open addressing is to keep a separate array called the *overflow table*, into which all items that collide with an occupied location are put. They can either be inserted with another hash function, or simply inserted in order, with sequential search used for retrieval. Discuss the advantages and disadvantages of this method.

8. In a chained hash table, suppose that the items in each chain are kept in order by key. Then a search can be terminated as soon as it passes the place where the key should be, if present. How many fewer probes will be done, on average, in an unsuccessful search? In a successful search? How many probes are needed, on average, to insert a new item in the right place? Compare your answers with the corresponding numbers derived in the text for the case of chains not ordered.

9. In our discussion of chaining, the hash table itself contained only pointers, list headers for each of the chains. One variant method is to place the first actual item of each chain in the hash table itself. (An empty position is indicated by an impossible key, as with open addressing.) With a given load factor, calculate the effect on space of this method, as a function of the number of words (except links) in each item. (A link takes one word.)

10. Write an algorithm for deleting an item from a chained hash table.

11. Write a deletion algorithm for a hash table with open addressing, using a second special key to indicate a deleted item (see part 8 of Section 3.7.3). Change the retrieval and insertion algorithms accordingly.

12. With linear probing it is possible to delete an item without using a second special key, as follows. Mark the deleted entry empty. Search until another empty position is found. If the search finds a key whose hash address is at or before the first empty position, then move it back there, make its previous position empty, and continue from the new empty position. Write an algorithm to implement this method. Do the retrieval and insertion algorithms need modification?

3.8 Conclusions: Comparison of methods.

This chapter has studied four quite different methods of information retrieval: sequential search, binary search, table lookup, and hashing. If we ask which of these is best, we must select the criteria by which to answer. In regard both to speed and convenience, ordinary lookup in contiguous tables is certainly superior, but there are many applications (sparse tables) to which it is inapplicable. It is also inappropriate whenever insertions or deletions are frequent, since such actions in contiguous storage may require moving large amounts of information. Which of the other three methods is best depends on other criteria, such as the form of the data.

Sequential search is certainly the most flexible of our methods. The data may be stored in any order, with either contiguous or linked representation. Binary search is much more demanding. The keys must be in order, and the data in random-access representation (contiguous storage). Hashing requires even more, a peculiar ordering of the keys well suited to retrieval from the hash table, but generally useless for any other purpose. If the data are to be available immediately for human inspection, then some kind of order is essential, and a hash table is inappropriate.

Finally, there is the question of the unsuccessful search. Sequential search and hashing, by themselves, say nothing except that the search was unsuccessful. Binary search can determine which data have keys closest to the target, and perhaps thereby can provide useful information.

3.9 The Life game revisited.

At the end of Chapter 1 we noted that the bounds we used for the arrays in Conway's game of Life were highly restrictive and artificial. The Life cells are supposed to be on an unbounded grid. In other words, we would really like to have the Pascal declaration

type grid = **array** [integer, integer] **of** cell;

which is, of course, illegal. Since only a limited number of these cells will actually be occupied at any one time, we should really regard the grid for the Life game as a sparse table, and therefore a hash table proves an attractive way to represent the grid.

3.9.1 Choice of algorithm.

Before we specify our data structures more precisely, let us consider the basic algorithm that we might use. We already have two versions of the Life simulation, and we should not introduce a third unless we know that it will prove a significant improvement. The first version scanned the entire grid at each generation, an action that is not suitable for a sparse array (where it would be impossibly slow). The second version, on the other hand, was designed essentially to treat the grid as a sparse array. It never explicitly scans through cells that are dead, but uses four lists to locate all cells that need attention. Rather than writing a complete new program from scratch, let us therefore see how far we can go to use the overall structure and design of the second program Life2 in conjunction with a hash table to represent the sparse array.

3.9.2 Specification of data structures.

We have already decided to represent our sparse array of cells in a hash table, but we have not yet decided between open addressing and chaining. For each cell we must keep the status of the cell (alive or dead), the number of living neighbors, and (since the key itself must be explicitly kept when using a hash table) the row and column of the cell. With these four entries in each record, there are few space considerations to advise our decision. With chaining, the size of each record will increase 25% to accommodate the necessary pointer, but the hash table itself will be smaller, and can take a higher load factor than with open addressing. With open addressing, the records will be smaller, but more room must be left vacant in the hash table to avoid long searches and possible overflow.

After space considerations, the second question we should ask concerns flexibility. Do we need to make deletions, and, if so, when? We could keep track of all cells until the memory is full, and then delete those that are not needed. But this would require re-hashing the full array, which would be slow and painful. With chaining we can easily dispose of cells as soon as they are not needed, and thereby reduce the number of cells in the hash table as much as possible.

Finally, we should review the ways and means of accessing the cells. As we work with a given cell, we need to locate its eight neighbors, and we can use the hash table to do so. Some of these neighbors may be inserted into the four lists **live, die, nextlive,** and **nextdie.** When we later retrieve a cell from one of these lists, we could again use the hash table to find it, but doing so would be repeating work. If we use chaining, then we can add a cell to a list either by inserting the cell itself or a pointer to it, rather than by inserting its coordinates as before. In this way we can locate the cell directly with no need for any search. At the same time, linked lists can help to avoid problems with unnecessary overflow.

For reasons both of flexibility and time-saving, therefore, let us decide to use dynamic memory allocation, a chained hash table, and linked lists.

The most obvious way to represent the four lists is by connecting the cells into one of the lists by means of a pointer field. This would need to be a second pointer field in the record for a cell, since the first pointer field is used for chains from the hash table. A subtle problem arises, however. We have no guarantee that the same cell may not simultaneously be on two of the lists, and with only one available pointer field, the entries of the two lists will become mixed up. The obvious way to cure this problem is to keep a total of five pointer fields for each cell, one for the hash-table chain, and four for possible use in the four lists. This solution wastes a great deal of space, since many of the cells will not be on any of the four lists, and very few (if any) will be on more than one.

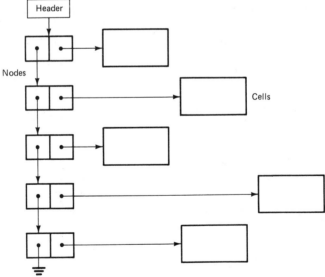

Figure 3.17. An indirect linked list

A much better way is to put pointers to cells into the four lists, not the cells themselves. The result is illustrated in Figure 3.17. Each node of the list thus contains two pointers, one to a cell, and one to the next node of the list.

3.9.3 The main program.

With these decisions made, we can now tie down the representation and notation for our data structures by writing the main program. Since we are following the method of Life2, the action part is identical with that of Life2.

```
program Life3(Input, Output);
{Simulation of Conway's game of Life on an unbounded grid}
{Version 3.}
const
  hashsize    = 997;                      {Choose a convenient prime}
  hashmax     = 996;                          { = hashsize − 1}
type
  status      = (alive, dead);
  count       = 0..8;                     {count of living neighbors}
  pcell       = ↑cell;
  pnode       = ↑node;
  cell        = record
                  state:    status;
                  numnbrs:  count;
                  row,
                  col:      integer;
                  nextcell: pcell
                end;
  node        = record
                  entry:    pcell;
                  nextnode: pnode
                end;

var
  hashtable:        array[0..hashmax] of pcell;
  live, die,
  nextlive,
  nextdie:          pnode;               {headers for linked lists}
  generation,
  lastgeneration:   integer;
begin
  Initialize;
  WriteMap;
  for generation : = 1 to lastgeneration do
  begin
    Vivify;
    Kill;
    WriteMap;
    AddNeighbors;
    SubtractNeighbors;
    CopyLive;
    CopyDie
  end                                    {processing one generation}
end.                                          {Program  Life3. }
```

3.9.4 Procedures.

Let us now write several of the procedures, so as to show how processing of the cells and of the lists transpires. The remaining procedures and functions will be left as exercises.

1. Procedure Vivify.

The task of the procedure Vivify is to traverse the list live, determine whether each cell on it satisfies the conditions to become alive, and vivify it if so, else delete it from the list. The usual way to facilitate deletion from a linked list is to keep two pointers in lock step, one position apart, while traversing the list. This method appears as an exercise, but here we use another that gives a simpler program at the expense of a little time and (temporarily) space.

Let us take advantage of the indirect linkage of our lists, and when we wish to delete an entry from the list, let us leave the node in place but set its entry field to **nil**. In this way, the node will be flagged as empty when it is again encountered in the procedure AddNeighbors.

```
procedure Vivify;
var
  p : pnode;                          {used to traverse list live}
begin
  p : = live;
  while p <> nil do
  with p↑ do begin
    with entry↑ do                    {entry↑ is the cell being examined.}
    if (state = dead) and (numnbrs = 3) then
      state: = alive
    else
      entry: = nil;                   {Remove the cell from list live.}
    p : = nextnode
  end                                 {processing node p↑}
end;
```

2. Procedure AddNeighbors.

The task of this procedure is to increase the neighbor count by 1 for each neighbor of all the cells that remain on list live, and to add cells to lists nextlive and nextdie when appropriate. The ordering of the cells on these lists is unimportant; hence we shall treat them as stacks, since stacks are the easiest lists to process. We shall use an auxiliary procedure Insert(p: pnode; q: pcell) to create a new node pointing to the given cell, and push it onto the given list.

Finding the neighbors of a given cell will require using the hash table; we shall postpone this task by referring to a function

function GetCell(row, col: integer): pcell;

that will return a pointer to the cell being sought, and create the cell if it was not previously in the hash table.

The procedure can now be written.

```
procedure AddNeighbors;
var
  i,j :       integer;              {row and column of a neighbor}
  p,                                {used to traverse list live}
  q :         pnode;                {used to delete nodes}
  neighbor : pcell;                 {points to the cell with coords i,j}

begin                               {Procedure AddNeighbors}
  p : = live;
  while p <> nil do
    with p↑ do
    begin
      if entry <> nil then
        with entry↑ do
          for i : = row − 1 to row + 1 do
          for j : = col − 1 to col + 1 do
          if (i <> row) or (j <> col) then   {exclude row, col itself}
          begin
            neighbor : = GetCell(i,j);
            with neighbor↑ do
            begin
              numnbrs : = numnbrs + 1;
              case numnbrs of
                0:    Writeln('Impossible case in AddNeighbors.');
                1,2:;                         {no action needed}
                3:    if state = dead then Insert(nextlive, neighbor);
                4:    if state = alive then Insert(nextdie, neighbor);
                5,6,7,8:;                     {no action needed}
              end                             {Case statement}
            end                   {With statement processing one neighbor}
          end;                                {looping through neighbors}
      q : = p;       {Prepare to dispose of the node p↑ from list live.}
      p : = nextnode;
      Dispose(q)
    end                                       {processing list node}
end;                                          {procedure}
```

3. Processing the hash table.

If you compare the two preceding procedures with the corresponding procedures for program Life2 in Chapter 1, you will find that they are almost a direct translation from contiguous storage to linked storage. We now turn to the first basic difference, the function that explicitly references the hash table. The task of the function

GetCell(i,j: integer): pcell

is first to look in the hash table for the cell with the given coordinates. If the search is successful, then the function returns a pointer to the cell; otherwise, it must create a new cell, assign it the given coordinates, initialize its other fields to the default values, and put it in the hash table, as well as return a pointer to it.

This outline translates into the following Pascal function. The part accessing the hash table is identical in substance to the corresponding procedure given in part 3 of Section 3.7.4.

```
function GetCell(i,j: integer): pcell;
{Gets cell from hash table if present; else creates cell}
var
  p :          pcell;                       {general purpose pointer}
  loc :        integer;                     {location returned by hash function }
begin
  loc : = Hash(i,j);
  p : = hashtable[loc];  {p now points to start of chain containing cell at
                                                                      i,j.}
                         {Search the chain for the desired cell.}
  if p <> nil then       {otherwise chain is empty and retrieval fails}
  begin
    while ((p↑.row <> i) or (p↑.col <> j)) and (p↑.nextcell <> nil)
    do
      p : = p↑.nextcell;
    if (p↑.row <> i) or (p↑.col <> j) then
      p := nil                              {Search has failed.}
  end;                                      {processing non-empty chain}
  if p <> nil then
    GetCell := p                            {Return cell from hash table.}
```

```
else begin          {Create new cell; initialize; insert in hash table.}
  New(p);
  with p↑ do begin
    row := i;
    col := j;
    state := dead;
    numnbrs := 0;
    nextcell := hashtable[loc];     {Push onto chain in hash table.}
    hashtable[loc] := p
  end;                              {inserting new cell into hash table}
  GetCell := p
end                                 {creating new cell}
end;                                {procedure}
```

4. The hash function.

Our hash function will differ slightly from those earlier in the chapter, in that its argument already comes in two parts (row and column), so that some kind of folding can be done easily. Before deciding how, let us for a moment consider the special case of a small array, where the function is one-to-one, and is exactly the index function. When there are exactly **maxrow** entries in each row, the index i, j maps to

$$i + maxrow * j$$

to place the rectangular array into contiguous storage, one row after the next.

It should prove effective to use a similar mapping for our hash function, where we replace **maxrow** by some convenient number (like a prime) that will maximize the spread and reduce collisions. Hence we obtain:

```
function Hash(i,j: integer): integer;
const
  factor = 101;                  {Choose a convenient prime.}
begin
  Hash := Abs(i + factor * j) mod hashsize
end;
```

5. Other subprograms.

The remaining subprograms all bear considerable resemblance either to one of the preceding procedures,or to the corresponding procedure in **Life2**, and therefore can safely be left as exercises.

Exercises

1. Rewrite the procedure **Vivify** to use two pointers in traversing the list **live**, and dispose of redundant nodes when they are encountered. Also make the accompanying simplifications in the procedure **AddNeighbors**.

2. Write the procedure Kill.

3. Write the procedure SubtractNeighbors. You will need to remove a cell from the hash table and dispose of it when it reaches the default case: the cell is dead and has a neighbor count of 0.

4. Write the procedure Insert.

5. Write the procedures for copying lists. [Your versions should run much faster than those used in Life2.]

6. The program as we have written it contains a bug, that of dangling pointers. When procedure SubtractNeighbors disposes of a cell, it may still be on one of the lists nextlive or nextdie, since these are allowed to contain redundant entries. Vivify and Kill may then err in the next generation. Correct the bug as follows.

   (a) Implement the plan of keeping space-available stacks, as discussed in Section 2.4.3. You will need to keep two stacks, one for available cells and one for available nodes. You will need to write four procedures for obtaining and disposing of cells and nodes.

   (b) Suppose that there are some (dangling) pointers to cells that have been placed on the available stack. Show that, when the next generation starts, the procedures Vivify and Kill will safely remove all such dangling pointers. before the available cells are reused.

7. Estimate the number of statements executed per generation in Life3 under the same assumptions that were used for Life2 in Section 1.6.5. Compare the results for the two versions.

8. Run the complete program Life3. Use the same configurations tested on Life2, and compare the time and space requirements.

3.10 References for further study.

The primary reference for this chapter is KNUTH, volume 3. (See the end of Chapter 2 for bibliographic details.) Sequential search occupies pages 389–405; binary search covers pages 406–414; then comes Fibonacci search, and a section on history. Hashing is the subject of Volume 3, pages 506–549. KNUTH studies all the methods we have touched, and many others besides. He does algorithm analysis in considerably more detail than we have, writing his algorithms in a pseudo-assembly language, and counting operations in detail there.

An alternative treatment that includes careful analysis of algorithms for searching, hashing, as well as other topics, is:

LYDIA I. KRONSJO, *Algorithms: Their Complexity and Efficiency,* John Wiley and Sons, New York, 1979.

Theorem 3.4 (successful and unsuccessful searches take almost the same time on average) is due to

> T. N. HIBBARD, *Journal of the ACM,* 9 (1962), 16–17.

Interpolation search is presented in

> C. C. GOTLIEB and L. R. GOTLIEB, *Data Types and Structures,* Prentice-Hall, Englewood Cliffs N.J.,1978, pages 133–135.

This book (pages 156–185) also considers arrays of various kinds, index functions, and access tables in considerable detail.

Extensions of the birthday surprise are considered in:

> M. S. KLAMKIN and D. J. NEWMAN, *Journal of Combinatorial Theory,* 3 (1967), 279–282.

Chapter 4

Sorting

This chapter studies several important methods for sorting lists, both contiguous and linked. At the same time, we shall develop further tools that help with the analysis of algorithms.

4.1 Introduction and notation.

We live in a world obsessed with keeping information, and to find it, we must keep it in some sensible order. Librarians make sure that no one misplaces a book; income tax authorities trace down every dollar we earn; credit bureaus keep track of almost every detail of our actions. I once saw a cartoon in which a keen filing clerk, anxious to impress the boss, said frenetically, "Let me make sure these files are in alphabetical order before we throw them out." If we are to be the masters of this explosion instead of its victims, we had best learn how to keep track of it all!

A few years ago, it was estimated, more than half the time on many commercial computers was spent in sorting. This is perhaps no longer true, since sophisticated methods have been devised for organizing data, methods that do not require that it be kept in any special order. Eventually, nonetheless, the information does go out to people, and then it must be sorted in some way. Because sorting is so important, a great many algorithms have been devised for doing it. In fact, so many good ideas appear in sorting methods that an entire course could easily be built around this one theme. Amongst the differing environments that require different methods, the most important is the distinction between *external* and *internal*, that is, whether there are so many records to be sorted that they must be kept in external files on disks, tapes, or the like, or whether they can all be kept internally in high-speed memory. In this chapter we consider only internal sorting.

It is not our intention to present anything close to a comprehensive treatment of internal sorting methods. For such a treatment, see Volume 3 of the monumental work of D. E. KNUTH (reference given at end of Chapter 2). KNUTH expounds about twenty-five sorting methods, and claims that they are "only a fraction of the algorithms that have been devised so far." We shall study only five methods, chosen, first, because they are good—each one can be the best choice under some circumstances; second, because they illustrate much of the variety appearing in the full range of methods; and third, because they are easy to write and understand, without too many details to complicate their presentation. Several variations of these methods will also appear as exercises.

Throughout this chapter we use the same notation as in the previous chapter, so that L will be a list of n items to be sorted. Each item x will have a key x.key by which the items are to be sorted. If we have a contiguous list L, then it will be indexed from 1 to n, and both the list L and the index n will be calling parameters for the procedures we write. If we have a linked list, then each item will contain a field called next of type pointer, and head will point to the first item in the list. The pointer head will be the only calling parameter for sorting procedures for linked lists.

In studying searching algorithms it soon became clear that the total amount of work done was closely related to the number of comparisons of keys. The same observation is true for sorting algorithms, but sorting algorithms must also either change pointers or move items around within the list, and therefore time spent this way is also important, especially in the case of large items kept in a contiguous list. Our analyses will therefore concentrate on these two basic actions.

As before, both the worst-case performance and the average performance of a sorting algorithm are of interest. To find the average we shall consider what would happen if the algorithm were run on all possible orderings of the list (with *n* items, there are *n*! such orderings altogether) and take the average of the results.

4.2 Insertion Sort.

Every avid player of a card game learns to sort a hand of cards almost automatically. One of the most common approaches is to look at the cards one at a time, and when each new card is seen, to insert it in the proper place in the (partial) hand of cards. This approach leads easily to an algorithm for computer sorting that is so natural that it should be in every programmer's repertoire.

To develop the algorithm, it is better to think of the cards not as held in one's hand, but as being placed face up in a row on a table one at a time as they are being sorted. As each new card is seen, then, it is compared with the row of cards, and some of them are pushed one position to the right to make room to insert the new one. An example is shown in Figure 4.1.

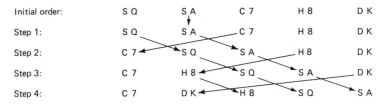

Figure 4.1. Example of insertion sort

The *insertion sort* algorithm thus proceeds on the idea of keeping the first part of the list, when once examined, in the correct order. An initial list with only one item is automatically in order. If we suppose that we have already sorted the first i−1 items, then we take item i and search through this sorted list of length i−1 to see where to insert item i.

4.2.1 Contiguous version.

For a contiguous list, we could use either sequential or binary search to find the place to insert item i. Binary search produces a slightly more complicated algorithm, and this will be pursued in the exercises. To make our algorithm even simpler, however, we shall here choose sequential search instead. A small trick will simplify the algorithm: If we do the search from the last toward the first item in the sorted list, then at the same time as we search we can move the items to make room to insert L[i] when we find the proper place. Let us now write the algorithm.

```
procedure InsertSort( var L: list; n: index);
var
  i,                              {i will be index of first unsorted item}
  j :            index;          {j searches sorted part of list}
  t :            item;           {t is used to swap entries}
  found:         Boolean;  {Has the proper place for L[i] been found?}
begin
  for i : = 2 to n do
    if L[i].key < L[i−1].key then    {otherwise, L[i] is in proper place}
    begin
      j : = i;
      t : = L[i];                           {Pull L[i] out of list.}
      repeat                     {Shift entries one place down list until}
        j : = j−1;                          {proper place is found.}
        L[j+1] : = L[j];         {Position j is now available for insertion.}
        if j = 1 then
          found : = true
        else
          found : = (L[j−1].key <= t.key)
      until found;
      L[j] : = t
    end
end;
```

The action of the program is nearly self-explanatory. Since a list with only one item is automatically sorted, the loop on i starts with the second item. If it is in the correct place, nothing needs to be done. Otherwise, the new item is pulled out of the list into the variable t, and the **repeat** ... **until** loop pushes items one position down the list until the correct position is found, and finally t is inserted there before proceeding to the next unsorted item. The case when t belongs in the first position of the list must be treated specially, since in this case there is no item with a smaller key that would terminate the search. We treat this special case by introducing the Boolean variable **found** and using an **if** statement to set its value.

4.2.2 Linked version.

For a linked version of insertion sort, we shall traverse the original list, break off one item at a time, and insert it in the proper place in a new, sorted list. To find where to insert p↑ we must search until we find an item in the sorted list with a greater key, and insert p↑ before this item. One effective way to insert an item before another (see Section 2.4.5) is to keep two pointers, which we call q and r, in lock step one position apart. Finally, let us note that a list with 0 or 1 item is already sorted, so that we can check these cases separately and thereby avoid trivialities elsewhere. Since we are breaking up the original list as we go, we shall keep separate pointers to traverse the sorted and unsorted parts of the list.

A *sentinel* is an extra item added to one end of a list to ensure that a loop will terminate without having to include a separate check. When we wish to insert p↑ into the sorted list, we shall first place it after the end of the sorted list, so that it will serve as a sentinel to stop the search. The details appear in the following procedure.

```
procedure InsertSort( var head: pointer);        {Linked version  sort}
var
  p,                                      {p↑ is item being inserted}
  tail,                                      {tail of sorted sublist}
  q,                                 {used to traverse sorted sublist}
  r :  pointer;                       {always one item in front of q↑}
begin
 if head <> nil then
 begin                              {Need only consider nonempty lists}
  tail : = head;
  while tail↑.next <> nil do
  begin
    p : = tail↑.next;                  {p is the next item to be inserted}
    if p↑.key < head↑.key then
    begin                              {insert p↑ at head of sorted list}
      tail↑.next : = p↑.next;            {advance sentinel down the list}
      p↑.next : = head;
      head : = p;
    end
```

```
        else begin                      {search sorted sublist to insert p↑}
          q : = head;
          r : = q↑.next;
          while p↑.key > r↑.key do
          begin
            q : = r;
            r : = q↑.next
          end;
          if p = r then
            tail : = p
          else begin
            tail↑.next : = p↑.next;
            p↑.next : = r;               {insert p↑ between q and r}
            q↑.next : = p
          end                           {inserting p↑ between q and r}
        end                             {searching list and inserting p↑}
      end                               {loop through nodes of list}
    end                                 {case where list length is > 0 }
  end;                                  {procedure InsertSort}
```

Even though the mechanics of the linked version are quite different from those of the contiguous version, you should be able to see that the basic method is the same. The only real difference is that the contiguous version searches the sorted sublist in reverse order, while the linked version searches it in increasing order of position within the list.

4.2.3 Analysis.

Since the basic ideas are the same, let us analyze only the performance of the contiguous version of the program. We also restrict our attention to the case when the list L is initially in random order (meaning that all possible orderings of the keys are equally likely). When we deal with item i, how far back must we go to insert it? There are i possible positions: not moving it at all, moving it one position, up to moving it $i-1$ positions to the front of the list. Given randomness, these are equally likely. The probability that it need not be moved is thus $1/i$, in which case only one comparison of keys is done, with no moving of items.

The contrary case, when item i must be moved, occurs with probability $(i-1)/i$. Let us begin by counting the average number of iterations of the **repeat** loop. Since all of the $i-1$ possible positions are equally likely, the average number of iterations is

$$\frac{1+2+\cdots+(i-1)}{i-1} \;=\; \frac{(i-1)i}{2(i-1)} \;=\; \frac{i}{2}.$$

One key comparison and one assignment are done for each of these iterations, with one more key comparison done outside the loop, along with two assignments of items. Hence, in this second case, item i requires, on average, $\frac{1}{2}i+1$ comparisons and $\frac{1}{2}i+2$ assignments.

When we combine the two cases with their respective probabilities, we have

$$\frac{1}{i}\times 1 \;+\; \frac{i-1}{i}\times(\frac{i}{2}+1) \;=\; \frac{i+1}{2}$$

comparisons and

$$\frac{1}{i}\times 0 \;+\; \frac{i-1}{i}\times(\frac{i}{2}+2) \;=\; \frac{i+3}{2}-\frac{2}{i}$$

assignments.

We must add these numbers from $i = 2$ to $i = n$. The result gives

$$\tfrac{1}{4}n^2+\tfrac{3}{4}n-1$$

comparisons of keys and approximately

$$\tfrac{1}{4}n^2+1\tfrac{3}{4}n-2\ln n-1.4$$

assignments of items. The latter calculation requires the result from Appendix A.2.7 that

$$1+\frac{1}{2}+\frac{1}{3}+\cdots+\frac{1}{n} \;\approx\; \ln n+0.7.$$

So far we have nothing with which to compare these numbers, but we can note that as n becomes larger the contributions from the terms involving n^2 become much larger than any of the other terms. Hence as the size of the list grows, the time needed by insertion sort grows like the square. Notice also that terms involving n^2 appear in both the counts of key comparisons and of item assignments.

The worst-case analysis of insertion sort will be left as an exercise, but we can observe quickly that the best case for insertion sort occurs when the list is already in order, when insertion sort will do nothing except $n-1$ comparisons of keys. We can now show that there is no sorting method that can possibly do better in this case.

THEOREM 4.1.   *Verifying that a list of n items is in order requires*
$n-1$ comparisons.

PROOF.   Consider an arbitrary program that checks whether a list of n items is in order or not (and perhaps sorts it if not). The program will do some comparison first, and this will involve two elements from the list. Sometime later, at least one of these two items must be compared with a third, or else there would be no way to decide where these two should be in the list relative to the third. Thus this second comparison involves only one new item not previously in a comparison. Continuing in this way, we see that there must be another comparison involving some one of the first three items and one new one. Note that we are not necessarily selecting the comparisons in the order in which the algorithm does them. Thus, after the first comparison, each one that we select involves only one new item not previously compared. All n of the items must enter some comparison, for there is no way to decide whether an item never compared to is in the right place. Thus to involve all n items requires at least $n-1$ comparisons.

Exercises

1. By hand trace through the steps insertion sort will use on the following list of 14 names to be sorted into alphabetical order:

   Tim Dot Eva Roy Tom Kim Guy Amy Jon Ann Jim Kay Ron Jan

   Count the number of comparisons that will be made, and the number of times a name will be moved.

2. Write programs that can be used to test and evaluate the performance of insertion sort (and, later, other methods). The following outline may be used.

   (a) Write the main program for the case of contiguous lists. The main program should declare the data types (such as item, list and index), and use procedures to set up the list of items to be sorted, print out the unsorted list if the user wishes, sort the list, and print the sorted list if the user wishes. The program should also determine the amount of CPU time required in the sorting phase.

   (b) Use a random number generator to construct lists of numbers (either integers or reals) to be sorted. Suitable sizes of the lists would be $n = 10$, 20, 100 and 300. It may be best to keep the lists in permanent files, so that the same lists can be used to evaluate different sorting methods.

   (c) Write a procedure to put the random numbers into the keys of records to be sorted. Do at least two cases: first, the records (of type item) should consist of the key alone, and, second, the records should be larger, with about 100 words of storage in each record. The fields other than the key need not be initialized.

   (d) Run the program to test the performance of contiguous insertion sort for short lists and long ones, and for small records and large ones.

   (e) Rewrite the main program for the case of linked lists instead of contiguous lists.

   (f) Rewrite the procedure to set up the records as a linked list. Either incorporate the possibility of both small and large records, or explain why there is no need to do so.

   (g) Run the program to test the performance of linked insertion sort.

3. What initial order for a list of keys will produce the worst case for insertion sort in the contiguous version? In the linked version?

4. How many key comparisons and item assignments does contiguous insertion sort make in its worst case?

5. Modify the linked version of insertion sort so that a list that is already sorted, or nearly so, will be processed rapidly.

6. Recall that a *sentinel* is an extra item added to one end of a list to ensure that a loop will terminate without having to check separately that the index has reached

its limit. Modify the contiguous version of procedure InsertSort to insert a sentinel into the list, so that the phrase "j = 1" can be removed from the termination condition for the loop. Compare the time required for the modified procedure with the original version for the same lists.

7. Rewrite the contiguous procedure InsertSort so that it uses binary search to locate where to insert the next item. Compare the time needed to sort a list with that of the original procedure InsertSort. Is it reasonable to use binary search in the linked version of InsertSort? Why or why not?

8. There is an even easier sorting method, which instead of using two pointers to move through the list, uses only one. We can call it *Scan Sort*, and it proceeds by starting at one end and moving forward, comparing adjacent pairs of keys, until it finds a pair out of order. It then swaps this pair of items, and starts moving the other way, continuing to swap pairs until it finds a pair in the correct order. At this point it knows that it has moved the one item as far back as necessary, so that the first part of the list is sorted, but, unlike insertion sort, it has forgotten how far forward has been sorted, so it simply reverses direction and sorts forward again, looking for a pair out of order. When it reaches the far end of the list, then it is finished.

    (a) Write a Pascal program to implement scan sort for contiguous lists. Your program should use only one index variable (other than n), one variable of type item to be used in making swaps, and no other local variables.

    (b) Compare the timings for your program with those of InsertSort.

9. A well-known algorithm called *Bubble Sort* proceeds by scanning the list from left to right, and whenever a pair of adjacent keys is found to be out of order then those items are swapped. In this first pass the largest key in the list will have "bubbled" to the end, but the earlier keys may still be out of order. Thus the pass scanning for pairs out of order is put in a loop that first makes the scanning pass go all the way to n, and at each iteration stops it one position sooner. Write a Pascal procedure for bubble sort, find the number of key comparisons and swaps it makes on average, and compare the results with those for insertion sort.

4.3 Selection Sort.

Insertion sort has one major disadvantage. Even after most items have been sorted properly into the first part of the list, the insertion of a later item may require that many of them be moved. All the moves made by insertion sort are moves of only one position at a time. Thus to move an item 20 positions up the list requires 20 separate moves. If the items are small, perhaps a key alone, or if the items are in linked storage, then the many moves may not require excessive time. But if the items are very large, records containing hundreds of components like personnel files or student transcripts, and must be kept in contiguous storage, then it would be far more efficient if, when it is necessary to move an item, then it could be moved immediately to its final position. Our next method accomplishes this goal.

This method is also modeled on sorting a hand of cards, but this time the hand held by a player who likes to look at all his cards at once. As he looks over his cards, he selects the highest one and puts it where it belongs, selects the second highest and puts it in its place, and continues in this way until they are all sorted.

This method (applied to the same hand used to illustrate insertion sort) is demonstrated in Figure 4.2.

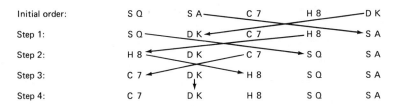

Initial order: S Q   S A   C 7   H 8   D K

Step 1: S Q   D K   C 7   H 8   S A

Step 2: H 8   D K   C 7   S Q   S A

Step 3: C 7   D K   H 8   S Q   S A

Step 4: C 7   D K   H 8   S Q   S A

Figure 4.2.Example of selection sort

This method translates into the following algorithm. Since its objective is to minimize data movement, selection sort is primarily useful with contiguous lists, and we therefore give only a contiguous version. The algorithm uses function MaxKey, which finds the maximum key on the part of the list L given as the calling parameters. The procedure Swap simply swaps the items with the given indices. For convenience in the discussion to follow, we write these two as separate subprograms.

```
procedure SelectSort( var L: list; n: index);
var
  i,                            {index of place being correctly filled}
  m : index;                    {index of largest key left (goes to i)}

{Declarations of function MaxKey and procedure Swap go here}

begin
  for i : = n downto 2 do
    begin
      m : = MaxKey(1, i);
      Swap(m,i)
    end
end;
```

Note that when all items in a list but one are in the correct place, then the remaining one must be also. Thus the **for** loop stops at 2.

```
function MaxKey( low, high: index): index;
var
  m,                                    {index of largest key so far}
  j :  index;                           {scans list for largest key}
begin
  m : = low;
  for j :  = low+1 to high do
    if L[m].key < L[j].key then
      m : = j;
  MaxKey :  = m
end;

procedure Swap( x, y: index);
var
  t : item;                             {temporary storage}
begin
  t :  = L[x];  L[x] := L[y];   L[y] := t
end;
```

A propos of algorithm analysis, the most remarkable fact about this algorithm is that both of the loops that appear are of the form **for** $\cdots$ **do** $\cdots$, which means that we can calculate in advance exactly how many times they will iterate. In the number of comparisons it makes, selection sort pays no attention to the original ordering of the list. Hence for a list that is nearly correct to begin with, selection sort is likely to be much slower than insertion sort. On the other hand, selection sort does have the advantage of predictability: its worst-case time will differ little from its best.

The primary advantage of selection sort regards data movement. If an item is in its correct final position, then it will never be moved. Every time any pair of items is swapped, then at least one of them moves into its final position, and therefore at most $n-1$ swaps are done altogether in sorting a list of n items. This is the very best that we can expect from any method that relies entirely on swaps to move its items.

We can analyze the performance of procedure SelectSort in the same way that it is programmed. The main procedure does nothing except some bookkeeping and calling the subprograms. Procedure Swap is called $n-1$ times, and each call does 3 assignments of items, for a total count of $3(n-1)$. The function MaxKey is called $n-1$ times, with the length of the sublist ranging from n down to 2. If t is the number of items on the list for which it is called, then MaxKey does exactly $t-1$ comparisons of keys to determine the maximum. Hence, altogether, there are

$$(n-1)+(n-2)+ \cdots +1 = \tfrac{1}{2}n(n-1)$$

comparisons of keys.

Let us pause for a moment to compare the counts for selection sort with those for insertion sort. The results are:

	Selection	*Insertion (average)*
Assignments of items	$3.0n - 3.0$	$0.25n^2 + 1.75n - 2 \ln n - 1.4$
Comparisons of keys	$0.5n^2 - 0.5n$	$0.25n^2 + 0.75n - 1.0$

The relative advantages of the two methods appear in these numbers. When n becomes large, $0.25n^2$ becomes much larger than $3n$, and if moving items is a slow process, then insertion sort will take far longer than selection sort. But the amount of time taken for comparisons is, on average, only about half as much for insertion sort as for selection sort. Under other conditions, then, insertion sort will be better.

Exercises

1. By hand, trace through the steps selection sort will use on the following list of 14 names to be sorted into alphabetical order:

   Tim Dot Eva Roy Tom Kim Guy Amy Jon Ann Jim Kay Ron Jan

   Count the number of comparisons and of moves that are made in sorting these names.

2. Run test programs to compare selection sort with insertion sort (contiguous version). Run at least four cases: with small lists (about 20 entries) and large (about 300), and with small items (key only) and large (about 100 words per item). The keys should be placed in random order.

3. The function MaxKey discards much of the information it discovers, since it returns only the index of the largest key. Suppose that the function was written in line in the main procedure, and consider the following modification. Introduce an additional variable x of type index, and set it to 1 before starting the outer loop. Before the inner loop initialize m to x rather than to 1. Before changing m to j in the **if** statement, set x to the old value of m. In this way, x points to a candidate for the second largest key, and subsequent passes of MaxKey will do fewer comparisons. Is this change worthwhile, and, if so, how many comparisons will it save on average?

4. Write a linked version of selection sort.

5. There is a simple algorithm called ***count sort*** that will construct a new, sorted list from L, provided we are guaranteed that all the keys in L are different from each other. Count sort goes through L once, and for each key L[i].key scans L to count how many keys are less than L[i].key. If c is this count, then the proper position in the sorted list for this key is $c+1$. Determine how many comparisons of keys will be done by count sort. Is it a better algorithm than selection sort?

4.4 Shell sort.

As we have seen, in some ways insertion sort and selection sort behave in opposite ways. Selection sort moves the items very efficiently but does many redundant comparisons. In its best case, insertion sort does the minimum number of comparisons, but is inefficient in moving items only one place at a time. Our goal now is to derive another method avoiding as much as possible the problems with both of these. Let us start with insertion sort and ask how we can reduce the number of times it moves an item.

The reason why insertion sort can move items only one position is that it compares only adjacent keys. If we were to modify it so that it first compares keys far apart, then it could sort the items far apart. Afterward the items closer together would be sorted, and finally the increment between keys being compared would be reduced to 1, to ensure that the list is completely in order. This is the idea implemented in 1959 by D. L. SHELL in the sorting method bearing his name. This method is also sometimes called *diminishing increment* sort. Before describing the algorithm formally, let us work through a simple example of sorting names.

Figure 4.3 shows what will happen when we first sort all names that are at distance 5 from each other (so there will be only two or three names on each such list), then re-sort the names using increment 3, and finally we do an ordinary insertion sort (increment 1).

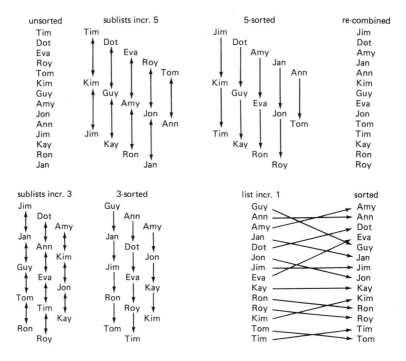

Figure 4.3. Example of Shell sort

You can see that, even though we make three passes through all the names, the early passes move the names close to their final positions, so that at the final pass (which does an ordinary insertion sort), all the items are very close to their final positions so the sort goes rapidly.

There is no magic about the choice of 5, 3 and 1 as increments. Many other choices might work as well or better. It would, however, probably be wasteful to choose powers of 2, such as 8, 4, 2 and 1, since then the same keys compared on one pass would be compared again at the next, whereas by choosing numbers that are not multiples of each other there is a better chance of obtaining new information from more of the comparisons. Although several studies have been made of Shell sort, no one has been able to prove that one choice of the increments is greatly superior to all others. Various suggestions have been made. If the increments are chosen close together, as we have done, then it will be necessary to make more passes, but each one will likely be quicker. If the increments decrease rapidly then fewer but longer passes will occur. The only essential feature is that the final increment be 1, so that at the conclusion of the process the list will be checked to be completely in order. For simplicity in the following algorithm, we start with increment $=$ n and at each pass reduce the increment by

$$\text{increment} := \text{increment } \textbf{div } 3 + 1.$$

We can now outline the algorithm for contiguous lists.

```
procedure ShellSort( var L: list; n: index);
var
  increment,                          {spacing of entries in sublist}
  start : index;                      {starting point of sublist}
begin
  increment : = n;
  repeat
    increment : = increment div 3 + 1;
    for start : = 1 to increment do
      Sort(start, increment)
  until increment = 1
end
```

The procedure Sort(start, increment) is exactly the procedure InsertSort except that the list starts at the variable start instead of 1, and the increment between successive values is as given instead of 1. The details of translating InsertSort are left as an exercise.

The analysis of ShellSort turns out to be exceedingly difficult, and to date good estimates on the number of comparisons and moves have been obtained only under special conditions. It would be very interesting to know how these numbers depend on the choice of increments, so that the best choice might be made. But even without a complete mathematical analysis, running a few large examples on a computer will convince you that ShellSort is quite good. Very large empirical studies have been made of ShellSort, and it appears that the number of moves, when n is large, is in the range of $n^{1.25}$ to $1.6n^{1.25}$. This constitutes a substantial improvement over insertion sort.

Exercises

1. By hand, sort the list of 14 names at the beginning of this section using Shell sort with increments of
    (a) 8, 4, 2, 1.
    (b) 7, 3, 1.
    Count the number of comparisons and moves that are made in each case.

2. Rewrite the procedure InsertSort to serve as the procedure Sort embedded in ShellSort.

3. Explain why Shell sort is ill suited for use with linked lists.

4. Run Shell sort on the same data used to compare sorting algorithms in the previous sections, and check its performance against that of insertion sort and selection sort.

4.5 Lower bounds.

Now that we have seen a method that performs much better than our first attempts, it is appropriate to ask,

How fast is it possible to sort?

In order to answer, we shall limit our attention (as we did when answering the same question for searching) to sorting methods that rely entirely on comparisons between pairs of keys to do the sorting.

Let us take an arbitrary sorting algorithm of this class and consider how it sorts a list of n items. Imagine drawing its comparison tree. Sample comparison trees for insertion sort and selection sort applied to three numbers a, b, c are shown in Figure 4.4. As each comparison of keys is made, it corresponds to an interior vertex (drawn as a circle). The leaves (square nodes) show the order that the numbers have after ordering.

The comparison tree of a sorting algorithm displays all the possible sequences of comparisons that can be made, as all the different paths from the root to the leaves. Since these comparisons control how the items are rearranged during sorting, any two different orderings of the list must result in some different decisions, hence in different paths through the tree, which must then end in different leaves. The number of ways that the list containing n items could originally have been ordered is $n!$, and thus the number of leaves in the tree must be at least $n!$. Lemma 3.2 now implies that the height of the tree is at least $\lg n!$. Since the height is an integer, we move up to the ceiling, $\lceil \lg n! \rceil$. This height is the number of comparisons made on the longest path through the tree. This is the number of comparisons in the worst case of sorting n objects. We restate this result formally.

THEOREM 4.2. *Any algorithm that sorts a list of n items by use of key comparisons must, for at least some ordering of the items, perform at least $\lceil \lg n! \rceil$ comparisons.*

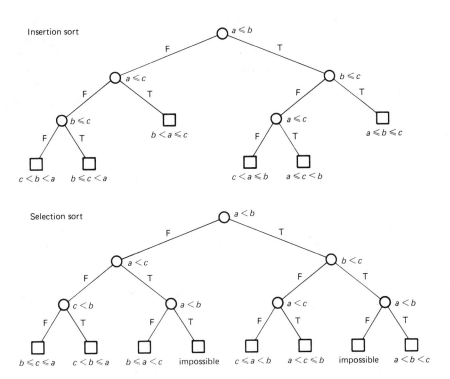

Figure 4.4. Comparison trees, insertion and selection sort, $n = 3$

Stirling's Formula from Appendix A gives an approximation to the factorial of an integer, which, after taking the base 2 logarithm, gives

$$\lg n! \approx (n + \tfrac{1}{2}) \lg n - (\lg e)\, n + \lg \sqrt{2\pi} + \frac{1}{12n}$$

The constants in this expression have the approximate values

$$\lg e \approx 1.442695041$$

$$\lg \sqrt{2\pi} \approx 1.325748069.$$

This approximation to $\lg n!$ is very close indeed, much closer than we shall ever need for analyzing sorting algorithms. For almost all purposes the following rough approximation will prove quite satisfactory:

$$\lg n! \approx (n + \tfrac{1}{2})(\lg n - 1\tfrac{1}{2}) + 2.$$

With a little additional effort we can prove a stronger theorem, showing that not only in the worst case, but on average, any sorting method relying on comparisons of keys must do at least $\lg n!$ comparisons. Take an arbitrary algorithm of this class, and consider its comparison tree for sorting lists of length n. It is possible that some of its leaves may be at levels less than lg $n!$ (for example, if the list turns out to be nearly in order insertion sort will do fewer than lg $n!$ comparisons). To show that the average level of leaves is at least lg $n!$ we shall first prove a lemma. Let T be an arbitrary 2-tree and denote by $E(T)$ its external path length.

> LEMMA 4.3.   *If a 2-tree T has q leaves, then its external path length*
> *$E(T)$ is at least q lg q, and the minimum of $E(T)$ occurs when all*
> *leaves of T are on the same level or on two adjacent levels.*

PROOF.   We prove the second assertion first. Suppose that there is a leaf on level u and a leaf on level v, where $u \geq v+2$. Then if we detach the two leaves on level u with the same parent and attach them under a leaf at level v, then we have not increased $E(T)$, and we may have decreased it. Continuing in this way, we can moves leaves upward in the tree until all leaves are on the same level or adjacent levels, and $E(T)$ will be less than or equal to its former value.

To prove the first assertion, we may now assume that T has minimum external path length. Then all leaves of T are on levels $u-1$ and u for some integer u. Let x of the leaves be on level $u-1$, and $q-x$ on level u. By Lemmas 3.1 and 3.2 we have no more than $2^{u-1}-x$ non-leaves on level $u-1$, each of which parents at most two leaves on level u, so that

$$q-x \quad \leq \quad 2(2^{u-1}-x),$$

which becomes

$$x \quad \leq \quad 2^u-q.$$

We now have

$$
\begin{aligned}
E(T) \quad &= \quad (u-1)\,x+u(q-x) \\
&= \quad qu-x \\
&\geq \quad qu-(2^u-q) \quad = \quad q(u+1)-2^u.
\end{aligned}
$$

Since we are choosing T to have minimal external path length, we have

$$2^{u-1} \quad < \quad q \quad \leq \quad 2^u.$$

If we set $u = $ lg $q+\epsilon$, then ϵ satisfies $0 \leq \epsilon < 1$, and substituting ϵ into the bound for $E(T)$ we obtain

$$E(T) \quad \geq \quad q(\text{ lg } q+1+\epsilon-2^\epsilon).$$

It turns out that, for $0 \leq \epsilon < 1$, the quantity $1+\epsilon-2^\epsilon$ is between 0 and 0.0861. Thus the minimum path length is quite close to q lg q, but may be slightly larger, as was to be shown.

To obtain a lower bound on the average number of key comparisons in a sorting algorithm, we now let T be the decision tree of the algorithm, and apply the lemma with $q = n!$, since $n!$ is a lower bound for the number of leaves in a comparison tree for sorting n objects. The average number of comparisons done is the average length of a path from the root to a leaf; that is, the external path length divided by the number of leaves. Hence we obtain:

> THEOREM 4.4. *Any algorithm that sorts lists of n items by comparing keys must, over all n! orderings of the list, perform on average at least*
>
> $$\lg n! \approx (n+0.5)(\lg n - 1.5) + 2$$
>
> *comparisons.*

Before ending this section, we should note that there are sometimes methods for sorting that do not use comparisons and can be faster. For example, if you know in advance that you have 100 items and that their keys are exactly the integers between 1 and 100 in some order, with no duplicates, then the best way to sort them is not to do any comparisons, but simply, if a particular item has key i, then place it in location i in the list. Exercise 3 suggests an extension of this idea to an algorithm.

Exercises

1. Draw the comparison trees for insertion and selection sort applied to four objects.

2. Find a sorting method for four keys that is optimal in the sense of doing the smallest possible number of key comparisons, on average.

3. Construct a list of 1000 (pseudo-)random numbers between 0 and 1. Write a program to sort them into a new list via the following *interpolation sort*. First clear the new list (to all 0). For each number from the old list, multiply it by 1000, take the integer part, and look in that position of the new list. If it is 0, put the number there. If not, move left or right (according to the relative size of the current number and the one in its place) to find the place to insert the new number, pushing the entries in the new list over if necessary to make room (as in the fashion of insertion sort). Show that your algorithm will really sort the numbers correctly. Compare its running time with that of the other sorting methods applied to the same unsorted list.

4. [Suggested by BERNIE LEE] Write a program to perform a linked distribution sort, as follows. Take the keys to be numbers, as in Exercise 3, and distribute them into linked lists according to their magnitude. The linked lists can either be kept sorted as the numbers are inserted, or sorted during a second pass, during which the lists are all connected together into one sorted list. Experiment to determine the optimum number of lists to use. (It seems that it works well to have enough lists so that the average length of each list is about 3.)

4.6 Divide and conquer.

If you compare the lower bounds derived in the last section with the expected performance of insertion sort and selection sort, then you will see that there is a considerable gap. If $n = 1000$, for example, then insertion sort does about 250,000 comparisons, and selection sort about 500,000, whereas the lower bound is about 8,500. An optimal method, therefore, should run almost 30 times faster than insertion sort when $n = 1000$. In this section we shall derive more sophisticated sorting algorithms that come close to providing the best performance that the lower bounds will allow.

4.6.1 The main ideas.

Making a fresh start is often a good idea, and we shall do so by forgetting (temporarily) almost everything that we know about sorting. Let us try to apply only one important principle that has shown up in every method we have done, and that we know from common experience: It is much easier to sort short lists than long ones. If the number of items to be sorted doubles, then the work more than doubles (in our first two methods it quadruples, roughly). Hence, if we can find a way to divide the list into two roughly equal-sized lists and sort them separately, then we will save work. If you were working in a library and were given a thousand index cards to put in alphabetical order, then a good way would be to distribute them into piles according to the first letter, and sort the piles separately.

The idea of dividing a problem into smaller but similar subproblems is called *divide and conquer*. First we note that comparisons by computer are usually two-way branches, so we shall divide the items to sort into two lists at each stage of the process.

What method, you may ask, should we use to sort the reduced lists? Since we have (temporarily) forgotten all the other methods we know, let us simply use the same method, divide-and-conquer, again, repeatedly subdividing the list. But we won't keep going forever: sorting a list with only one item doesn't take any work, even if we know no formal sorting methods.

In summary, let us informally outline divide-and-conquer sorting:

```
procedure Sort( list )
   if the length of the list is greater than 1 then
   begin
      Partition the list into lowlist, highlist;
      Sort( lowlist );
      Sort( highlist);
      Combine( lowlist, highlist)
   end.
```

We still must decide how we are going to partition the list into two sublists, and, after they are sorted, how we are going to combine the sublists into a single list. There are two methods, each of which works very well in different circumstances.

1. Mergesort.

In the first method we simply chop the list into two sublists of sizes as nearly equal as possible, then sort them separately. Afterward we carefully merge the two sorted sublists into a single sorted list. Hence this method is called *mergesort.*

2. Quicksort.

The second method does more work in the first step of partitioning the list into two sublists, and the final step of combining the sublists then becomes trivial. This method was invented and christened *Quicksort* by C. A. R. HOARE. To partition the list we first choose some key from the list for which, we hope, about half the keys will come before and half after. Call this key the *pivot.* Then we partition the items so that all those with keys less than the pivot come in one sublist, and all those with greater keys come in another. Then we sort the two reduced lists separately, put the sublists together, and the whole list will be in order.

4.6.2 An example.

Before we refine our methods into detailed procedures, let us work through a specific example. We take the following seven numbers to sort:

26 33 35 29 19 12 22.

1. Mergesort example.

The first step of mergesort is to chop the list into two. When (as in this example) the list has odd length, let us establish the convention of making the left sublist one entry larger than the right sublist. Thus we divide the list into

26 33 35 29   and   19 12 22

and first consider the left sublist. It is again chopped in half as

26 33   and   35 29.

For each of these sublists we again apply the same method, chopping each of them into sublists of one number each. Sublists of length 1, of course, require no sorting. Finally, then, we can start to merge the sublists to obtain a sorted list. The sublists 26 and 33 merge to give the sorted list 26 33, and the sublists 35 and 29 merge to give 29 35. At the next step we merge these two sorted sublists of length 2 to obtain a sorted sublist of length 4,

26 29 33 35.

Now that the left half of the original list is sorted, we do the same steps on the right half. First we chop it into the sublists

19 12   and   22.

The first of these is divided into two sublists of length 1, which are merged to give 12 19. The second sublist, 22, has length 1 so needs no sorting. It is now merged with 12 19 to give the sorted list

$$12 \quad 19 \quad 22.$$

Finally, the sorted sublists of lengths 4 and 3 are merged to produce

$$12 \quad 19 \quad 22 \quad 26 \quad 29 \quad 33 \quad 35.$$

2. Quicksort example.

Let us again work through the same example, this time applying the methods of quicksort, and keeping careful account of the execution of steps from our outline of the method. To use quicksort we must first decide, in order to partition the list into two pieces, what key to choose as the pivot. We are free to choose any number, but for consistency will use a definite rule. Perhaps the simplest rule is to choose the first number on a list as the pivot.

Our first pivot, then, is 26, and the list partitions into sublists

$$19 \quad 12 \quad 22 \quad \text{and} \quad 33 \quad 35 \quad 29,$$

consisting, respectively, of the numbers less than and greater than the pivot. (We have left the order of the items in the sublists unchanged from that in the original list, but this decision also is arbitrary.)

We now arrive at the next line of the outline, which tells us to sort the first sublist. We thus start the algorithm over again from the top, but this time applied to the shorter list

$$19 \quad 12 \quad 22.$$

The pivot of this list is 19, which partitions its list into two sublists of one number each, 12 in the first and 22 in the second. With only one entry each, these sublists do not need sorting, so we arrive at the last line of the outline, and therefore combine the two sublists with the pivot between them to obtain the sorted list

$$12 \quad 19 \quad 22.$$

Now the call to the sort procedure is finished for this sublist, so it returns whence it was called. It was called from within the sort procedure for the full list of seven numbers, so we now go on to the next line of that procedure.

We have now used the procedure twice, with the second instance occurring within the first instance. Note carefully that the two instances of the procedure are working on different lists, and are as different from each other as executing the same code twice within a loop. It may help to think of the two instances as having different colors, so that the instructions in the second (inner) call could be written out in full in place of the call, but in a different color of ink, thereby clearly distinguishing them as a separate instance of the procedure.

Returning to our example, we find the next line of the first instance of the procedure to be another call to sort another list, this time the three numbers

33 35 29.

As in the previous (inner) call, the pivot 33 immediately partitions the list, giving sublists of length 1, which are then combined to produce the sorted list

29 33 35.

Finally, this call to sort returns, and we reach the last line of the (outer) instance that sorts the full list. At this point, the two sorted sublists of length three are combined with the original pivot of 26 to obtain the sorted list

12 19 22 26 29 33 35

and the process is complete.

4.6.3 Recursion.

A procedure like divide-and-conquer, that calls itself (or calls one procedure that calls another and so on until the first is called again) is termed *recursive*. Recursive procedures are often the easiest and most natural way to solve a problem. At first some people feel slightly uncomfortable with recursive procedures. Recursion may perhaps appear at first to be an infinite process, but there is no more danger of writing infinite recursion than of writing an infinite iterative loop. In fact, the dangers are less, since an infinite recursion will soon run out of space and terminate the program, while infinite iteration may continue until manually terminated. In our procedure we have deliberately ensured that when the list has size 1 or less there is no recursion. When the list is longer, each recursive call is with a list strictly smaller than before. The process will therefore terminate in a finite number of steps.

The importance of recursion makes it the major topic of Chapter 7, and by that time we shall have seen several other important examples of recursive procedures. In Chapter 7 we shall also explain some details of how a recursive procedure works on most computer systems. Appendix B, finally, describes methods for converting recursive procedures into equivalent non-recursive procedures. These methods are useful if you need to program in one of the older languages (such as FORTRAN, COBOL or BASIC) that do not provide for recursion.

4.6.4 Tree of subprogram calls.

With all the recursive calls through which we worked our way, the examples we have studied may lead you to liken recursion to the fable of the Sorcerer's Apprentice, who, when he had enchanted a broom to fetch water for him, did not know how to stop it and so chopped it in two, whereupon it started duplicating itself until there were so many brooms fetching water that disaster would have ensued had the master not returned.

The easy way to keep track of all the calls in our quicksort example is to draw a tree, as in Figure 4.5. The two calls to Sort at each level are shown as the children of the vertex. The sublists of size 1 or 0, that need no sorting, are drawn as the leaves. In the other vertices (to save space) we include only the pivot that is used for the call.

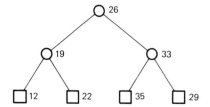

Figure 4.5. Recursion tree, quicksort of 7 numbers

Drawing a tree can prove a good way to study the structure of subprogram calls, even when recursion is not involved. The main program is shown as the root of the tree, and all the calls that the main program makes directly are shown as the vertices directly below the root. Each of these subprograms may, of course, call other subprograms, which are shown as further vertices on lower levels. In this way the tree grows into a form like the one in Figure 4.6. We shall call such a tree a ***tree of subprogram calls.*** We are especially interested in recursion, so that often we draw only the part of the tree showing the recursive calls, and call it a ***recursion tree.***

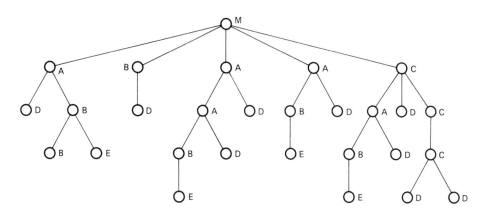

Figure 4.6. A tree of subprogram calls

From Figure 4.6 you should notice, first, that in drawing the tree recursion is in no way an exception: different recursive calls appear simply as different vertices that happen to have the same name of a subprogram. Second, note carefully that the tree shows the calls to subprograms, not the nesting of declarations of subprograms. Hence a subprogram called from only one place, but within a loop executed more than once, will appear several times in the tree, once for each execution of the loop. Similarly, if a subprogram is called from a conditional statement that is not executed, then the call will not appear in the tree.

A closely related picture of recursion is that of *stack frames*; refer for a moment to Figure 2.2. The stack frames show the nesting of recursive calls, and also illustrate the storage requirements for recursion. If a procedure calls itself recursively several times, then separate copies of the variables declared in the procedure are created for each recursive call. In the usual implementation of recursion, these are kept on a stack. Note that the amount of space needed for this stack is proportional to the height of the recursion tree, not to the total number of nodes in the tree. That is, the amount of space needed to implement a recursive procedure depends on the *depth* of recursion, not on the *number* of times the procedure is invoked.

If you are still uneasy about the workings of recursion, then you will find it helpful to pause and work through sorting the list of fourteen names introduced in previous sections, using both mergesort and quicksort. As a check, Figure 4.7 provides the tree of calls for quicksort in the same abbreviated form used for the previous example. This tree is given for two versions, one where the pivot is the first key in each sublist, and one where the central key (center left for even-sized lists) is the pivot.

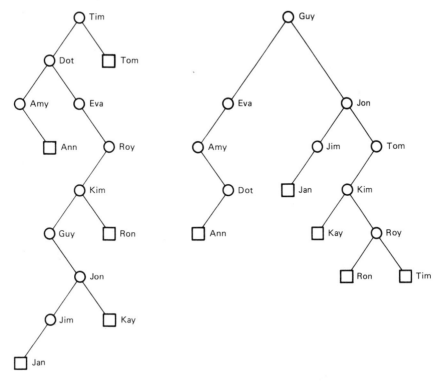

Figure 4.7. Recursion trees, quicksort of 14 names

Exercises

1. Apply quicksort to the list of seven numbers considered in this section, where the pivot in each sublist is chosen to be (a) the last number in the sublist, and (b) the center (or left-center) number in the sublist. In each case, draw the tree of recursive calls.

2. Apply mergesort to the list of 14 names considered for previous sorting methods:

    Tim Dot Eva Roy Tom Kim Guy Amy Jon Ann Jim Kay Ron Jan

3. Apply quicksort to this list of 14 names, and thereby sort them by hand into alphabetical order. Take the pivot to be (a) the first key in each sublist and (b) the center (or left-center) key in each sublist.

4. In both divide-and-conquer methods we have attempted to divide the list into two sublists of approximately equal size, but the basic outline of sorting by divide-and-conquer remains valid without equal-sized halves. Consider dividing the list so that one sublist has size only 1. This leads to two methods, depending on whether the work is done in splitting one element from the list, or in combining the sublists.

    (a) Split the list by finding the item with the largest key, and making it the sublist of size 1. After sorting the remaining items, the sublists are combined easily by placing the item with the largest key last.

    (b) Split off the last item from the list. After sorting the remaining items, merge this item into the list.

    Show that one of these methods is exactly the same method as insertion sort, and the other is the same as selection sort.

4.7 Mergesort for linked lists.

Let us now turn to the writing of formal procedures for each of our sorting methods. In the case of mergesort we shall write a version for linked lists and leave the case of contiguous lists as an exercise. For quicksort we shall do the reverse.

4.7.1 The procedures.

Our outline of the basic method for mergesort translates directly into the following procedure, which should be invoked from the calling program with its calling parameter being a pointer to the head of the list to be sorted.

```
procedure MergeSort(var p: pointer);
                {Divides list in half, sorts recursively, and merges.}
var
  q :            pointer;
begin
  if p <> nil then if p↑.next <> nil then
  begin       {Otherwise, list has 0 or 1 entry, with no need to sort.}
    Divide(p, q);
    MergeSort(p);
    MergeSort(q);
    p : = Merge(p, q)
  end
end;
```

Subsidiary to MergeSort are the procedure Divide(p, q), that takes the list to which p points, divides it in half, and returns with q pointing to the start of the second half, and the function Merge(p, q), that merges the lists to which p and q point, returning a pointer to the merged list as the function value. These subsidiary subprograms follow.

```
procedure Divide(var p, q: pointer);
{Takes list to which p points, divides it in half, and returns with p point-
ing to head of the first half, and q to the head of second half. Requires
that original list contain at least two items, or error occurs}
var
    r : pointer
begin
    q : = p;                      {Start q at position 1, r at position 3}
    r : = p↑.next;
    r : = r↑.next;
    while r <> nil do      {Move r two positions for each move of q}
    begin
        r : = r↑.next;
        q : = q↑.next;
        if r <> nil then
            r : = r↑.next
    end;
    {Break list into halves after q↑.}
    r : = q↑.next;
    q↑.next : = nil;
    q : = r
end;
```

```
function Merge (p, q: pointer): pointer;
{Merges two sorted lists into one, that will begin at the function name.
Requires that both lists be non-empty.}
var
    r : pointer ;                    {always points to last node of sorted list}
begin
    if (p = nil) or (q = nil ) then
        Writeln('Merge called with empty list(s).');
    if p↑.key <= q↑.key then
    begin
        r : = p;
        p : = p↑.next
    end
    else begin
        r : = q;
        q : = q↑.next
    end;
    Merge : = r;
    while (p <> nil) and (q <> nil) do
    if p↑.key <= q↑.key then
    begin
        r↑.next : = p;
        r : = p;
        p : = p↑.next
    end
    else begin
        r↑.next : = q;
        r : = q;
        q : = q↑.next
    end;
    if p = nil then r↑.next : = q  else  r↑.next : = p
end;
```

4.7.2 Analysis of mergesort.

Now that we have a functional algorithm, it is time to pause and determine its behavior, so that we can make reasonable comparisons with other methods. As with other algorithms on linked lists, we need not be especially concerned with the time needed to move items, and concentrate instead on the number of comparisons of keys that the procedure will do.

1. Counting comparisons.

    Comparison of keys is done at only one place in the complete mergesort procedure. This place is within the main loop of the merge (sub-)procedure. After each comparison one of the two items is sent to the output list. Hence the number of comparisons certainly cannot exceed the number of items being merged. To find the total lengths of these lists, let us again consider the recursion tree of the algorithm, which for simplicity we draw in Figure 4.8 as the case when $n = 2^m$ is a power of 2.

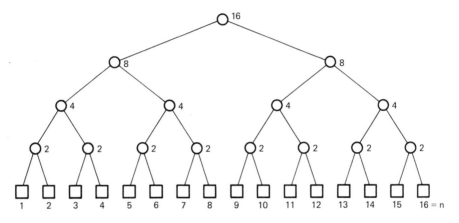

Figure 4.8. Length of sublist merges

    It is clear from the tree of Figure 4.8 that the total lengths of the lists on each level is precisely n, the total number of items. In other words, every item is treated in precisely one merge on each level. Hence the total number of comparisons done on each level cannot exceed n. The number of levels, excluding the leaves (for which no merges are done), is $\lceil \lg n \rceil$. The number of comparisons of keys done by mergesort on a list of n items, therefore, is certainly no more than

$$n \lceil \lg n \rceil.$$

2. Contrast with insertion sort.

    Recall (Section 4.2.3) that insertion sort does more than $\frac{1}{4}n^2$ comparisons of keys, on average, in sorting n items. As soon as n becomes greater than 16, $\lg n$ becomes less than $\frac{1}{4}n$, and when n is of practical size for sorting a list, $\lg n$ is far less than $\frac{1}{4}n$. Therefore the number of comparisons done by mergesort is far less than the number done by insertion sort. When $n = 1024$, for example, then $\lg n = 10$, so that the bound on comparisons for mergesort is 10,240, whereas the average number that insertion sort will do is more than 250,000. A problem requiring a half-hour of computer time using insertion sort will probably require hardly a minute using mergesort.

The appearance of the expression $n \lg n$ in the preceding calculation is by no means accidental, but relates closely to the lower bounds established in Section 4.5, where it was proved that any sorting method that uses comparisons of keys must do at least

$$\lg n! \approx n \lg n - 1.44n + 0.5 \lg n + 1$$

comparisons of keys. When n is large, the first term of this expression becomes much more important than the others. We have now found, in mergesort, an algorithm that comes within reach of this lower bound.

3. Improving the count.

By being somewhat more careful we can, in fact, obtain a more accurate count of comparisons made by mergesort that will show that its actual performance comes even closer to the best possible number of comparisons of keys allowed by the lower bound.

First, let us observe that merging two lists of total size k never requires k comparisons, but instead at most $k-1$, since after the second largest key has been put out, there is nothing left to which to compare the largest key, so it goes out without another comparison. Hence we should reduce our total count of comparisons by 1 for each merge that is performed. The total number of merges is essentially

$$\frac{n}{2} + \frac{n}{4} + \frac{n}{8} + \cdots + 1 \ = \ n-1.$$

(This calculation is exact when n is a power of 2, and is a good approximation otherwise.) The total number of key comparisons done by mergesort is therefore less than

$$n \lg n - n + 1.$$

Second, we should note that it is possible for one of the two lists being merged to be finished before the other, and then all items in the second list will go out with no further comparisons, so the number of comparisons may well be less than we have calculated. Every element of one list, for example, might precede every element of the second list, so all elements of the second list would come out using no comparisons. The exercises outline a proof that the total count can be reduced, on average, to

$$n \lg n - 1.1583n + 1,$$

and the correct coefficient of n is likely close to -1.25. We thus see that, not only is the leading term as small as the lower bound permits, but the second term is also quite close. By refining the merge procedure even more, the method can be brought within a few percent of the theoretically optimal number of comparisons (see references).

4. Conclusions.

From these remarks it may appear that mergesort is the ultimate sorting method, and, indeed, for linked lists in random order it is difficult to surpass. We must remember, however, that considerations other than comparing keys are important. The program we have written spends significant time finding the center of the list, so that it can break it in half. The exercises discuss one method for saving some of this time, and at the end of Chapter 7 we shall develop a variation that will give further improvement. The linked version of mergesort uses space efficiently. It needs no large auxiliary arrays or other lists, and since the depth of recursion is only lg n, the amount of space needed to keep track of the recursive calls is very small.

5. Contiguous mergesort.

For contiguous lists, unfortunately, mergesort is not such an unqualified success. The difficulty is in merging two contiguous lists without substantial expense in one of (1) space, (2) computer time, or (3) programming effort. The first and most straight-forward way to merge two contiguous lists is to use an auxiliary array large enough to hold the combined list, and to copy the entries into the array as the lists are merged. This method requires extra space proportional to n. For a second method, we could put the sublists to be merged next to each other, forget the amount of order they already have, and use a method like insertion sort to put the combined list into order. This approach uses almost no extra space, but uses computer time proportional to n^2, compared to time proportional to n for a good merging algorithm. Finally (see references), algorithms have been invented that will merge two contiguous lists in time proportional to n, using only a small, fixed amount of extra space. These algorithms, however, are very complicated.

Exercises

1. Implement mergesort for linked lists on your computer. Use the same conventions and the same test data used for implementing and testing the linked version of insertion sort. Compare the performance of mergesort and insertion sort for short and long lists, and for lists nearly in correct order and in random order.

2. Our mergesort program for linked lists spends significant time locating the center of each sublist, so that it can be broken in half. Implement the following mod-ification that will save most of this time. First set up a record to describe a linked list that will contain not only (1) a pointer to the head of the list, but also (2) a pointer to the center of the list and (3) the length of the list. At the beginning, the original list must be traversed once to determine this information. With this information it becomes easy to break the list in half and obtain the lengths of the sublists. The center of a sublist can be found by traversing only half the sublist. Rewrite the mergesort procedure to pass the records describing linked lists as calling parameters, and use them to simplify the subdivision of the lists.

3. The count of key comparisons in merging is usually too high, since it does not account for the fact that one list may be finished before the other. It might happen, for example, that all entries in the first list come before any in the second list, so that the number of comparisons is just the length of the first list.

(a) Show that the average number of comparisons performed by our algorithm to merge two lists of length 2 is 8/3. [*Hint:* Start with the ordered list 1, 2, 3, 4. Write down the six ways of putting these numbers into two ordered lists of length 2, and show that four of these ways will use 3 comparisons, and two will use 2 comparisons.]

(b) Show that the average number of comparisons done to merge two lists of length 3 is 4.5.

(c) Show that the average number of comparisons done to merge two lists of length 4 is 6.4.

(d) Use the above results to obtain the improved total count of key comparisons for mergesort.

(e) Show that, as m tends to infinity, the average number of comparisons done to merge two lists of length m approaches $2m - 2$.

4. Our mergesort procedure pays little attention to whether or not the original list was partially in the correct order. In **natural mergesort** the list is broken into sublists at the end of an increasing sequence of keys, instead of arbitrarily at its half-way point. This exercise requests the implementation of two versions of natural mergesort.

In the first version the original list is traversed only once, and only two sublists are used. As long as the order of the keys is correct, the nodes are placed in the first sublist. When a key is found out of order, the first sublist is ended and the second started. When another key is found out of order, the second sublist is ended, and the second sublist merged into the first. Then the second sublist is repeatedly built again, and merged into the first. When the end of the original list is reached, the sort is finished. This first version is simple to program, but, as it proceeds, the first sublist is likely to become much longer than the second, and the performance of the procedure will degenerate to that of insertion sort.

The second version ensures that the lengths of sublists being merged are closer to being equal, and therefore that the advantages of divide-and-conquer are fully used. This method keeps a (small) auxiliary array containing (1) the lengths and (2) pointers to the heads of the ordered sublists that are not yet merged. The entries in this array should be kept in order according to the length of sublist. As each (naturally ordered) sublist is split from the original list, it is put into the auxiliary array. If there is another list in the array whose length is between half and twice that of the new list, then the two are merged, and the process repeated. When the original list is exhausted then any remaining sublists in the array are merged (smaller lengths first), and the sort is finished.

There is nothing sacred about the ratio of 2 in the criterion for merging sublists. Its choice merely ensures that the number of entries in the auxiliary array cannot exceed lg n (prove it!). A smaller ratio (required to be greater than 1) will make the auxiliary table larger, and a larger ratio will lessen the advantages of divide-and-conquer. Experiment with test data to find a good ratio to use.

5. Devise a version of merge sort for contiguous lists. The difficulty is to produce a procedure to merge two sorted lists in contiguous storage. It is necessary to use some additional space other than that needed by the two lists. The easiest solution is to use two arrays, each large enough to hold all the items in the two original lists. The two sorted sublists occupy different parts of the same array. As they are merged, the new list is built in the second array. After the merge is complete, the new list can, if desired, be copied back into the first array. Otherwise, the roles of the two arrays can be reversed for the next stage.

6. *[Challenging]* The merging method described in Exercise 5 uses extra space proportional to the number of items in the two lists, but can be written to run efficiently, with time proportional to the number of items. Try to devise a merging method for contiguous lists that will require as little extra space as possible, but that will still run in time (linearly) proportional to the number of items in the lists. [There is a solution using only a small, constant amount of extra space. See references.]

7. *[Radix sort]* A formal sorting algorithm predating computers was first devised for use with punched cards, but can be developed into a very efficient sorting method for linked lists. The idea is to consider the key one character at a time, and to divide the items, not into two sublists, but into as many sublists as there are possibilities for the given character from the key. If our keys, for example, are words or other alphabetic strings, then we divide the list into twenty-six sublists at each stage. Punched cards have twelve rows; hence mechanical card sorters work on only one column at a time, and divide the cards into twelve piles.

   A person sorting words by this method would first distribute the words into twenty-six lists according to the initial letter, then divide each of these sublists into further sublists according to the second letter, and so on. The following idea eliminates this multiplicity of sublists: Partition the items into sublists first by the least significant position, not the most significant. After this first partition, the sublists are put back together as a single list, in the order given by the character in the least significant position. The list is then partitioned according to the second least significant position and recombined as one list. When, continuing in this way, the list has been partitioned by the most significant place and recombined, then it will be completely sorted.

   Implement this method in Pascal for linked lists, where the keys are strings of letters or blanks of fixed length. The sublists should be treated as linked queues, and you will need an array of 27 such queues, indexed by the letters and by the character blank (or some substitute character). Within a loop running from the least to most significant positions, you should traverse the linked list, and add each item to the end of the appropriate queue. After the list has been thus partitioned, recombine the queues into one list by linking the tail of each queue to the head of the next. At the end of the major loop on positions, the list will be completely sorted.

Run radix sort on the same data used to check linked mergesort, and compare the results. Note that the time used by radix sort is proportional to *nk*, where *n* is the number of items being sorted, and *k* is the number of characters in a key. The time for mergesort is *n* lg *n*. The relative performance of the methods will therefore relate in some ways to the relative sizes of *k* and lg *n*.

4.8 Quicksort for contiguous lists.

We now turn to the method of quicksort, in which the list is first partitioned into lower and upper sublists for which all keys are, respectively, less than some pivot key or greater than the pivot key. Quicksort can be developed for linked lists with very little difficulty, and this project will be pursued in the exercises. The most important applications of quicksort, however, are to contiguous lists, where it can prove to be very fast, and where it has the advantage over contiguous mergesort of not requiring a choice between using substantial extra space for an auxiliary array or investing great programming effort in implementing a complicated and sophisticated merge algorithm.

4.8.1 The main procedure.

Our task in developing contiguous quicksort consists essentially in writing an algorithm for partitioning items in an array by use of a pivot key, swapping the items within the array so that all those with keys before the pivot come first, then the item with the pivot key, and then the items with larger keys.

Since the sublists are kept in the same array, in the proper relative positions, the final step of combining sorted sublists is completely vacuous, and thus is omitted.

Contiguous quicksort is started by a call

QuickSort(1, n)

to the following procedure, where the array L that holds the list, and the number n of items, are defined outside the procedure. In accordance with the conventions used for other methods, we can implement these requirements by writing:

```
procedure MainQuickSort( var L: list; n: index);
{Main procedure to invoke recursive quicksort.}
{Declare procedure QuickSort here.}
begin   QuickSort(1, n)   end;

procedure QuickSort( head, tail: index);
{Sorts the contiguous list stored in array L, where the list begins at
                              index head and ends at index tail}
var
    lowhead,   lowtail,                        {bounds of lower sublist}
    highhead,  hightail:  index;               {bounds of upper sublist}
```

```
        begin
          if head < tail then                    {list of length < 2 is sorted}
          begin
            Partition ( head, tail, lowhead, lowtail, highhead, hightail );
            Quicksort ( lowhead, lowtail );
            Quicksort ( highhead, hightail );
          end
        end;                                      {procedure Quicksort}
```

4.8.2 Partitioning the list.

Now we must construct the procedure **Partition**. First we must calculate the pivot. We could choose any key from the list as our pivot: we hope that our choice will partition the keys so that about half come on each side of the pivot. Often the first key in the list is chosen as pivot, but this will prove to be a poor choice if the keys are already in order, or are nearly so. Let us instead choose an item near the center of the list, and take its key as our pivot.

Second, we must compare each key in the list with the pivot, and if it is on the wrong side of the pivot, then move it to the other side. We shall do this task by using an index i to scan the list from its head until we find a key at least as large as the pivot, which gives an item that belongs to the right of the pivot instead of to its left. Then we use another index j to scan down from the high end until we find a key at least as small as the pivot, which therefore belongs on its left. Thus the items at indices i and j can now be swapped. We then continue to scan right on i and left on j until we find another pair out of place. Since we allow equality with the pivot to stop both of the scans, the pivot will serve as a sentinel to terminate both loops. When, finally, i and j meet or cross (so that i is to the right of j) then all keys in the list have been examined, and the list will be properly partitioned.

We thus obtain the following algorithm.

```
        procedure Partition( head, tail: index;
                    var lowhead, lowtail, highhead, hightail: index);
        var
          pivot : keytype;                   {will be taken from center of list}
          t : item;                          {used to swap two items in list}
          i,                                 {scan from head of list}
          j : index;                         {scan from tail of list}
        begin
          pivot := L[ (head + tail) div 2 ].key;
          i := head − 1;                     {i will be increased before use}
          j := tail + 1;
          repeat
            repeat i := i + 1 until L[i].key >= pivot;
            repeat j := j − 1 until L[j].key <= pivot;
            if i < j then                    {swap items at i and j}
```

```
          begin t := L[i]; L[i] := L[j]; L[j] := t end
      until i >= j;
      lowhead := head;  hightail := tail;
      if i = j then
         begin   lowtail := j − 1;  highhead := i + 1 end
         else begin lowtail := j;    highhead := i    end
   end;                                           {procedure Partition}
```

1. Verifying the algorithm.

The manipulation of indices in this procedure may appear somewhat mysterious; let us therefore pause to establish formally that it works correctly. We shall use the method of loop invariants introduced in Section 1.6.4. The invariants for the outer repeat loop are:

At the beginning of the loop, all items between head *and* i, *inclusive, have keys less than or equal to* pivot; *and all items between* j *and* tail, *inclusive, have keys greater than or equal to* pivot.

At the first iteration of the outer loop these invariants are vacuously true, since i < head, so there are no items in the specified range, and j > tail, so there are no items between. Now assume that the invariants are true at the beginning of some iteration. After the two inner repeat loops, items may have been found that violate the invariants, but when they are swapped the invariants become true again. Hence the invariants remain true as long as the swap is done, that is, as long as i < j. In the contrary case, i ≥ j, the outer loop terminates. Hence the proof is complete.

When the outer loop terminates, all items strictly before i have keys less than or equal to pivot, and item i has key greater than or equal to pivot. All items strictly after j have keys greater than or equal to pivot, and item j has key less than or equal to pivot. If the loop terminates with i = j, then the item in that position has pivot as its key, and should be put in neither of the two sublists. If, on the contrary, the loop terminates with j < i, then item j belongs in the lower sublist and item i belongs in the upper sublist, but the items (if any) between j and i all have keys equal to pivot, and hence go to neither sublist.

Check to ensure that you understand how this procedure works, and try it on several simple examples to convince yourself that it treats extreme cases correctly.

4.8.3 Analysis of Quicksort.

It is now time to examine the quicksort algorithm carefully, to determine when it works well and when not, and how much computation it performs.

1. Choice of pivot.

Our choice of a key at the center of the list to be the pivot is arbitrary. This choice may succeed in dividing the list nicely in half, or we may be unlucky and find that one sublist is much larger than the other. Some other methods for choosing the pivot are considered in the exercises. An extreme case for our method occurs for the following list, where every one of the pivots selected turns out to be the smallest key in its sublist:

$$2 \ 6 \ 4 \ 1 \ 3 \ 5 \ 7$$

Check it out, using the Partition procedure in the text. When quicksort is applied to this list, its label will appear to be quite a misnomer, since at the first recursion the non-empty sublist will have length 6, at the second 5, and so on.

If we were to choose the pivot as the first key in each sublist, then the extreme case would occur when the keys are in their natural order, or in their reverse order. These orders, of course, are more likely to happen than some random order, and therefore choosing the first or last key as pivot is likely to cause problems.

2. Count of comparisons and swaps.

Let us determine the number of comparisons and swaps that contiguous quicksort makes. Let $C(n)$ be the number of comparisons of keys made by quicksort when applied to a list of length n, and let $S(n)$ be the number of swaps of items. We have $C(1) = C(0) = 0$. The partition procedure compares every key in the list with the pivot exactly once, although we cannot tell in advance which of the loops (i or j) covers a particular key. Thus procedure Partition accounts for exactly n key comparisons. If one of the two sublists it creates has length r, then the other sublist will have length at most $n-r$. The number of comparisons done in the two recursive calls will then be $C(r)$ and $C(n-r)$. Thus we have

$$C(n) \ = \ n \ + \ C(r) \ + \ C(n-r).$$

To solve this equation we need to know r. In fact, our notation is slightly deceptive, in that the values of $C(\ )$ depend not only on the length of the list, but on the exact ordering of the items in it. Thus we shall obtain different answers in different cases, depending on the ordering.

3. Comparison count, worst case.

First consider the worst case for comparisons. We have already seen that this occurs when the pivot fails to split the list at all, so that one sublist has $n-1$ entries and the other is empty. In this case, since $C(0) = 0$, we obtain $C(n) = n+C(n-1)$. An expression of this form is called a *recurrence relation* because it expresses its answer in terms of earlier cases of the same result. We wish to solve the recurrence, which means to find an equation for $C(n)$ that does not involve $C(\ )$ on the other side. Various (sometimes difficult) methods are needed to solve recurrence relations, but in this case we can do it easily by starting at the bottom instead of the top:

$$C(1) = 0.$$
$$C(2) = 2 + C(1) \ = 2.$$
$$C(3) = 3 + C(2) \ = 3 + 2.$$
$$C(4) = 4 + C(3) \ = 4 + 3 + 2.$$
$$\cdot \ \cdot \ \cdot \ \cdot \ \cdot \ \cdot \ \cdot$$
$$C(n) = n + C(n-1) = n + (n-1) + \cdots + 3 + 2$$
$$= \frac{n(n+1)}{2} - 1$$
$$= \tfrac{1}{2}n^2 + \tfrac{1}{2}n - 1.$$

Recall that selection sort makes about

$$\tfrac{1}{2}n^2 - \tfrac{1}{2}n$$

key comparisons, and making too many redundant comparisons was the weak point of selection sort (as compared with insertion). Hence in its worst case, quicksort is worse than the worst case of selection sort.

4. Swap count, worst case.

Next let us determine how many times quicksort will swap items, again in its worst case. If the partition algorithm has performed k swaps, then it will have put k items into each of the sublists, so that each of the sublists is guaranteed to have length at least k (it may be more, since some items may already have been on the proper side of the pivot, and thus do not participate in a swap). It turns out, then, that the maximum number of swaps that can occur within the partition algorithm for a list of size n is almost $\tfrac{1}{2}n$. To this must be added the counts for the two recursive calls, each on a list of size about $\tfrac{1}{2}n$. With $S(n)$ the total number of swaps on a list of length n, we then have

$$S(n) \ = \ \tfrac{1}{2}n + 2S(\tfrac{1}{2}n)$$

in the worst case. This time let us solve the recurrence by substituting earlier cases of the formula into itself, terminating when we reach $S(1) = 0$. We obtain

$$
\begin{aligned}
S(n) \ &= \ \tfrac{1}{2}n + 2S(\tfrac{1}{2}n) \\
&= \ \tfrac{1}{2}n + 2(\tfrac{1}{4}n + 2S(\tfrac{1}{4}n)) \\
&= \ \tfrac{1}{2}n + \tfrac{1}{2}n \ + 4(\tfrac{1}{8}n + 2S(\tfrac{1}{8}n)) \\
&= \ \tfrac{1}{2}n + \tfrac{1}{2}n + \tfrac{1}{2}n + 8S(\tfrac{1}{8}n)
\end{aligned}
$$
$$\cdot \ \cdot \ \cdot \ \cdot \ \cdot \ \cdot \ \cdot$$

The number of times $\tfrac{1}{2}n$ is added is the same as the number of times n can be divided by 2 before reaching 1, which is $\lg n$. Thus we obtain

$$S(n) \ = \ \tfrac{1}{2}n \lg n$$

in the worst case.

5. Comparison with selection sort.

Recall that selection sort performs $n-1$ swaps to sort a list of size n. Thus quicksort (so-called) not only does more comparisons than selection sort, but more swaps as well (as long as $n \geq 4$). Indeed, in the worst-case analysis, quicksort is a disaster, and its name is nothing less than false advertising.

It must be for some other reason that quicksort was not long ago consigned to the scrap heap of programs that never worked. The reason is the average behavior of quicksort when applied to lists in random order, which turns out to be one of the best of any sorting methods (using key comparisons and applied to contiguous lists) yet known!

4.8.4 Average-case analysis of quicksort.

To do the average-case analysis we shall assume that all possible orderings of the list are equally likely, and for simplicity we take the keys to be just the integers from 1 to n. When we select the pivot in the procedure **Partition** it is equally likely to be any one of the keys.

Denote by p whatever key is selected as pivot. Then after the partition, key p is guaranteed to be in index p, since the keys $1, \cdots, p-1$ are all to its left, and $p+1, \cdots, n$ are to its right.

1. Counting swaps.

The number of swaps that will have been made in one call to **Partition** is the number of keys in positions 1 through $p-1$ (i.e., before p) that are greater than or equal to p, plus one more if the key at index p is not p itself before the partition. The probability that any particular key is greater than or equal to p is $(n-p+1)/n$. To obtain the number of swaps expected we shall add all these probabilities. The answer, however, is only approximate, since we do not know that whether one key is greater than or equal to p is or is not independent of the same property for another key. We obtain:

$$\frac{(p-1)(n-p+1)}{n} + \frac{n-1}{n} = \frac{(n+2)p-p^2-2}{n}.$$

We must now take the average of all these numbers, since p is random, by adding them from $p = 1$ to $p = n$ and dividing by n. The calculation requires the identities in Appendix A.1, and the result is $(n/6)+1-(7/n)$ swaps, which we approximate to $n/6$ swaps.

We thus obtain the recurrence relation for the average number of swaps in the complete sort:

$$S(n) = \frac{n}{6} + S(r) + S(n-r-1)$$

where r is the length of the lower sublist.

2. Solving the recurrence relation.

Next we wish to eliminate r from this expression. Since the pivot is equally likely to be any of the n keys, r is equally likely to take any value from 0 to $n-1$. Thus we obtain the average value for the expression by adding it for $r = 0$ to $r = n-1$ and dividing by n:

$$S(n) = \frac{n}{6} + \frac{2}{n}(S(0)+S(1)+ \cdots +S(n-1)).$$

If we were sorting a list of length $n-1$ we would obtain the same expression with n replaced by $n-1$:

$$S(n-1) = \frac{n-1}{6} + \frac{2}{n-1}(S(0)+S(1)+ \cdots +S(n-2)).$$

Multiplying the first expression by n, the second by $n-1$, and subtracting, we obtain

$$nS(n) - (n-1)S(n-1) = \frac{2n-1}{6} + 2S(n-1),$$

or

$$\frac{S(n)}{n+1} = \frac{S(n-1)}{n} + \frac{2n-1}{6n(n+1)}.$$

We can solve this recurrence relation as we solved a previous one by recalling that $S(1) = 0$ and starting at the bottom. The result is

$$\frac{S(n)}{n+1} = \sum_{k=2}^{n} \frac{2k-1}{6k(k+1)}.$$

To evaluate this summation we first note (without proof) that

$$\sum_{k=2}^{\infty} \frac{1}{k(k+1)} < 0.65.$$

Moreover, from the study of harmonic numbers in Appendix A we obtain

$$\sum_{k=2}^{n} \frac{1}{k+1} \approx \ln(n+1)+ \gamma - 1.5 \approx \ln n - 0.92.$$

Combining these approximations we finally obtain

$$\frac{S(n)}{n+1} \approx \tfrac{1}{3}\ln n$$

so that

$$S(n) \approx \tfrac{1}{3}(n+1)\ln n.$$

In order to compare this result with those for other sorting methods, we note that

$$\ln n \;=\; (\ln 2)(\lg n)$$

and $\ln 2 \approx 0.69$, so that

$$S(n) \;\approx\; 0.23(n+1)(\lg n).$$

3. Counting comparisons

Since each call to the partition procedure makes as many comparisons as there are items in the list, the recurrence relation for the number of comparisons made in the average case will differ from that for swaps in only one way: Instead of $n/6$ swaps in the partition procedure, there are n comparisons. Hence:

$$C(n) \;=\; n + C(r) + C(n-r-1).$$

Since the recurrence for the number $C(n)$ of key comparisons differs from that for $S(n)$ only by the factor of $1/6$ in the latter, the same steps used to solve for $S(n)$ will yield

$$C(n) \;\approx\; 2(n+1)(\ln n) \;\approx\; 1.39n \lg n.$$

4.8.5 Comparison with other sorting methods.

The calculation just completed shows that, on average, quicksort does about 39% more comparisons of keys than required by the lower bound, and therefore also about 39% more than mergesort. The reason is that mergesort is carefully designed to divide the list into halves of essentially equal size, whereas the sizes of the sublists for quicksort cannot be predicted in advance. Hence it is possible that quicksort's performance can be seriously degraded, but such an occurrence is unlikely in practice, so averaging the times of poor performance with those of good performance yields the result just obtained.

Concerning data movement, we did not derive detailed information for mergesort, since we were primarily interested in the linked version. If, however, we consider the version of contiguous mergesort that builds the merged sublists in a second array, and reverses the use of arrays at each pass, then it is clear that, at each level of the recursion tree, all n items will be copied from one array to the other. The number of levels in the recursion tree is $\lg n$, and it therefore follows that the number of assignments of items in contiguous mergesort is $n \lg n$. For quicksort, on the other hand, we obtained a count of about $0.23n \lg n$ swaps, on average. A good implementation should accomplish a swap of items in two assignments. On average, therefore, contiguous quicksort performs fewer than half as many assignments of data items as contiguous mergesort.

Exercises

1. Implement quicksort (for contiguous lists) on your computer, and test it with the same data used with previous sorting algorithms. Compare the number of comparisons of keys, assignments of items, and total time required for sorting.

2. How will the quicksort algorithm (as presented in the text) proceed if all the keys in the list are equal (a possibility we have generally excluded)?

3. [due to KNUTH] Describe an algorithm that will arrange a contiguous list whose keys are real numbers so that all the items with negative keys will come first, then those with non-negative keys. The final list need not be completely sorted. Make your algorithm do as few movements of items and as few comparisons as possible. Do not use an auxiliary array.

4. [due to HOARE] Suppose that, instead of sorting, we wish only to find the mth smallest key in a given list of size n. Show how quicksort can be adapted to this problem, doing much less work than a complete sort.

5. [due to WIRTH] Suppose that the **repeat** loop in procedure Partition is replaced by the following "obvious" and simpler version:

```
repeat
  repeat i := i + 1 until L[i].key >= pivot;
  repeat j := j - 1 until L[j].key <= pivot;
  t := L[i]; L[i] := L[j]; L[j] := t
until i >= j;
```

Find a list of keys for which this version fails.

6. Write a version of quicksort for linked lists, and run it on your computer for the same test data used for previous methods. The simplest choice for pivot is the first key in the list being sorted. You should find the partition procedure conceptually easier and more straightforward than the contiguous version, since items need not be swapped, but only links changed. You will, however, require a short additional procedure to re-combine the sorted sublists into a single linked list.

7. A different method for choosing the pivot in quicksort is to take the median of the first, last and central keys of the list. Describe the modifications needed to the procedure QuickSort (contiguous version) to implement this choice. How much extra computation will be done? For $n = 7$ find an ordering of the keys

$$1, \ 2, \ \cdots, \ 7$$

that will force the algorithm into its worst case. How much better is this worst case than that of the original algorithm?

8. [Requires elementary probability theory] A good way to choose the pivot is to use a random-number generator to choose the index for the next pivot at each call to Sort. Using the fact that these choices are independent, find the probability that quicksort will happen upon its worst case. First do the problem for $n = 7$, and then for general n.

9. Because it may involve more overhead, quicksort may be inferior to simpler methods for very short lists. Find experimentally a value where, on average, quicksort becomes more efficient than insertion sort. Write a hybrid sorting procedure that starts with quicksort, and, when the sublists are sufficiently short, switches to insertion sort. Determine if it is better to do the switch-over within the recursive procedure, or to terminate the recursive calls when the sublists are sufficiently short to change methods, and then at the very end of the process run through insertion sort once on the whole list.

4.9 Comparison of methods.

In this chapter we have studied and carefully analyzed quite a variety of sorting methods. Perhaps the best way to summarize this work is to emphasize in turn each of the three important efficiency criteria:

▶ Use of storage space;

▶ Use of computer time;

▶ Programming effort.

1. Use of space.

In regard to space, most of the algorithms we have discussed use little space other than that occupied by the original list, which is rearranged in its original place to be in order. The exceptions are quicksort and mergesort, where the recursion does require a small amount of extra storage to keep track of the sublists that have not yet been sorted. But in a well-written algorithm the amount of extra space used for recursion is proportional to $\lg n$, and will be trivial in comparison with that needed for other purposes.

Finally, we should recall that a major drawback of mergesort for contiguous lists is that the most straightforward version requires extra space equal to that occupied by the original list.

In many applications the list to be sorted is much too large to be kept in high-speed memory, and when this is the case, a great many other methods become necessary. A frequent approach is to divide the list into sublists that can be sorted internally within high-speed memory, and then merge the sorted sublists externally. Hence much work has been invested in developing merging algorithms, primarily when it is necessary to merge many sublists at once. We shall not discuss this topic further.

2. Computer time.

The second efficiency criterion is use of computer time, which we have already carefully analyzed, and shall discuss further in more general terms in the next section.

3. Programming effort.

The third efficiency criterion is often the most important of all: this criterion is the efficient and fruitful use of the programmer's time.

If a list is small, the sophisticated sorting techniques designed to minimize computer time requirements are usually worse or only marginally better in achieving their goal than the simpler methods. If a program is to be run only once or twice and there is enough machine time, then it would be foolish for a programmer to spend days or weeks investigating many sophisticated algorithms that might, in the end, only save a few seconds of computer time.

The saving of programming time is an excellent reason for choosing a simple algorithm, even if it is inefficient, but two words of caution should always be remembered. First, saving programming time is never an excuse for writing an incorrect program, one that may usually work but can sometimes misbehave. Murphy's law will then inevitably come true. Second, simple programs, designed to be run only a few times and then discarded, often instead find their way into applications not imagined when they were first written. Lack of care in the early stages will then prove exceedingly costly later.

For many applications, insertion sort can prove to be the best choice. It is easy to write and maintain, and runs efficiently for short lists. Even for long lists, if they are nearly in the correct order, insertion sort will be very efficient. If the list is completely in order, then insertion sort verifies this condition as quickly as can be done.

4. Statistical analysis.

The final choice of algorithm will depend not only on the length of list, the size of records, and their representation in storage, but very strongly on the way in which the records can be expected to be ordered at the start. The analysis of algorithms from the standpoint of probability and statistics is of great importance. For most algorithms we have been able to obtain results on the mean (average) performance, but the experience of quicksort shows that the amount by which this performance changes from one possible ordering to another is also an important factor to consider. The *standard deviation* is a statistical measure of this variability. Quicksort has an excellent mean performance and the standard deviation is small, which signifies that the performance is likely to differ little from the mean. For algorithms like selection sort and like merge sort, the best-case and worst-case performances differ little, which means that the standard deviation is almost 0. Other algorithms, like insertion sort, will have a much larger standard deviation in their performance. The particular distribution of the orderings of the incoming lists is therefore an important consideration in choosing a sorting method. To enable intelligent decisions, the professional computer scientist needs to be knowledgeable about important aspects of mathematical statistics as they apply to algorithm analysis.

5. Empirical testing.

Finally, in all these decisions we must be careful to temper the theoretical analysis of algorithms with empirical testing. Different computers and compilers will produce different results. Therefore, it is most instructive to see by experiment how the different algorithms behave in different circumstances.

Exercises

1. A sorting algorithm is called *stable* if, whenever two items have equal keys, then after sorting the two items will be in the same order in the list as before sorting. Stability is important if a list has already been sorted by one key and is now being sorted by another key, and it is desired to keep as much of the original ordering as the new one allows. Determine which of the sorting methods of this chapter are stable and which are not. For those which are not, produce a list (as short as possible) containing some items with equal keys whose orders are not preserved. In addition, see if you can discover simple modifications to the algorithm that will make it stable.

2. Which of the methods we studied would be a good choice in each of the following applications? Why? If the representation of the list in contiguous or linked storage makes a difference in your choice, state how.

   (a)   You wish to write a general-purpose sorting program that will be used by many people in a variety of applications.

   (b)   You wish to sort a thousand numbers once. After you finish, you will not keep the program.

   (c)   You need to sort five items in the middle of a long program. Your sort will be called hundreds of times by the long program.

   (d)   Each week you are given a computer file containing hundreds of names. Usually these are already all in alphabetical order, but sometimes a few names are not. You must sort the names.

3. Discuss the advantages and disadvantages of designing a general sorting procedure as a hybrid between quicksort and Shellsort. What criteria would you use to switch from one to the other? Which would be the better choice for what kinds of lists?

4. Summarize the results of the test runs of the sorting methods of this chapter for your computer. Also include any variations of the methods that you have written as exercises. Make charts comparing (a) the number of key comparisons, (b) the number of assignments of items, (c) the total running time, (d) the working storage requirements of the program, (e) the length of the program, and (f) the amount of programming time required to write and debug the program.

4.10 Asymptotics.

The time has come to distill important generalizations from our analyses of searching and sorting algorithms. As we have progressed we have been able to see more clearly which aspects of algorithm analysis are of great importance and which parts can safely be neglected. It is, for example, certainly true that sections of a program that are performed only once outside loops can contribute but negligibly little to the running time. We have studied two different versions of binary search and found that the most significant difference between them was a small amount of work in the innermost loop, that might make one slightly preferable to the other sometimes, but that both versions would run far faster than sequential search for lists of moderate or large size. We have also seen two sorting methods—insertion and selection—for which the difference in performance could be significant but for both of which the amount of work increased much faster relative to the size of the list than for more sophisticated sorting methods.

The design of efficient methods to work on small problems is an important subject to study, since a large program may need to do the same or similar small tasks many times during its execution. As we have discovered, however, for small problems the large overhead of a sophisticated method may make it inferior to a simpler method. To improve efficiency in the algorithm for a small problem the programmer must necessarily devote attention to details specific to the computer system and programming language.

4.10.1 Analysis of functions.

The design of efficient algorithms for large problems is an entirely different matter. We have seen that the overhead becomes relatively unimportant; it is the basic idea that will make all the difference between success and a problem too large to be attacked.

The word *asymptotics*, which titles this section, means the study of functions of a parameter n, as n becomes larger and larger without bound. In comparing sorting algorithms we have seen that a count of the number of comparisons of keys and of the number of movements of data items accurately reflects the total running time for large problems, since it has generally been true that all the other operations (such as incrementing and comparing indices) have gone in lock step either with comparison of keys or movement of items.

In fact, the frequency of these two basic actions is much more important than a total count of all operations including the housekeeping. The total including housekeeping is too dependent on the choice of programming language and on the programmer's particular style, so dependent that it tends to obscure the general methods. Variations in housekeeping details or programming technique can easily triple the running time of a program, but such a change probably will not make the difference between whether the computation is feasible or not. But a change in fundamental method, on the other hand, can make a vital difference. If the number of basic actions is proportional to the size n of the input, then doubling n will about double the running time, no matter how the housekeeping is done. If the number of basic actions is proportional to lg n, then doubling n will hardly change the running time. If the number of basic actions is proportional to n^2, then the time will quadruple, and the computation may still be feasible, but may be uncomfortably long. If the number of basic operations is proportional to 2^n, then doubling n will square this number. A computation that took 1 second might involve a million (10^6) basic operations, and doubling the input might require 10^{12} basic operations, moving the time from 1 second to 11½ days.

Our desire in formulating general principles that will apply to the analysis of other classes of algorithms, then, is to have a notation that will accurately reflect the way in which the computation time will increase with the size, but that will ignore superfluous details with little effect on the total. We wish to concentrate on one or two basic operations within the algorithm, without too much concern for all the housekeeping operations that will accompany them. If an algorithm does $f(n)$ basic operations when the size of its input is n, then its total running time will be at most $cf(n)$, where c is a constant that depends on the algorithm, on the way it is programmed, and on the computer used, but c does not depend on the size n of the input (at least when n is past a few initial cases; for example, if $n = 1$ then a sorting algorithm does 0 comparisons and swaps, but it will still take a little time).

4.10.2 The big Oh notation.

These ideas are embodied in the following notation:

DEFINITION. If $f(n)$ and $g(n)$ are functions defined for positive integers n, then to write

$$f(n) \quad \text{is} \quad O(g(n))$$

(read: "$f(n)$ is *big Oh* of $g(n)$") means that there exists a constant c such that $|f(n)| \le c\, |g(n)|$ for all sufficiently large positive integers n.

Under these conditions we also say that "$f(n)$ has *order* at most $g(n)$", or "$f(n)$ grows no more rapidly than $g(n)$".

When we apply this notation, $f(n)$ will normally be the operation count or time for some algorithm, and we wish to choose the form of $g(n)$ to be as simple as possible. We thus write $O(1)$ to mean computing time that is a constant (not dependent on n); $O(n)$ means that the time is directly proportional to n, and is called *linear time*. We call $O(n^2)$ *quadratic time*, $O(n^3)$ *cubic*, and $O(2^n)$ *exponential*. These five orders, together with *logarithmic time* $O(\log n)$ and $O(n \log n)$, are almost the only ones commonly used in analyzing algorithms.

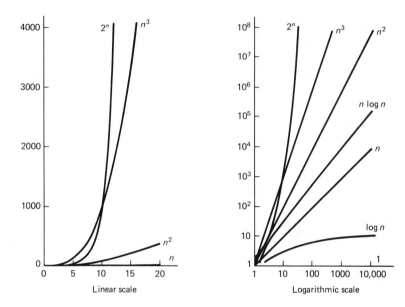

Figure 4.9. Growth rates of common functions

Figure 4.9 shows how these seven functions (with constant 1) grow with n. Notice especially how much slower $n \lg n$ grows than n^2; this is essentially the reason why the sophisticated sorting algorithms are far superior for large lists. Notice also how much more rapidly 2^n grows than any of the other functions. An algorithm for which the time grows exponentially with n will prove usable only for very small values of n.

Note that the constant c in the definition of the big Oh notation depends on which functions $f(n)$ and $g(n)$ are under discussion. Thus we can write that $17n^3 - 5$ is $O(n^3)$ (here $c = 17$ will do, as will any larger c), and also $35n^3$ is $O(n^3)$ (here $c \geq 35$). Some authors write $f(n) = O(g(n))$, but we shall refrain from doing so, since such an equation might encourage algebraic manipulations that are not allowable because of the different constants (such as deducing the absurd $35n^3 = 17n^3 - 5$ in the preceding example).

4.10.3 The Theta notation.

Note that it is equally correct to write that $35n^3$ is $O(n^7)$ as that $35n^3$ is $O(n^3)$. It is correct but uninformative to write that all our sorting algorithms have time that is $O(n^5)$. If $h(n)$ is any function that grows faster than $g(n)$, then clearly a function that is $O(g(n))$ must also be $O(h(n))$. We would like to have a more precise measure, which we can obtain as follows:

DEFINITION. If $f(n)$ and $g(n)$ are functions defined for positive integers, then to write

$$f(n) \quad \text{is} \quad \Theta(g(n))$$

(read: "$f(n)$ is **big theta** of $g(n)$") means that there exist positive constants c and d such that

$$|f(n)| \leq c |g(n)| \quad \text{and} \quad |g(n)| \leq d |f(n)|$$

for all sufficiently large positive integers n.

We also say that $f(n)$ has the **same order** (or **order of magnitude**) as $g(n)$.

We can now summarize easily how the amount of work done by the algorithms of the last two chapters grows with the size n of the list:

▶ Sequential search is $\Theta(n)$.

▶ Binary search is $\Theta(\log n)$.

▶ Hash table retrieval is $\Theta(1)$ on average, but $\Theta(n)$ in the worst case.

▶ Insertion sort and selection sort are $\Theta(n^2)$.

▶ Quicksort is $\Theta(n \log n)$ in the average case, but $\Theta(n^2)$ in the worst case.

▶ Merge sort is $\Theta(n \log n)$ in both average and worst cases.

▶ Empirical evidence suggests that Shellsort may be one of $\Theta(n^{1.25})$ or $\Theta(n(\log n)^2)$.

4.10.4 Ordering of common functions.

The theta relation divides functions into (equivalence) classes, such that $f(n)$ is in the same class with $g(n)$ if and only if $f(n) = \Theta(g(n))$. These classes can be given an order, with the class of constant functions lowest (they do not grow at all as n increases), according to how fast the functions grow with n. A few simple rules about the ordering of these classes will suffice for all our purposes:

1. The classes of powers of n are ordered according to the exponent: n^a is in a lower class than n^b if and only if $a < b$.

2. The class of $\log n$ is independent of the base taken for the logarithms, and is in a lower class than n^a for any $a > 0$.

3. Any exponential class a^n for $a > 1$ grows faster than any power of n, and a^n grows faster than b^n if $a > b$.

4. If $g(n)$ is in a lower class than $f(n)$, then $f(n)$ and $f(n)+g(n)$ are in the same class. In particular, in a sum of terms, the most rapidly growing term alone determines the class, and all other terms may be ignored.

5. If a function is multiplied by any non-zero constant, then its class does not change. More generally, if $f(n)$ is in the same [a lower] class than $g(n)$, and $h(n)$ is any non-zero function, then $f(n)h(n)$ is in the same [a lower] class as [than] $g(n)h(n)$. (Example: $n \log n$ is in a lower class than n^2, since $\log n$ is in a lower class than n.)

6. The preceding rules may be applied recursively (a chain rule) by substituting a function of n for n. (Example: $\log \log n$ grows more slowly than $(\log n)^{\frac{1}{2}}$.)

4.10.5 Asymptotic equality.

An even stronger relationship between functions, that no longer ignores the constant coefficient that appears in the definitions of order of magnitude, is the following:

> DEFINITION. If $f(n)$ and $g(n)$ are functions defined for positive integers, then $f(n)$ and $g(n)$ are **asymptotically equal** provided that the limit as n tends to infinity of $f(n)/g(n)$ is 1.

We can now write:

▶ The number of comparisons made in the second version of binary search is asymptotically equal to double that for the first version.

▶ Stirling's Approximation (Appendix A) says that $n!$ is asymptotically equal to

$$\sqrt{2\pi n}\left(\frac{n}{e}\right)^n.$$

▶ The number of comparisons of keys done by mergesort is asymptotically equal to the smallest number allowed by the lower bound.

Exercises

1. For each of the following pairs of functions find the smallest integer value of n for which the first becomes larger than the second.

   (a) n^2, $15n + 5$.

   (b) 2^n, $8n^4$.

   (c) $0.1n$, $10 \lg n$,   when $n > 1$.

   (d) $0.1n^2$, $100n \lg n$, when $n > 1$.

2. Divide the following functions into classes so that two functions $f(n)$ and $g(n)$ are in the same class if and only if $f(n)$ is $\Theta(g(n))$. Arrange the classes in the lowest order to the highest. (A function may be in a class by itself, or several functions may be in the same class.)

$$n \qquad (\lg n)^3 \qquad 2^n$$
$$n \lg n \qquad n^3 - 100n^2 \qquad \ln n!$$
$$\lg n \qquad n + \lg n \qquad n^3$$
$$\lg \lg n \qquad n^{0.1} \qquad n^2$$
$$1000000 \qquad 1000n \lg n \qquad \lg n^2$$

3. Write a program to test on your computer how long it takes to do $n \lg n$, n^2, 2^n, n^5, and $n!$ additions for $n = 5, 10, 15, 20$.

4. Show that a function $f(n)$ is $\Theta(g(n))$ if and only if $f(n)$ is $O(g(n))$ and $g(n)$ is $O(f(n))$.

5. Let x and y be real numbers with $0 < x < y$. Prove that n^x is $O(n^y)$ but n^y is not $O(n^x)$.

6. Show that logarithmic time $\Theta(\log_a n)$ does not depend on the base a chosen for the logarithms. That is, prove that

$$\log_a n \quad \text{is} \quad \Theta(\log_b n)$$

for any real numbers $a > 1$ and $b > 1$.

4.11 References for further study.

The primary reference for this chapter is the comprehensive series by D. E. KNUTH (bibliographic details in Chapter 2).

Internal sorting occupies Volume 3, pages 73–180. KNUTH does algorithm analysis in considerably more detail than we have. He writes all algorithms in a pseudo-assembly language, and does detailed operation counts there. He studies all the methods we have, several more, and many variations.

The original references to Shell sort and quicksort are, respectively:

> D. L. SHELL, "A high-speed sorting procedure," *Communications of the ACM*, 2 (1959), 30–32.

> C. A. R. HOARE, "Quicksort," *Computer Journal*, 5 (1962), 10–15.

The unified derivation of mergesort and quicksort, that can also be used to produce insertion sort and selection sort, is based on the work:

> JOHN DARLINGTON, "A synthesis of several sorting algorithms," *Acta Informatica*, 11 (1978), 1–30.

Mergesort can be refined to bring its performance very close to the optimal lower bound. One example of such an improved algorithm, whose performance is within 6% of the best possible, is:

> R. MICHAEL TANNER, "Minimean merging and sorting: an algorithm," *SIAM J. Computing*, 7 (1978), 18–38.

A contiguous merge algorithm that operates in linear time with a small, constant amount of additional space was devised by:

M. A. KRONROD, *Doklady Akad. Nauk SSSR,* 186 (1969), 1256–1258.

Several interesting variations of the procedure to partition the list for contiguous quicksort appear in:

D. E. KNUTH, "Structured programming with goto statements,"*Computing Surveys,* 6 (1974), 261–302.

More extensive analysis is given in:

ROBERT SEDGEWICK, "The analysis of quicksort programs,"*Acta Informatica* 7 (1976/77), 327–355.

Expository surveys of various sorting methods are:

W. A. MARTIN, "Sorting,"*Computing Surveys,* 3 (1971), 148–174.

H. LORIN, *Sorting and Sort Systems,* Addison-Wesley, Reading, Mass., 1975.

Programs in Pascal for most of the methods we discuss, along with analysis and empirical results, appear in:

N. WIRTH, *Algorithms + Data Structures = Programs,* Prentice-Hall, Englewood Cliffs, N.J., 1976, pages 56–124.

There is, of course, a vast literature in probability and statistics with potential applications to computers. A classic treatment of elementary probability and statistics is:

W. FELLER, *An Introduction to Probability Theory and its Applications,* second edition, volume 1, Wiley-Interscience, New York, 1957.

Chapter 5

Binary Trees

Linked lists have great advantages of flexibility over the contiguous representation of data structures, but they have one weak feature. They are sequential lists, that is, they are arranged so that it is necessary to move through them only one position at a time. In this chapter we overcome these disadvantages by studying trees as data structures, using the methods of pointers and linked lists for their representation. Data structures organized as trees will prove valuable for a range of applications, especially for problems of information retrieval.

Consider the problem of searching an ordinary linked list for some target key. There is no way to move through the list other than one node at a time, and hence searching through the list must always reduce to a sequential search. As you know, sequential search is usually very slow in comparison with binary search. The pivotal question for this chapter is,

Can we find a method for rearranging the nodes of a linked list so that we can search in time $O(\log n)$ instead of $O(n)$?

If we consider applying binary search to the list of names in Figure 5.1, then the order in which comparisons will be made is shown in the accompanying comparison tree.

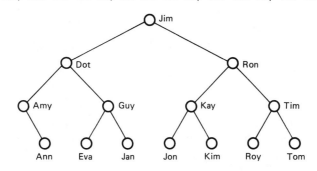

Figure 5.1. Comparison tree for binary search

From the diagram it may already be clear that the way in which we can keep the advantages of linked storage and obtain the speed of binary search is to store the nodes in the structure of the comparison tree itself, with links used to describe the relations of the tree.

5.1 Definitions.

In binary search, when we make a comparison with a key we then move either left or right depending on the outcome of the comparison. It is thus important to keep the relation of left and right in the structure we build. It is also possible that the part of the tree on one side or both below a given node is empty. In the example of Figure 5.1, the name Amy has an empty left subtree. For all the leaves, both subtrees are empty.

We can now give the formal definition of a new data structure.

> DEFINITION. A *binary tree* is either empty, or it consists of a node called the *root* together with two binary trees called the *left subtree* and the *right subtree* of the root.

Note that this definition is that of a data structure, and makes no reference to the way in which it is represented in memory. As we shall presently see, a linked representation is natural and easy to use, but other methods are possible as well. Note also that this definition makes no reference to keys or the way in which they are ordered. Binary trees are used for many purposes other than searching; hence we have kept the definition general. Information retrieval is, nonetheless, one of the most important uses for binary trees, and therefore we use a special term for binary trees in which there are keys with a special order:

> DEFINITION. A binary *search tree* is a binary tree that is either empty or in which each node contains a key that satisfies the conditions:
>
> 1. All keys (if any) in the left subtree of the root precede the key in the root.
>
> 2. The key in the root precedes all keys (if any) in its right subtree.
>
> 3. The left and right subtrees of the root are again search trees.

Before we consider search trees further, let us return to the general definition of binary trees, and see how the recursive nature of the definition works out in the construction of small binary trees.

The first case, which involves no recursion, is that of an empty binary tree. For ordinary trees we would never think of allowing an empty tree, but for binary trees it is convenient, not only in the definition, but in algorithms, since the empty binary tree will be naturally represented by a **nil** pointer.

The only way to construct a binary tree with one node is to make that node its root, and to make both the left and right subtrees empty. Thus a single node with no branches is a binary tree.

With two nodes in the tree, one of them will be the root and the other will be in a subtree. Thus one of the left or right subtrees must be empty, and the other will contain one node. Hence there are two different binary trees with two nodes.

At this point you should note that the concept of a binary tree differs from that of an ordinary tree, in that left and right are important. The two binary trees with two nodes can be drawn as

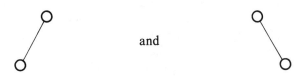

and

which are different from each other, but neither can be distinguished from

as ordinary trees.

Binary trees, moreover, are not the same class as the 2-trees studied in the analysis of algorithms. Each node in a 2-tree has either 0 or 2 children, never 1 as can happen with a binary tree. Left and right are not important for 2-trees, but they are crucial in working with binary trees.

For the case of a binary tree with three nodes, one of these will be the root, and the others will be partitioned between the left and right subtrees in one of the ways

$$2 + 0 \qquad 1 + 1 \qquad 0 + 2.$$

Since there are two binary trees with two nodes and only one empty tree, the first case gives two binary trees. The third case does similarly. In the second case, the left and right subtrees both have one node, and there is only one binary tree with one node, so there is one binary tree in the second case. Altogether, then, there are five binary trees with three nodes.

These binary trees are all drawn in Figure 5.2. Before proceeding, you should pause to construct all fourteen binary trees with four nodes. This exercise will further help you establish the ideas behind the definition of binary trees.

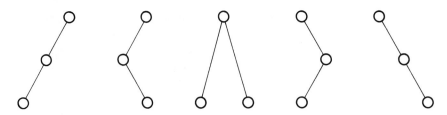

Figure 5.2.The binary trees with three nodes

A binary tree has a natural representation in linked storage. As usual, we shall wish all the nodes to be acquired as dynamic storage, so we shall need a separate pointer variable to enable us to find the tree. Our usual name for this pointer variable will be *root,* since it will point to the root of the tree. With this pointer variable it is easy to recognize an empty binary tree as precisely the condition

$$root = \textbf{nil.}$$

Each node of a binary tree (as the root of some subtree) has both a left and a right subtree, which we can reach with pointers by declaring:

```
type  pointer = ↑node;
      node  = record
            {information fields within the node go here}
            left,
            right: pointer
      end
```

These declarations turn the comparison tree for the fourteen names from Figure 5.1 into the linked binary tree of Figure 5.3. As you can see, the only difference between the comparison tree and the linked binary tree is that we have explicitly shown the nil links in the latter, whereas it is customary in drawing trees to omit all empty subtrees and the branches going to them. The tree of Figure 5.3, furthermore, is automatically a binary search tree, since the decision to move left or right at each node is based on the same comparisons of keys used in the definition of a search tree.

5.2 Treesearch.

At this point we should tie down some of the major ideas by writing a little procedure to search through a linked binary tree for the item with a particular key. First let us write some declarations that would appear in the main program, in a form somewhat similar to those introduced for searching in Chapter 3. Recall that we

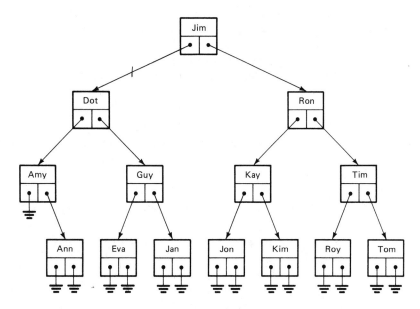

Figure 5.3. A linked binary tree

used item as the name for the records in the list, each of which contained a key field. We leave **keytype** undefined, assuming that it is some type, such as a number or a string, for which any two keys can be compared to determine which should be first. As in previous chapters, we assume that no two items have the same key.

```
type pointer    = ↑item;
     item       = record
        key: keytype;

     {other information fields go here}

        left,
        right: pointer
     end;

var  root,                          {pointer to root of binary tree}
     p:     pointer;     {temporary pointer that moves through tree}
     target: keytype;                       {key for which we search}
```

To search for the target we first compare it with the key at the root of the tree. If it is not the same, we go to the left subtree or right subtree as appropriate and repeat the search in that subtree. What event will be the termination condition? Clearly if we find the key, the procedure succeeds. If not, then we continue searching until we hit an empty subtree. By using a pointer p to move through the tree, we can use p also to send the results of the search back to the calling program. Thus:

> Procedure TreeSearch uses a pointer p as its calling parameter. Before calling the procedure the pointer should be set to the root of the tree:
>
> $$p := root.$$
>
> When the procedure returns, p will point to the node containing the target if the search was successful, and p will be **nil** if it was unsuccessful.

Perhaps the simplest way to write the procedure is to use recursion:

```
procedure TreeSearch (var p: pointer;  target: keytype);
begin
  if p <> nil then
    if target <> p↑.key then
      if target < p↑.key then
        begin p := p↑.left; TreeSearch(p, target) end
      else
        begin p := p↑.right; TreeSearch(p, target) end
end;
```

The recursion in this procedure can easily be removed, essentially by writing a loop in place of the nested **if** statements. The body of the procedure then consists essentially of the statement:

```
while (p <> nil) and (target <> p↑.key) do
  if target < p↑.key then p := p↑.left else p := p↑.right
```

With standard Pascal, however, this statement must be rewritten to avoid a run-time error when the search is unsuccessful, since it may attempt to look up p↑.key even though p = **nil**. Perhaps the simplest way is to introduce a Boolean variable, as implemented in the following procedure.

```
procedure TreeSearch( var p: pointer; target: keytype);
var finished: Boolean;
begin
  repeat
    if p = nil then finished := true
    else if p↑.key = target then finished := true
```

```
   else begin
      finished := false;
      if target < p↑.key then p := p↑.left else p := p↑.right
   end
 until finished
end;
```

5.3 Traversal of binary trees.

In many applications it is necessary, not only to find a node within a binary tree, but to be able to move through all the nodes of the binary tree, visiting each one in turn. If there are *n* nodes in the binary tree, then there are *n*! different orders in which they could be visited, but most of these have little regularity or pattern. When we write an algorithm to traverse a binary tree we shall almost always wish to proceed so that the same rules are applied at each node. At a given node, then, there are three tasks we shall wish to do in some order: We shall visit the node itself; we shall traverse its left subtree; and we shall traverse its right subtree. If we name these three tasks *V, L,* and *R*, respectively, then there are six ways to arrange them:

$$V\ L\ R \qquad L\ V\ R \qquad L\ R\ V \qquad V\ R\ L \qquad R\ V\ L \qquad R\ L\ V$$

By standard convention these six are reduced to three by considering only the ways in which the left subtree is traversed before the right. The other three are clearly similar. These three remaining ways are given names:

$$V\ L\ R \qquad\qquad L\ V\ R \qquad\qquad L\ R\ V$$
Preorder   *Inorder*   *Postorder*

These three names are chosen according to the step at which the given node is visited. With *preorder traversal* the node is visited before the subtrees, with *inorder traversal* it is visited between them, and with *postorder traversal* the root is visited after both of the subtrees.

Inorder traversal is also sometimes called *symmetric order,* and postorder traversal may be called *endorder.*

The translation from the definitions to formal procedures to traverse a linked binary tree in these ways is especially easy. As usual, we take root to be a pointer to the root of the tree, and we assume the existence of another procedure Visit( ) that does the desired task for each node.

```
procedure Preorder(root: pointer);    procedure Inorder(root: pointer);
begin                                 begin
   if root <> nil then                   if root <> nil then
   begin                                 begin
     Visit(root);                          Inorder(root↑.left);
     Preorder(root↑.left);                 Visit(root);
     Preorder(root↑.right)                 Inorder(root↑.right)
   end                                   end
end;                                  end;
```

```
procedure Postorder(root: pointer);
begin
 if root <> nil then
 begin
  Postorder(root↑.left);
  Postorder(root↑.right);
  Visit(root)
 end
end;
```

The choice of the names *preorder, inorder* and *postorder* is not accidental, but relates closely to a motivating example of considerable interest, that of expression trees. An *expression tree* is built up from the simple operands and operators of an (arithmetical or logical) expression by placing the simple operands as the leaves of a binary tree, and the operators as the interior nodes. For each binary operator the left subtree contains all the simple operands and operators in the left operand of the given operator, and the right subtree contains everything in the right operand. For a unary operator one subtree will be empty.

We traditionally write some unary operators to the left of their operands, such as '−' (unary negation) or the standard functions like log( ) and cos( ). Others are written on the right, such as the factorial function ( )!, or the function that takes the square of a number, ( )². Sometimes either side is permissible, such as the derivative operator, which can be written as d/dx on the left, or as ( )′ on the right, or the incrementing operator ++ in the language "C" (where the actions on the left and right are different). If the operator is written on the left, then in the expression tree we take its left subtree as empty. If it appears on the right, then its right subtree will be empty.

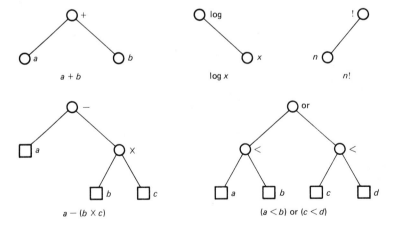

Figure 5.4.Expression trees

The expression trees of a few simple expressions are shown in Figure 5.4, together with the slightly more complicated example of the quadratic formula in Figure 5.5, where we denote exponentiation by ↑.

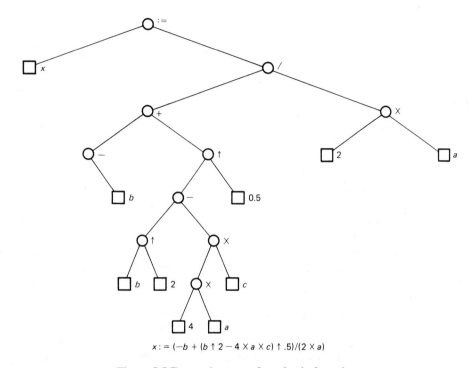

$$x := (-b + (b \uparrow 2 - 4 \times a \times c) \uparrow .5)/(2 \times a)$$

Figure 5.5. Expression tree of quadratic formula

If you apply the traversal algorithms to these trees, you will immediately see how their names are related to the well-known *Polish forms* of expressions: Traversal of an expression tree in preorder yields the *prefix form* of the expression, in which every operator is written before its operand(s); inorder traversal gives the *infix form* (the customary way to write the expression); and postorder traversal gives the *postfix form,* in which all operators appear after their operand(s). A moment's consideration will convince you of the reason: The left and right subtrees of each node are its operands; and the relative position of an operator to its operands in the three Polish forms is the same as the relative order of visiting the components in each of the three traversal methods.

5.4 Treesort.

As a further example, let us take the binary tree of fourteen names from Figure 5.1 or Figure 5.3, and write them in the order given by each traversal method:

preorder:

Jim Dot Amy Ann Guy Eva Jan Ron Kay Jon Kim Tim Roy Tom

inorder:

Amy Ann Dot Eva Guy Jan Jim Jon Kay Kim Ron Roy Tim Tom

postorder:

Ann Amy Eva Jan Guy Dot Jon Kim Kay Roy Tom Tim Ron Jim

It is no accident that inorder traversal produces the names in alphabetical order. A search tree is set up so that all the nodes in the left subtree of a given node come before it in the ordering, and all the nodes in its right subtree come after it. Hence inorder traversal produces all the nodes before a given node first, then the given node, and then all the later nodes.

We now have the idea for an interesting sorting method, called **treesort.** We simply take the items to be sorted, build them into a binary search tree, and use inorder traversal to put them out in order. This method has the great advantage, as we shall see, that it is easy to make changes in the list of items considered. Adding and deleting items in a sorted contiguous list is oppressively slow and painful; searching for an item in a sequential linked list is equally inefficient.

Treesort has the considerable advantages that it is almost as easy to make changes as in a linked list; the sort is as fast as quicksort; and searches can be made with the efficiency of binary search.

5.4.1 Insertion into a search tree.

The first part of treesort is to build the items into a binary search tree. We can do so by starting with an empty binary tree and inserting one item at a time into the tree, always making sure that the properties of a search tree are preserved. The first case, inserting an item into an empty tree, is easy. We need only create a new node, with root pointing to it, and put the item in the node. If the tree is not empty, then we must compare the key with the one in the root. If it is less, then the new item must be inserted into the left subtree; if it is more, then it must be inserted into the right subtree. If the keys are equal, then our assumption that no two items have the same key is violated.

From this outline we can now write our procedure, using the same declarations employed for the procedure TreeSearch.

```
procedure Insert(var root: pointer;  newitem: pointer);
begin
  if root = nil then
  begin
    root := newitem;
    root↑.left := nil;
    root↑.right := nil
  end
```

```
    else with root↑ do
    if newitem↑.key < key then
      Insert(left, newitem)
    else if newitem↑.key > key then
      Insert(right, newitem)
    else Error                                        { duplicate key}
end;
```

The use of recursion in this procedure is not essential. In Chapter 7 we shall see that, when the only recursive call that a procedure makes is the last statement that it executes, then the recursion can always be replaced by an iterative loop. (This is called *tail-end recursion,* or often simply *tail* recursion.) To replace recursion with iteration we must introduce a local pointer variable p that will move to the left or right subtree. We use the condition p = **nil** to terminate the loop.

```
procedure Insert(var root: pointer; newitem: pointer);
var p:            pointer;                      {used to move through tree}
begin
  p := root;
  while p <> nil do with p↑ do
    if newitem↑.key < key then
      if left <> nil then
        p := left
      else
        begin left : = newitem; p : = nil end
    else if newitem↑.key > key then
      if right <> nil then
        p := right
      else
        begin right : = newitem; p : = nil end
    else Error;                                 {duplicate key}
  newitem↑.left := nil;
  newitem↑.right := nil;
  if root = nil then root := newitem            {care for empty tree}
end;
```

5.4.2 The treesort algorithm.

Now that we can insert new items into the search tree, we can build it up, and thus devise the new sorting method. In the resulting procedure we assume the existence of a procedure GetItem( ) that will provide a pointer to the next item to be sorted. GetItem(p) returns the value p = **nil** when there are no more items to be inserted. The procedure will return as its result the pointer root to the search tree it builds.

```
procedure TreeSort(var root: pointer);
var  p: pointer;
begin
  root := nil;
  GetItem(p);
  while p <> nil do
  begin
    Insert(root, p)
    GetItem(p);
  end;
  Inorder(root)                              {Traverse the final tree.}
end;
```

Note carefully that, if the same set of items is presented to **Treesort** in a different order, then the search tree that is built may have a different shape. When it is traversed in inorder, the keys will still be properly sorted, but the particular location of items within the tree depends on the way in which they were initially presented to **Treesort**. If the fourteen names of Figure 5.1, for example, are presented in the order

Tim Dot Eva Roy Tom Kim Guy Amy Jon Ann Jim Kay Ron Jan

then the resulting search tree will be the one in Figure 5.6. If the names are presented sorted in their alphabetical order, then the search tree will degenerate into a chain.

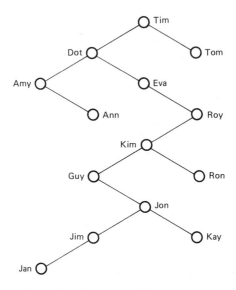

Figure 5.6. Search tree of fourteen names

Let us briefly study what comparisons of keys are done by treesort. The first key goes directly into the root of the search tree, with no key comparisons. As each succeeding key comes in it is first compared to the key in the root and then goes either into the left subtree or the right subtree. Notice the similarity with quicksort, where at the first stage every key is compared with the first pivot key, and then put into the left or the right sublist. In treesort, however, as each key comes in it goes into its final position in the linked structure. The second key becomes the root of either the left or right subtree (depending on its comparison with the root key). From then on all keys going into the same subtree are compared to this second key. Similarly, in quicksort all keys in one sublist are compared to the second pivot, the pivot for that sublist. Continuing in this way, we can make the following observation.

> THEOREM 5.1. *Treesort makes exactly the same comparisons of keys as does quicksort when the pivot for each sublist is chosen to be the first key in the sublist.*

As we know, quicksort is usually an excellent method. On average, only mergesort among the methods we have studied makes fewer key comparisons. Hence, on average, we can expect treesort also to be an excellent sorting method in terms of key comparisons. Quicksort, however, needs to have access to all the items to be sorted throughout the process. With treesort, the items need not all be available at the start of the process, but are built into the tree one by one as they become available. Hence treesort is preferable for applications where the items are received one at a time. The major advantage of treesort is that its search tree remains available for later insertions and deletions, and that the tree can subsequently be searched in logarithmic time, whereas all our previous sorting methods either required contiguous lists, for which insertions and deletions are difficult, or produced simply linked lists for which only sequential search is available.

The major drawback of treesort is already implicit in Theorem 5.1. Quicksort has a very poor performance in its worst case, and, although a careful choice of pivots makes this case extremely unlikely, the choice of pivot to be the first key in each sublist makes the worst case appear whenever the items are already sorted. If the items are presented to treesort already sorted, then treesort too will be a disaster—the search tree it builds will reduce to a chain. Treesort should never be used if the items are already sorted, or are nearly so. There are few other reservations about treesort that are not equally applicable to all linked structures. For small problems with small items contiguous storage is usually the better choice, but for large problems and bulky records linked storage comes into its own.

5.4.3 Deletion from a search tree.

At the beginning of the discussion of treesort, the ability to make changes in the search tree was mentioned as an advantage. We have already obtained an algorithm that adds a new item to the search tree, and it can be used to update the tree as easily as to build it from scratch. But we have not yet considered how to delete an item from the tree. If the item to be deleted is a leaf, then the process is easy: We need only replace the link to the deleted node by **nil**. The process remains easy if the deleted item has only one subtree: We adjust the link from the parent of the deleted node to point to its subtree.

When the item to be deleted has both left and right subtrees non-empty, however, the problem is more complicated. To which of the subtrees should the parent of the deleted item now point? What is to be done with the other subtree? This problem is illustrated in Figure 5.7, together with one possible solution. (An exercise outlines another, sometimes better solution.) What we do is to attach the right subtree in place of the deleted node, and then hang the left subtree onto an appropriate node of the right subtree.

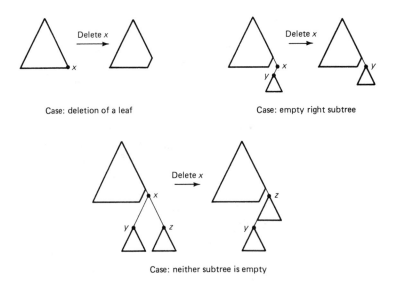

Figure 5.7. Deletion of a node from a search tree

To which node of the right subtree should the former left subtree be attached? Since every key in the left subtree precedes every key of the right subtree, it must be as far to the left as possible, and this point can be found by taking left branches until an empty left subtree is found.

We can now write a procedure to implement this plan. As a calling parameter it will use a pointer p to the node to be deleted. Since the object is to update the search tree, we must assume that the corresponding actual parameter is one of the links of the tree, and not just a copy, or else the tree structure itself will not be changed as it should. In other words, if the node at the left of x↑ is to be deleted, the call should be

Delete(x↑.left)

and if the root is to be deleted, the call should be

Delete(root).

On the other hand, the following call will not work properly:

y := x↑.left; Delete(y).

```
procedure Delete(var p: pointer);
var
  q:  pointer;                {used to look for place to hang left subtree}
begin
  if p := nil then
    Error                       {attempt to delete non-existent node}
  else if p↑.right := nil then
  begin                         {re-attach left subtree in place of p↑}
    q := p;
    p := p↑.left;
    Dispose(q)
  end
  else if p↑.left := nil then
  begin                         {re-attach right subtree in place of p↑}
    q := p;
    p := p↑.right;
    Dispose(q)
  end
  else                                    {neither subtree is empty}
  begin
    q := p↑.right;              {move right, then as far left as possible}
    while q↑.left <> nil do q := q↑.left;
    q↑.left := p↑.left;
    q := p;
    p := p↑.right;
    Dispose(q)
  end
end;
```

You should trace through this procedure to check that all pointers are updated properly, especially in the case when neither subtree is empty. Note the steps needed to make the loop stop at a vertex with empty left subtree, but not to end at the empty subtree itself.

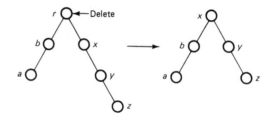

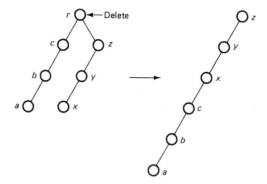

Figure 5.8. Deletions from two search trees

This procedure is far from optimal, in that it can greatly increase the height of the tree. Two examples are shown in Figure 5.8. When the roots are deleted from these two trees, the one on the top reduces its height, but the one below increases its height. Thus the time required for a later search can substantially increase, even though the total size of the tree has decreased. There is, moreover, often some tendency for insertions and deletions to be made in sorted order, that will further elongate the search tree. Hence, to optimize the use of search trees, we need methods to make the left and right subtrees more nearly balanced. We shall consider this important topic at the end of the chapter, and continue its study in Chapter 9 .

Exercises

1. Construct the fourteen binary trees with four nodes.

2. Write a function that will count all the nodes of a linked binary tree.

3. Determine the order in which the vertices of the following binary trees will be visited under (1) preorder, (2) inorder, and (3) postorder traversal.

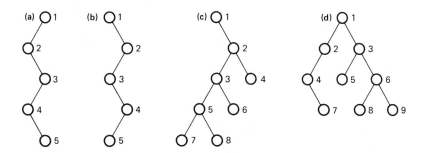

4. Write a function that will count the leaves (i.e., the nodes with both subtrees empty) of a linked binary tree.

5. Write a function that will find the height of a linked binary tree.

6. Write a procedure to perform a *double-order traversal* of a binary tree, meaning that at each node of the tree the procedure first visits the node, then traverses its left subtree (in double order), then visits the node again, then traverses its right subtree (in double order).

7. For each of the binary trees in Exercise 3, determine the order in which the nodes will be visited in the mixed order given by invoking **procedure** A :

```
procedure A(p: pointer);           procedure B(p: pointer);
begin                              begin
  if p <> nil then begin             if p <> nil then begin
    Visit(p);                          A(p↑.left);
    B(p↑.left);                        Visit(p);
    B(p↑.right);                       A(p↑.right)
  end                                end
end;                               end;
```

8. Write a procedure that will make a copy of a linked binary tree. The procedure should obtain the necessary new nodes from the system, and copy the information fields from the nodes of the old tree to the new one.

9. Write a procedure that will print the keys from a binary tree in the *bracketed form*

$$(\text{ key} : \text{LT} , \text{RT})$$

where **key** is the key in the root, **LT** denotes the left subtree of the root printed in bracketed form, and **RT** denotes the right subtree in bracketed form. *Optional part:* Modify the algorithm so that it prints nothing instead of (:,) for an empty tree, and x instead of (x:,) for a tree consisting of only one node with key x.

10. Write a procedure that will interchange all left and right subtrees in a linked binary tree. (See the example in Figure 5.9.)

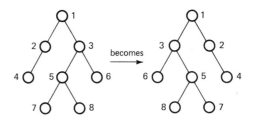

Figure 5.9. Reversal of a binary tree

11. Draw the search trees that procedure **TreeSort** will construct for the list of fourteen names presented in each of the following orders.

   (a) Jan Guy Jon Ann Jim Eva Amy Tim Ron Kim Tom Roy Kay Dot
   (b) Amy Tom Tim Ann Roy Dot Eva Ron Kim Kay Guy Jon Jan Jim
   (c) Jan Jon Tim Ron Guy Ann Jim Tom Amy Eva Roy Kim Dot Kay
   (d) Jon Roy Tom Eva Tim Kim Ann Ron Jan Amy Dot Guy Jim Kay

12. Write a procedure that will delete a node from a linked binary tree, using the following method in the case when the node to be deleted has both subtrees non-empty. First find the immediate predecessor of the node under inorder traversal (the immediate successor would work just as well), by moving to its left child and then as far right as possible. This immediate predecessor is guaranteed to have at most one child (why?), so it can be deleted from its current position without difficulty. It can then be placed into the tree in the position formerly occupied by the node that was supposed to be deleted, and the properties of a search tree will still be satisfied (why?).

13. Write a procedure for searching, using a binary search tree with sentinel as follows. Introduce a new sentinel node, and keep a pointer to it. See Figure 5.10. Replace all the **nil** links within the search tree with links to the sentinel. Then, for each search, first store the target into the sentinel. Run both this procedure and the original procedure **TreeSearch** to compare the time needed both for successful and unsuccessful search.

14. Write a procedure that will traverse a binary tree level by level. That is, the root is visited first, then the immediate children of the root, then the grandchildren of the root, etc. [*Hint:* Use a queue.]

15. Write a function that will return the width of a linked binary tree, that is, the maximum number of nodes on the same level.

16. Write a procedure that converts a binary tree into a doubly linked list, in which the nodes have the order of inorder traversal of the tree. At the conclusion of the procedure, the pointer **root** should point to the leftmost node of the doubly linked list, and the links **right** and **left** should be used to move through the list, and be **nil** at the two ends of the list.

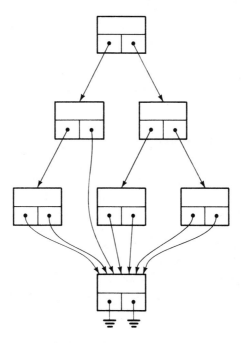

Figure 5.10. Binary search tree with sentinel

For the following exercises, it is assumed that the keys stored in the nodes of the binary trees are all distinct, but it is not assumed that the trees are search trees. That is, there is no necessary connection between the ordering of the keys and their location in the trees. If a tree is traversed in a particular order, and each key printed when its node is visited, the resulting sequence is called the sequence corresponding to that traversal.

17. Suppose that you are given two sequences that supposedly correspond to the preorder and inorder traversals of a binary tree. Prove that it is possible to reconstruct the binary tree uniquely.

18. Either prove or disprove (by finding a counterexample) the analogous result for inorder and postorder traversal.

19. Either prove or disprove the analogous result for preorder and postorder traversal.

20. Find a pair of (short) sequences of the same keys that could not possibly correspond to the preorder and inorder traversals of any binary tree.

5.5 Orchards, trees, and binary trees.

Binary trees, as we have seen, are a powerful and elegant form of data structures. Even so, the restriction to no more than two children at each node is severe, and there are many possible applications for trees as data structures where the number of children of a node can be arbitrary. This section elucidates a pleasant and helpful surprise: Binary trees provide a convenient way to represent what first appears to be a far broader class of trees.

5.5.1 On the classification of species.

Since we have already sighted several kinds of trees in the applications we have studied, we should, before exploring further, put our gear in order by settling the definitions. In mathematics the term *tree* has a quite broad meaning: it is any set of points (called vertices) and any set of pairs of distinct vertices (called edges or branches) such that (1) there is a sequence of edges (a path) from any vertex to any other, and (2) there are no circuits, that is, no paths starting from a vertex and returning to the same vertex.

In computer applications we rarely need to study trees in such generality, and when we do, for emphasis we call them *free trees.* Our trees are almost always tied down by having one particular vertex singled out as the *root,* and for emphasis we call such a tree a *rooted tree.*

A rooted tree can be drawn in our usual way by picking it up by its root and shaking it so that all the branches and other vertices hang downward, with the leaves at the bottom. Even so, rooted trees still do not have all the structure that we usually use. In a rooted tree there is still no way to tell left from right, or, when one vertex has several children, to tell which is first, second, and so on. If for no other reason, the restraint of sequential execution of instructions (not to mention sequential organization of storage) usually imposes an order on the children of each vertex. Hence we define an *ordered tree* to be a rooted tree in which the children of each vertex are assigned an order.

Note that ordered trees for which no vertex has more than two children are still not the same class as binary trees. If a vertex in a binary tree has only one child, then it could be either on the left side or on the right side, and the two resulting binary trees are different, but both would be the same as ordered trees.

As a final note related to the definitions, let us note that the 2-trees that we studied as part of algorithm analysis are rooted trees (but not necessarily ordered trees) with the property that every vertex has either 0 or 2 children. Thus 2-trees do not coincide with any of the other classes we have introduced.

Figure 5.11 shows what happens for the various kinds of trees with a small number of vertices. Note that each class of trees after the first can be obtained by taking the trees from the previous class and distinguishing those that differ under the new criterion. Compare the list of five ordered trees with four vertices with the list of fourteen binary trees with four vertices constructed as an exercise in Section 5.4. You will find that, again, the binary trees can be obtained from the appropriate ordered trees by distinguishing a left branch from a right branch.

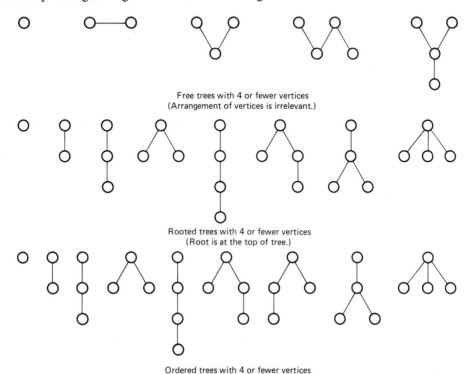

Free trees with 4 or fewer vertices
(Arrangement of vertices is irrelevant.)

Rooted trees with 4 or fewer vertices
(Root is at the top of tree.)

Ordered trees with 4 or fewer vertices

Figure 5.11. Various kinds of trees

5.5.2 Ordered trees.

1. Computer representation.

If we wish to use an ordered tree as a data structure, the obvious way to represent it in computer memory would be to extend the standard way to represent a binary tree, keeping as many fields in each node as there may be subtrees, in place of the two links needed for binary trees. Thus in a tree where some nodes have as many as ten subtrees, we would keep ten link fields in each node. But this will result in a great many of the link fields being **nil**. In fact, we can easily determine exactly how many. If the tree has n nodes and each node has k link fields, then there are $n \times k$ links altogether. There is exactly one link that points to each of the $n-1$ nodes other than the root, so the proportion of **nil** links must be

$$\frac{(n \times k)-(n-1)}{n \times k} \;>\; 1 - \frac{1}{k}.$$

Hence if a vertex might have ten subtrees, then more than ninety percent of the links will be **nil.** Clearly, this method of representing ordered trees is very wasteful of space. The reason is that, for each node, we are maintaining a contiguous list of links to all its children, and these contiguous lists reserve much unused space. We now investigate a way that replaces these contiguous lists with linked lists and leads to an elegant connection with binary trees.

2. Linked representation.

In order to keep the children of each node in a linked list, we shall need two kinds of links. First comes the header for each such list; this will be a link from each node to its leftmost child, which we may call firstchild. Second, each node except the root will appear in one of these lists, and hence requires a link to the next node on the list, that is, to the next child of the parent. We may call this second link nextchild. This representation is illustrated in Figure 5.12.

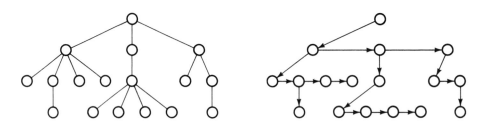

Figure 5.12. Linked representation of an ordered tree

3. The natural correspondence.

For each node of the ordered tree we have defined two links (that will be **nil** if not otherwise defined), firstchild and nextchild. By using these two links we now have the structure of a binary tree; that is, the linked representation of an ordered tree is a linked binary tree. If we wish, we can even form a better picture of a binary tree by taking the linked representation of the ordered tree and rotating it a few degrees clockwise, so that downward (firstchild) links point leftward, and the horizontal (nextchild) links point downward and to the right.

4. Inverse correspondence.

Suppose that we reverse the steps of the preceding process, by beginning with a binary tree, and trying to recover an ordered tree. The first observation that we must make is that not every binary tree is obtained from a rooted tree by the above process: Since the nextchild link of the root is always **nil,** the root of the corresponding binary tree will always have an empty right subtree. To study the inverse correspondence more carefully, we must consider another class of data structures.

5.5.3 Forests and orchards.

In our work so far with binary trees we have profited from using recursion, and for other classes of trees we shall continue to do so. Employing recursion means reducing a problem to a smaller one. Hence we should see what happens if we take a rooted tree or an ordered tree and strip off the root. What is then left is (if not empty) a set of rooted trees, or an ordered set of ordered trees, respectively.

The standard term for an arbitrary set of trees is *forest,* but when we use this term we generally assume that the trees are rooted. The phrase *ordered forest* is sometimes used for an ordered set of ordered trees, but we shall adopt the equally descriptive (and more colorful) term **orchard** for this class. (Although this term is not yet in common use, perhaps it will soon become standard.)

Note that not only can we obtain a forest or an orchard by removing the root from a rooted tree or an ordered tree, respectively, but we can build a rooted or an ordered tree by starting with a forest or an orchard, attaching a new vertex at the top, and adding branches from the new vertex (which will be the root) to the roots of all trees in the forest or the orchard.

We shall use this observation to give a new, recursive definition of ordered trees and orchards, one that yields a formal proof of the connection with binary trees. First let us consider how to start. Recall that it is possible that a binary tree be empty; that is, it may have no vertices. It is also possible that a forest or an orchard is empty; that is, that it contain no trees. It is, however, not possible that a rooted or an ordered tree be empty, since it is guaranteed to contain a root, at least. If we wish to start building trees and forests, we can note that the tree with only one vertex is obtained by attaching a new root to an empty forest. Once we have this tree, we can make a forest consisting of as many one-vertex trees as we wish, and attach a new root to build all rooted trees of height 1. In this way we can continue to construct all the rooted trees in turn in accordance with the following mutually recursive definitions.

> DEFINITION. A *rooted tree* consists of a single vertex v, called the *root* of the tree, together with a forest F, whose trees are called the **subtrees** of the root.
>
> A *forest* F is a (possibly empty) set of rooted trees.

A similar construction works for ordered trees and orchards.

> DEFINITION. An *ordered tree* T consists of a single vertex v, called the *root* of the tree, together with an orchard O, whose trees are called the **subtrees** of the root v. We may denote the ordered tree with the ordered pair
>
> $$T = \{v, O\}.$$

An *orchard* O is either the empty set $\varnothing$, or consists of an ordered tree T, called the *first tree* of the orchard, together with another orchard O' (which contains the remaining trees of the orchard). We may denote the orchard with the ordered pair

$$O = (T, O').$$

Notice how the ordering of trees is implicit in the definition of orchard. A non-empty orchard contains a first tree, and the remaining trees form another orchard, which again has a first tree, which is the second tree of the original orchard. Continuing to examine the remaining orchard yields the third tree, and so on, until the remaining orchard is the empty one.

5.5.4 The formal correspondence.

We can now obtain the principal result of this section.

THEOREM 5.2. *Let S be any finite set of vertices. There is a one-to-one correspondence f from the set of orchards whose set of vertices is S to the set of binary trees whose set of vertices is S.*

PROOF. Let us use the notation introduced in the definitions to prove the theorem. First, we need a similar notation for binary trees: A binary tree B is either the empty set $\varnothing$, or consists of a root vertex v with two binary trees B_1 and B_2. We may thus denote a binary tree with the ordered triple

$$B = [v, B_1, B_2].$$

The first case to consider is the empty orchard $\varnothing$, which will correspond to the empty binary tree:

$$f(\varnothing) = \varnothing.$$

If the orchard O is not empty, then it is denoted by the ordered pair

$$O = (T, O_2)$$

where T is an ordered tree and O_2 another orchard. The ordered tree T is denoted as the pair

$$T = \{v, O_1\}$$

where v is a vertex and O_1 is another orchard. We substitute this expression for T in the first expression, obtaining

$$O = (\{v, O_1\}, O_2).$$

We define the correspondence f from the orchard to a binary tree by

$$f(\{v, O_1\}, O_2) = [v, f(O_1), f(O_2)].$$

It is now obvious that the function *f* is a one-to-one correspondence between orchards and binary trees with the same vertices. For any way to fill in the symbols v, O_1, O_2 on the left side, there is exactly one way to fill in the same symbols on the right, and vice versa.

5.5.5 Rotations.

We can also use this notational form of the correspondence to help us form the picture of the transformation from orchard to binary tree. In the binary tree $[v, f(O_1), f(O_2)]$ the left link from v goes to the root of the binary tree $f(O_1)$, which in fact was the first child of v in the ordered tree $\{v, O_1\}$. The right link from v goes to the vertex that was formerly the root of the next ordered tree to the right. That is, 'left link' in the binary tree corresponds to 'first child' in an ordered tree, and 'right link' corresponds to 'next sibling'. In geometrical terms the transformation reduces to the rules:

1. Draw the orchard so that the first child of each vertex is immediately below the vertex, rather than centering the children below the vertex.

2. Draw a vertical link from each vertex to its first child, and draw a horizontal link from each vertex to its next sibling.

3. Remove the remaining original links.

4. Rotate the diagram 45 degrees clockwise, so that the vertical links appear as left links, and the horizontal links as right links.

This process is illustrated in Figure 5.13.

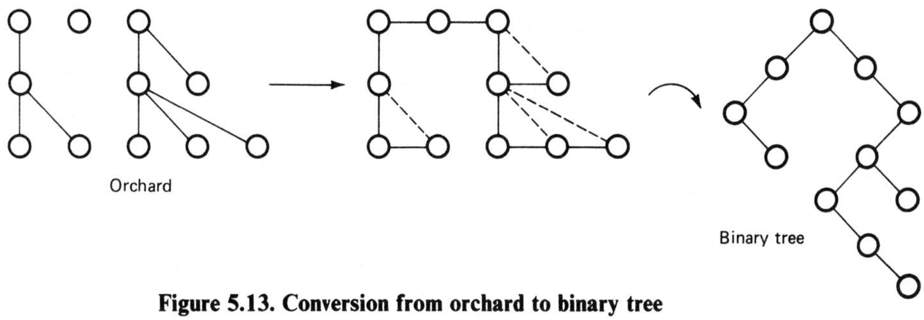

Figure 5.13. Conversion from orchard to binary tree

5.5.6 Summary.

We have seen three ways to describe the correspondence between orchards and binary trees:

▶ firstchild and nextchild links,

▶ rotations of diagrams,

▶ formal notational equivalence.

Most people find the second way, rotation of diagrams, the easiest to remember and to picture. It is the first way, setting up links to give the correspondence, that is usually needed in actually writing computer programs. The third way, the formal correspondence, finally, is the one that proves most useful in constructing proofs of various properties of binary trees and orchards.

Exercises

1. Convert each of the following orchards into a binary tree.

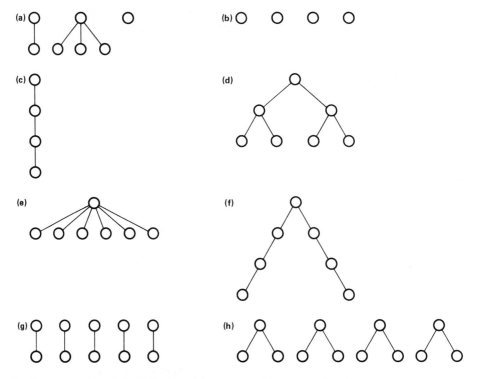

2. Convert each of the following binary trees into an orchard.

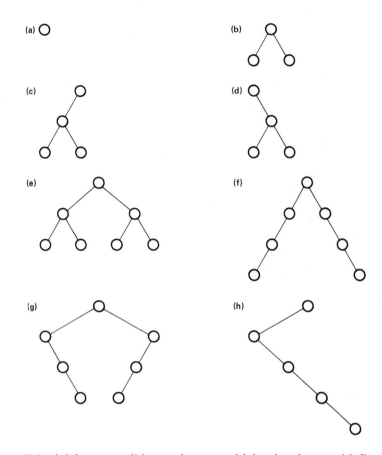

3. Draw all the (a) free trees, (b) rooted trees, and (c) ordered trees with five vertices.

4. We can define the ***preorder traversal*** of an orchard as follows. If the orchard is empty, do nothing. Otherwise, first visit the root of the first tree, then traverse the orchard of subtrees of the first tree in preorder, and then traverse the orchard of remaining trees in preorder. Prove that preorder traversal of an orchard and preorder traversal of the corresponding binary tree will visit the vertices in the same order.

5. We can define the ***inorder traversal*** of an orchard as follows. If the orchard is empty, do nothing. Otherwise, first traverse the orchard of subtrees of the first tree's root in inorder, then visit the root of the first tree, and then traverse the orchard of remaining subtrees in inorder. Prove that inorder traversal of an orchard and inorder traversal of the corresponding binary tree will visit the vertices in the same order.

6. Describe a way of traversing an orchard that will visit the vertices in the same order as postorder traversal of the corresponding binary tree. Prove that your traversal method visits the vertices in the correct order.

5.6 Building a binary search tree.

Suppose that we have a list of items that is already in order, perhaps a file of records, with keys already sorted alphabetically. If we wish to use these items to look up information, add additional items, or make other changes, then we would like to take the list or file of items and make it into a binary search tree.

We could, of course, start out with an empty binary tree and simply use the tree insertion algorithm to insert each item into it. But the items were given already in order, so the resulting search tree will become one long chain, and using it will be too slow—with the speed of sequential search rather than binary search. We wish instead, therefore, to take the items and build them into a tree that will be as bushy as possible, so as to reduce both the time to build the tree and all subsequent search time. When the number of nodes, n, is 31, for example, we wish to build the tree of Figure 5.14.

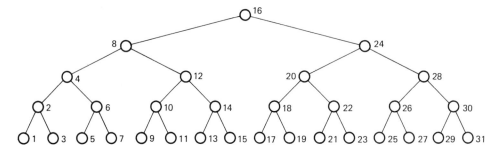

Figure 5.14. Complete binary tree with 31 nodes

In Figure 5.14 the vertices are numbered in their natural order, that is, in inorder sequence, which is the order in which they will be received and built into the tree. If you examine the diagram for a moment, you may notice an important property of the labels. The labels of the leaves are all odd numbers, that is, they are not divisible by 2. The labels of the nodes one level above the leaves are 2, 6, 10, 14, 18, 22, 26 and 30. These numbers are all double an odd number, that is, they are all even, but are not divisible by 4. On the next level up, the labels are 4, 12, 20 and 28, numbers that are divisible by 4, but not by 8. Finally, the nodes just below the root are labeled 8 and 24, and the root itself is 16. The key observation is:

> *If the nodes of a complete binary tree are labeled in inorder sequence, then each node is exactly as many levels above the leaves as the highest power of 2 that divides its label.*

Let us now put one more constraint on our problem: Let us suppose that we do not know in advance how many items will be built into the tree. If the items are coming from a file or a linked list, then this assumption is quite reasonable, since we may not have any convenient way to count the items before receiving them.

This assumption also has the advantage that it will stop us from worrying about the fact that, when the number of nodes is not exactly one less than a power of 2, then the resulting tree will not be complete and cannot be as symmetric as the one in Figure 5.14. Instead, we shall design our algorithm as though it were completely symmetric, and after receiving all items we shall determine how to tidy up the tree.

5.6.1 Getting started.

There is no doubt what to do with node number 1 when it arrives. It will be a leaf, and therefore its left and right pointers should both be set to **nil**. Node number 2 goes above node 1, as shown in Figure 5.15. Since node 2 links to node 1, we obviously must keep some way to remember where node 1 is. Node 3 is again a leaf, but it is in the right subtree of node 2, so we must remember a pointer to node 2.

Does this mean that we must keep a list of pointers to all nodes previously processed, to determine how to link in the next one? The answer is no, since when node 3 is received, all connections for node 1 are complete. Node 2 must be remembered until node 4 is received to establish the left link from node 4, but then a pointer to node 2 is no longer needed. Similarly node 4 must be remembered until node 8 has been processed.

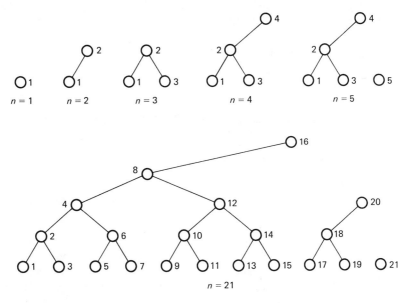

Figure 5.15. Building the first nodes into a tree

It should now be clear that to establish future links, we need only remember pointers to one node on each level, the last node processed on that level. We keep these pointers in an array called **lastnode**, that will be quite small. For example, a tree with 20 levels can accommodate

$$2^{20} - 1 \quad > \quad 1,000,000$$

nodes.

As each new node arrives, it is clearly the last one received in the order, so we can set its right pointer to **nil** (at least temporarily). The left pointer of the new node is **nil** if it is a leaf, and otherwise is the entry in **lastnode** one level lower than the new node. So that we can treat the leaves in the same way as other nodes, we consider the leaves to be on level 0, index the array **lastnode** from -1 to the maximum height allowed, and ensure that **lastnode**[-1] = **nil**.

5.6.2 Declarations and the main procedure.

We can now write down declarations of the variables needed for our task, and, while we are at it, we can outline the main procedure. The first step will be to receive all the nodes and insert them into the tree. To obtain each new node we assume the existence of an auxiliary procedure

GetNode(p)

that returns with **p** pointing to the new node, or **p** = **nil** when all nodes have been delivered. After all the nodes have been inserted, then we must find the root of the tree, and then connect any right subtrees that may be dangling (see Figure 5.15 in the case of 5 or 21 nodes).

The main procedure thus becomes:

```
procedure BuildTree(root: pointer);
{Uses auxiliary procedure GetNode(p) to obtain a list of items in proper
order of keys, and builds them into a binary search tree.}

const maxheight = 20;

type
  level    = −1 .. maxheight;          {number of steps above leaves}

var
  lastnode:     array[level] of pointer;          {contains pointer to
                                          last node processed on each level}
  counter:      integer;          {number of nodes read in so far}
  p:      pointer;                          {p↑ is present input node}
  lev:    level;                                  {level of p↑}
```

```
begin                                    {Procedure BuildTree}
  for lev := −1 to maxheight do lastnode[lev] := nil;
  counter := 0;
  GetNode(p);
  while p <> nil do
  begin
    counter := counter + 1;
    Insert(p);
    GetNode(p)
  end;                                   {receiving and processing input}
  FindRoot;
  ConnectSubtrees
end;                                     {Procedure BuildTree}
```

5.6.3 Inserting a node.

The discussion in the previous section shows how to set up the left links of each node correctly, but for some of the nodes the right link should not permanently have the value **nil.** When a new node arrives, it cannot yet have a proper right subtree, since it is the latest node (under the ordering) so far received. The node, however, may be the right child of some previous node. On the other hand, it may instead be a left child, in which case its parent node has not yet arrived. We can tell which case occurs by looking in the array lastnode. If lev denotes the level of the new node, then its parent has level lev + 1. We look at lastnode[lev + 1]↑. If its right link is still **nil,** then its right child must be the new node; if not, then its right child has already arrived, and the new node must be the left child of some future node.

We can now formally describe how to insert a new node into the tree.

```
procedure Insert(p: pointer);
{Inserts p↑ as rightmost node of a partial binary search tree.}

var
  lev :   level;                         {level of p↑}

begin                                    {Procedure Insert}
  lev := Power2(counter);
  p↑.right := nil;
  p↑.left := lastnode[lev − 1];
  lastnode[lev] := p;
  if lastnode[lev + 1] <> nil then
    with lastnode[lev + 1]↑ do
    if right = nil then right := p
end;                                     {Procedure Insert}
```

This procedure uses a short function to find the level of p↑:

```
function Power2(c: integer): level;
{Finds the highest power of 2 that divides c. Requires c ≠ 0.}
var
  lev :   level;
begin                                          {Function Power2}
  lev := 0;
  while not odd(c) do
    begin c := c div 2; lev := lev + 1 end;
  Power2 := lev
end;                                           {Function Power2}
```

5.6.4 Finishing the task.

Finding the root of the tree is easy: the root is the highest node in the tree; hence its pointer is the highest non-nil entry in the array **lastnode**. We therefore have:

```
procedure    FindRoot;
var
  lev: level;

begin                                          {Procedure FindRoot}
  if counter = 0 then
    root := nil                                {Tree is empty.}
  else begin                                   {Non-empty tree}
    lev := maxheight;    {Find highest occupied level; it gives root}
    while lastnode[lev] = nil do lev := lev − 1;
    root := lastnode[lev]

  end
end;                                           {Procedure FindRoot}
```

Finally, we must determine how to tie in any subtrees that may not yet be connected properly after all the nodes have been received. The difficulty is that some nodes in the upper part of the tree may still have their right links set to **nil,** even though further nodes have come in that belong in their right subtrees.

Any node for which the right child is still **nil** will be one of the nodes in **lastnode.** Its right child should be set to the highest node in **lastnode** that is not already in its left subtree. We thus arrive at the following algorithm.

```
procedure ConnectSubtrees;
var
  p:    pointer;
  lev:  level;
  s:    level;
begin                                    {Procedure ConnectSubtrees}
  lev := maxheight;
  while (lastnode[lev] = nil) and (lev > 1) do
    lev := lev − 1;                      {Find highest node: root}
  while lev > 1 do          {Nodes on levels 1 and 0 are already OK}
    with lastnode[lev]↑ do
    if right <> nil then
      lev := lev − 1             {Search down for highest dangling node}
    else begin                   {Case: right subtree is undefined.}
      p := left;                 {Find highest entry in lastnode that}
      s := lev − 1;                         {is not in left subtree.}
      repeat
        p := p↑.right;
        s := s − 1
      until (p = nil) or (p <> lastnode[s]);
      right := lastnode[s];
      lev := s          {Nodes on levels between lev and s are on left.}
    end                          {Connecting dangling subtrees}
end;                                      {Procedure ConnectSubtrees}
```

5.6.5 Evaluation.

The algorithm of this section produces a binary search tree that is not always completely balanced. If 32 nodes come in, then node 32 will become the root of the tree, and all 31 remaining nodes will be in its left subtree. Thus the leaves are five steps removed from the root. If the root were chosen optimally, then most of the leaves would be four steps from it, and only one would be five steps. Hence one comparison more than necessary will usually be done.

One extra comparison in a binary search is not really a very high price, and it is easy to see that a tree produced by our method is never more than one level away from optimality. There are sophisticated methods for building a binary search tree that is as balanced as possible, but much remains to recommend a simpler method, one that does not need to know in advance how many nodes are in the tree.

The exercises outline ways in which our algorithm can be used to take an arbitrary binary search tree and rearrange the nodes to bring it into better balance, so as to improve search times. Again, there are more sophisticated methods (which, however will likely be slower) for rebalancing a tree. In Chapter 9 we shall study AVL trees, in which we perform insertions and deletions in such a way as always to maintain the tree in a state of near-balance. For many practical purposes, however, the simpler algorithm described in this section should prove sufficient.

5.6.6 Random search trees and optimality.

To conclude this section, let us ask whether it is worthwhile on average to keep a search tree balanced, or to rebalance it. If we assume that the keys have arrived in random order, then, on average, how many more comparisons are needed in a search of the resulting tree than would be needed in a completely balanced tree?

In answering the question we first convert the binary search tree into a 2-tree, as follows. Think of all the vertices of the binary tree as drawn as circles, and add on new, square vertices replacing all the empty subtrees (**nil** links). This process is shown in Figure 5.16. All the vertices of the original binary tree become internal vertices of the 2-tree, and the new vertices are all external (leaves). A successful search terminates at an interior vertex of the 2-tree, and an unsuccessful search at a leaf. Hence the internal path length gives us the number of comparisons for a successful search, and the external path length the number for an unsuccessful search.

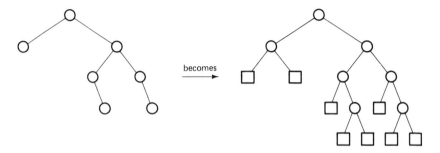

Figure 5.16. Conversion of a binary tree into a 2-tree

We shall assume that the $n!$ possible orderings of keys are equally likely in building the tree. When there are n nodes in the tree, we denote by $S(n)$ the number of comparisons done in the average successful search, and by $U(n)$ the number in the average unsuccessful search.

The number of comparisons needed to find any key in the tree is exactly one more than the number of comparisons that were needed to insert it in the first place, and inserting it required the same comparisons as the unsuccessful search showing that it was not yet in the tree. We therefore have the relationship

$$S(n) \;=\; 1 + \frac{U(0)+U(1)+\cdots+U(n-1)}{n}.$$

The relation between internal and external path length, as presented in Theorem 3.4, states that

$$S(n) \;=\; (1+1/n)U(n)-1.$$

The last two equations together give

$$(n+1)U(n) \;=\; 2n+U(0)+U(1)+\cdots+U(n-1).$$

We solve this recurrence by writing the equation for $n-1$ instead of n:

$$nU(n-1) \quad = \quad 2(n-1)+U(0)+U(1)+\cdots+U(n-2),$$

and subtracting, to obtain

$$U(n) \quad = \quad U(n-1) + \frac{2}{n+1}.$$

The sum

$$H_n \quad = \quad 1+\frac{1}{2}+\frac{1}{3}+\cdots+\frac{1}{n}$$

is called the nth **harmonic number,** and it is shown in Appendix A.2.7 that this number is approximately the natural logarithm $\ln n$. Since $U(0) = 0$, we can now evaluate $U(n)$ by starting at the bottom and adding:

$$U(n) \quad = \quad 2\left[1 + \frac{1}{2} + \cdots + \frac{1}{n+1} \right] \quad = \quad 2H_{n+1} \quad \approx \quad 2\ln n.$$

By Theorem 3.4 the number of comparisons for a successful search is also approximately $2\ln n$. By Theorem 3.6, the optimal number of comparisons in a search of n items is the base 2 logarithm, $\lg n$. But (see Appendix A.2.5)

$$\ln n \quad = \quad (\ln 2)(\lg n).$$

Finally, therefore, we have

> THEOREM 5.3.   *The average number of comparisons needed in the average binary search tree with n nodes is approximately* $2 \ln n = (2 \ln 2)(\lg n)$.

> COROLLARY 5.4.   *The average binary search tree requires approximately* $2 \ln 2 \approx 1.39$ *times as many comparisons as a completely balanced tree.*

In other words, the average cost of not balancing a search tree is approximately 39% more comparisons. In applications where optimality is important, this cost must be weighed against the extra cost of balancing the tree, or of maintaining it in balance. Note especially that these latter tasks involve not only the cost of computer time, but the cost of the extra programming effort that will be required.

Exercises

1. Draw the sequence of partial search trees (like Figure 5.15) that the method in this section will construct for $n = 6$ through $n = 16$.

2. Write a procedure GetNode(p) that will traverse a linked list and get each node from the list in turn.

3. Combine the algorithm for converting a binary tree to a doubly-linked list (requested in Exercise 16 of Section 5.4) with Exercise 2 and the algorithm of this section to obtain a self-contained procedure to balance a binary search tree.

4. Write a version of procedure GetNode(p) that traverses a binary tree in inorder without first converting it into a linked sequential list. Make sure that the algorithm of this section will not change any links in the tree until your traversal algorithm no longer needs them. Thereby obtain a self-contained procedure for balancing a binary search tree with only one pass through its nodes.

5. Write a procedure GetNode(p) that will read a record from a file, check that the key is in the proper order, and return a new node containing the record. Thereby obtain a self-contained procedure for reading a balanced binary search tree from an ordered sequential file.

6. Suppose that the number of nodes in the tree is known in advance. Modify the algorithm of this section to take advantage of this knowledge, and produce a tree in which any imbalance is of at most one level, and occurs at the leaves rather than near the root.

7. There are $6 = 3!$ possible orderings of three keys, but only 5 distinct binary trees with three nodes. Therefore these binary trees are not equally likely to occur as search trees. Find which search tree corresponds to each possible order, and thereby find the probability for building each of the binary search trees from randomly ordered input.

8. Repeat Exercise 7, with the $4! = 24$ orderings of four keys, and the 14 binary trees with four nodes.

5.7 References for further study.

One of the most thorough available studies of binary trees is in the series of books by KNUTH. The properties of binary trees, other classes of trees, traversal, path length, and history, altogether occupy pages 305–405 of Volume 1. Volume 3, pages 422–480, discusses binary search trees, balancing trees, and related topics. The proof of Theorem 5.3 is from Volume 3, page 427.

An alternative study of binary trees, with Pascal programs presented in detail, is

N. WIRTH, *Algorithms + Data Structures = Programs,* Prentice-Hall, Englewood Cliffs, N.J., 1976.

Chapter 6

Case Study:
An Index Writer

This chapter develops a program that makes a list of all the distinct words appearing in a text. This case study illustrates both principles of program design and of data structuring, exhibiting applications and interactions of arrays, files, hash tables, linked lists, and binary search trees.

6.1 Specifying the problem.

There are several good reasons for making a list, in alphabetical order, of all the distinct words that appear in a document. First, a list of the important words is helpful in preparing an index for the document, especially if page numbers are included along with the words. Second, we may wish, for a broader class of words, to be able to locate all the occurrences of each word, so that we can quickly find the context of a short section that we remember. Such a list of words with all their occurrences is called a *concordance*. Third, we might like to have a list of all the words with a count of how many times each word is used. Different authors use different styles; and often substantial differences occur in the relative frequencies of using common words. Word counts provide important clues to scholars attempting to determine doubtful authorships. Fourth (but not least important), a word list is of great help in recognizing inconsistencies in spelling words. The word list cannot, by itself, serve as a spelling corrector, but it can certainly recognize many misprints that might otherwise not be detected. It is often reasonable to expect that an author is inconsistent in spelling a word if he is not sure of its correct spelling, and these inconsistencies can be spotted quickly in the list, and used to flag words whose spelling should be checked.

You may already have guessed that the first major application of the program we develop in this chapter is the very text of this book itself. The first and fourth reasons are clearly important for this application, with the second and third capabilities being interesting by-products. A document of about 150,000 words is clearly much too large to keep in the high-speed memory of a computer at one time, and sorting 150,000 items is a very big task. Hence our first restriction on our project: We must spurn the simple solution of reading the whole document into memory, splitting it into a long list of words, and sorting the list. Instead, we shall assume that we have memory enough for two or three thousand words, but no more.

Our second restriction is that the program should run efficiently, so that, if possible, it will run on a microcomputer in reasonable time, or, if that is not possible, it will at least run successfully on a quite small computer system. The program will probably also need to request some information from the user. It should therefore run quickly enough to be used interactively on a time-sharing system, without frustrating the user with long delays.

With these restrictions in mind, let us describe the task of our project more precisely. We wish to have a list of the distinct words in the text, arranged in alphabetical order. For some words (as specified by the user), we wish a list of all the pages on which the word appears. For some words (as specified by the user), we wish a count of the number of appearances of the word. There may remain other words for which we desire no special information. Hence we may regard the words as going into one of three categories, which we shall call *index, count,* and *forget.*

At the first appearance of each word, the program must ask the user which of these three dispositions to make. The program should never ask the user twice about the same word.

At this point it may appear that we have spelled out the requirements for the program completely, but we have not. For example, we have not specified exactly what constitutes a word; this task we postpone to a later section. Nor have we specified the form of input and output. For documents of any significant size we shall clearly wish to read the document from a file, rather than typing it in as input from a terminal. We could type the word list out at the terminal, but this would be prohibitively long for a large document, and not as useful as making the word list into another file that can later be examined and appropriate information extracted. Finally, in the future we will presumably wish to run the program on other documents. If so, we may not wish to specify the disposition of each word all over again. Hence the program should set up a master word list, update it with the new words from the current document, and keep the updated list as another file. For backup purposes the previous master word list should not be destroyed or altered.

Note carefully that, at this point, although we have a good idea of what the program should do and the way in which it will communicate with its environment (via files and the interactive user), we have said nothing about the way the data will be kept while the program is running, nor of the method that will be used to process the data (other than to eschew one obvious possible method). By the time we have settled these questions we shall have devised the essence of the program, and in a project this large it is essential that we avoid jumping to premature decisions.

6.2 Structuring the data: The main program.

6.2.1 Requirements on data organization.

Our problem includes several conflicting requirements that greatly limit the ways of representing our data. The master word list, first of all, will be much too large to be kept in memory all at once. Second, our program is supposed to run efficiently, and accesses to files (on disk or otherwise outside high-speed memory) are very slow compared to operations within memory. It is therefore impractical to consider looking up each word separately in the master word list. With a large document it will, in any case, take significant time for the program to read all the way through the document, so we should, if possible, avoid reading the same information more than once from a file. Finally, as we have previously noted, the input text will be too large to fit into memory. Hence we would like to be able to read the input text only once; read the master word list only once; and in this single pass produce the word list for the input document in alphabetical order with page references or frequency counts as desired.

1. Two-phase program.

This goal is unattainable. It might happen that the first word of the input text belongs at the very end of the word list. Since we cannot keep all the words in memory at once, it will be necessary to use some kind of auxiliary files to remember the words from the input text until they can be compared to the master word list and processed accordingly. Thus the first phase of our program will read the input text, split it into individual words, and put them away for further processing.

2. Common words.

It now appears as though we must read the entire input at least twice, once as a document, and again after it has been split into a long list of words. One simple observation, fortunately, will spare most of the words from going into the auxiliary files and having to be processed further in a second phase. This observation is that, in English (or any other human language) some words occur far more frequently than others. A dictionary of reasonable size contains perhaps 50,000 entries; an unabridged dictionary more than 100,000, but only a few common words make up the bulk of the words in almost any text. In the present book, for example, a vocabulary of fewer than 1000 words will cover more than 80% of all words in the text. In ordinary English discourse, it usually takes only 134 distinct words to account for half of all the words in a text.

During the input phase, therefore, let us keep a list of the most common words in memory, and look up each word in this list as soon as it is read in. If it is in the list, then we can process it at once; if not, then it must be put into an auxiliary file for later processing.

In what kind of data structure should we keep these common words? Our use of the list is that of table lookup: for each incoming word we wish to determine as quickly as possible whether it is in the list or not. The keys are the words themselves, and there are too many possible words to use simple array indexing; the study in Chapter 3 shows this task to be an appropriate application for a hash table. Our list of common words will not (after it is constructed) be subject to insertions or deletions; with a good hash function open addressing will probably prove better than chaining. Let us therefore reach the decision to keep the list of common words in memory during the first phase as a hash table with open addressing.

For simplicity we shall (arbitrarily) decide that the list of common words in the hash table coincides with the common words for which no information is to be kept. Hence, when a word is found in the hash table, no further processing is needed, and we sometimes write the category *hash* in place of *forget*.

3. Auxiliary files.

Our next task is to decide how to store the words that do require further processing in the second phase. The simplest way is to set up an auxiliary file and write the words into it one at a time. The file is then reset and read in the second phase. If there is enough room to read all these words into memory at once, then the second phase can proceed efficiently: the words can first be sorted alphabetically and then compared with the master word list as it is read. If we are sure that the program will never be used for documents of more than about 10,000 words, and the first phase disposes of about 80% of them, then there may be enough room to proceed in this way, and it is then a good choice of method.

For generality, however, we would like to be able to process larger documents. The time required for sorting, moreover, grows faster than the number of words, and therefore, if we can find a way to divide the problem into a series of smaller problems, then the total time required for sorting will be shortened, and the available memory can accommodate a larger document.

The idea that we shall use to subdivide the problem is the same idea used in radix sort: instead of putting the words into one auxiliary file, we divide them into twenty-six auxiliary files, according to the first letter of the word. As we shall see, this requires essentially no extra time in the first phase, and it divides the second phase into twenty-six similar but smaller problems that will, together, run faster than one large sorting problem.

4. The third phase.

Recall that the words from the current document were to be used to update the master word list (keeping a backup copy). This task could be done while the second phase is in progress, but for simplicity and clarity we shall instead use a third phase, that will merge the word list for the current document with the master word list, and will also update the list of common words kept as the hash table.

5. Filters.

Our program design as it has developed is typical of many applications where the work to be done splits naturally into a series of tasks or phases that can be considered separately. A good way to think of the work is as starting with raw input and passing it through a series of *filters*, each of which converts the data into a form closer to the desired result. This approach is the basis of the popular UNIX® operating system, which is made up of a large number of filters, each of which does only one task, usually quite a simple task. The power of the operating system comes from the flexibility and generality of the ways in which filters can be combined.

In our program, too, we should consider each of the three phases as independently from the others as we can. Not only will this approach help to keep the design simple, but we may find that one or another part of the program will prove to be useful for some unanticipated application. Within a UNIX or UNIX-like system it would probably be best to write each of the three phases as a separate program. With other systems, however, it is not so convenient to direct the output of one program to become the input of another, and therefore we shall consider the more difficult case of writing the three phases within one program. Even so, we can improve the modularity of the project by keeping the interface between phases as simple as we can, and by insisting, for example, that all temporary files remain in human-readable form.

6.2.2 The main program.

At this point, let us reinforce our decisions concerning data representation by establishing the notation that will be used both for communication with the outside environment and for sending information from the first phase to the second phase. These notations constitute the declarations placed in the main program.

The **const** declaration section includes all constants used in the program, even those used in only one phase or subprogram. By collecting all the constants in one place, it becomes easier to see what changes must be made to adapt the program to a particular computer system.

A program that manipulates words or other character strings will necessarily have some dependence on the way in which characters are represented in computer memory. For definiteness, this chapter has been written for the ASCII representation. A comment is inserted at every point where this assumption makes a difference, noting what changes may be needed for other representations.

```
program IndexText(InText, InIndex, NewIndex, OutIndex, HashFile,
                  Input, Output);

{Produces word counts and list of references for the document file
InText. Uses the master word list in file InIndex, if provided. Output word
list for the new text goes to file NewIndex. The merger of these two files
becomes OutIndex. HashFile contains the common words to be ig-
nored. If not specified, it is created on output, containing the words so
flagged by the user.}
```

* UNIX is a trademark of Bell Laboratories

```
const
  maxwd        = 20;        {More letters in a word will be ignored.}
  minwd        = 3;                {Shorter words will be ignored .}
  hashsize     = 2003;      {should be a prime; size of hash table}
  linesperpage = 66;        {assumes standard spacing and paper}
  maxheight    = 20;              {for building binary tree in phase 2}
  A            = 'A';
  Z            = 'Z';
  hyphen       = '-';
  blank        = ' ';
  apostrophe   = '''';            {requires two ''s to represent one}
  underscore   = '_';
  ordbackspace = 8;         {ASCII control character for backspace}
  ordformfeed  = 12;        {ASCII control character for new page}
  changecase   = 32;        {ASCII difference between upper and lower
                                                              case}

type
  word        = packed array[1..maxwd] of char;
  reference   = record
                     wd: word;
                     pg: integer;                        {page number}
                end;
  fileref     = file of reference;           {used for local files}
  letter      = A..Z;
  hashentry   = 1..hashsize;

var
  InText,                             {Document being processed}
  InIndex,                                    {Master word list}
  NewIndex,                         {Word list of current document}
  OutIndex:   text;                      {Updated master word list}
  HashFile:   file of word;
  NewHashFile:file of word;  {Local file, used to update HashFile}
  RefFile:    array[letter] of fileref;   {Local files used forauxiliary
                          storage of words from phase 1 to phase 2:
                          separate file for each initial letter}
  blankword:  word;                          {will contain all blanks}

begin                                              {Main program}
  SplitWords;                                             {Phase 1}
  ClassifyWords;                                          {Phase 2}
  UpdateHashFile;                              {Phase 3, first part}
  MergeIndices;                               {Phase 3, second part}
end.
```

6.2.3 Word processing.

1. Storage of a word.

Our program needs to keep a considerable number of different words in storage, and must be able to compare, move, and change these words efficiently. The length of a word varies considerably: one reasonable approach would be to keep words stored as a linked list of characters. This method, however, would use considerable space for links, and would make comparison of two words a fairly slow process. For simplicity, therefore, we shall represent a word as a (packed) array of characters of fixed length maxwd = 20. All positions in the array after the end of the word will be filled with blanks.

We shall frequently need to perform various standard tasks with words. Standard Pascal allows two arrays to be checked for equality, but does not necessarily provide the other facilities we need, which we therefore write as auxiliary subprograms. Many Pascal compilers, however, do provide these other capabilities, which should then probably be used in place of the subprograms given here.

2. Comparing words.

```
function Lt(u,v: word): Boolean;
{Determine if word u precedes word v lexicographically.}

var
  i: 1..maxwd;                              {loop variable}

begin                                       {Function Lt}
  i := 1;
  while (i < maxwd) and (u[i] = v[i]) do  i := i + 1;
  Lt := (u[i] < v[i])
        {Above is the version that works with ASCII code. For codes
         where blank comes after letters, modifications are necessary.}
end;                                        {Function Lt}
```

3. Reading and writing a word.

For convenience in processing, we shall treat all the words put in the files generated by our program in the same way as words in memory, that is, as having the fixed length of maxwd = 20 characters, with blanks added to make up this length. The procedures below are applied only to files whose words are of this fixed length (not, for example, to the terminal input, where the user could not be expected to type in extra blanks to complete a word).

```
procedure ReadWord( var F: text; var w: word);
{Reads word w from text file F. Assumes not at end of file.}

var
  c: 1..maxwd;
begin                                          {Procedure ReadWord}
  for c := 1 to maxwd do
    Read(F, w[c])
end;                                           {Procedure ReadWord}


procedure WriteWord( var F: text; w: word);
{Writes word w to text file F}

var
  c: 1..maxwd;
begin                                          {Procedure WriteWord}
  for c := 1 to maxwd do
    Write(F, w[c])
end;                                           {Procedure WriteWord}
```

6.3 Phase 1: Splitting the text into words.

The task of this phase is, briefly, to read the input text, split it into individual words, look up each word in the hash table, and, if it is not there, put it in the appropriate auxiliary file for later processing.

6.3.1 The main procedure.

This action translates into the outline coded as the following procedure, which in turn invokes three other procedures. Initialize sets up the hash table and the necessary variables; GetWord splits off a single word from the input text; and Conclude tidies up after the input text has been completely read.

As we did in the main program, we declare in this main procedure several variables that are used only in the sub-procedures. These include various counters and other information needed to identify words and determine the page number corresponding to each word.

```
procedure SplitWords;
{Sets up hash table, reads text, and divides into 26 word lists}

type
  hashentry      = 1..hashsize;
var
  hash:          array[hashentry] of word;           {hash table}
  pagecount,                            {keeps the current page number}
  addpage,                      {amount to increase pagecount after word}
```

linecount:	integer;	{line number on the current page}
outcount:	**array**[letter] **of** integer;	{counters for word files}
wordcount:	integer;	{count of all words in the text}
w:	word;	{word currently being processed}
x:	hashentry;	{location of w, if in hash table}
endinput:	Boolean;	{true if and only if input has all been read}
firstletter:	char;	{Into which file does word w go?}

{The following variables are kept for use in procedure GetWord, and for efficiency are set up only once in procedure Initialize.}

backspace,		
formfeed:	char;	{ASCII control characters}
contchar,		{characters OK in the middle of a word}
alphabet:	**set of** char;	{letters only—to start a word}

{Implementation dependent. A good implementation should allow "set of char". Otherwise, a restricted range is required.}

```
begin                                      {Procedure SplitWords}
  Initialize;                    {Sets up files, hash table, constants}
  GetWord(w);                    {Obtains a single word from InText}
  while not endinput do
  begin
    x := HashAddress(w);
    if w <> hash[x] then
    begin                        {not in hash table; put into RefFile}
      firstletter := w[1];
      outcount[firstletter] := outcount[firstletter] + 1;
      with RefFile[firstletter]↑ do
      begin
        wd := w;
        pg := pagecount
      end;
      Put(RefFile[firstletter])
    end;
    GetWord(w);
  end;
  Conclude                               {Writes word counts to Output.}
end;                                      {Procedure SplitWords}
```

6.3.2 Designing the hash function and table.

The first auxiliary subprogram needed in phase 1 concerns the processing of the hash table. We have already decided to use open addressing in the hash table of common words used in the above procedure. An unoccupied position in the table will

contain the special word blankword consisting of all blanks. Since the table will run a
load factor of perhaps 0.5, linear probing may prove unsatisfactory; let us instead use
quadratic probing. Finally comes the question of error processing: what if we attempt
to insert a word into a completely full table? We could either check for this condition
in the function determining the hash address, or in phase 3 when inserting additional
words into the file. If we do the check in the function, then it will be needlessly invoked
for every access to the hash table; hence instead we postpone the check to phase 3.

```
function HashAddress(w: word): hashentry;
{Calculates the location in hash table of word w, or, if none, returns
pointing to the blank word where w should go}

var
  x,                                              {calculated location}
  inc;            integer;          {increment for open addressing}

begin                                      {Function HashAddress}
  x := (ord(w[1])*ord(w[3])*ord(w[4])+ord(w[6])) mod hashsize+1;
{Hash function assumes long word length. For short word machines,
must ensure that the result is non-negative, and worry about overflow.}
  if (hash[x] <> w) and (hash[x] <> blankword) then
  begin
    inc := 1;
    repeat
      x := x + inc;
      if x > hashsize then x := x - hashsize;
      inc := inc + 1
    until (w = hash[x]) or (blankword = hash[x])
  end;
  HashAddress := x
end;                                        {Function HashAddress}
```

6.3.3 Initialization.

The procedure initializing all the variables involves no really new
ideas. Nevertheless, you should especially note the error-checking included at several
points.

```
procedure Initialize;
{Sets up constant-valued sets for use in GetWord. Opens the text file
and initializes various counters. Opens file holding hash table (if any),
and reads or otherwise initializes the table.}

var
  ch: char;                                {general purpose character}
  i: integer;                            {general purpose loop control}
```

```
begin                                        {Procedure Initialize}
  backspace := chr(ordbackspace);
  formfeed := chr(ordformfeed);   {Initialize ASCII control characters}
  alphabet := ['A'..'Z', 'a'..'z'];            {Letters only, to start a word}
  contchar  :=  alphabet  +  [hyphen, apostrophe, backspace,
                                                       underscore];
                        {characters that will not terminate the word}
  for i := 1 to maxwd do
    blankword[i] := blank;

  Reset(InText);
  endinput := eof(InText);
  repeat
    Write( 'What is the page number on which the text begins?');
    Readln(pagecount);
    if pagecount < 0 then
      Writeln('Must be a non-negative integer.')
  until pagecount >= 0;
  linecount := 0;
  addpage := 0;
  wordcount := 0;

  for ch := A to Z do
  begin
    Rewrite( RefFile[ch] );
    Outcount[ch] := 0
  end;

  Reset(HashFile);
  if eof(HashFile) then
  begin    {There is no previous table; initialize the table to all blanks.}
    Writeln('Cannot open file for hash table. Creating a new table.');
    for i := 1 to hashsize do
      hash[i] := blankword
  end else begin                     {retrieve the previous hash table}
    i := 0;
    repeat
      i := i + 1;
      hash[i] := HashFile↑;
      Get(HashFile)
    until eof(HashFile) or (i >= hashsize);
    if (not eof(HashFile)) or (i <> hashsize) then
      Writeln('Error in reading hash table. Incorrect number of entries.')
  end;
end;                                          {Procedure Initialize}
```

6.3.4 Finding one word.

Before we can begin to write the procedure that obtains one word from the input text, we must finally address the question:

What is a word?

The naive answer is: "any sequence of letters," but a few moments' consideration will show that our problems are considerably more complicated.

1. Numerals.

Should numerals be allowed in words? Numbers like "1000" or "1728" are frequently written with numerals (as done here), but treated like words. In computer programs names like A1 and A2 are considered distinct. For the sake of completeness, it might be a good idea to allow numerals within words, and treat them in the same way as letters. For simplicity, however, we shall follow the practice of dictionaries and shall exclude numerals. Hence digits appearing between words will be ignored, and the appearance of a digit will terminate a word.

2. Upper and lower case.

Perhaps the simplest way to treat upper and lower case letters is to regard them as identical. This way, however, loses information. The acronym "SAM" (Sequential Access Method) is not the same as the man's name "Sam." The name "IBM" would be misspelled in lower case letters. On the other hand, a word should not be considered different because it happens to appear at the beginning of a sentence, and is therefore capitalized. Let us therefore adopt the same convention used in dictionaries: The first letter of every word will be converted to upper case, but the remaining letters will be left in the same case in which they appear. In comparisons upper and lower case will be considered different.

3. Separators.

A word ends when a blank is encountered, the line ends, or any character other than a letter or numeral appears (such as punctuation), except for a few special characters that we shall consider separately. All characters in the input should then be ignored until the next word starts, and this will be with the next letter that appears.

4. Hyphens.

Hyphens are used for two purposes. At the end of a line, a hyphen means that a word continues on the next line. In this case, we shall delete both the hyphen and the end of line, combining the two parts into a single word. When not at the end of a line, a hyphen connects two words (or radicals) to form a single word. It is quite reasonable to regard each constituent as a separate word, but we shall instead elect to treat a hyphenated word as a single unit. In a word like "pre-empt" neither half is an independent word, and a term like "Come-by-chance" (a town in Newfoundland) has meaning quite distinct from any of its constituent words. Note that our conventions will have the effect of stripping the hyphen from a hyphenated word that happens to be divided after its hyphen between two lines. This situation should arise infrequently. Finally, hyphens are occasionally attached to the end of words, as in the phrase "in-, post- or preorder traversal." We shall delete such hyphens.

Note that hyphens are not the same as dashes—such as the one in this sentence. In typewritten or computer-input text, however, a dash is frequently represented as two consecutive hyphens. Hence we shall treat two consecutive hyphens as the termination of a word.

5. Apostrophes.

Apostrophes have three common uses. They frequently appear as quotation marks, in which case they should terminate words like other punctuation. Second, they appear within contractions, where they should be treated like letters and allow the word to continue. Third, they denote the possessive form of a noun. There is little reason to regard the word "cat's" as different from "cat"; hence we remove a final apostrophe followed by "s." The possessive form "s'" causes no difficulty, of course, since its apostrophe will terminate the word like other punctuation. Finally, within the inner part of a hyphenated term we shall leave the possessive form intact: an early version of this chapter's program produced a strange result by stripping the possessive from *bird's-eye*, a term appearing both in Chapter 6 and in Chapter 1.

The only time when the rules formulated here will go wrong is that they regard the possessive form "its" as distinct from its variant "it," and fail to recognize the contraction "it's," instead converting it to the word "it."

6. Underlining.

Some texts contain the underscore character '_' together with associated backspace characters to produce underlined words. We shall ignore all such characters, removing them from the words before further processing.

6.3.5 Getting a word from InText.

We can now build all these decisions into the key procedure of phase 1, which reads through the file InText and returns the next word. We use a subsidiary procedure GetChar to obtain a single character from InText, and at the same time keep track of ends of lines and the end of file, via the variables endln and endinput, respectively. Since the end of file is discovered in the subsidiary procedure, a statement label and **goto** are used to exit from the outer procedure when the file ends. The end of a page is also detected by GetChar, but the page number associated with a word should be that where the word begins, which might not be the same as where it ends. Hence the variable keeping track of page numbers is updated in GetWord rather than in GetChar.

A second subsidiary procedure, AddChar, appends a character to the word currently being read, and ensures that the word does not exceed maxwd characters (The

constant maxwd = 20 is declared in the main program). Longer words are truncated. The program also ignores all words less than minwd = 3 characters, in order
to speed the program.

Since the end of a word is determined by finding the first character not in the
word, and since the treatment of several of the special characters depends on what
comes after the character, the character buffer ch will often contain the character *after*
the one being currently processed.

procedure GetWord(**var** w: word);
{Gets words from input file InText, and returns only words at least
minwd characters long. Parameter endinput becomes true if and only if
the end of InText is reached with no word to return. This parameter is
set by the subsidiary procedure GetChar. Procedure also updates
global variables wordcount and linecount. Updates global variable
pagecount after each linesperpage cr's, or after each formfeed, whichever comes first. Uses the sets alphabet and contchar, and various
character constants.}

label 1;   {used by GetChar to exit procedure on eof(InText)}

var c: 0..maxwd;   {count of characters in word}
    ch: char;   {character currently processed}
    endln: Boolean;   {At the end of a line?}

begin   {Procedure GetWord}
  repeat   {until current word is at least minwd chars long}
    repeat
      GetChar(ch)   {Find a letter that will start the word.}
    until ch **in** alphabet;
    pagecount := pagecount + addpage;
    addpage := 0;
    c := 0;
    if ch **in** ['a'..'z'] **then**   {Translate first letter to upper case.}
      ch := chr(ord(ch) − changecase);   { System dependent}
    AddChar(ch);   {Put first letter into the word}
    GetChar(ch);
    while ch **in** contchar **do**
      if ch **in** alphabet **then**   {Add letters directly to word}
      begin   {processing letter}
        AddChar(ch);
        GetChar(ch)
      end   {processing letter}

```
          else if ch = hyphen then
          begin                                    {processing hyphen}
            GetChar(ch);              {Find what comes after hyphen.}
            if endln then
              GetChar(ch)          {Delete both the hyphen and end of line}
            else if ch = hyphen then    {Two hyphens represent a dash}
              ch := blank               {Use a blank to terminate the word}
            else if ch in alphabet then
              AddChar(hyphen)           {Include hyphens between letters}
            else {nothing}                  {Delete all other hyphens}
          end                                    {processing hyphen}
          else if ch= apostrophe then
          begin                                  {processing apostrophe}
            GetChar(ch);
            if ch   = 's' then         {Delete "s' at end of word only}
            begin
              GetChar(ch);
              if ch in contchar then
              begin
                AddChar(apostrophe);
                AddChar('s')
              end
            end
            else if ch in alphabet then
              AddChar(apostrophe)              {Allow contractions.}
          end                                  {processing apostrophe}
          else    {Remaining possibilities are backspace and underscore.}
            GetChar(ch);                        {Delete these characters.}
          {While loop on continuing characters ends here.}
          wordcount := wordcount + 1
        until c >= minwd;               {Skip over short words.}

        while c < maxwd do                       {Fill with blanks}
        begin
          c := c + 1;
          w[c] := blank
        end;
      1:          {When end of file occurs, will exit to here from GetChar}
      end;                                      {Procedure GetWord}
```

1. Getting one character.

```
procedure GetChar(var ch: char);
{Gets a character from input text into ch. Checks for eof. Updates
page count and line count.}
```

```
begin                                    {Procedure GetChar}
  if eof(InText) then
    if c >= minwd then
      ch := '.'          {special character to end the current word}
    else begin                    {no word to return; set endinput}
      endinput := true;
      goto 1                              {exit from GetWord}
    end
  else begin            {not at end of file. Process next character.}
    ch := InText↑;
    endln := eoln(InText);
    Get(InText);
    if endln then
    begin
      linecount := linecount + 1;
      if linecount >= linesperpage then
        begin
          addpage := addpage + 1;
          linecount := 0
        end
    end;
    if ch = formfeed then
      begin
        addpage := addpage + 1;
        linecount := 0;
        endln := true;              {Treat formfeed like end of line.}
        ch := blank
      end
  end
end;                                      {Procedure GetChar}
```

2. Adding a character to the word.

```
procedure AddChar(ch: char);
{adds given character to word, if possible}

begin                                     {Procedure AddChar}
  if c < maxwd then
  begin
    c := c + 1;
    w[c] := ch
  end
end;                                      {Procedure AddChar}
```

6.3.6 Tidying up.

To complete the first phase of the program, we need only close or reset all the files so that the second phase can read them.

```
procedure Conclude;
{Writes out counts of various word lists. For some systems, it is neces-
sary to close files, which should be done in this procedure.}

var
   ch: char;                                        {loop index}

begin                                        {Procedure Conclude}
   Writeln('The total number of words read in is ', wordcount:7);
   Writeln;
   Writeln('The number of words to process further in the next stage,');
   Writeln('beginning with each letter, is below.');
   Writeln;
   for ch := 'A' to 'M' do Write(' ', ch:1, ' ');
   Writeln;
   for ch := 'A' to 'M' do Write(outcount[ch]:4, ' ');
   Writeln;
   Writeln;
   for ch := 'N' to 'Z' do Write(' ', ch:1, ' ');
   Writeln;
   for ch := 'N' to 'Z' do Write(outcount[ch]:4, ' ');
   Writeln;
   Writeln
end;                                         {Procedure Conclude}
```

Exercises

1. As written, the program ignores all words with fewer than three letters. What single change will make the program keep track of shorter words?

2. What would be the easiest way to modify the program to translate all letters to upper case, and hence ignore the distinction between upper and lower case?

3. Describe the modifications needed in the program so that it would treat digits in the same way as letters.

4. Describe the changes needed so that the program will regard the parts of a hyphenated term as separate words (except when a hyphen is at the end of a line).

5. Some dialects of Pascal (such as those usually used for microcomputers), unfortunately, do not allow an array of files. First describe how to simplify the

program so that all words requiring further processing go into a single auxiliary file. Second, devise a scheme by which some of the advantages of sorting with multiple files can be kept, but using fewer than twenty-six files, and not in an array.

6. Some operating systems limit the number of files that can be simultaneously open to fewer than twenty-six. Describe how to modify the program to use an array of fewer than twenty-six files, where now words with several different initial letters go to the same file. If, for example, the array has eight files, then dividing the letters as follows will achieve a fairly uniform spread of (English) words among the files:

A — B   C — D   E — G   H — L   M — O   P — R   S   T — Z.

6.4 Phase 2: Classifying the words.

Our task in phase 2 is to process the words that were put in the temporary files in phase 1. More specifically, for each initial letter from A to Z, we wish to read the references from the appropriate temporary file, read the entries from the master word list InIndex with the same initial letter, produce a word count or list of page numbers for words in the master word list, and, on the first occurrence of a word not in InIndex, request the user to assign it to the appropriate category.

6.4.1 Choosing data structures.

There are several ways to store the data in memory, each of which brings both advantages and disadvantages. Let us first recall the requirements for the data in this second phase. One requirement is that the finished word lists are to be in alphabetical order, available for human inspection. Hence the words must be sorted at some stage in the process. Second, the process is to run efficiently. Sorting tends to be a slow process, so we must exercise care how and when to do it. Third, memory is limited, so we must attempt to avoid storing duplicate information and otherwise try to avoid overflow.

1. Sort, then merge.

If there is enough room in memory for all the references from one of the temporary files, then perhaps the easiest way to solve the problem is, first, to read in all these references, second, sort them alphabetically, and, finally, read through the master word list, comparing entries as we go. This comparison stage is akin to merging two files. If the same word appears in both lists, then the word list can be updated. If a word is in the new list but not the old, then its disposition can be learned by asking the user, and the proper action can then be taken.

2. Collect, then sort and merge.

The major difficulty with the preceding method is that there may not be enough room for all the references from the temporary file. Any writer, working on one document, tends to use a somewhat restricted vocabulary, but to use the same words many times (This observation is especially true of technical writing). Hence the total number of references may be too large for memory, but the total number of distinct words will probably not be. As we read the temporary file, therefore, we should amalgamate the references belonging to the same word.

One commendable method (left as an exercise) to do this is to set up a new hash table, and insert each reference as it is received, amalgamating those that are found to belong together. After the file is exhausted, the hash table is sorted and compared to the master word list.

3. Collect, sort and compare simultaneously.

In yet another method (the one that we shall develop), the references are amalgamated and sorted and compared with the master word list as they are received. Instead of concentrating on the file of references, we read in the appropriate part of the master word list and build it into a binary tree. The master word list is already in alphabetical order, so this task will go very quickly—its time is linear in the number of words. As each reference is read in, we search for it in the binary tree with the speed of binary search. If it is present, then the corresponding node is updated; if not, then it is inserted into the tree at the appropriate place. A final inorder traversal of the tree yields the new word list in alphabetical order.

6.4.2 The main procedure.

We can now establish our notation by writing the main procedure for phase 2. We shall, of course, use linked storage for the binary tree, and the type **node** is a record with variants according to the disposition of the associated word. The list of page numbers for each word is kept as a simply linked list, with nodes of type **reflist**. The two associated pointer types are called **pointer** and **pointref**, respectively.

```
procedure ClassifyWords;
{For each letter of the alphabet, reads in a list of words from InIndex;
builds into a binary tree; supplements with entries fromRefFile; and
writes result to NewIndex and NewHashFile.}

type
  wordtype = (hash, count, index);   {three ways to process a word}
  pointref = ↑reflist;
  reflist = record                              {list of references}
              pg: integer;
              next: pointref
            end;
```

```
pointer  =  ↑node;
node  =  record                          {vertex of the binary tree}
            wd:    word;
            left,
            right: pointer;
         case kind: wordtype of
            hash:
               ();  {empty}
            count:
               (ct: integer);
            index:
               (ref: pointref)
         end;

var
   root: pointer;                        {root of the binary tree}
   ch: char;                             {loop on first letter of word.}


begin                                    {Procedure ClassifyWords}
Writeln('At the appearance of each word, give its disposition:');
Writeln('  F — Forget all occurrences of this word.');
Writeln('  C — Count how many times this word appears.');
Writeln('  I — Index this word: list the pages on which it appears.');

Reset(InIndex);
Rewrite(NewIndex);


for ch := A to Z do        {Start main loop on first letter of word.}
   begin
   BuildTree(root, ch);    {Get the part of master wordlist starting with
                           ch from the file InIndex, and build into binary tree.}
   Reset(RefFile[ch]);
   while not eof(RefFile[ch]) do
   begin
     Process(RefFile[ch]↑);
                  {Use new words from RefFile[ch] to update tree.}
     Get( RefFile[ch] )
   end;


   OutputTree(root)
   {Writes the contents of the tree into files NewIndex and NewHash.}
   end                                   {main loop on letters of alphabet}
end;                                     {Procedure ClassifyWords}
```

6.4.3 Setting up the search tree.

The entries in the master word list InIndex are already sorted alphabetically; hence they can be built into the search tree by the method developed in Section 5.6. The procedure BuildTree needed here is precisely the procedure BuildTree developed in Section 5.6. The only difference is that the character ch should be passed through as a second calling parameter. The letter ch is not used in BuildTree itself, but should be passed to the subsidiary procedure GetNode(p, ch). Here it determines which entries should be read from InIndex, and when the reading should stop.

Since the procedures are almost identical to those developed there, we refer to Section 5.6 for the procedure BuildTree and its subsidiary subprograms Insert, Power2, FindRoot and ConnectSubtrees. For our present application we need only write the procedure GetNode.

1. File structure.

Note that, up to this late time in writing the program, we have not needed to decide the format of the master word file InIndex. Now, however, we shall write the procedure to read this file and must therefore specify its structure. First, this file is to be accessible for human inspection or for use by other programs; hence the file should be of type text rather than of some privately defined type not available to other programs or systems. Hence, although we shall regard the entries of the file as a kind of record, they will not be treated as such by Pascal. We shall, instead, place all of the information for a single word as one *line* of the file in Pascal.

The first piece of information in each entry is, of course, the word itself. This will occupy maxwd characters. Next we must indicate whether the word is to be indexed, or its occurrences counted. We do so by placing either the letter 'i' or 'c' after the word. Finally comes a list of page numbers for 'i' words, or a single integer count for 'c' words.

2. Setting up a node.

```
            procedure GetNode( var p: pointer; ch: char);
            {Reads a word from file InIndex and sets node correspondingly.}
            {Returns p = nil at eof or when next word starts later than ch.}

            var
              wordcode:char;                      {letter indicating type of word}

            begin                                        {Procedure GetNode}
              while (not eof(InIndex)) and (InIndex↑ = blank) do
                Get(InIndex);                            {Skip all leading blanks.}
              if eof(InIndex) then
                p := nil
```

```
    else if InIndex↑ > ch then
      p := nil
    else begin
      New(p);
      with p↑ do begin
        ReadWord(InIndex, wd);
        Read(InIndex, wordcode);
        if wordcode = 'i'
          then begin kind := index; ref := nil end
        else if wordcode = 'c'
          then begin kind := count; ct := 0  end
        else
          Writeln('Erroneous word code in file InIndex.');
      end;                              {with statement setting up node}
      Readln(InIndex)                   {Advance to start of next entry.}
    end
  end;                                             {Procedure GetNode}
```

Note that this procedure sets either the reference list to be empty or the count to be 0 (depending on the word type) for each word. The values to be put into the tree concern the new input document only; these values will be combined with the former values in InIndex during the third phase of the program.

6.4.4 Processing a reference.

Now that the binary tree has been built, the next task to be done in phase 2 is to process the references from the temporary file. The references are read in by the main procedure; we now can write the subsidiary procedure that processes a single reference, updating the binary tree appropriately. This procedure, of course, invokes several others. Its basic task is to search the binary tree for a node corresponding to the reference given as its calling parameter. If it finds such a node, then it invokes UpdateNode; if not, then it invokes NewWord to create a new node for the word, and InsertTree to put it into the binary tree.

The basic structure of these procedures is similar to that of corresponding procedures developed in Chapter 5, but the differences required by the specific application are enough that they are rewritten here in full.

1. The tree search.

```
    procedure Process( r: reference);
    {Takes word and page reference r, and updates binary tree.}

    var
      p:     pointer;                   {trace through tree}
      found: Boolean;                   {Is the word in the tree?}
```

```
begin                                        {Procedure Process}
  if root = nil then                         {The tree might be empty.}
    NewWord(root, r)
  else begin                                 {case of non-empty tree}
    p := root;                               {Begin a tree search.}
    found := false;
    repeat
      if r.wd = p↑.wd then
        found := true
      else if Lt(r.wd, p↑.wd) then
        p := p↑.left
      else
        p := p↑.right
    until found or (p = nil);

    if found then UpdateNode(p, r)
    else begin                               {p↑ was not found: add to tree.}
      NewWord(p, r);
      InsertTree(root, p)
    end
  end
end;                                         {Procedure Process}
```

2. Updating a node.

```
procedure UpdateNode( p: pointer; r: reference);
{Uses reference r to update information in node p↑}

var
  q: pointref;                               {used to add reference to list}

begin
  with p↑ do
    case kind of
      hash:;                                 {no action needed}
      count: ct := ct + 1;
      index: if ref = nil then
               begin
                 New(ref);
                 ref↑.pg : = r.pg;
                 ref↑.next: = nil
               end
```

```
                     else if ref↑.pg <> r.pg then
                     begin                          {Add the new reference to list.}
                       New(q);
                       q↑.pg: = r.pg;
                       q↑.next := ref;
                       ref: = q
                     end

              end                          {Case statement to update tree}
            end;                           {Procedure UpdateNode}
```

3. Creating a new node.

```
          procedure NewWord(var p: pointer; r: reference);
          {Creates a node for the first occurrence of a new reference r. A
          pointer to the new node is returned in p.}

          var
            response: char;                    {answer received from user}

          begin                                {Procedure NewWord}
            New(p);
            with p↑ do
            begin
              wd := r.wd;
              left := nil;
              right := nil;
              repeat                           {Ask user what kind of word}
                WriteWord(output, wd);
                Write('is (F, C, I)?');
                Read(response)
              until response in ['F', 'C', 'I' ,'f', 'c', 'i'];
              case response of
                'F','f': kind := hash;
                'C','c': begin
                           kind := count;
                           ct := 1
                         end;
                'I','i':  begin
                           kind := index;
                           New(ref);
                           ref↑.pg := r.pg;
                           ref↑.next := nil;
                         end
              end                                {Case statement}
            end                                  {With statement}
          end;                                   {Procedure NewWord}
```

4. Inserting a new node into the tree.

procedure InsertTree(r, p: pointer);
{Adds node p↑ to the tree with root r↑. Requires that r ≠ **nil** and p↑ not
be in tree. Proceeds by recursion.}

begin   {Procedure InsertTree}
  if Lt(p↑.wd, r↑.wd) **then**
    if r↑.left = **nil then** r↑.left := p
    else InsertTree(r↑.left, p)
  else
    if r↑.right = **nil then** r↑.right := p
    else InsertTree(r↑.right, p)
end;   {Procedure InsertTree}

6.4.5 Output the tree.

The only remaining task in phase 2 is to write the information from the binary tree into the output files. The overall structure of this task is a simple inorder traversal of the binary tree, as follows.

1. Binary tree traversal.

procedure OutputTree(p: pointer);
{Traverses the tree for which p↑ is the root in inorder.}

begin   {Procedure OutputTree}
  if p <> **nil then**
  with p↑ **do**
  begin
    OutputTree(left);   {Traverse left subtree}
    PutNode(p);
    OutputTree(right);   {Traverse right subtree}
    Dispose(p)
  end
end;   {Procedure OutputTree}

2. Output one node.

The information in a node of the binary tree will be written out in the same format as it was read from the text file InIndex. For nodes of types index or count, the information is written to file NewIndex, which in phase 3 will be merged with InIndex. For the nodes of type forget (hash), the words should not go into the word lists, but into a temporary file NewHashFile, which in phase 3 will be used to update the permanent HashFile.

```
procedure PutNode( p: pointer);

var
  q: pointref;                          {used to traverse list of references}

begin                                                {Procedure PutNode}
  with p↑ do
    case kind of
      hash: begin
              NewHashFile↑ := wd;
              Put( NewHashFile )
            end;
      count: if ct <> 0 then       {Otherwise, word is not in document}
             begin
               WriteWord(NewIndex, wd);
               Write(NewIndex, 'c');
               Writeln( NewIndex, ct:5)
             end;
      index: if ref <> nil then
             begin
               WriteWord(NewIndex, wd);
               Write(NewIndex, 'i');
               q := ref;
               repeat
                 Write( NewIndex, q↑.pg:5);
                 q := q↑.next
               until q = nil;
               Writeln( NewIndex )
             end
    end                                              {case statement}
end;                                                 {Procedure PutNode}
```

Exercises

1. Some Pascal systems provide facilities for returning blocks of storage to the system that are more efficient than the **dispose** procedure. If your system has such a facility, show how it can be used in this chapter's program.

2. Describe the changes needed to keep lists of unused space and reuse this space instead of relying on the standard procedures **new** and **dispose**.

3. Suppose that the temporary files of references are small enough that each of them will fit in memory. Implement the first plan for phase 2, wherein the list of references is first sorted and then compared with the master word list InIndex.

4. Implement the second plan for phase 2, in which each reference is first inserted into a hash table, and multiple entries are amalgamated. Afterward, the contents of the hash table are sorted and compared with the master word list InIndex.

5. The master word list can become a large file (for this book it is about 150,000 characters). A great deal (perhaps half) of this space is taken by blanks, since we represent each word as a blank-filled sequence of exactly maxwd characters. Describe the changes needed so that each word in the file will be terminated by its first blank, and extra blanks will not be stored in the file.

6.5 Phase 3: Updating the permanent files.

6.5.1 The hash file.

The new entries for the hash table are in the file NewHashFile. We need only use the same function HashAddress written in phase 1 to insert these entries into the table, and write the resulting table out to HashFile.

We now face a small organizational problem. If the same function HashAddress is needed both in phase 1 and in phase 3, should it not be declared at the level immediately within the main program, so that it will be available in both phases? It would certainly be reasonable to do so, but if we do, then we must also save space for the hash table at the same time, since the function refers to the table, and we would otherwise have undeclared variables. But in phase 2 we do not use the hash table, and cannot afford to lose the space that it would occupy. We are therefore unable to declare the table and its function at the outer level, and must instead write the same declarations out twice, once in phase 1 and once in phase 3.

The preceding problem points out a major deficiency of Pascal. Declarations have a strictly hierarchical range of validity in Pascal, which does not always meet the requirements of a program. In the current project, we would really like to use a *package* that would combine the hash table with its associated function, declare the package only once, and instruct the compiler that it should be included in phase 1 and phase 3, but not in phase 2. A good name for packages such as this is *information hiding module*, since we have no need to access the hash table except through the function in the one specific way.

With the conventions of standard Pascal, however, we have no choice except to write the function HashAddress a second time. While we are doing so, we can make a slight change in the function to include error checking. It is conceivable that the hash table becomes full, in which case the function will search interminably for an empty position. This search should be prevented by inserting a condition such as

if inc > (hashsize **div** 2) **then** $\cdots$

after inc is incremented by 1. The conditional statement should take appropriate action for overflow.

```
procedure UpdateHashFile;
{Reads in old hash table, inserts file of new entries; writes out to
HashFile}

var
  hash: array[hashentry] of word;
  x: hashentry;
  w: word;

begin                                   {Procedure UpdateHashFile}
  Reset(HashFile);
  if eof(HashFile) then       {HashFile is empty; create new table.}
    for x := 1 to hashsize do
      hash[x] := blankword
  else
    for x := 1 to hashsize do
      Read(HashFile, hash[x]);
  {Some versions of Pascal do not allow procedures Read and
Write for files other than text. For such systems, expand to use Get
                                                       and Put.}

  Reset(NewHashFile);
  while not eof(NewHashFile) do
  begin
    Read(NewHashFile, w);
    hash[HashAddress(w)] := w
    {If table is full, new entries will replace old ones.}
  end;

  Rewrite(HashFile);
  for x := 1 to hashsize do
    Write(HashFile, hash[x])

end;                                    {Procedure UpdateHashFile}
```

6.5.2 Merging the word lists.

The procedure for merging the new word list into the master word list involves no really new ideas, but the procedure is somewhat complicated by the need to combine two records into one when the same word appears in both lists. This task is assisted by the subsidiary procedure CopyLine. This procedure uses two Boolean parameters to determine whether it is beginning a new line (so that it should write out the word being processed) and whether it should end the current line. The procedure also reads in the word from the next record, in order to continue the usual buffering of one record.

```
procedure MergeIndices;
{Merges files NewIndex and InIndex into file OutIndex}

var
  u, v: word;
  m, n: integer;
  ukind,
  vkind: char;                              {Is the word of kind i or c?}

begin                                       {Procedure MergeIndices}
  Reset(NewIndex);
  Reset(InIndex);
  Rewrite(OutIndex);

  if eof(NewIndex) or eof(InIndex) then
    Writeln('One of the indices is empty. No merge done.')
  else begin
    ReadWord(NewIndex, u);
    ReadWord( InIndex, v);
    repeat
      if Lt(u,v) then
        CopyLine(u, NewIndex, true, true)
        {Boolean parameters mean, respectively: start new line; end
                                                                  line.}
      else if Lt(v,u) then
        CopyLine(v, InIndex, true, true)
      else begin            {Words are equal. Determine kind of word.}
        Read(NewIndex, ukind);
        Read( InIndex, vkind);
        if ukind <> vkind then
          Writeln('Inconsistent word types found in merge.');
        WriteWord(OutIndex, u);
        Write(OutIndex, ukind);
        if ukind = 'c' then
        begin
          Readln(NewIndex, m);
          Readln( InIndex, n);
          m := m + n;
          Writeln(OutIndex, m:5);
          if not eof(NewIndex) then ReadWord(NewIndex, u);
          if not eof( InIndex) then ReadWord( InIndex, v)
        end
```

```
    else begin                    {copy both lists of page numbers}
      CopyLine(u, NewIndex, false, false);
      CopyLine(v, InIndex, false, true)
    end
  end
until eof(NewIndex) or eof(InIndex);

while not eof(NewIndex) do
  CopyLine(u, NewIndex, true, true);
while not eof(InIndex) do
  CopyLine(v, InIndex, true, true)
{At most one of the two loops above will iterate.}

end
end;                              {Procedure MergeIndices}
```

1. Copying a line.

```
procedure CopyLine( var w: word; var F: text;  newline, endline:
                                                            Boolean);
{Copies the remainder of a line from the file F to OutIndex. If newline
is true, then the word w is also written, and kind is copied. If endline
is true, then the line written to OutIndex is ended.  The procedure also
reads a new word w from the next line in F.}

var
  n: integer;                     {number copied from file to file}
  kind: char;                     {word code copied from file to file}

begin                             {Procedure CopyLine}
  if newline then
  begin
    WriteWord(OutIndex, w);
    Read(F, kind);
    Write(OutIndex, kind)
  end else
    while (not eof(F)) and (not eoln(F)) and (F↑ = blank) do
      Get(F);

  while (not eof(F)) and (not eoln(F)) do
  begin
    Read(F, n);
    Write(OutIndex, n:5);
    while(not eoln(F)) and (F↑ = blank) do
      Get(F);                                        {Skip blanks}
  end;
```

```
ReadIn(F);
if not eof(F) then
  ReadWord(F, w);

if endline then WriteIn(OutIndex)
end;                                        {Procedure CopyLine}
```

6.5.3 Summary.

With this procedure, the program has been completely written. It is, as you can see, by far the longest program that has appeared in this book. It illustrates an

```
1.    program IndexText(InText, InIndex, NewIndex, OutIndex,
                  HashFile, Input, Output);        {main program}
2.        function Lt(u, v: word): Boolean;
3.        procedure ReadWord(var F: text; var w: word);
4.        procedure WriteWord(var F: text; w: word);

5.        procedure SplitWords;                      {phase 1}
6.            function HashAddress(w: word): hashentry;
7.            procedure Initialize;
8.            procedure GetWord;
9.                procedure GetChar(var ch: char);
10.               procedure AddChar(ch: char);
11.           procedure Conclude;

12.       procedure ClassifyWords;                   {phase 2}
13.           procedure BuildTree(var root: pointer; ch: char);
14.               procedure Insert(p: pointer);
15.               function Power2(c: integer): level;
16.               procedure FindRoot;
17.               procedure ConnectSubtrees;
18.               procedure GetNode(var p: pointer; ch: char);
19.           procedure Process(r: reference);
20.               procedure UpdateNode(p: pointer; r: reference);
21.               procedure NewWord(var p: pointer; r: reference);
22.               procedure InsertTree(r, p: pointer);
23.           procedure OutputTree(p: pointer);
24.               procedure PutNode(p: pointer);

25.       procedure UpdateHashFile;                  {phase 3}
26.           function HashAddress(w: word): hashentry;
27.       procedure MergeIndices;
28.           procedure CopyLine
```

Table 6.1.   Nesting of subprogram declarations

inescapable feature of large programs: it is impossible to keep all the details in mind at once. By concentrating first on the overall outline, and then on one section at a time, it is possible to write and debug the entire program. In the end, even so, the program must be put together to function as a single unit. At this stage the skills of a librarian become important, simply to keep track of all the subprograms and to put them in their proper places. In summary, then, the organizational structure of our program is shown in Table 6.1. All the necessary subprograms are listed, and the indenting shows the appropriate nesting of declarations.

6.6 Review, analysis, and maintenance.

Experience can either reinforce or change priorities, desires and goals. Experience in working with a program can show which features are strong and which are not, which capabilities are valuable and which should be modified. The index writing program of this chapter is by no means in final form. In fact, it is not presented here in the form in which it is actually used. The program is, instead, presented in a form as close as possible to that in which it was first designed and written (with bugs removed). The reason for this presentation is to illustrate that computer programming, like engineering or art, is an experimental subject where a first effort will usually need further refinement and polishing before it achieves complete satisfaction.

This section discusses some proposed changes for the program, some possible extensions of its capabilities, and some improvements that can be made in its structure. This section should be regarded as an extended set of exercises, an outline of various projects, some of which can be pursued almost indefinitely.

6.6.1 Convenience of use.

In its current form, our program is not as friendly as it might be. With a good-sized file the first phase will take significant time, during which the user is left in total silence. The program should keep the user informed of its progress during execution. At a minimum, one line might be printed for each page processed, indicating how the work is going. On the other hand, it is certainly possible to make the program too verbose. Printing the entire text as it is read would probably be excessive.

Failures can occur in the execution of any program, but every effort should be made to make them unlikely, and to minimize their effects. The input and output of our program should be refined (according to the features and requirements of a particular system) so that file-handling errors are completely processed and will not cause catastrophic failure. A large program like ours is always in danger of being manually interrupted by the user or the system (for example, time limits). At the moment, such interruption may destroy all the work already complete. All the files opened for output, for example, may be lost. If your system provides facilities for programmed processing of interrupts, or allows the program to complete an orderly shutdown, then by all means these facilities should be included in the program. If it is possible to salvage the incomplete files, then auxiliary programs should be written to do so, and, if possible, to allow the program to continue from where it was interrupted.

6.6.2 Flexibility and generality.

As written, our program tacitly assumes that the document is in its final form, with no errors and ready to be completely indexed. The major application of the program, however, will be to documents that are not in final form. The program is especially useful in checking spelling and consistency of word choice in different parts of a document. The output files should therefore not necessarily become part of a permanent record. The third phase of the program, which merges these output files into the permanent hash table and master word list, should probably be a separate program that could be run if the document is in final form, and otherwise need not be.

The program treats misspelled words in exactly the same way as correctly spelled words. There should be a special category for misspelled words or others that are questionable. After the program finishes, the words in this category should be collected for the user in some form to facilitate their investigation and correction. In fact, I find it convenient to split the "index" category of the program into three categories: category "i" contains the important terms that will be placed in an index; category "p" contains words that occur only a few times, and for which page references (a concordance) will be given. Category "?" includes the misspelled words and others that will probably be changed. Words in this last category are never merged into the permanent records.

Just because a word occurs frequently, it is not necessarily uninteresting. Frequency counts could certainly be kept for the words in the hash table, and would be of interest for some purposes. When first running the program to set up the initial word lists, it may not be evident to the user into which category to place some words. Words placed in the hash table may turn out to be not so common as other words. An interesting extension of phase 3 of the program would be another program to reallocate words among the various categories. The relative frequencies of words in the hash table, in category "c" and category "p" (give page references) would be determined, and appropriate criteria used to move words from one category to another.

A related project is to re-hash the hash table, according to frequency. The order in which words are inserted in the hash table is that in which they first appear. If the table is nearly full, then searches of several entries may be needed to find a particular word. Depending on the order of first appearance, common words can require longer searches than less common ones. Future runs of the program can therefore be speeded up by sorting all the words in the hash table according to frequency, and then inserting them all over again into an empty table according to this order.

Finally, it would probably be better to write the program as a series of several independent programs (*filters*), as proposed in part 5 of Section 6.2.1. In this way, different parts of the program could be used separately if needed in a particular application.

6.6.3 Use of space.

Our decision to represent words as fixed-length arrays of exactly maxwd = 20 characters wastes a great deal of space. Space in the files can easily be saved by eliminating trailing blanks from the words (as proposed in an exercise). Saving space in high-speed memory is more difficult, given the constraints of standard Pascal. It might be practical to use linked storage, with blocks of several letters in each node, but the programming would then become more complicated.

A more sophisticated method is to recognize that the usual way of representing individual letters in computer storage takes up a great deal of space, much more than is actually needed. Eight binary digits are usually used for each character. Within our words we allow upper and lower case letters, hyphens and apostrophes, for a total of only 54 characters. In six binary digits we can represent 64 distinct characters. Hence by using six instead of eight bits we can immediately reduce our space requirements by 25%. With a little more work we can save a great deal more. Not all characters are equally likely. The letter 'e' occurs much more frequently than 'z' or 'j'. A *Huffman encoding* is a system that produces a representation in which the common characters have very short codes, and the uncommon characters much longer codes, and thereby reduces the average space needed for a word.

If we look at sequences of letters we can do even better. In English the pair of letters 'th' occurs very frequently, while 'jj' or 'qb' almost never occur. In one large experiment (see the paper of McMahon, Cherry and Morris in the references) considering triples of letters and blanks, of the 21952 possible combinations, only 4923, or 22.4%, actually occur in a large text of about a half-million words. By using this and further methods, it is possible to devise representations of English text that will reduce the space needed, on average, to little more than 1.5 bits per character.

Such packing of characters requires execution time, of course. On the other hand, the speed of reading and writing files is slow compared to calculation. It is necessary, therefore, to reach a balance between a system that requires a great deal of calculation, but can minimize file accesses by keeping more information in high-speed memory, and a system that calculates very quickly but requires more file processing.

6.6.4 Spelling correction.

A highly desirable extension of the program is that it should not only detect words that are probably misspelled, but that it should be able to suggest or make corrections in the spelling. Such a goal cannot be completely within our reach until we can devise programs that understand the meaning rather than just the form of a text. Nonetheless, misprints tend to occur in predictable ways, and it is possible to use some of these patterns to suggest corrections. This topic is open-ended and the subject of considerable current work. See the references for summaries of some of this activity.

6.7 References for further study.

A good, starting point for learning some of the various approaches for designing programs like that of this chapter is the following survey paper.

> JAMES L. PETERSON, "Computer programs for detecting and correcting spelling errors," *Communications of the ACM* 23 (1980), 676–687; related correspondence and comments: *Ibid.* 24 (1981), 322, 331–332, 608–609, 618–619.

As you see from this list of pages, this survey paper has elicited considerable correspondence regarding alternative methods. This correspondence reflects substantial current interest in the development of spelling-correcting programs.

This paper includes an annotated bibliography of 44 items, constituting excellent source material for further study of the topics raised in this chapter. Let us single out a few of these sources, with some further references.

First is a book in which the author describes a much more elaborate spelling checking and correcting program (made up of 105 procedures).

> JAMES L. PETERSON, *Design of a spelling program: An experiment in program design,* Lecture Notes in Computer Science, volume 96, Springer-Verlag, Berlin, Heidelberg, New York, 1980.

A simple spelling corrector is described in:

> PETER ROBINSON and DAVE SINGER, "Another spelling correction program," *Communications of the ACM* 24 (1981), 296–297.

An interesting idea for a spelling checker, using multiple hashing functions to determine with high probability if a word is misspelled while using only 20% of the space needed for a dictionary, is:

> ROBERT NIX, "Experience with a space efficient way to store a dictionary," *Communications of the ACM,* 24 (1981), 297–298.

The observations in this chapter about word frequencies are taken from the following paper, which provides a good tutorial on a statistical approach to spelling checking and text compression:

> L. E. MCMAHON, L. L. CHERRY, and R. MORRIS, "Statistical text processing," *Bell System Tech. J.* 57 (1978), 2137–2154.

Word frequencies and other statistical information for a text of more than a million words are given in:

> H. KUCERA and W. FRANCIS, *Computational Analysis of Present-Day American English,* Brown University Press, Providence, R. I., 1967.

A very elementary exposition of techniques for text compression by (variable-length) Huffman codes is:

> HAROLD CORBIN, "An introduction to data compression," *Byte* 6, no. 4 (April, 1981), 218–226, 246–250.

Since the ability to locate a passage containing a given term is important for scholars, concordances have been used for many years, and, before the advent of computers, a great deal of labor was invested in developing such concordances. One of the best examples is the following book, which lists the chapter and verse of every word appearing in the King James translation of the Bible, and except for the forty-seven most common words, lists every occurrence of each word with its surrounding context.

> JAMES STRONG, *Exhaustive Concordance of the Bible,* Methodist Book, 1894 (available in many reprint editions).

Chapter 7

Recursion

As we have seen from studying sorting methods and binary trees, recursion is a valuable programming tool. This chapter presents several applications of recursion that further illustrate its usefulness. Some of these applications are simple; others are quite sophisticated. Later in the chapter we analyze how recursion is usually implemented on a computer. In the process, we shall obtain guidelines regarding good and bad uses of recursion, when it is appropriate, and when it should best be avoided.

The first several sections of this chapter study various applications of recursion, in order to illustrate a range of possible uses. The programs we write are chosen to be especially simple, but to illustrate features that often appear in much more complicated applications.

7.1 Divide and conquer.

All the uses that we have made of recursion so far are of the form called *divide-and-conquer*, which can be defined generally as the method of solving a problem by dividing it into two or more subproblems, each of which is similar to the original problem in nature, but smaller in size. Solutions to the subproblems are then obtained separately and combined to produce the solution of the original problem. Hence we can sort a list by dividing it into two sublists, sort them separately, and combine the results. We can traverse a binary tree by traversing the left and right subtrees of the root separately.

An even easier application of divide-and-conquer is the following recreational problem.

7.1.1 The Towers of Hanoi.

In the nineteenth century a game called the *Towers of Hanoi* appeared in Europe, together with promotional material (undoubtedly apocryphal) explaining that the game represented a task underway in the Temple of Brahma. At the creation of the world, the priests were given a brass platform on which were three diamond needles. On the first needle were stacked sixty-four golden disks, each one slightly smaller than the one under it. (The less exotic version sold in Europe had eight cardboard disks and three wooden posts.) The priests were assigned the task of moving all the golden disks from the first needle to the third, subject to the conditions that only one disk can be moved at a time, and that no disk is ever allowed to be placed on top of a smaller disk. The priests were told that when they had finished moving the sixty-four disks, it would signify the end of the world. See Figure 7.1.

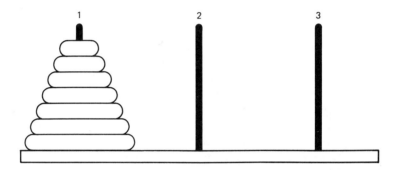

Figure 7.1. The Towers of Hanoi

Our task, of course, is to write a computer program that will type out a list of instructions for the priests. We can summarize our task by the instruction

Move(64,1,3,2)

which means: Move 64 disks from needle 1 to needle 3 using needle 2 for intermediate storage.

7.1.2 The solution.

The idea that gives a solution is to concentrate our attention not on the first step (which must be to move the top disk somewhere), but rather on the hardest step: moving the bottom disk. There is no way to reach the bottom disk until the top 63 disks have been moved, and, furthermore, they must all be on needle 2 so that we can move the bottom disk from needle 1 to needle 3. This is because only one disk can be moved at a time and the bottom (largest) one can never be on top of any other, so that when we move the bottom one, there can be no other disks on needles 1 or 3. Thus we can summarize the steps of our algorithm as:

```
Move(63,1,2,3);
Writeln('Move a disk from needle 1 to needle 3.');
Move(63,2,3,1)
```

We now have a small step toward the solution, only a very small one since we must still describe how to move the 63 disks two times, but a significant step nonetheless, since there is no reason why we cannot move the 63 remaining disks in the same way. (In fact, we must do so in the same way since there is again a largest disk that must be moved last.)

This is exactly the idea of recursion. We have described how to do the key step and asserted that the rest of the problem is done in essentially the same way.

7.1.3 Refinement.

To write the algorithm formally we shall need to know at each step which needle may be used for temporary storage, and thus we will invoke the procedure in the form

Move(n,a,b,c)

which will mean: *Move n disks from needle* a *to needle* b *using needle* c *as temporary storage.*

Supposedly our task is to be finished in a finite number of steps (even if it does mark the end of the world!), and thus there must be some way that the recursion stops. The obvious stopping rule is that, when there are no disks to be moved, there is nothing to do. We can now write the complete program to embody these rules.

```
program Hanoi(output);
const          ndisks = 64;
type           disk  = 0..ndisks;
               needle = 1..3;

procedure Move(n:disk; a,b,c: needle);
{moves n disks from a to b using c for temporary storage}
begin
  if n > 0 then begin
    Move(n — 1, a, c, b);
    Writeln('Move a disk from', a:2, ' to', b:2);
    Move(n — 1, c, b, a)
  end
end;                           {declaration of Procedure Move}

begin                                    {main program}
  Move(ndisks, 1, 3, 2)
end.
```

7.1.4 Analysis.

Note that this program not only produces a complete solution to the task, but it produces the best possible solution, and, in fact, the only solution that can be found except for the possible inclusion of redundant and useless sequences of instructions such as:

> *Move a disk from needle 1 to needle 2.*
> *Move a disk from needle 2 to needle 3.*
> *Move a disk from needle 3 to needle 1.*

This uniqueness of the irreducible solution is because, at every stage, the task to be done can be summarized as to move a certain number of disks from one needle to another, and there is no way to do this task except to move all the disks except the bottom one first, then perhaps make some redundant moves, then move the bottom one, possibly make more redundant moves, and finally move the upper disks again.

Next, let us find out how many times the recursion will proceed before starting to return and back out. The first time procedure **Move** is called it is with $n = 64$, and each recursive call reduces the value of n by 1. Thus, if we exclude the calls with $n = 0$, which do nothing, we have a total depth of recursion of 64. That is, if we were to draw the tree of recursive calls for the program, it would have 64 levels above its leaves. Except for the leaves, each vertex results in two recursive calls (as well as in writing out one instruction), and so the number of vertices on each level is exactly double that of the level above. The recursion tree for the somewhat smaller task that moves 3 disks instead of 64 appears as Figure 7.2.

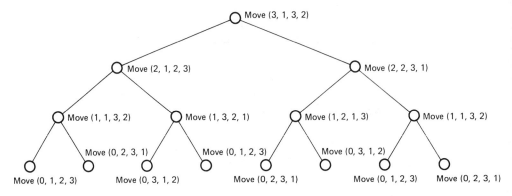

Figure 7.2. Recursion tree for 3 disks

From the recursion tree we can easily calculate how many instructions are needed to move 64 disks. One instruction is printed for each vertex in the tree, except for the leaves (which are calls with $n = 0$). The number of non-leaves is

$$1 + 2 + 4 + \cdots + 2^{63} = 2^{64} - 1,$$

and this is the number of moves required altogether.

We can estimate how large this number is by using the approximation

$$10^3 = 1000 < 1024 = 2^{10}.$$

There are about 3.2×10^7 seconds in one year. Suppose that the instructions could be carried out at the rather frenetic rate of one every second (the priests have plenty of practice). Since

$$2^{64} \;=\; 2^4 \times 2^{60} \;>\; 2^4 \times 10^{18} \;=\; 1.6 \times 10^{19},$$

the total task will then take about 5×10^{11} years. If astronomers estimate the age of the universe at about 10 billion (10^{10}) years, then according to this story the world will indeed endure a long time—50 times as long as it already has!

7.2 Postponing the work.

Divide and conquer, by definition, involves two or more recursive calls within the algorithm being written. In this section we illustrate two applications of recursion each using only one recursive call. In these applications one case or one phase of the problem is solved without using recursion, and the work of the remainder of the problem is postponed to the recursive call.

7.2.1 Generating permutations.

Our first example is the problem of generating the $n!$ permutations of n objects as efficiently as possible. If we think of the number $n!$ as the product

$$n! \;=\; 1 \times 2 \times 3 \times \cdots \times n,$$

then the process of multiplication can be pictured as the tree in Figure 7.3 (Ignore the labels for the moment).

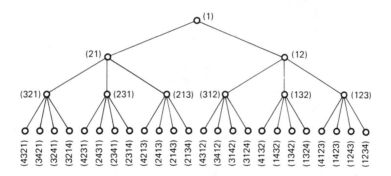

Figure 7.3. Permutation generation by multiplication, $n = 4$

1. The idea.

We can identify permutations with the nodes as given by the labels in Figure 7.3. At the top is 1 by itself. We can obtain the two permutations of $\{1, 2\}$ by writing 2 first on the left, then on the right of 1. Similarly, the six permutations of $\{1, 2, 3\}$

can be obtained by starting with one of the permutations (2, 1) or (1, 2) and inserting 3 into one of the three possible positions (left, center, or right). The task of generating permutations of $\{1, 2, \cdots, k\}$ can now be summarized as:

> *Take a given permutation of* $\{1, 2, \cdots, k-1\}$ *and regard it as an ordered list. Insert k, in turn, into each of the k possible positions in this ordered list, thereby obtaining k distinct permutations of* $\{1, 2, \cdots, k\}$.

This algorithm illustrates the use of recursion to complete tasks that have been temporarily postponed. That is, we can write a procedure that will first insert 1 into an empty list, and then use a recursive call to insert the remaining numbers from 2 to n into the list. This first recursive call will insert 2 into the list containing only 1, and postpone further insertions to a recursive call. On the nth recursive call, finally, the integer n will be inserted. In this way, having begun with a tree structure as motivation, we have now developed an algorithm for which the given tree becomes the recursion tree.

2. Refinement.

Let us restate the algorithm in slightly more formal terms. We shall invoke our procedure as

$$\text{Permute}(1, n)$$

which will mean to insert all integers from 1 to n to build all the $n!$ permutations. When it is time to insert the integer k, the remaining task is:

```
procedure Permute(k, n);
begin
  for each possible position in the list L do
  begin
    Insert k into the given position;
    if k = n        then ProcessPermutation
                    else Permute(k + 1, n);
    Remove k from the given position
  end
end;
```

The procedure ProcessPermutation will make whatever disposition is desired of a complete permutation of $\{1, 2, \cdots, n\}$. We might wish only to print it out, or we might wish to send it as input to some other task.

3. Data structures.

Let us now make some decisions regarding representation of the data. We use an ordered list to hold the numbers being permuted. This list is global to the recursive invocations of the procedure, that is, there is only the master copy of the list, and each recursive call updates the entries in this master list. Since we must continually insert and delete entries into and from the list, linked storage will be more flexible than keeping the entries in a contiguous list. But the total number of entries in the list never exceeds *n*, so we can (probably) improve efficiency by keeping the linked list within an array, rather than using dynamic memory allocation. Our links are thus integer indices relative to the start of the array. With an array, furthermore, the index of each entry, as it is assigned, will happen to be the same as the value of the number being inserted, so the need to keep this numerical value explicitly disappears, so that only the links need to be kept in the array.

Insertions and deletions are further simplified if we put an artificial first node at the beginning of the list, so that insertions and deletions at the beginning of the (actual) list can be treated in the same way as those at other positions, always as insertions or deletions after a node.

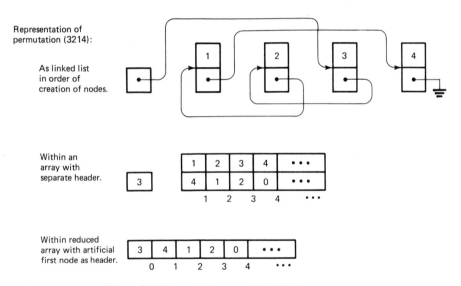

Figure 7.4. Permutation as a linked list in an array

This representation of a permutation as a linked list within an array is illustrated in Figure 7.4.

4. Final program.

With these decisions we can write our algorithm as a formal program.

```
program PermutationGenerator( Input, Output );
const
  maxdegree  = 20;              {maximum number of elements allowed}
type
  pointer  = 0..maxdegree;       {0 will always denote a nil pointer}
var
  L: array[ pointer ] of pointer;
  n: integer;

procedure Permute( k, n: pointer );
var
  p: pointer;                              {pointer to traverse list in L.}
begin
  p := 0;
  repeat
    L[k] := L[p];  L[p] := k;       {First insert k after entry p of list}
    if k = n then  ProcessPermutation              {defined externally}
              else  Permute(k + 1, n);
    L[p] := L[k];                              {Remove k from list.}
    p := L[p]                         {Advance p one position.}
  until p = 0                         {p = 0 at the end of list.}
end;                                            {Procedure Permute}

begin                                            {Main program}
  Write('Number of elements to permute?');
  Readln( n );
  if (n < 1) or (n > maxdegree) then Error       {defined externally}
  else begin
    L[0] := 0;                    {Set the list to be initially empty}

    Permute( 1, n)
  end
end.
```

Recall that the array L describes a linked list of pointers, and does not contain the objects being permuted. If, for example, it is desired to print the integers $\{1, \cdots, n\}$ being permuted, then the auxiliary procedure becomes:

```
procedure ProcessPermutation;
var q :pointer;                          {used to traverse linked list}
begin
  q := 0;
  while L[q] <> 0 do
  begin
    Write( L[q] );
    q := L[q]
  end;
  Writeln
end;
```

5. Comparisons.

It may be interesting to note that the simple algorithm developed here has execution time comparable with the fastest of all published algorithms for permutation generation. R. SEDGEWICK (reference at end of chapter) gives a survey of such algorithms, and singles out the following algorithm, devised by B. R. HEAP, as especially efficient.

```
procedure Permute(n : integer);
var
  c : integer;                           {pointer to traverse list in L.}
  t : integer;                           {used to swap entries in list.}
begin
  c := 1;
  if n > 2 then  Permute(n − 1)
           else  ProcessPermutation;
  while c < n do
  begin
    if odd(n) then begin t := L[n]; L[n] := L[1]; L[1] := t end
              else begin t := L[n]; L[n] := L[c]; L[c] := t end;
    c := c + 1;
    if n > 2 then  Permute(n − 1)
             else  ProcessPermutation
  end
end;
```

On a microcomputer running (interpretive) UCSD Pascal[*], this algorithm requires 101.4 seconds to generate the 40,320 permutations of 8 objects, whereas the linked-list algorithm accomplishes the task in 91.8 seconds, an improvement of about 10%. With other implementations these numbers will differ, of course, but it is safe to

[*] UCSD Pascal is a trademark of the Regents of the University of California.

conclude that the linked-list algorithm is at least comparable in efficiency. The correctness of the linked-list method, moreover, is obvious, whereas a proof that this other method actually generates all $n!$ distinct permutations of n objects is much more involved.

7.2.2 Backtracking : Non-attacking queens.

For our second example of an algorithm where recursion allows the postponement of all but one case, let us consider the puzzle of how to place eight queens on a chessboard so that no queen can take another. Recall that a queen can take another piece that lies on the same row, the same column, or the same diagonal (either direction) as the queen. The chessboard has eight rows and columns.

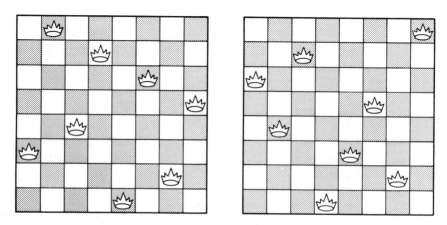

Figure 7.5. Two configurations showing eight non-attacking queens

It is by no means obvious how to solve this puzzle, and its complete solution defied even the great C. F. GAUSS, who attempted it in 1850. It is typical of puzzles that do not seem amenable to analytic solutions, but require either luck coupled with trial and error, or else much exhaustive (and exhausting) computation. To convince you that solutions to this problem really do exist, two of them are shown in Figure 7.5.

1. Solving the puzzle.

A person attempting to solve the eight queens problem will usually soon abandon attempts to find all (or even one) of the solutions by being clever, and will start to put queens on the board, perhaps randomly or perhaps in some logical order, but always making sure that no queen placed can take another already on the board. If the person is lucky enough to get eight queens on the board by proceeding in this way, then he has found a solution; if not, then one or more of the queens must be removed and placed elsewhere to continue the search for a solution. To start formulating a program, let us sketch this method in algorithmic form. We denote by n the number of queens on the board; initially $n = 0$. The key step is described as follows.

```
procedure AddQueen;
    for every unguarded position p on the board  do
    begin
        Place a queen in position p;
        n := n + 1;
        if n = 8 then print the configuration  else  AddQueen;
        Remove the queen from position p;
        n := n - 1
    end.
```

This sketch illustrates the use of recursion to mean "Continue to the next stage and repeat the task." Placing a queen in position p is only tentative; we leave her there only if we can continue adding queens until we have eight. Whether we reach eight or not, the procedure will return when it finds that it has finished or there are no further possibilities to investigate. After the inner call has returned, then, it is time to remove the queen from position p, because all possibilities with her there have been investigated.

2. Backtracking.

This procedure is typical of a broad class called **backtracking algorithms** that attempt to complete a search for a solution to a problem by constructing partial solutions, always ensuring that the partial solutions remain consistent with the requirements of the problem. The algorithm then attempts to extend a partial solution toward completion, but when an inconsistency with the requirements of the problem occurs, then the algorithm backs up (**backtracks**) by removing the most recently constructed part of the solution, and trying another possibility.

Backtracking proves useful in situations where many possibilities may first appear, but few survive further tests. In scheduling problems, for example, it will likely be easy to assign the first few matches, but as further matches are made the constraints drastically reduce the number of possibilities. Or consider the problem of designing a compiler. In some languages (but not Pascal) it is impossible to determine the meaning of a statement until almost all of it has been read. Consider, for example, the pair of FORTRAN statements

$$\text{DO 17 K} = 1,6$$
$$\text{DO 17 K} = 1.6$$

Both of these are legal : the first initiates a loop, and the second assigns the number 1.6 to the variable DO17K. In such cases where the meaning cannot be deduced immediately, backtracking is a useful method in *parsing* (that is, splitting apart to decipher) the text of a program.

3. Refinement : Choosing the data structures.

To fill in the details of our algorithm for the eight queens problem, we must first decide how we will determine which positions are unguarded at each stage, and how we will loop through the unguarded positions. This amounts to reaching some decisions about the representation of data in the program.

A person working on the eight-queens puzzle with an actual chessboard will probably proceed to put queens into the squares one at a time. We can do the same in a computer by introducing an 8×8 array with Boolean entries, and by defining an entry to be true if a queen is there and false if not. To determine if a position is guarded, the person would scan the board to see if a queen is guarding the position, and we could do the same, but doing so would involve considerable searching.

A person working the puzzle on paper or on a blackboard often observes that when a queen is put on the board, time will be saved in the next stage if all the squares that the new queen guards are marked off, so that it is only necessary to look for an unmarked square to find an unguarded position for the next queen. Again, we could do the same by defining each entry of our array to be true if it is free and false if it is guarded. A problem now arises, however, when we wish to remove a queen. We should not necessarily change a position that she has guarded from false to true, since it may well be that some other queen still guards that position. We can solve this problem by making the entries of our array integers rather than Boolean, each entry denoting the number of queens guarding the position. Thus, to add a queen we increase the count by 1 for each position on the same row, column, or diagonal as the queen, and to remove a queen we reduce the appropriate counts by 1. A position is unguarded if and only if it has a count of 0.

In spite of its obvious advantages over the previous attempt, this method still involves some searching to find unguarded positions, and some calculation to change all the counts at each stage. The algorithm will be adding and removing queens a great many times, so that this calculation and searching may prove expensive. A person working on this puzzle soon makes another observation that saves even more work.

Once a queen has been put in the first row, no person would waste time searching to find a place to put another queen in the same row, since the row is fully guarded by the first queen. There can never be more than one queen in each row. But our goal is to put eight queens on the board, and there are only eight rows. It follows that there must be a queen, exactly one queen, in every one of the rows. (This is called the *pigeonhole principle* : If you have n pigeons and n pigeonholes, and no more than one pigeon ever goes in the same hole, then there must be a pigeon in every hole.)

Thus we can proceed by placing the queens on the board one row at a time, starting with the first row, and we can keep track of where they are with a single array

var col : **array**[1..8] **of** 1..8

where col[i] gives the column containing the queen in row i. To make sure that no two queens are on the same column or the same diagonal, we need not keep and search through an 8×8 array, but we need only keep track of whether each column is free or guarded, and whether each diagonal is likewise. We can do this with three Boolean arrays, colfree, upfree, and downfree, where diagonals from the lower left to the upper right are considered upward, and those from the upper left to lower right are considered downward.

How do we identify the positions along a single diagonal? Along the main (downward) diagonal the entries are

$$[1,1], [2,2], \cdots, [8,8]$$

which have the property that the row and column indices are equal, that is, their difference is 0. It turns out that along any downward diagonal the row and column indices will have a constant difference. This difference is 0 for the main diagonal, and ranges from $1-8 = -7$ for the downward diagonal of length 1 in the upper right corner, to $8-1 = 7$ for the one in the lower left corner. Similarly, along upward diagonals the sum of the row and column indices is constant, ranging from $1+1 = 2$ to $8+8 = 16$.

After making all these decisions, we can now define all our data structures formally, and, at the same time, we can write the main program.

```
program Queen(Output);
var  col:       array[1..8] of 1..8;        {column with the queen}
     colfree:   array[1..8] of Boolean;         {Is the column free?}
     upfree:    array[2..16] of Boolean;
                                      {Is the upward diagonal free?}
     downfree:  array[-7..7] of Boolean;
                                      {Is the downward diagonal free?}
     row :      0 .. 8;          {row whose queen is currently placed}
     x :        integer;              {index to initialize arrays}

{Declaration of Procedure AddQueen to be inserted here}

begin
  row := 0;
  for x := 1 to 8     do colfree[x] := true;
  for x := 2 to 16    do upfree[x] := true;
  for x := -7 to 7    do downfree[x] := true;
  AddQueen
end.
```

Translation of the sketch of the procedure AddQueen into a program is straightforward, given the use of the arrays that have now been defined.

```
procedure AddQueen;
var  c  :1 .. 8;                              {Column being tried for queen}
begin
row := row + 1;
for c := 1 to 8 do
  if colfree[c] and upfree[row+c] and downfree[row−c] then
  begin                                       {Put a queen in position [row, c].}
    col[row] := c;    colfree[c] := false;
    upfree[row+c] := false; downfree[row−c] := false;
    if row = 8 then WriteBoard else AddQueen;
    {Now backtrack by removing the queen.}
    colfree[c] := true;
    upfree[row+c] := true; downfree[row−c] := true;
  end;                                        {processing queen at column c}
row := row − 1
end                                           {procedure AddQueen};
```

4. Local and global variables.

Note that in program **Queen** almost all the variables and arrays are declared in the main program, whereas in program **Hanoi** the variables were declared in the recursive procedure. If variables are declared within a procedure then they are local to the procedure and not available outside it. In particular, variables declared in a recursive procedure are local to a single occurrence of the procedure, so if the procedure is called again recursively, the variables are new and different, and the original variables will be remembered after the procedure returns. The copies of variables set up in an outer call are not available to the procedure during an inner recursive call. In program **Queen** we wish the same information about guarded rows, columns and diagonals to be available to all the recursive occurrences of the procedure, and to do this, the appropriate arrays are declared not in the procedure, but in the main program. The only reason for the array col[   ] is to communicate the positions of the queens to the procedure **Write-Board**. The information in this array is also preserved in the eight local copies of the variable c set up during the recursive calls, but only one of these local copies is available to the program at a given time.

5. Analysis of backtracking.

Finally, let us estimate the amount of work that our program will do. If we had taken the naive approach by writing a program that first placed all eight queens on the board, and then rejected the illegal configurations, then we would be investigating as many configurations as choosing eight places out of sixty-four, which is

$$\binom{64}{8} = 4,426,165,368.$$

The observation that there can be only one queen in each row immediately cuts this number to

$$8^8 \quad = \quad 16,777,216.$$

This number is still large, but our program will not investigate nearly this many positions. Instead, it rejects positions whose column or diagonals are guarded. The requirement that there be only one queen in each column reduces the number to

$$8! \quad = \quad 40,320$$

which is quite manageable by computer, and the actual number of cases the program considers will be much less than this (see exercises), since positions with guarded diagonals in the early rows will be rejected immediately, with no need to make the fruitless attempt to fill the later rows.

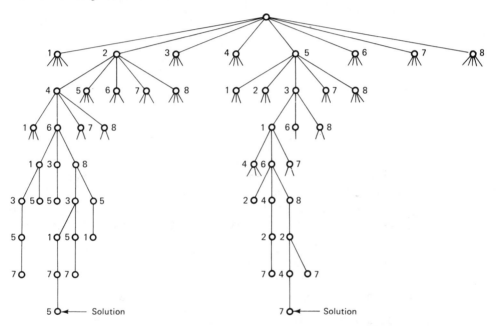

Figure 7.6. Part of the recursion tree, eight queens problem

This behavior summarizes the effectiveness of backtracking: positions that are early discovered to be impossible prevent the later investigation of many fruitless paths.

Another way to express this behavior of backtracking is to consider the tree of recursive calls to procedure **AddQueen**, part of which is shown in Figure 7.6. It appears formally that each vertex might have up to eight children corresponding to the recursive calls to **AddQueen** for the eight possible values of c. Even at levels near the root, however, most of these branches are found to be impossible, and the removal of one vertex on an upper level removes a multitude of its descendents. Backtracking is a most effective tool to prune a recursion tree to manageable size.

Exercises

1. What is the maximum depth of recursion in program Queen?

2. Starting with the following partial configuration of five queens on the board, construct the recursion tree of all situations that program Queen will consider in trying to add the remaining three queens. Stop drawing the tree at the point where the program will backtrack and remove one of the original five queens.

3. Run program Queen on your computer. You will need to write procedure Write-Board to do the output. In addition, find out exactly how many positions are investigated by including a counter that is incremented every time procedure AddQueen is started. [Note that a method that placed all eight queens before checking for guarded squares would be equivalent to eight calls to AddQueen.]

4. Modify the linked-list algorithm for generating permutations so that the position occupied by each number does not change by more than one to the left or to the right from any permutation to the next one generated. [This is a simplified form of one rule for *campanology* (ringing changes on church bells).]

5. Write a program that will read a molecular formula such as H_2SO_4 and will write out the molecular weight of the compound that it represents. Your program should be able to handle bracketed radicals such as in $Al_2(SO_4)_3$. [*Hint:* Use recursion to find the molecular weight of a bracketed radical. *Simplifications:* You may find it helpful to enclose the whole formula in brackets ($\cdots$). You will need to set up a table of atomic weights of elements, indexed by their abbreviations. For simplicity the table may be restricted to the more common elements. Some elements have one-letter abbreviations, and some two. For uniformity you may add blanks to the one-letter abbreviations.]

6. Describe a rectangular maze by indicating its paths and walls within an array. Write a backtracking program to find a way through the maze.

7. Another chessboard puzzle (this one reputedly solved by GAUSS at the age of four) is to find a sequence of moves by a knight that will visit every square of the board exactly once. Recall that a knight's move is to jump two positions either vertically or horizontally and at the same time one position in the perpendicular direction. Such a move can be accomplished by setting x to either 1 or 2, setting y to $3 - x$, and then changing the first coordinate by $\pm x$ and the second by $\pm y$ (providing the resulting position is still on the board). Write a backtracking program that will input an initial position and search for a knight's tour starting at the given position and going to every square once and no square more than once. If you find that the program runs too slowly, a good method to help the knight find his way is to order the list of squares to which he can move from a given position so that he will first try to go to the squares with the least accessibility, that is, to the squares from which there are the fewest knight's moves to squares not yet visited.

8. [Stable marriage problem] Suppose that there are n men and n women, and that each woman has ranked all the men according to her preferences, and each man has ranked all the women according to his preferences. Write a backtracking algorithm that will pair all the men with all the women so that the following stability criterion is satisfied. Suppose that man M and woman W have been paired. This pair is stable provided that, for all other pairs of man N and woman X, either M prefers W to X, or X prefers N to M. If the pair were not stable, then M might desert W and run off with X, leaving W and N unmatched. The total matching is stable provided that all its pairs are stable.

7.3 Tree-structured programs: Look-ahead in games.

In games of mental skill the person who can anticipate what will happen several moves in advance has a substantial advantage over a competitor who looks only for immediate gain. In this section we develop a computer algorithm to play games by looking at possible moves several steps in advance. This algorithm can be described most naturally in terms of a tree; afterward we show how recursion can be used to program this tree structure.

7.3.1 Game trees.

We can picture the sequences of possible moves by means of a *game tree*, in which the root denotes the initial situation and the branches from the root denote the legal moves that the first player could make. At the next level down, the branches correspond to the legal moves by the second player in each situation, and so on, with branches from vertices at even levels denoting moves by the first player, and branches from vertices at odd levels denoting moves by the second player.

The complete game tree for the trivial game of *Eight* is shown in Figure 7.7. In this game the first player chooses one of the numbers 1, 2 or 3. At each later turn the appropriate player chooses one of 1, 2 or 3, but the number previously chosen is not allowed. A running sum of the numbers chosen is kept, and if a player brings this sum to exactly 8, then the player wins. If the player takes the sum over 8, then the other player wins. No draws are possible. In the diagram, F denotes a win by the first player, and S a win by the second player.

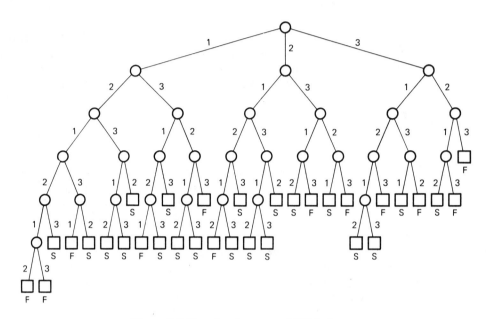

Figure 7.7. Tree for the game of "Eight"

Even a trivial game like "Eight" produces a good-sized tree. Games of real interest like *Chess* or *Go* have trees so huge that there is no hope of investigating all the branches, and a program that runs in reasonable time can examine only a few levels below the current vertex in the tree. People playing such games are also unable to see every possibility to the end of the game, but they can make intelligent choices, because, with experience, a person comes to recognize that some situations in a game are much better than others, even if they do not guarantee a win. Thus for any interesting game that we propose to play by computer, we shall need some kind of evaluation function that will examine the current situation and return a number assessing its benefits. To be definite, we shall assume that large numbers reflect favorable situations for the first player, and therefore small (or more negative) numbers show an advantage for the second player.

7.3.2 The minimax method.

Part of the tree for a fictional game appears in Figure 7.8. Since we are looking ahead, we need the evaluation function only at the leaves of the tree (that is, the positions from which we shall not look further ahead in the game), and from this information we wish to select a move. The move we eventually select is a branch coming from the root, and we take the evaluation function from the perspective of this player, which means that this player selects the maximum value possible. At the next level down the other player will select the smallest value possible, and so on. By

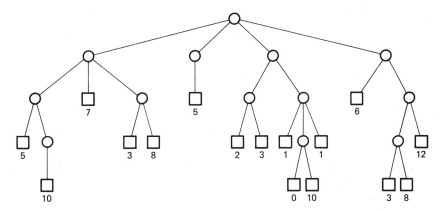

Figure 7.8. A game tree with values assigned at the leaves

working up from the bottom of the tree we can assign values to all the vertices. Since we alternately take minima and maxima, this process is called a ***minimax*** procedure. The result is shown in Figure 7.9 (the dotted lines will be explained later, in one of the exercises). The value of the current situation is 7, and the current (first) player should choose the leftmost branch.

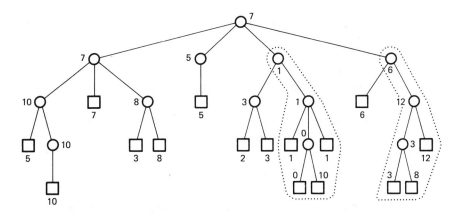

Figure 7.9. Minimax evaluation of a game tree

7.3.3 Algorithm development.

Next let us see how the minimax method can be embodied in a formal algorithm for looking ahead in a game-playing program. We wish to write a general-purpose algorithm that can be used with any two-player game; we shall therefore leave various types and data structures unspecified, since their choice will depend on the particular game being played. First, we shall need to use a procedure that we call

procedure Recommend(P: player; **var** L: list; **var** v: value)

that will return a list L of recommended moves for the player P, as well as a value v that depends on the current situation in the game (but not yet on which of the recommended moves is eventually made). For the player we use the simple type declaration

type player = (first, second)

and always take the first player as the one who wishes to maximize the value, while the second player wishes to minimize the value. The value will normally be a number.

How the list of recommended moves is to be stored depends on the game. In some games the moves can be described concisely and only a few different kinds of moves are appropriate; for such games contiguous storage may be best. In other games the number of recommended moves can change greatly from one turn to another, and a linked list may prove better. Hence we leave the type list unspecified and use auxiliary procedures FirstEntry(L, m) and NextEntry(L, m) to obtain the first and subsequent moves m from the list, a Boolean function Finished(L) to determine when traversing the list is complete, and an integer function Size(L) to return the number of entries.

Before writing the procedure that looks ahead in the tree, we should decide when the algorithm is to stop looking further. For a game of reasonable complexity, we must establish a number of levels maxdepth beyond which the search will not go. But there are at least two other conditions under which exploring the tree is unnecessary. The first occurs when the procedure Recommend returns a list with only one recommended move, and the other occurs when the outcome of the game is already completely determined (it is a certain win, loss, or tie). We coalesce these two conditions by requiring procedure Recommend to return only one move when the outcome of the game is certain. Thus, even if procedure Recommend finds several winning moves, it must return only one of them.

The basic task of looking ahead in the tree can now be described with the following recursive algorithm.

procedure LookAhead(depth: integer; P: player;
                                     var m: move; **var** v: value);
    {Searches as many as depth levels through the game tree; returns the
    move m for player P, and the value v as an assessment of the situation.}

begin
  Recommend(P, L, v);
  if the list L contains only one recommended move **then**
    Return the one move and associated value
  else begin
    for each recommended move **do**
      Tentatively make the move and recursively LookAhead for the
      other player's best move;
      Select the best value for P among the values returned in the loop
      above;
      Return the corresponding move and value as the result
  end
end.

7.3.4 Refinement.

To specify the details of this algorithm we must, finally, employ two more procedures that depend on the game:

  MakeMove(P: player; m: move) and UndoMove(P: player; m: move)

that make and undo tentative moves as indicated. In the formal procedure we also
rearrange some of the steps from the outline.

  procedure LookAhead(depth: integer; P: player; **var** m: move;
                                                    var v: value);
  {Searches as many as depth levels through the game tree; returns the
  move m for player P, and the value v as an assessment of the situation.}

  var
    opponent: player;   {opponent of P}
    om: move;   {recommended move for opponent}
    ov: value;   {value returned for opponent's move}
    L: list;   {list of recommended moves for P}
    tm: move;   {tentative move being tried in tree}
  begin
    Recommend(P, L, v);
    if Size(L) <= 0 **then**
      Forfeit   {cannot make any move}
    else if (Size(L) = 1) **or** (depth = 0) **then**
      FirstEntry(L, m)   {return the one move as answer;
                                  the value v has been set by Recommend}

```
        else begin
          if P = first then
          begin
            opponent := second;
            v := −infinity       {set to a value less than any that occurs}
          end else begin
            opponent := first;
            v := infinity
          end;
          FirstEntry(L, tm);
          repeat
            MakeMove(P, tm);
            LookAhead( depth − 1, opponent, om, ov);
            UndoMove(P, tm);
            if (P = first) and (ov > v) then
              begin v := ov;  m := tm end
            else if (P = second) and (ov < v) then
              begin v := ov;  m := tm  end;
            NextEntry(L, tm)
          until Finished(L)
        end
      end;
```

Exercises

1. Assign values of +1 for a win by the first player and −1 for a win by the second player in the game of "Eight", and apply the minimax procedure to its tree as shown in Figure 7.7.

2. A variation of the game of *Nim* begins with a pile of sticks, from which a player can remove 1, 2, or 3 sticks at each turn. The player must remove at least 1 (but no more than remain on the pile). The player who takes the last stick loses. Draw the complete game tree that begins with (a) 5 and (b) 6 sticks. Assign appropriate values for the leaves of the tree, and evaluate the other nodes by the minimax method.

3. Draw the game tree, assign values to the leaves, and apply the minimax evaluation for the game of *tic-tac-toe (noughts and crosses)*. Stop the game when it becomes a certain tie (or one player wins). You may reduce the size of the tree by taking advantage of symmetries: At the first move, for example, show only three possibilities (the center square, a corner, or a side square) rather than all nine. Further symmetries near the root will reduce the size of the game tree.

4. Write the auxiliary subprograms FirstEntry(L, m), NextEntry(L, m), Finished(L), and Size(L) for the case when the list is (a) contiguous and (b) linked.

5. Write a main program and the other procedures needed to play "Eight" against a human opponent. Procedure **Recommend** can return all legal moves at each turn.

6. Write a look-ahead program for playing tic-tac-toe. In the simplest version, procedure **Recommend** returns all empty positions as recommended moves. Approximately how many possibilities will then be investigated in a complete search of the game tree? Implement this simple method. Second, modify the procedure **Recommend** so that it searches for two marks in a row with the third empty, and thereby recommends moves more intelligently. Compare the running times of the two versions.

7. Consider the following game played on an $n \times n$ board. Each player alternately puts a 1 or a 0 into an empty square (either player can use either number), and the game continues until the board is completely filled. The numbers along each row, column, and the two main diagonals are then added. If there are more odd sums than there are even sums, then the first player wins. If the number of even sums is greater, then the second player wins. Otherwise, the game is a tie. Write a look-ahead program to play this game against a human opponent, who chooses the value of n.

8. [*Major project*] Write a look-ahead program that plays three dimensional tic-tac-toe. This game is played on a $4 \times 4 \times 4$ cube, with the usual rules. There are 76 possible winning lines (rows, columns, stacks and diagonals) with four in a row.

9. [*Major project*] Write a look-ahead program for the game of *Kalah* (see references at end of chapter for rules and strategy).

10. If you have worked your way through the tree in Figure 7.8 in enough detail, you may have noticed that it is not necessary to obtain the values for all the vertices while doing the minimax process, for there are some parts of the tree in which the best strategy certainly cannot appear. Let us suppose that we work our way through the tree starting at the lower left, and filling in the value for a parent vertex as soon as we have the values for all its children. After we have done all the vertices in the two main branches on the left, we find values of 7 and 5, and therefore the maximum value will be at least 7. When we go to the next vertex on level 1 and its left child, we find that the value of this child is 3. At this stage we are taking minima, so the value to be assigned to the parent on level 1 cannot possibly be more than 3 (it is actually 1). Since 3 is less than 7, the first player will take the leftmost branch instead, and we can exclude the other branch. The vertices that, in this way, need never be evaluated, are shown within dotted lines in Figure 7.9. The process of eliminating vertices in this way is generally called **alpha-beta pruning**. The letters α (alpha) and β (beta) are generally used to denote the cutoff points found.

    Modify the procedure **LookAhead** so that it uses alpha-beta pruning to reduce the number of branches investigated. Compare the performance of the two versions in playing several games.

7.4 Compilation by recursive descent.

Consider the problem of designing a compiler that translates a program written in Pascal into machine language. As the compiler reads through the source program written in Pascal, it must understand the syntax and translate each line into the equivalent instructions in machine language.

The first part of a Pascal program (or subprogram) contains declarations of labels, constants, types and variables. The compiler will use this information to allocate space for variables, and to determine what kinds of operations can be done with the variables. At the same time, the compiler must remember the identifiers that have been declared as names of types, variables, and the like, so that these identifiers can be interpreted correctly when they appear later in the program. Hence the compiler sets up a *symbol table* to keep track of the identifiers. Some compilers use a binary tree to contain the symbol table; others use a hash table; still other compilers use some combination or some other data structure. Although many interesting ideas appear in the design and use of symbol tables, our goal here is only to obtain an overview of how a compiler can use recursion, so we shall not study symbol tables further.

The next part of a Pascal program contains declarations of procedures and functions, and the final part consists of the action (statements) of the program. When we come to the declarations of procedures and functions, we can see a good application of recursion. Pascal syntax is designed so that the overall form of a subprogram is the same as that of the main program. Hence there is no need to write another complete section of the compiler to translate the declarations and statements within a subprogram. Instead, the compiler can in essence call itself recursively to compile each subprogram, and after the recursive call returns, it will go on to compile the next subprogram. After all subprograms are compiled, it will translate the statements in the main program. The main program itself, in fact, can be regarded as a subprogram within a mythical outer block in which all the standard identifiers (such as the constant maxint, the types Boolean and text, the procedures writeln and dispose) have already been declared. In this way the main program can be treated almost completely symmetrically with subprograms.

7.4.1 The main program.

The overall task of the compiler is thus described as follows:

```
program PascalCompiler;
begin
  Set up symbol table and declarations for all standard identifiers;
  Check that first word of the input is 'program';
  DoModule
  Check that the last symbol is a period '.'
end.
```

The procedure DoModule translates a program, procedure, or function.

Note that the compiler must continually check what is the next word or symbol in the program. Depending on what this word or symbol is, various actions will be taken. Such a word or symbol is called a *token*, and for our purposes we take a token to be any one of a Pascal reserved word, identifier, literal constant, operator, or punctuation mark. Note, furthermore, that the only way to tell that many constructions in Pascal have terminated is when a token is found that is *not* part of the construction. A statement, for example, terminates when the next token is a semicolon or one of the words **end, else,** or **until.** Hence whenever we start to process part of the program, the variable nexttoken will be the token that initiates that part, and when the processing is complete, then nexttoken will be the first token not in the part just processed. The procedure GetToken will split out the next token.

With this understanding, we can expand the procedure DoModule. The first step it will do is to obtain the next token, so it will effectively skip over the word **program, procedure,** or **function,** and it is essentially irrelevant which of these is being processed.

```
procedure DoModule;
begin
  Initialize the symbol table for the symbols in this module.
  GetToken(nexttoken);
  if nexttoken  = '(' then DoParameters;  {returns after matching ')'}
  if nexttoken  = 'label' then DoLabelSection;
  if nexttoken  = 'const' then DoConstantSection;
  if nexttoken  = 'type' then DoTypeSection;
  if nexttoken  = 'var' then DoVariableSection;
  while (nexttoken  = 'function') or (nexttoken ='procedure')
          do DoModule;
  if nexttoken  = 'begin' then DoCompoundStatement else Error
end;
```

7.4.2 Type declarations.

In order to see a further application of recursion, let us take a slightly more detailed look at the declaration of types. In Pascal, arrays may contain arrays; records may contain records. A well-designed compiler will use a separate procedure to process each of the standard categories of types. Thus there will be a procedure DoType that will, as required, invoke procedures that we call DoArray, DoRecord, DoSet, and DoScalarType (amongst others). The way in which these procedures work is closely related to their syntax diagrams. In particular, DoArray will invoke DoScalarType to determine the type by which the array is indexed, and DoType to determine the type of the entries. DoRecord will invoke a procedure called DoVariable for each of the fields within the record. DoVariable will, in turn, invoke DoType to find out the type of the variable. These recursive calls thus eventually work their way down to the simple types, and the meaning of the entire construction is then determined.

The process of splitting a text or expression into pieces to determine its syntax is called ***parsing***. Parsing can proceed either by first examining the atomic (indivisible) building blocks and how they are put together (called ***bottom-up parsing***), or by splitting the text or expression into simpler components (called ***top-down parsing***). Hence comes the motivation for the term ***recursive descent***: the compiler parses large constructions by splitting them into smaller pieces, and recursively parses each of the pieces. It thereby descends to simpler and smaller constructions, which are finally split apart into their atomic components, which can be evaluated directly.

As a simple example, consider the following declaration, which results in the tree of procedure calls shown in Figure 7.10. **Index** is a scalar type previously defined in the program:

```
type item = array[ index ] of
    record
        a: record u: integer; v: index end;
        b: set of index;
        c: array[ index ] of real;
    end;
```

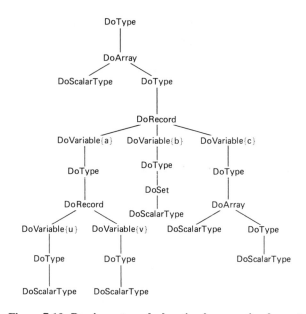

Figure 7.10. Parsing a type declaration by recursive descent

7.4.3 Parsing statements.

Parsing the action part of a program also proceeds by recursive descent. The action part is a compound statement, and is parsed by the procedure Do-

CompoundStatement. A compound statement is made up of 0 or more statements, each of which will be parsed by DoStatement, which, in turn, invokes a different procedure for each possible kind of statement.

As an example, let us see how an **if** statement might be parsed and translated into an assembler language (that is, into a language that corresponds directly with machine-level instructions, but still allows symbolic names and statement labels). From its syntax diagram, we know that an **if** statement consists of the token **if** followed by a Boolean expression, followed by the token **then** and a statement, and finally optionally followed by the token **else** and another statement. See Figure 7.11.

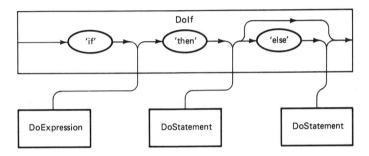

Figure 7.11. Parse tree for an if statement

The assembler-language equivalent of the **if** statement will first evaluate the expression, and then use conditional jumps (**goto** statements) to branch around the assembler code corresponding to the statements in the **then** or **else** clauses, as appropriate. The syntax diagram therefore translates into the following procedure.

```
procedure DoIf;
begin
    GetToken(nexttoken);
    DoExpression;                          {This will write the assembler code to
                                            evaluate the Boolean expression.}

    if nexttoken <> 'then' then Error
    else begin
    Generate a new assembler-language label x;
    Write assembler code that will cause a conditional jump
            to label x when the Boolean expression is false;
    GetToken(nexttoken);
    DoStatement;  {This will write the assembler code that corresponds to the
                                            statement in the then clause.}
```

if nexttoken $=$ **'else' then**
begin
   Generate a new assembler-language label y;
   Write an assembler unconditional jump to label y;
   Write the label x at this point in the assembler code;
   GetToken(nexttoken);
   DoStatement;   {This will write the assembler code that corre-
                           sponds to the statement in the else clause.}
   Write the label y at this point in the assembler code
end
else begin   {case with no else clause}
   Write the label x at this point in the assembler code
end
end;

Finally, as an exercise you should apply this algorithm to the statement

if a $>$ 0 **then** b $:=$ 1 **else if** a $=$ 0 **then** b $:=$ 2 **else** b $:=$ 3;

Since this line is made up of two **if** statements, the parsing procedure will call itself recursively, and generate a total of four labels. The parse tree for this statement is shown in Figure 7.12.

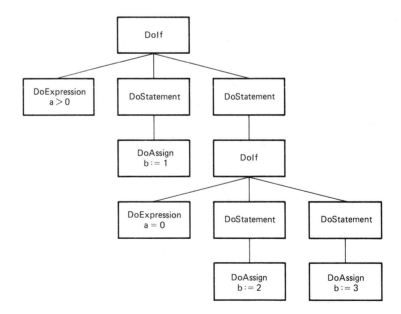

Figure 7.12. Parse tree for nested if statement

In practice, an actual compiler may rearrange some of the jumps and thereby produce an answer superficially different from yours. The output of one such compiler (OMSI Pascal® for the PDP/11®) applied to the preceding statement is given in Figure 7.13, where the only changes made from the actual output of the compiler are to replace some numeric displacements calculated by the compiler by their symbolic forms. This particular compiler generates extra statement labels because, for technical reasons, it must follow the wasteful practice of generating branch instructions to do nothing but branch around other jump instructions. In the resulting PDP/11 assembler language, the instruction TST tests the sign of an integer; BEQ branches if the integer is equal to 0, BGT if it is greater than 0. JMP is an unconditional jump. MOV moves the first number given to the second location specified.

```
        TST     A       ; if a > 0 then
        BGT     L0
        JMP     L1
L0:     MOV     #1,B    ; b := 1
        JMP     L2      ; else if a = 0 then
L1:     TST     A
        BEQ     L3
        JMP     L4
L3:     MOV     #2,B    ; b := 2
        JMP     L5      ; else
L4:     MOV     #3,B    ; b := 3
L5:
L2:
```

Figure 7.13. Output from a Pascal compiler

As you can see from all this, the construction of a compiler is quite a complicated process. A typical Pascal compiler (when written in Pascal) may be five to ten thousand lines of code. The index-writing program of Chapter 6, by comparison, is only about one thousand lines. The present section has attempted only to give a broad overview of the way in which recursion proves useful in writing a compiler. If you take a more detailed view, you will find that we have not only omitted programming steps, but that it is necessary to address many problems that we have not considered at all (for example, error processing). Many interesting ideas arise in the consideration of these problems, so that compiler design and construction constitute a major subject within computer science, one worthy of extensive study in its own right.

® OMSI Pascal is a trademark of Oregon Software, Inc. PDP is a trademark of Digital Equipment Corporation.

Exercises

1. For each of the following declarations, draw a tree similar to Figure 7.10 showing the subprogram calls that will occur in parsing the declaration.

   (a) **type** complex = **record** x: real; y: real **end;**
   (b) **type** list = **record** count: index; L: **array**[index] **of** item **end;**
   (c) **var** X: list;
   (d) **var** A: **array**[index] **of set of** index;

2. For each of the following statements, draw a tree similar to Figure 7.12 showing the subprogram calls that will occur in parsing the statement. You may assume the existence of subprograms such as DoCase, DoWhile, etc.

   (a) **while** x > 0 **do if** x > 10 **then** x := −x **else** x := y − x;
   (b) **if** a > b **then if** c > d **then** x := 1 **else if** e > f **then** x := 3;
   (c) **begin end;**

3. Draw parse trees and write outlines of procedures for parsing the following kinds of statements.

   (a) **while** expression **do** statement.
   (b) Compound statement: **begin** statement(s) **end.**
   (c) **case** ··· **end.**
   (d) **for** variable := expression **to** (or **downto**) expression **do** statement.

4. Write a Pascal procedure GetToken that will read through an input text and return each token (as defined in this section) one at a time as the procedure is invoked.

7.5 Principles of recursion.

7.5.1 Guidelines for using recursion.

Recursion is a tool to allow the programmer to concentrate on the key step of an algorithm, without having initially to worry about coupling that step with all the others. As usual with problem solving, the first approach should usually be to consider several simple examples, and as these become better understood, to attempt to formulate a method that will work more generally. In regard to using recursion, you may begin by asking yourself, "How can this problem be divided into parts?" or "How will the key step in the middle be done?" Be sure to keep your answer simple but generally applicable. Do not come up with a multitude of special cases that work only for small problems or at the beginning and end of large ones. Once you have a simple, small step toward the solution, ask whether the remainder of the problem can be done in the same or a similar way, and modify your method if necessary so that it will be sufficiently general.

Once the key step is determined, find a stopping rule that will indicate that the problem or a suitable part of it is done. Build this stopping rule into your key step. You should now be able to write the main program and a recursive procedure that will describe how to carry the step through.

Next, and of great importance, is a verification that the recursion will always terminate. Start with a general situation and check that in a finite number of steps the stopping rule will be satisfied and the recursion terminate. Be sure also that your algorithm correctly handles extreme cases. When called on to do nothing, any algorithm should be able to return graciously, but it is especially important that recursive algorithms do so, since a call to do nothing is often the stopping rule.

The key tool for the analysis of recursive algorithms is the recursion tree. As we shall see in the next section, the height of the tree is closely related to the amount of memory that the program will require, and the total size of the tree reflects the number of times the key step will be done, and hence the total time the program will use. It is usually highly instructive to draw the recursion tree for one or two simple examples appropriate to your problem.

7.5.2 How recursion works.

The question of how recursion is actually done in a computer should be carefully separated in our minds from the question of using recursion in designing algorithms. In the design phase, we should use all problem-solving methods that prove to be appropriate, and recursion is one of the most flexible and powerful of these tools. In the implementation phase, we may need to ask which of several methods is the best under the circumstances. There are at least two ways to accomplish recursion in computer systems. At present, the first of these is experimental and not generally available in commercial systems, but with changing costs and capabilities of computer equipment, it will probably soon be regarded as quite practical. Our major point in considering two different implementations is that, although restrictions in space and time do need to be considered, they should be considered separately from the process of algorithm design, since different kinds of computer equipment in the future may lead to different capabilities and restrictions.

1. Multiple processors: Concurrency.

Perhaps the most natural way to think of implementing recursion is to think of each subprogram not as occupying a different part of the same computer, but to think of each subprogram as running on a separate machine. In that way, when one subprogram invokes another, it starts the corresponding machine going, and when the other machine completes its work, then it sends the answer back to the first machine, which can then continue its task. If a procedure makes two recursive calls to itself, then it will simply start two other processors working with the same instructions that it is using. When these processors complete their work, they will send the answers back to the processor that started them going. If they, in turn, make recursive calls, then they will simply start still more processors working.

At one time, the central processor was the most expensive component of a computer system, and any thought of a system including more than one processor would have been considered extravagant. The price of processing power compared to other computing costs has now dropped radically, and in all likelihood we shall, before long, see large computer systems that will include hundreds, if not thousands, of identical microprocessors among their components. When this occurs, implementation of recursion via multiple processors will become commonplace if not inevitable.

With multiple processors, programmers will no longer consider algorithms solely as a linear sequence of actions, but will instead realize that some parts of the algorithm can be done at the same time as other parts. In divide-and-conquer algorithms such as quicksort or binary tree traversal, for example, the two halves into which the problem is divided often do not depend on each other, and can be worked on simultaneously by multiple processors.

Processes that take place simultaneously are called **concurrent**. The study of concurrent processes and the methods for communication between them is, at present, an active subject for research in computing science, one in which important developments will undoubtedly improve the ways in which algorithms will be described and implemented in coming years.

2. Single processor implementation: Storage areas.

In order to determine how recursion can be efficiently implemented in a system with only one processor, let us for the moment leave recursion to consider the question of what steps are needed to call a subprogram, on the primitive level of machine-language instructions in a simple computer. The hardware of any computer has a limited range of instructions, that includes (amongst other instructions) doing arithmetic on specified words of storage or on registers, moving data to and from the memory, and branching (jumping) to a specified address. When a calling program branches to the beginning of a subprogram the address of the place whence the call was made must be stored in memory, or else the subprogram could not remember where to return. The addresses or values of the calling parameters must also be stored where the subprogram can find them, and where the answers can in turn be found by the calling program after the subprogram returns. When the subprogram starts, it will do various calculations on its local variables and storage areas. Once the subprogram finishes, however, these local variables are lost, since they are not available outside the subprogram. The subprogram will of course have used the registers within the CPU for its calculations, so normally these would have different values after the subprogram finishes than before it is called. It is traditional, however, to expect that a subprogram will change nothing except its calling parameters or global variables (side effects). Thus it is customary that the subprogram will save all the registers it will use, and restore their values before it returns.

In summary, when a subprogram is called, it must have a storage area (perhaps scattered as several areas); it must save the registers or whatever else it will change, using the storage area also for its return address, calling parameters, and local variables. As it returns it will restore the registers and the other storage that it was expected to restore. After the return it no longer needs anything in its local storage area.

In this way we implement subprogram calls by changing storage areas, an action that takes the place of changing processors that we considered before. In these considerations it really makes no difference whether the subprogram is called recursively or not, providing that, in the recursive case, we are careful to regard two recursive calls as being different, so that we do not mix the storage areas for one call with those of another, any more than we would mix storage areas for different subprograms, one called from within the other. For a non-recursive subprogram the storage area can be one fixed area, permanently reserved, since we know that one call to the subprogram will have returned before another one is made, and after the first one returns the information stored is no longer needed. For recursive subprograms, however, the information stored must be preserved until the outer call returns, so an inner call must use a different area for its temporary storage.

Note that the common practice of reserving a permanent storage area for a non-recursive subprogram can in fact be quite wasteful, since a considerable amount of memory may be consumed in this way, memory that might be useful for other purposes while the subprogram is not active.

3. Re-entrant programs.

Essentially the same problem of multiple storage areas arises in a quite different context, that of *re-entrant* programs. In a large time-sharing system there may be many users simultaneously using the BASIC interpreter or the text-editing system. These systems programs are quite large, and it would be very wasteful of high-speed memory to keep thirty or forty copies of exactly the same large set of instructions in memory at once, one for each user. What is generally done instead is to write large systems programs like the BASIC interpreter or the text editor with the instructions in one area, but with the addresses of all variables or other data kept in a separate area. Then in the memory of the time-sharing system there will be only one copy of the instructions, but a separate data area for each user.

This situation is somewhat analogous to students writing a test in a room where the questions are written on the blackboard. There is then only one set of questions that all students can read, but each student separately writes answers on different pieces of paper. There is no difficulty for different students to be reading the same or different questions at the same time, and with different pieces of paper their answers will not be mixed with each other.

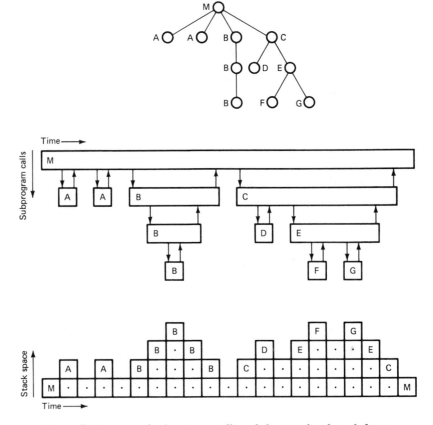

Figure 7.14. A tree of subprogram calls and the associated stack frames

4. Data structures: Stacks and trees.

We have yet to specify the data structure that will keep track of all these storage areas for subprograms; to do so let us look at the tree of subprogram calls. So that an inner subprogram can access variables declared in an outer block, and so that we can return properly to the calling program, we must, at every point in the tree, remember all vertices on the path from the given point back to the root. As we move through the tree, vertices are added to and deleted from one end of this path; the other end (at the root) remains fixed. Hence the vertices on the path form a stack; the storage areas for subprograms likewise are to be kept as a stack. This process is illustrated in Figure 7.14.

From Figure 7.14 and our discussion we can immediately conclude that the amount of space needed to implement recursion (which of course is related to the number of storage areas in current use) depends on the height of the recursion tree. Programmers who have not carefully studied recursion sometimes think mistakenly that the space requirement relates to the total number of vertices in the tree. The *time* requirement of the program is related to the number of times subprograms are done, and therefore to the total number of vertices in the tree, but the *space* requirement is only that of the storage areas on the path from a single vertex back to the root. Thus the space requirement is reflected in the height of the tree. A well-balanced, bushy recursion tree hence signifies a recursive process that can do much work with little need for extra space.

Figure 7.14 can, in fact, be interpreted in a broader context than as the process of invoking subprograms. It thereby elucidates an easy but important observation, providing an intimate connection between arbitrary (ordered rooted) trees and stacks:

THEOREM 7.1. *During the traversal of any (rooted ordered) tree, vertices are added to or deleted from the path back to the root in the fashion of a stack. Given any stack, conversely, a (rooted ordered) tree can be drawn to portray the life history of the stack, as items are added to or deleted from it.*

In most modern computers efficient means are provided to allow the same instructions to refer to different storage areas as desired. In the IBM 370[*] series, for example, every instruction that refers to memory calculates the address it uses by adding some value (displacement) to the contents of a specified register called the base register. If the value in the base register is set to the beginning of one storage area then all later instructions will refer to that area. Changing only the one value in the base register will make all the instructions refer to another storage area. A second example consists of the machines in the PDP/11 series and most microcomputers. Most of the instructions on these machines can be made to automatically push or pop a stack as they refer to memory for their operands.

---

[*]IBM 370 is a registered trademark of International Business Machines, Inc.

5. Conclusion.

The moral of the story is that, when properly implemented, recursion is neither inefficient nor expensive, except perhaps on some machines of quite old design that are rapidly being retired. Some compilers, unfortunately, do make a mess out of recursive procedures, but on a well-designed system there is essentially no additional time overhead for using recursion, and no reason to avoid it when it is the natural method.

7.5.3 Tail-end recursion

Suppose that the very last action of a procedure is to make a recursive call to itself. In the stack implementation of recursion, as we have seen, the local variables of the procedure will be pushed onto the stack as the recursive call is initiated. When the recursive call terminates, these local variables will be popped from the stack and thereby restored to their former values. But doing so is pointless, because the recursive call was the last action of the procedure, so the procedure now terminates and the just-restored local variables are immediately discarded.

When the very last action of a procedure is a recursive call to itself, it is thus pointless to use the stack, as we have seen, since no local variables need to be preserved. All that is needed is to set the dummy calling parameters to their new values and branch to the beginning of the procedure. We summarize this principle for future reference.

THEOREM 7.2.   *If the last executed statement of a procedure is a recursive call to itself, then this call can be eliminated by changing the values of the calling parameters to those specified in the recursive call, and repeating the whole procedure.*

This special case when a recursive call is the last executed statement of the procedure is especially important because it frequently occurs. It is called **tail-end recursion**, or, often, simply **tail recursion**. You should carefully note that tail-end recursion means that the last executed statement is a recursive call, not necessarily that the recursive call is the last statement appearing in the procedure. Tail-end recursion may appear, for example, within one clause of a **case** statement or an **if** statement where other program lines appear later.

With most modern compilers there will be little difference in execution *time* whether tail-end recursion is left in a program or is removed. If *space* considerations are important, however, then the principle of Theorem 7.2 should usually be followed if it is applicable, whether other recursion is being removed or not. By rearranging the termination condition if needed, it is usually possible to repeat the procedure without using a **goto**.

Consider, for example, a divide-and-conquer algorithm like that devised for the Towers on Hanoi in Section 7.1. By removing tail-end recursion, procedure **Move** of the original recursive program can be expressed as:

```
procedure Move(n: disk; a,b,c: needle);
{Moves n disks from a to b using c for temporary storage}
var
  t: needle;                        {temporary storage to swap needles}
begin
  while n > 0 do begin
    Move(n — 1, a, c, b);
    Writeln('Move a disk from', a:2, 'to', b:2);
    n := n — 1;   t := a;   a := c;   c := t
  end                                          {looping down on n}
end;                                  {declaration of Procedure Move}
```

We should have been quite clever had we thought of this version of the procedure when we first looked at the problem, but now that we have discovered it via other considerations, we can give it a natural interpretation. Think of the two needles a and c as in the same class: we wish to use them for intermediate storage as we slowly move all the disks onto b. To move a stack of n disks onto b, then, we must move all except the bottom to the other one of a and c, then move the bottom disk to b, and repeat after interchanging a and c, continuing to shuffle all except the bottom disk between a and c, and at each pass getting a new bottom one onto b.

7.5.4 When not to use recursion.

1. Factorials.

Many textbooks present the calculation of factorials as the first example of a recursive program:

```
function Factorial(n: integer): integer;
begin
  if n <= 1 then Factorial := 1
    else Factorial := n * Factorial(n—1)
end;
```

Although this program is simple and easy, there is an equally simple iterative program:

```
function Factorial(n: integer): integer;
var i, p: integer;
begin
  p := 1;
  for i := 2 to n do p := p * i;
  Factorial := p
end;
```

Which of these programs uses less storage space? At first glance it might appear that the recursive one does, since it has no local variables, and the iterative program has two. But actually (see Figure 7.15) the recursive program will set up a stack and fill it with the $n-1$ numbers

$$n, \; n-1, \; n-2, \; \cdots \; , \; 2$$

that are its calling parameters before each recursion, and will then, as it works its way out of the recursion, multiply these numbers in the same order as does the second program. Thus the recursive program keeps considerably more storage, and will take more time as well, since it must store and retrieve all the numbers as well as multiply them.

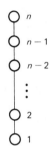

Figure 7.15. Recursion tree for calculating factorials

2. Fibonacci numbers.

A far more wasteful example than factorials (and one that also appears as an apparently recommended program in some textbooks) is the computation of the *Fibonacci Numbers*, which are defined by the recurrence relation

$$F_0 \; = \; 0, \qquad F_1 \; = \; 1, \qquad F_n \; = \; F_{n-1}+F_{n-2} \qquad \text{for } n \geq 2.$$

(If you are interested, consult Appendix A.4 for a discussion of the properties of these numbers.) The recursive program closely follows the definition:

```
function Fib(n: integer): integer;
begin
  if n <= 0 then      Fib := 0
  else if n = 1 then  Fib := 1
  else                Fib := Fib(n-1) + Fib (n-2)
end;
```

In fact, this program is quite attractive, since it is of the divide-and-conquer form: The answer is obtained by calculating two simpler cases. As we shall see, however, in this example it is not "divide-and-conquer," but "divide-and-complicate."

To assess this algorithm, let us consider, as an example, the calculation of F_7, whose recursion tree is shown in Figure 7.16. The procedure will first have to obtain F_6 and F_5. To get F_6 requires F_5 and F_4, and so on. But after F_5 is calculated on the way to F_6, then it will be lost and unavailable when it is later needed to get F_7. Hence, as

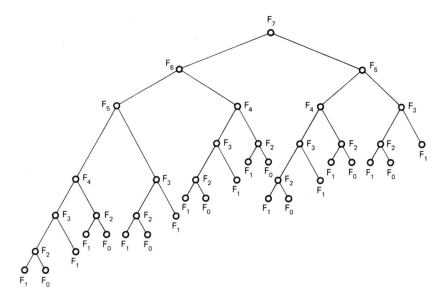

Figure 7.16. Recursion tree for calculation of F_7

the recursion tree shows, the recursive program needlessly repeats the same calculations over and over. Further analysis appears as an exercise. It turns out that the amount of time used by the recursive function to calculate F_n grows exponentially with n.

As with factorials, we can produce a simple iterative program by noting that we can start at 0 and keep only three variables, the current Fibonacci number and its two predecessors.

```
function Fib(n: integer): integer;
var i, a, b, c: integer;
begin
  if n <=0 then
    Fib := 0
  else if n = 1 then
    Fib := 1
```

```
      else begin
      a := 0;  b := 1;
      for i := 2 to n do
      begin
        c := a + b;
        a := b; b := c
      end;
      Fib := c
    end
  end;
```

The iterative function obviously uses time that is $\Theta(n)$, so that, as we saw in Section 4.10, the time difference between this function and the exponential time of the recursive function will be vast.

If you regard this non-recursive program as too tricky, then you can write a straightforward iterative program that sets up a list of length n, and calculates F_n simply by starting with F_0 and calculating and storing all the Fibonacci numbers up through F_n. Even this program will use only about n words of storage, which is less than the recursive program will use.

3. Comparisons between recursion and iteration.

What is fundamentally different between these two examples and the proper uses of recursion that were illustrated in the previous sections of this chapter? To answer this question we shall again turn to the examination of recursion trees. It should already be clear that a study of the recursion tree will provide much useful information to help us decide when recursion should or should not be used.

If a function or a procedure makes only one recursive call to itself, then its recursion tree has a very simple form: it is a chain; that is, each vertex has only one child. This child corresponds to the single recursive call that occurs. Such a simple tree is easy to comprehend. For the factorial function it is simply the list of requests to calculate the factorials from $(n-1)!$ down to 1!. By reading the recursion tree from bottom to top instead of top to bottom, we immediately obtain the iterative program from the recursive one. When the tree does reduce to a chain, then transformation from recursion to iteration is often easy, and will likely save both space and time.

Note that a procedure's making only one recursive call to itself is not at all the same as having the recursive call made only one place in the procedure, since this place might be inside a loop. It is also possible to have two places that issue a recursive call (such as both the **then** and **else** clauses of an **if** statement) where only one call can actually occur.

The recursion tree for calculating Fibonacci numbers is not a chain, but contains a great many vertices signifying duplicate tasks. When a recursive program is run, it sets up a stack to use while traversing the tree, but if the results stored on the stack are discarded rather than kept in some other data structure for future use, then a great deal of duplication of work may occur, as in the recursive calculation of Fibonacci numbers.

In such cases it is preferable to substitute another data structure for the stack, one that allows references to locations other than the top. The most obvious choice is that of an ordinary list holding all information calculated so far, and this in fact works nicely for the Fibonacci numbers. The iterative program that we wrote for the Fibonacci numbers, the one that uses only three temporary variables, is in one sense tricky, even though it is easy. The reason is that nothing similar is likely to be found for the numbers defined by the following recurrence relation, one that is similar in form to that for the Fibonacci numbers, and could likely not be separated from it by general programming methods:

$$G_0 \; = \; 0, \qquad G_1 \; = \; 1, \qquad G_n \; = \; G_{n-1} + G_k \qquad \text{for } n \geq 2,$$

where $k = \lceil \ln n \rceil$.

After removal of tail-end recursion, most of the programs written earlier in this chapter each involve only one recursive call, but note carefully that this call is within a loop, and therefore their recursion trees will not reduce to chains. In some cases, nonetheless, it is possible to predict what the parameters of each recursive call will be, and thereby to devise an equivalent non-recursive program with no stacks. In the next section we shall exploit the complete symmetry of the recursion tree for mergesort, in order to derive an efficient non-recursive version of this important sorting method.

Finally, by setting up an explicit stack, we can take any recursive program and rearrange it into non-recursive form. Appendix B describes methods for doing so. The resulting program, however, is often more complicated and harder to understand than the recursive version, and for many applications the saving of space and time is insignificant. On machines with hardware stack instructions, in fact, the non-recursive form may actually require more running time than the equivalent recursive program. Appendix B develops a non-recursive version of quicksort as an example.

7.5.5 Guidelines and conclusions.

In making a decision, then, about whether to write a particular algorithm in recursive or non-recursive form, a good starting point is to consider the recursion tree. If it has a simple form, the iterative version may be better. If it involves duplicate tasks, then data structures other than stacks will be appropriate, and the need for recursion may disappear. If the recursion tree appears quite bushy, with little duplication of tasks, then recursion is likely the natural method.

The stack used to resolve recursion can be regarded as a list of postponed obligations for the program. If this list can be easily constructed in advance, then iteration is probably better; if not, recursion may be. Recursion is something of a top-down approach to problem solving; it divides the problem into pieces or selects out one key step, postponing the rest. Iteration is more of a bottom-up approach; it begins with what is known and from this constructs the solution step by step.

It is always true that recursion can be replaced by iteration and stacks. It is also true, conversely, (see references for the proof) that any (iterative) program that manipulates a stack can be replaced by a recursive program with no stack. Thus the careful programmer should not only ask whether recursion should be removed, but should also ask, when a program involves stacks, whether the introduction of recursion might produce a more natural and understandable program that could lead to improvements in the approach and in the results.

At this point let us pause to summarize some general principles we have developed about the use of recursion.

1. Recursion should be used freely in the initial design of algorithms. It is especially appropriate where the main step toward solution consists of reducing a problem to one or more smaller cases.

2. Tail-end recursion should be removed if space considerations are important (Theorem 7.2).

3. The recursion tree should be studied to see whether the recursion is needlessly repeating work, or if the tree represents an efficient division of the work into pieces.

4. A tree that reduces to a chain implies that recursion can be replaced by iteration.

5. If the recursion tree shows complete regularity that can be determined in advance, then sometimes this regularity can be built into the algorithm in a way that will improve efficiency and perhaps remove the recursion.

6. Recursive procedures and iterative procedures using stacks can accomplish exactly the same tasks. Consider carefully whether recursion or iteration will lead to a clearer program and give more insight into the problem.

7. Recursion can always be translated into iteration, but the general rules (Appendix B) will often produce a result that greatly obscures the structure of the program. Such obfuscation should be tolerated only when the programming language makes it unavoidable, and even then it should be well documented.

Exercises

1. In the recursive calculation of F_n, determine exactly how many times each smaller Fibonacci number will be calculated. From this determine the order-of-magnitude time and space requirements of the recursive function. [You may find out either by setting up and solving a recurrence relation (top-down approach), or by finding the answer in simple cases and proving it more generally by mathematical induction (bottom-up approach). Consult Appendix A.4.]

2. The **greatest common divisor** (GCD) of two positive integers is the largest integer that divides both of them. Thus the GCD of 8 and 12 is 4, the GCD of 9 and 18 is 9, and the GCD of 16 and 25 is 1. Write a recursive function GCD(x, y: integer)

that implements the ***division algorithm:*** If $y = 0$, then the GCD of x and y is x; otherwise the GCD of x and y is the same as the GCD of y and x **mod** y. Rewrite the function in iterative form.

3. The binomial coefficients may be defined by the following recurrence relation, which is the idea of ***Pascal's triangle***:

$$C(n, 0) = 1 \text{ and } C(n, n) = 1 \qquad\qquad \text{for } n \geq 0.$$
$$C(n, k) = C(n-1, k) + C(n-1, k-1) \quad \text{for } n > k > 0.$$

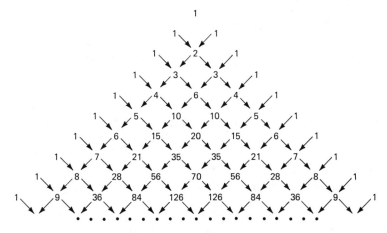

Figure 7.17. The top of Pascal's triangle of binomial coefficients

(a) Write a recursive function to generate $C(n, k)$ by the above formula.

(b) Draw the recursion tree for calculating $C(6, 4)$.

(c) Use a square array and write a non-recursive program to generate Pascal's triangle in the lower left half of the array.

(d) Write a non-recursive program with neither array nor stack to calculate $C(n, k)$ for arbitrary $n \geq k \geq 0$.

(e) Determine the asymptotic space and time requirements for each of the algorithms devised in parts (a), (c) and (d).

4. ***Ackermann's Function***, defined as follows, is a standard device to determine how well recursion is implemented on a computer.

$$A(0, n) = n+1 \qquad\qquad \text{for } n \geq 0.$$
$$A(m, 0) = A(m-1, 1) \qquad\qquad \text{for } m > 0.$$
$$A(m, n) = A(m-1, A(m, n-1)) \quad \text{for } m > 0 \text{ and } n > 0.$$

(a) Write a recursive function to calculate Ackermann's Function.

(b) Calculate the following values:

$$A(0, 0) \qquad A(0, 9) \qquad A(1, 8) \qquad A(2, 2) \qquad A(2, 0)$$
$$A(2, 3) \qquad A(3, 2) \qquad A(4, 2) \qquad A(4, 3) \qquad A(4, 0)$$

(c) Write a non-recursive function to calculate Ackermann's function.

7.6 Stackless recursion removal: Mergesort.

This final, optional section discusses point 5 of the guidelines for using recursion in Section 7.5.5; that is, the translation of a program into non-recursive form by exploiting the regularity of its recursion tree, thereby avoiding the need to use a stack. The program we develop in this section is not likely to prove a great improvement over the recursive version, since the stack space saved is only $O(\lg n)$. It is primarily a matter of taste which version to use.

Mergesort is one of the most efficient sorting methods we have studied; it is the only one we considered (although others exist) for which the number of comparisons in the worst case, as well as in the average case, is $\Theta(n \log n)$. Mergesort is therefore a good choice for large sorting problems when time constraints are critical. The recursion used in mergesort, however, may entail some overhead costs; hence let us consider how to rewrite mergesort in non-recursive form.

Let us begin by considering the tree of recursive calls that mergesort will make in sorting a list; this tree for $n = 16$ is drawn in Figure 7.18. In the recursive formulation of mergesort, we begin at the root of the tree and divide the list in half. We then look at the left list (move to the left subtree) and repeat the division. Afterward, we look at the right sublist and move to the right subtree. In other words,

Recursion in mergesort performs a preorder traversal of the tree.

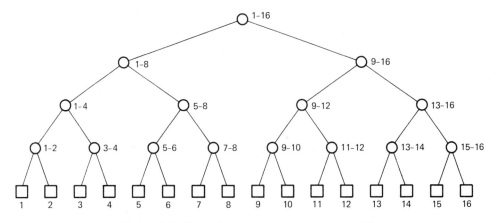

Figure 7.18. Recursion tree for mergesort, $n = 16$

Now let us determine the order in which the merges are actually done. No sublists are actually merged until the list has been divided all the way down to sublists of one element each. The first two one-element sublists, represented as the leftmost two leaves in the tree, are then merged. Then the next two one-element sublists are merged, and afterward the resulting two-element sublists are merged into a four-element sublist. In this way the process continues building small sublists into larger ones. In fact,

The order in which the merges are actually done
constitutes a postorder traversal of the tree.

Translating mergesort into non-recursive form amounts to rewriting the algorithm to perform a postorder traversal of the tree instead of a preorder traversal. We could, of course, use a stack to assist with the postorder traversal, but instead we shall take advantage of the fact that, when n is a power of 2, the tree has a completely symmetric structure. Using this structure we can obtain a non-recursive traversal algorithm with no need for a stack. The idea that we shall employ is the same as that used in Section 5.6, where we developed an algorithm for building elements from an ordered list into a balanced binary search tree. In fact, the algorithm we now need differs from that of Section 5.6 only in that we now wish to make a postorder traversal of the tree, whereas in Section 5.6 we did an inorder traversal.

We shall also find that, when n is not a power of 2 (as in Section 5.6), few further difficulties arise. The present algorithm will also have the advantage over the recursive form, that it is not necessary to know or calculate in advance how many items are in the list being sorted. (Recall that our original recursive version of mergesort spent significant time finding the center of a linked list.)

To design our algorithm, let us imagine receiving the elements of the unsorted list one at a time, and as each element arrives, let us continue the postorder traversal of the tree by doing as many merges as possible with the elements that we have available. When only the first element has arrived, no merge can be done; when the second element comes, the first two sublists of size 1 will be merged. Element 3 does not induce any merges, but element 4 is first compared with element 3, and the resulting two-element sublist is then merged with the first two-element sublist. Continuing in this way, we see that element 5 does not induce any merge, element 6 induces only 1, element 7 none, and element 8 induces 3 merges. Further study of the tree will convince you that:

When mergesort processes the item in position c of its input, then the
number of times that sublists are merged before proceeding to the
next element is exactly the highest power of 2 that divides c.

In writing our algorithm we shall, as in Section 4.7, consider only a version sorting linked lists. In this way, we can use the same function presented in Section 4.7 to merge two sorted sublists, and we need not consider the auxiliary space or complicated algorithms needed to accomplish merging in contiguous lists.

As we progress through the tree, we shall find that at various stages several sublists will have been constructed that have not yet been merged with each other. We shall keep track of these sublists by using an auxiliary array of pointers. At any point in the process, there can be at most one such sublist corresponding to each level in the tree; hence the size of this array grows only logarithmically with the length of the list being sorted, and the amount of additional memory that it requires is inconsequential.

The main part of our algorithm can now be described completely: we shall traverse the linked list of input, and use the function **Power2(c)** (taken from Section 5.6) to determine the number **mergecount** of times that sublists will be merged. We do these merges, using the sublists whose headers are in the auxiliary array. After the appropriate merges are made, a pointer to the resulting sorted sublist is placed in location **mergecount** of the auxiliary array.

It now remains only for us to describe what must be done to complete the sort after the end of the input list is reached. If n is an exact power of 2, then the list will be completely sorted at this point. Otherwise, it turns out that:

> *At the end of receiving input, the sorted sublists that must still be merged occupy precisely the same relative positions in the auxiliary array as those occupied by the non-zero digits in the representation of the counter c as a binary integer.*

We can prove this observation by mathematical induction. When $n = 1$ it is certainly true. In fact, when n is any exact power of 2, $n = 2^k$, the first part of the algorithm will have merged all the items as received into a single sorted sublist, and the integer n when written in binary has a single 1 in the digit position k corresponding to the power of 2, and 0's elsewhere. Now consider the algorithm for an arbitrary value of n, and let 2^k be the largest power of 2 such that $2^k \leq n$. The binary representation of n contains a 1 in position k (the count of digits starts at 0), which is its largest non-zero digit. The remaining digits form the binary representation of $m = n - 2^k$. When the first 2^k items have been received, the algorithm will have merged them into a single sublist, a pointer to which is in position k of the auxiliary array, corresponding properly to the digit 1 in position k of the binary representation of n. As the remaining m items are processed, they will, by induction hypothesis, produce sublists with pointers in positions corresponding to 1's in the binary representation of m, which, as we have observed, is the same as the remaining positions in the binary representation of n. Hence the proof is complete.

With this background, we can now produce a formal description of the algorithm. The notational conventions are those of Section 4.7.

```
procedure NRMergeSort(var head: pointer);
{Non-recursive version of mergesort.  Uses a counter c to determine the
   number of sublists to merge at each stage.}
```

```
const
  maxlog  = 20;                   {allows over 1,000,000 entries in list}
var
  sublist: array[0..maxlog] of pointer;
  p,                                        {first unsorted item from list}
  q:       pointer;                    {head of a (partial) merged list}
  i,                                          {used to control for loop}
  c,                                    {counter (index) of current item}
  mergecount,                        {largest power of 2 dividing c}
  d:       integer;          {a digit in binary representation of c}
begin                                       {Main procedure NRMergesort}
  p := head;
  c := 0;
  while p <> nil do                      {Traverse the unsorted list.}
  begin
    c := c + 1;
    mergecount := Power2(c);
    q := p;
    p := p↑.next;
    q↑.next := nil;                    {Split off q↑ as a sublist of size 1.}
    for i := 0 to mergecount − 1 do
      q := Merge(q, sublist[i]);
    sublist[mergecount] := q
  end;

  {At this point, the list has been traversed. The unmerged sublists
  correspond to the 1's in the binary representation of the  counter c.
  Note that p = nil at this point.}
  mergecount := − 1;
  while c <> 0 do
  begin
    d := c mod 2;                                 {d is a binary digit in c}
    c := c div 2;
    mergecount := mergecount + 1;
    if d <> 0 then
      if p = nil then
        p := sublist[mergecount]          {This case occurs only for first
                                                          non-zero d.}
      else
        p := Merge(p,sublist[mergecount])
                                      {This case occurs always thereafter.}
  end;

  head := p
end;
```

Exercises

1. Run the non-recursive mergesort of this section, and compare timings with those of the recursive version of Section 4.7.

2. The algorithm for the Towers of Hanoi has a completely symmetric recursion tree. Design a non-recursive program for this problem that uses no stacks, lists or arrays.

7.7 References for further study.

The examples and applications studied in this chapter come from a variety of sources. The Towers of Hanoi is quite well-known, and appears in several textbooks. A recent survey of related papers is

> D. Wood, "The Towers of Brahma and Hanoi revisited,"*Journal of Recreational Math.* 14 (1981–82), 17–24.

Our treatment of the eight-queens problem especially follows that given in:

> N. Wirth, *Algorithms + Data Structures = Programs,* Prentice-Hall, Englewood Cliffs, N.J. , 1976, pp. 143–147.

This book by Wirth also contains solutions of the Knight's Tour (pp. 137–142) and stable marriage (pp. 148–154) problems, as well as a chapter (pp. 280–349) on compiling and parsing.

Generalizations of the stable marriage problem form the subject for the small book:

> D. E. Knuth, *Mariages stables et leur relations avec d'autres problèmes combinatoires,* Les Presses de l'Université de Montréal, Montréal, Canada, 1976, 106 pages.

The algorithm that generates permutations by insertion into a linked list was published in the ACM *SIGCSE Bulletin,* 14 (February, 1982), 92–96. Useful surveys of many methods for generating permutations are:

> R. Sedgewick, "Permutation generation methods,"*Computing Surveys,* 9 (1977), 137–164; *addenda, ibid.*, 314–317.

> R. W. Topor, "Functional programs for generating permutations,"*Computer Journal* 25 (1982), 257–263.

The original reference for the efficient algorithm by Heap is:

> B. R. Heap, "Permutations by Interchanges,"*Computer Journal,* 6 (1963), 293–294.

The applications of permutations to campanology (change ringing of bells) produce interesting problems amenable to computer study. An excellent source for further information is:

F. J. BUDDEN, *The Fascination of Groups,* Cambridge University Press, Cambridge, England, 1972, pp. 451–479.

Compilation by recursive descent is a standard topic in compiler design, a topic treated in detail in most newer textbooks in compiler theory. Consult, for example:

ALFRED V. AHO and JEFFREY D. ULLMAN, *Principles of Compiler Design,* Addison-Wesley, Reading, Mass., 1977.

Many other applications of recursion appear in books such as:

E. HOROWITZ and S. SAHNI, *Fundamentals of Computer Algorithms,* Computer Science Press, Rockville, Md., 1978, 626 pp.

This book (pages 290–302) contains more extensive discussion and analysis of game trees and look-ahead programs. An outline of a programming project for the game of Kalah appears in:

CHARLES WETHERELL, *Etudes for Programmers,* Prentice-Hall, Englewood Cliffs, N. J., 1978.

The general theory of recursion forms a topic of current research. A readable presentation from a theoretical approach is:

R. S. BIRD, *Programs and Machines,* John Wiley & Sons, New York, 1976.

See also:

R. S. BIRD, "Notes on recursion elimination ," *Communications of the ACM,* 20 (1977), 434–439.

R. S. BIRD, "Improving programs by the introduction of recursion," *Communications of the ACM,* 20 (1977), 856–863.

The proof that stacks may be eliminated by the introduction of recursion appears in:

S. BROWN, D. GRIES, and T. SZYMANSKI, "Program schemes with push-down stores," *SIAM J. Computing,* 1 (1972), 242–268.

A non-recursive program using no stack is developed for the Towers of Hanoi in the paper:

HELMUT PARTSCH and PETER PEPPER, "A family of rules for recursion removal," *Information Processing Letters* 5 (1976), 174–177.

Chapter 8

Case Study:
The Polish Notation

This chapter studies the Polish notation for arithmetic or logical expressions, first in terms of problem solving, and then as applied to a program that interactively accepts an expression, compiles it, and evaluates it. This chapter illustrates uses of recursion, stacks and trees, as well as their interplay in problem solving and algorithm design.

8.1 The problem.

One of the most important accomplishments of the early designers of computer languages was allowing a programmer to write arithmetic expressions in something close to their usual mathematical form. It was a real triumph to design a compiler that understood expressions such as

$$(x + y) * \exp(x - z) - 4.0$$
$$a * b + c / d - c * (x + y)$$
$$\textbf{not (p and q) or } (x <= 7.0)$$

and produced machine-language output. In fact, the name FORTRAN stands for

FORmula TRANslator

in recognition of this very accomplishment. It often takes only one simple idea that, when fully understood, will provide the key to an elegant solution of a difficult problem, in this case the translation of expressions into sequences of machine-language instructions.

The triumph of the method to be developed in this chapter is that, in contrast to the first approach a person might take, it is not necessary to make repeated scans through the expression to decipher it, and, after a preliminary translation, neither parentheses nor priorities of operators need be taken into account, so that evaluation of the expression can be achieved with great efficiency.

8.1.1 The quadratic formula.

Before we discuss this idea, let us briefly imagine the problems an early compiler designer might have faced when confronted with a fairly complicated expression. Even the quadratic formula produces problems:

$$x \quad := \quad (-b + (b \uparrow 2 - (4 \times a) \times c) \uparrow \tfrac{1}{2}) / (2 \times a)$$

(Here, and throughout this chapter, we denote exponentiation by '$\uparrow$'. We limit our attention to one of the two roots.) Which operations must be done before others? What are the effects of parentheses? When can they be omitted? As you answer these questions for this example, you will probably look back and forth through the expression several times.

In considering how to translate such expressions, the compiler designers soon settled on the conventions that are familiar now: operations are ordinarily done left to right, subject to the priorities assigned to operators, with exponentiation highest, then multiplication and division, then addition and subtraction. This order can be altered by parentheses. For the quadratic formula the order of operations is:

$$x \quad := \quad (- b + (b \uparrow 2 - (4 \times a) \times c) \uparrow \tfrac{1}{2}) / (2 \times a)$$

	$\uparrow$	$\uparrow$	$\uparrow$	$\uparrow$	$\uparrow$	$\uparrow$	$\uparrow$	$\uparrow$	$\uparrow$	$\uparrow$
	10	1	7	2	5	3	4	6	9	8

Note that assignment '$:=$' really is an operator that takes the value of its right operand and assigns it to the left operand. The priority of '$:=$' will be the lowest of any operator, since it cannot be done until the expression is fully evaluated.

8.1.2 Unary operators and priorities.

With one exception, all the operators in the quadratic equation are **binary,** that is, they have two operands. The one exception is the leading minus sign in $-b$. This is a **unary** operator, and unary operators provide a slight complication in determining priorities. Normally we interpret -2^2 as -4, which means that negation is done after exponentiation, but we interpret 2^{-2} as ¼ and not as -4, so that here negation is done first. It is reasonable to assign unary operators the same priority as exponentiation, and in order to preserve the usual algebraic conventions, to evaluate operators of this priority from right to left. Doing this, moreover, also gives the ordinary interpretation of $2 \uparrow 3 \uparrow 2$ as

$$2^{(3^2)} \;=\; 512 \qquad \text{and not as} \qquad (2^3)^2 \;=\; 64.$$

Evaluation of some operators from right to left, and others from left to right, would require that we write more complicated algorithms, however, so we shall ignore this problem, and instead shall always require parentheses to override the convention of evaluating operators of equal priority from left to right. The exercises describe a method to correct this defect.

There are unary operators other than negation. These include such operations as taking the factorial of x, denoted $x!$, the derivative of a function f, denoted f', as well

as all functions of a single variable, such as the trigonometric, exponential and logarithmic functions. There is also the Boolean operator **not**, which negates a Boolean
variable.

Several binary operators also have Boolean results: the operators **and** and **or** as
well as the comparison operators '=', '≠', '<', '>', '≤', and '≥'. These comparisons
are normally done after the arithmetic operators, but before **and, not** and assignment.

We thus obtain the following list of priorities to reflect our usual customs in
evaluating operators:

Operators						*Priority*
↑,	all unary arithmetic operators					7
×	/	**div**	**mod**			6
+	− (binary)					5
=	≠	<	>	≤	≥	4
not						3
and	**or**					2
:=						1

Note that these priorities are not those used in Pascal, where **and** has priority 6 and **or**
has priority 5. As long as we are designing our own system, however, we are free to set
our own conventions, provided that they are consistent, reasonable and appropriate.

8.2 The idea.

8.2.1 Expression trees.

Drawing a picture is often an excellent way to gain insight into a problem. For
our current problem, the appropriate picture is the *expression tree*, as first introduced
in Section 5.3. Recall that an expression tree is a binary tree in which the leaves are
the simple operands, and the interior vertices are the operators. If an operator is
binary, then it has two non-empty subtrees that are its left and right operands (either
simple operands or sub-expressions). If an operator is unary, then only one of its
subtrees is non-empty, the one on the left or right according as the operator is written
on the right or left of its operand. You should review Figure 5.4 for several simple
expression trees, as well as Figure 5.5 for the expression tree of the quadratic formula.

Let us determine how to evaluate an expression tree such as, for example, the one
shown in part (a) of Figure 8.1. It is clear that we must begin with one of the leaves,
since it is only the simple operands for which we know the values when starting. To be
consistent, let us start with the leftmost leaf, whose value is 2.9. Since, in our example,
the operator immediately above this leaf is unary negation, we can apply it immediately, and replace both the operator and its operand by the result, −2.9. This step
results in the diamond-shaped node in part (b) of the diagram.

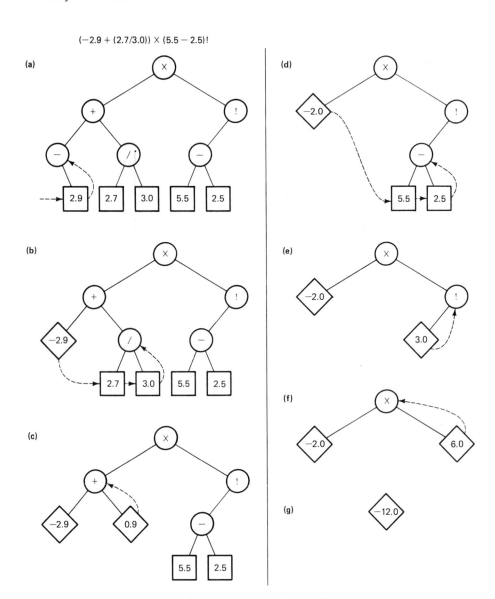

Figure 8.1. Evaluation of an expression tree

The parent of the diamond-shaped node in part (b) is a binary operator, and its second operand has not yet been evaluated. We cannot, therefore, apply this operator yet, but must instead consider the next two leaves, as shown by the dotted path. After moving past these two leaves, the path moves to their parent operator, which can now be evaluated, and the result placed in the second diamond-shaped node, as shown in part (c).

At this stage, both operands of the addition are available, so we can perform it, obtaining the simplified tree in part (d). And so we continue, until the tree has been reduced to a single node, which is the final result. In summary, we have processed the nodes of the tree in the order

$$2.9 \quad - \quad 2.7 \quad 3.0 \quad / \quad + \quad 5.5 \quad 2.5 \quad - \quad ! \quad \times$$

The general observation is that we should process the subtree rooted at any given operator in the order: "Evaluate its left subtree; Evaluate its right subtree; Perform the operator." (If the operator is unary, then one of these steps is vacuous.) This order is precisely a postorder traversal of the expression tree. We have already observed in Section 5.3 that the postorder traversal of an expression tree yields the postfix form of the expression, in which each operator is written after its operands, instead of between them.

This simple idea is the key to efficient calculation of expressions by computer.

As a matter of fact, our customary way to write arithmetic or logical expressions with the operator between its operands is slightly illogical. The instruction

Take the number 12 *and multiply by* $\cdots$.

is incomplete until the second factor is given. In the meantime it is necessary to remember both a number and an operation. From the viewpoint of establishing uniform rules it makes more sense either to write

Take the numbers 12 *and* 3; *then multiply.*

or to write

Do a multiplication. The numbers are 12 *and* 3.

8.2.2 Polish notation.

This method of writing all operators either before their operands, or after them, is called *Polish notation*, in honor of its discoverer, the Polish mathematician JAN ŁUKASIEWICZ. When the operators are written before their operands, it is called the *prefix form*. When the operators come after their operands, it is called the *postfix form*, or, sometimes, *reverse Polish form* or *suffix form*, Finally, in this context, it is customary to use the coined phrase *infix form* to denote the usual custom of writing binary operators between their operands.

The expression $a \times b$ becomes $\times a\, b$ in prefix form and $a\, b \times$ in postfix form. In the expression $a + b \times c$ the multiplication is done first, so we convert it first, obtaining first $a + (b\, c \times)$ and then $a\, b\, c \times +$ in postfix form. The prefix form of this expression is $+ a \times b\, c$. Note that prefix and postfix forms are not related by taking mirror images or other such simple transformation. Note also that all parentheses have been omitted in the Polish forms. We shall justify this omission later.

As a more complicated example we can write down the prefix and postfix forms of the quadratic formula, starting from its expression tree, as shown in Figure 5.5.

First, let us traverse the tree in preorder. The operator in the root is the assignment ':=', after which we move to the left subtree, which consists only of the operand x. The right subtree begins with the division '/', and then moves leftward to '+' and to the unary negation '−'.

We now have an ambiguity that will haunt us later if we do not correct it. The first '−' (minus) in the expression is unary negation, and the second is binary subtraction. In Polish form it is not obvious which is which. When we go to evaluate the prefix string we will not know whether to take one operand for '−' or two, and the results will be quite different. To avoid this ambiguity we shall reserve '−' to denote binary subtraction, and use the special symbol '∸' for unary negation (this terminology is certainly not standard. There are other ways to resolve the problem).

The preorder traversal up to this point has yielded

$$:=\quad x\quad /\quad +\quad \dot{-}\quad b$$

and the next step is to traverse the right subtree of the operator '+'. The result is the sequence

$$\uparrow\quad -\quad \uparrow\quad b\quad 2\quad \times\quad \times\quad 4\quad a\quad c\quad \tfrac{1}{2}$$

Finally, we traverse the right subtree of the division '/', obtaining

$$\times\quad 2\quad a$$

Hence the complete prefix form for the quadratic formula is:

$$:=\quad x\quad /\quad +\quad \dot{-}\quad b\quad \uparrow\quad -\quad \uparrow\quad b\quad 2\quad \times\quad \times\quad 4\quad a\quad c\quad \tfrac{1}{2}\quad \times\quad 2\quad a$$

You should verify yourself that the postfix form is:

$$x\quad b\quad \dot{-}\quad b\quad 2\quad \uparrow\quad 4\quad a\quad \times\quad c\,\times\quad -\quad \tfrac{1}{2}\quad \uparrow\quad +\quad 2\quad a\quad \times\quad /\quad :=$$

8.2.3 Pascal method.

Before concluding this section, we should remark that most Pascal compilers do not use Polish forms in translating expressions into machine language (although many other languages do). Most Pascal compilers, instead, use the method of recursive descent as introduced in section 7.4. In this method, each priority of operator requires a separate procedure for its compilation (and a separate syntax diagram for its definition). This requirement may partially explain why Pascal uses a truncated list of priorities in comparison with those employed throughout this chapter.

Translation of an expression by recursive descent is called **top-down parsing**, whereas this chapter's method of translating an expression by looking at each of its components in turn is an example of **bottom-up parsing**.

Exercises

(a) Draw the expression tree for each of the following expressions. Using the tree, convert the expression into (b) prefix and (c) postfix form. Use the table of priorities developed in this section, not those in Pascal.

1. $a + b < c$

2. $a < b + c$

3. $a - b < c - d$ **or** $e < f$

4. $n!$ **div** $(k! \times (n - k)!)$
   (Formula for binomial coefficients)

5. $s := (n / 2) \times (2 \times a + (n-1) \times d)$
   (This is the sum of the first n terms of an arithmetic progression.)

6. $g := a \times (1 - r{\uparrow}n)/(1-r)$
   (This is the sum of the first n terms of a geometric progression.)

7. $a = 1$ **or** $b \times c = 2$ **or** $(a > 1$ **and**   **not** $b < 3)$

8.3 Evaluation of Polish expressions.

We first introduced the postfix form as a natural order of traversing an expression tree in order to evaluate the corresponding expression. Later in this section we shall formulate an algorithm for evaluating an expression directly from the postfix form, but first (since it is even simpler) we consider the prefix form.

8.3.1 Evaluation of an expression in prefix form.

Preorder traversal of a binary tree works from the top down. The root is visited first, and the remainder of the traversal then divided into two parts. The natural way to organize the process is as a recursive, divide-and-conquer algorithm. The same situation holds for an expression in prefix form. The first symbol (if there is more than one) is an operator (the one that will actually be done last), and the remainder of the expression comprises the operand(s) of this operator (one for a unary operator, two for a binary operator). Our procedure for evaluating the prefix form should hence begin with this first symbol. If it is a unary operator, then the procedure should invoke itself recursively to determine the value of the operand. If the first symbol is a binary operator, then it should make two recursive calls for its two operands. The recursion terminates in the remaining case: When the first symbol is a simple operand, then it is its own prefix form and the procedure should only return its value.

The following outline thus summarizes the evaluation of an expression in prefix form:

```
procedure Evaluate(expression, result);
    Let t be the first symbol in expression, and move one position through
    the expression;
    if t is a unary operator then
    begin
        Evaluate(expression, x);
        Set the result to the value of operator t applied to x
    end
```

```
  else if t is a binary operator then
  begin
    Evaluate(expression, x);
    Evaluate(expression, y);
    Set the result to the value of operator t applied to x and y
  end
  else                                              {t is a simple operand}
    Set the result to the value of t
end;
```

8.3.2 Pascal conventions.

To tie down the details in this outline, let us establish some conventions and rewrite the algorithm in Pascal. The operators and operands in our expression may well have names that are more than one character long; hence we do not scan the expression one character at a time. Instead we define a *token* to be a single operator or operand from the expression. To emphasize that the procedure scans through the expression only once we shall employ an auxiliary procedure

GetToken(var t: token)

that will move through the expression and return one token at a time. We need to know whether the token is an operand, a unary operator or a binary operator, so we assume the existence of a function Kind( ) that will return one of the three words

operand, unaryop, binaryop

(In Pascal these identifiers together constitute an *enumerated type*.)

For simplicity we shall assume that all the operands and the results of evaluating the operators are of the same type, which we leave unspecified and call value. In many applications this type would be one of integer, real, complex or Boolean.

Finally, we must assume the existence of three auxiliary functions that return a result of type value.

DoUnary(t: token, x: value): value
DoBinary(t: token, x, y: value): value

actually perform the given operation on their operand(s). They need to recognize the symbols used for the operation t and the operands x and y, and invoke the necessary machine-language instructions. Similarly,

GetValue(t: token): value

returns the actual value of a simple operand t, and might need, for example, to convert a constant from decimal to binary form, or look up the value of a variable. The actual form of these functions will depend very much on the application. We cannot settle all these questions here, but want only to concentrate on designing one important part of a compiler or expression evaluator.

8.3.3 Pascal procedure for prefix evaluation.

With these preliminaries we can now translate our outline into a Pascal program to evaluate prefix expressions.

```
procedure EvaluatePrefix( var result: value);
var
  t:     token;
  x, y:  value;
begin
  GetToken(t);
  case Kind(t) of
    unaryop:   begin
                 EvaluatePrefix( x );
                 result  := DoUnary(t, x)
               end;
    binaryop:  begin
                 EvaluatePrefix( x );
                 EvaluatePrefix( y );
                 result  := DoBinary(t,x,y)
               end;
    operand:   result  := GetValue( t )
  end
end;
```

8.3.4 Evaluation of postfix expressions.

It is almost inevitable that the prefix form so naturally calls for a recursive function for its evaluation, since the prefix form is really a "top-down" formulation of the algebraic expression: the outer, overall actions are specified first, then later in the expression the component parts are spelled out. On the other hand, in the postfix form the operands appear first, and the whole expression is slowly built up from its simple operands and the inner operators, in a "bottom-up" fashion. Therefore iterative programs using stacks appear more natural for the postfix form. (It is of course possible to write either recursive or non-recursive programs for either form. We are here discussing only the motivation, or what first appears more natural.)

To evaluate an expression in postfix form, it is necessary to remember the operands until their operator is eventually found some time later. The natural way to remember them is to put them on a stack. Then when the first operator to be done is encountered, it will find its operands on the top of the stack. If it puts its result back on the stack, then its result will be in the right place to be an operand for a later operator. When the evaluation is complete, the final result will be the only value on the stack. In this way, we obtain a procedure to evaluate a postfix expression.

At this time we should note a significant difference between postfix and prefix expressions. There was no need, in the prefix procedure, to check explicitly that the end of the expression had been reached, since the entire expression automatically constituted the operand(s) for the first operator. Reading a postfix expression from left to right, however, we can encounter sub-expressions that are, by themselves, legitimate postfix expressions. For example, if we stop reading

$$b \quad 2 \quad \uparrow \quad 4 \quad a \quad \times \quad c \quad \times \quad -$$

after the '$\uparrow$', we find that it is a legal postfix expression. To remedy this problem we shall suppose that the expression ends with a special sentinel, and for this sentinel token the function Kind( ) returns the special value

endexpression.

The remaining defined types in Pascal, as well as the other auxiliary procedures and functions are the same as for the prefix evaluation. In addition, we shall represent the stack as an array declared in our procedure, with subsidiary procedures as follows.

```
procedure Push( v: value);              procedure Pop( var v: value);
begin                                   begin
  if nstack >= maxstack then error        if nstack <= 0 then error
  else begin                              else begin
    nstack := nstack + 1;                   v := stack[ nstack ];
    stack[ nstack ] := v                    nstack := nstack - 1
  end                                     end
end;                                    end;

procedure EvaluatePostfix( var result: value);
const
  maxstack = 100;                          {maximum size of stack}
var
  stack:    array[1 .. maxstack] of value;
  nstack:   0 .. maxstack;                 {number of values in stack}
  t:        token;                         {current operator or operand}
  x, y:     value;                         {operands of current operator}
begin                                      {Procedure EvaluatePostfix}
  nstack := 0;                             {Initialize stack to be empty.}
  repeat
    GetToken( t );
    case Kind( t ) of
      operand:
              Push( GetValue( t ) );
      unaryop:
              begin
                Pop( x );
                Push( DoUnary( t, x) )
              end;
```

```
binaryop:
        begin
          Pop( y );
          Pop( x );
          Push( DoBinary( t, x, y) )
        end;
    endexpression:
        if nstack = 1 then
          Pop( result )
        else
          Error                          {Must be exactly 1 entry at end}
  end                                    {case statement}
  until Kind( t ) = endexpression;
end;
```

In this program we have included error checking in the Push and Pop procedures, to catch the possibility that the appearance of an operator might call for popping the stack without enough operands on the stack. Similarly at the end there is an error if there is more than one result or no result on the stack.

8.3.5 Proof of the program: counting stack entries.

So far we have given only an informal motivation for the preceding program, and it may not be clear that it will produce the correct result in every case. Fortunately it is not difficult to give a formal justification of the program, and at the same time, to discover a useful criterion as to whether an expression is properly written in postfix form or not.

The method we shall use is to keep track of the number of entries in the stack. When each operand is obtained, it is immediately pushed onto the stack. A unary operator first pops, then pushes the stack, and thus makes no change in the number of entries. A binary operator pops the stack twice and pushes it once, giving a net decrease of one entry in the stack. More formally, we have:

> For a sequence E of operands, unary and binary operators, form a
> running sum by starting at the left end of E and counting +1 for
> each operand, 0 for each unary operator, and −1 for each binary
> operator. E satisfies the **running-sum condition** provided that this
> running sum never falls below 1, and is exactly 1 at the right-hand
> end of E.

The sequence of running sums for an evaluation of the postfix form of the quadratic formula is illustrated in Figure 8.2. We shall prove the following two theorems at the same time.

THEOREM 8.1.   *If E is a properly formed expression in postfix form, then E must satisfy the running sum condition.*

THEOREM 8.2.   *A properly formed expression in postfix form will be correctly evaluated by procedure* EvaluatePostfix.

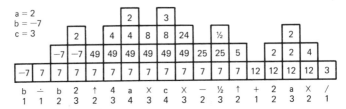

Figure 8.2. Stack frames and running sums, quadratic formula

PROOF.   We shall prove the theorems together by using mathematical induction on the length of the expression E being evaluated.

The starting point for the induction is the case that E is a single operand alone, with length 1. This operand contributes +1, and the running-sum condition is satisfied. The procedure, when applied to a simple operand alone, gets its value, pushes it on the stack (which was previously empty) and at the end pops it as the final value of the procedure, thereby evaluating it correctly.

For the induction hypothesis we now assume that E is a proper postfix expression of length more than 1, that the program correctly evaluates all postfix expressions of length less than that of E, and that all such shorter expressions satisfy the running-sum condition. Since the length of E is more than 1, E is constructed at its last step either as F *op*, where *op* is a unary operator and F a postfix expression, or as F G *op*, where *op* is a binary operator and F and G are postfix expressions. In either case the lengths of F and G are less than that of E, so by induction hypothesis both of them satisfy the running-sum condition, and the procedure would evaluate either of them separately and would obtain the correct result.

First take the case when *op* is a unary operator. Since F satisfies the running-sum condition, the sum at its end is exactly +1. As a unary operator, *op* contributes 0 to the sum, so the full expression E satisfies the running-sum condition. When the procedure reaches the end of F, similarly, it will, by induction hypothesis, have evaluated F correctly and left its value as the unique stack entry. The unary operator *op* is then finally applied to this value, which is popped as the final result.

Finally, take the case when *op* is binary. When the procedure reaches the last token of F, the value of F will be the unique entry on the stack. Similarly, the running sum will be 1. At the next token the program starts to evaluate G. By the induction hypothesis the evaluation of G will also be correct and its running sum alone never falls below 1, and ends at exactly 1. Since the running sum at the end of F is 1, the combined running sum never falls below 2, and ends at exactly 2 at the end of G. Thus the evaluation of G will proceed and never disturb the single entry on the bottom of the stack, which is the result of F. When the evaluation reaches the final binary operator *op*, the running sum is correctly reduced from 2 to 1, and the operator finds precisely its two operands on the stack, where after evaluation it leaves its unique result. This completes the proof of Theorems 8.1 and 8.2.

This error checking by keeping a running count of the number of entries on the stack provides a handy way to verify that a sequence of tokens is in fact a properly formed postfix expression, and is especially useful because its converse is also true:

> THEOREM 8.3.   *If E is any sequence of operands and operators that satisfies the condition on running sums, then E is a properly formed expression in postfix form.*

PROOF.   We shall again use mathematical induction to prove Theorem 8.3. The starting point is an expression containing only one token. Since the running sum (same as final sum) for a sequence of length 1 will be 1, this one token must be a simple operand. One simple operand alone is indeed a syntactically correct expression.

Now, for the inductive step, suppose that the theorem has been verified for all expressions strictly shorter than E, and E has length greater than 1. If the last token of E were an operand, then it would contribute $+1$ to the sum, and since the final sum is 1, the running sum would have been 0 one step before the end, contrary to the assumption that the running-sum condition is satisfied. Thus the final token of E must be an operator.

If the operator is unary, then it can be omitted and the remaining sequence still satisfies the condition on running sums, so by induction hypothesis is a syntactically correct expression, and all of E then also is.

Finally suppose that the last token is a binary operator *op*. To show that E is syntactically correct, we must find where in the sequence the first operand of *op* ends and the second one starts, by using the running sum. Since the operator *op* contributes -1 to the sum, it was 2 one step before the end. This 2 means that there were two items on the stack, the first and second operands of *op*. As we step backward through the sequence E, eventually we will reach a place where there is only one entry on the stack (running sum 1), and this one entry will be the first operand of *op*. Thus the place to break the sequence is at the last position before the end where the running sum is exactly 1. Such a position must exist, since at the far left end of E (if not before) we will find a running sum of 1. When we break E at its last 1, then it takes the form F G *op*. The subsequence F satisfies the condition on running sums, and ends with a sum of 1, so by induction it is a correctly formed postfix expression. Since the running sums during G of F G *op* never again fall to 1, and end at 2 just before *op*, we may subtract 1 from each of them and conclude that the running sums for G alone satisfy the condition. Thus by induction hypothesis G is also a correctly formed postfix expression. Thus both F and G are correct expressions, and can be combined by the binary operator *op* into a correct expression E. Thus the proof of the theorem is complete.

We can take the proof one more step, to show that the last position where a sum of 1 occurs is the *only* place where the sequence E can be split into syntactically correct subsequences F and G. For suppose it was split elsewhere. If at the end of F the running sum is not 1, then F is not a syntactically correct expression. If the running sum is 1 at the end of F, but reaches 1 again during the G part of F G *op*, then the sums for G alone would reach 0 at that point, so G is not correct. We have now shown that there is only one way to recover the two operands of a binary operator. Clearly there is only one way to recover the single operand for a unary operator. Hence we can recover the infix form of an expression from its postfix form, together with the order in which the operations are done, which we can denote by bracketing the result of every operation in the infix form with another pair of parentheses.

We have therefore proved:

> THEOREM 8.4.   *An expression in postfix form that satisfies the running-sum condition corresponds to exactly one fully bracketed expression in infix form. Hence no parentheses are needed to achieve the unique representation of an expression in postfix form.*

Similar theorems hold for the prefix form; their proofs are left as exercises. The theorems of this section provide both a theoretical justification of the use of Polish notation, and a convenient way to check an expression for correct syntax.

8.3.6 Recursive evaluation of postfix expressions.

Most people find that the recursive procedure for evaluating prefix expressions is easier to understand than the stack-based (non-recursive) procedure for evaluating postfix expressions. In this (optional) section we show how the stack can be eliminated in favor of recursion for postfix evaluation.

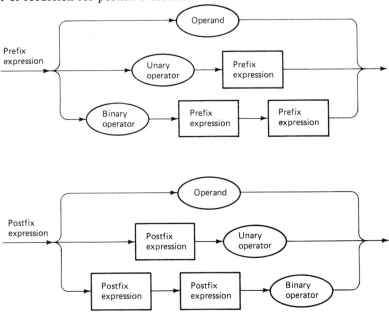

Figure 8.3. Syntax diagrams of Polish expressions

First, however, let us see why the natural approach leads to a recursive procedure for prefix evaluation but not for postfix. We can describe both prefix and postfix expressions by the syntax diagrams of Figure 8.3. In both cases there are three possibilities: the expression consists of only a single operand, or the outermost operator is unary or is binary.

In tracing through the diagram for prefix form, the first token we encounter in the expression determines which of the three branches we take, and there are then no further choices to make (except within recursive calls, which need not be considered just now). Hence the structure of the recursive procedure for prefix evaluation closely resembles the syntax diagram.

With the postfix diagram, however, there is no way to tell from the first token (which will always be an operand) which of the three branches to take. It is only when the last token is encountered that the branch is determined. This fact does, however, lead to one easy recursive solution: Read the expression from right to left; reverse all the arrows on the syntax diagram; and use the same procedure as for prefix evaluation!

If we wish, however, to read the expression in the usual way from left to right, then we must work harder. Let us consider separately each of the three kinds of tokens in a postfix form. We have already observed that the first token in the expression must be an operand; this follows directly from the fact that the running sum after the first token is (at least) 1. Since unary operators do not change the running sum, unary operators can be inserted anywhere after the initial operand. It is the third case, binary operators, whose study leads to the solution.

Consider the sequence of running sums, and the place(s) in the sequence where the sum drops from 2 to 1. Since binary operators contribute -1 to the sum, such places must exist if the postfix expression contains any binary operators, and must correspond to the places in the expression where the two operands of the binary operator constitute the whole expression to the left. Such situations are illustrated in the stack frames of Figure 8.2. The entry on the bottom of the stack is the first operand; a sequence of positions where the height is at least 2, starting and ending at exactly two, make up the calculation of the second operand, and, taken in isolation, this sequence is itself a properly formed postfix expression. A drop in height from 2 to 1 marks one of the binary operators in which we are interested.

After the binary operator more unary operators may appear, and then the process may repeat itself (if the running sums again increase) with more sequences that are self-contained postfix expressions followed by binary and unary operators. In summary, we have shown that postfix expressions are described by the syntax diagram of Figure 8.4, which translates easily into the recursive procedure that follows. The Pascal conventions are the same as in the previous procedures.

The situation appearing in the postfix diagram of Figure 8.3 is called *left recursion*, and the steps we have taken in the transition to the diagram in Figure 8.4 are typical of those needed to remove left recursion.

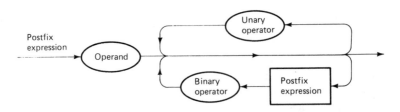

Figure 8.4. Alternative syntax diagram, postfix expression

```
procedure EvaluatePostfix( var result: value);        {recursive version}
var
  t:    token;
begin
  GetToken(t);
  if Kind(t) <> operand then
    Error
  else
    P( result );
  if Kind(t) <> endexpression then
    Error
end;
procedure P( var result: value );
{Recursively evaluates postfix expression beginning at token t, which is
guaranteed to be an operand when P is invoked.  At the conclusion, t is
the first token beyond the expression evaluated, and will be either a
binary operator or endexpression.}

var
  x: value;
begin
  result := GetValue(t);
  GetToken(t);
  while (Kind(t) = unaryop) or (Kind(t) = operand) do
  begin
    if Kind(t) = unaryop then
      result := DoUnary(t, result)
    else                                             {t must be an operand}
    begin
      P( x );
      if Kind(t) = binaryop then
        result := DoBinary(t, result, x)
```

```
        else
            Error
        end;
        GetToken(t)
    end
    end;
```

Exercises

1. Trace the action on each of the following expressions by the procedure EvaluatePostfix in (a) non-recursive and (b) recursive versions. For the recursive procedure draw the tree of recursive calls, indicating at each node which tokens are being processed. For the non-recursive procedure, draw a sequence of stack frames showing which tokens are processed at each stage.

   (a) a b $+$ c $\times$
   (b) a b c $+$ $\times$
   (c) a $!$ b $!$ $/$ c d $-$ a $!$ $-$ $\times$
   (d) a b $<$ **not** c d $\times$ $<$ e **or**

2. Trace the action of the procedure EvaluatePrefix on each of the following expressions, by drawing a tree of recursive calls showing which tokens are processed at each stage.

   (a) $/$ $+$ x y $!$ n
   (b) $/$ $+$ $!$ x y n
   (c) **and** $<$ x y **or**   **not** $=$ $+$ x y z $>$ x 0

3. Which of the following are syntactically correct postfix expressions? Show the error in each incorrect expression. Translate each correct expression into infix form, using parentheses as necessary to avoid ambiguities.

   (a) a b c $+$ $\times$ a $/$ c b $+$ d $/$ $-$
   (b) a b $+$ c a $\times$ b c $/$ d $-$
   (c) a b $+$ c a $\times$ $-$ c $\times$ $+$ b c $-$
   (d) a $\div$ b $\times$
   (e) a $\times$ b $\div$
   (f) a b $\times$ $\div$
   (g) a b $\div$ $\times$

4. Translate each of the following expressions from prefix form into postfix form.

   (a) $/$ $+$ x y $!$ n
   (b) $/$ $+$ $!$ x y n
   (c) **and** $<$ x y **or**   **not** $=$ $+$ x y z $>$ x 0

5. Write a Pascal algorithm to translate an expression from prefix form into postfix form. Use the Pascal conventions of this chapter.

6. Translate each of the following expressions from postfix form into prefix form.

    (a) *a*   *b*   +   *c*   ×
    (b) *a*   *b*   *c*   +   ×
    (c) *a*   !   *b*   !   /   *c*   *d*   −   *a*   !   −   ×
    (d) *a*   *b*   <   **not**   *c*   *d*   ×   <   *e*   **or**

7. Write a Pascal algorithm to translate an expression from postfix form into prefix form. Use the Pascal conventions of this chapter.

8. A *fully bracketed* expression is one of the following forms:

    (a) a simple operand;
    (b) (*op E*) where *op* is a unary operator and *E* is a fully bracketed expression;
    (c) (*E op F*) where *op* is a binary operator and *E* and *F* are fully bracketed expressions.

Hence, in a fully bracketed expression, the results of every operation are enclosed in parentheses. Examples of fully bracketed expressions are $((a+b)-c)$, $(-a)$, $(a+b)$, $(a+(b+c))$. Write Pascal algorithms that will translate expressions from (a) prefix and (b) postfix form into fully bracketed form.

9. Formulate and prove theorems analogous to Theorems 8.1, 8.3 and 8.4 for the prefix form of expressions.

8.4 Translation from infix form to Polish form.

Very few (if any) programmers habitually write algebraic or logical expressions in Polish form, or even in fully bracketed form. To make convenient use of the algorithms we have developed, we must have an efficient method to translate arbitrary expressions from infix form into Polish notation. As a first simplification, we shall consider only the postfix form. Secondly, we shall exclude unary operators that are placed to the right of their operands. Such operators cause no conceptual difficulty, but would make the algorithms more complicated.

One method that we could use would be to build the expression tree from the infix form, and traverse the tree to obtain the postfix form, but, as it turns out, constructing the tree is actually more complicated than constructing the postfix form directly. Since, in postfix form, all operators come after their operands, the task of translation from infix to postfix form is simply:

> *Delay each operator until its right-hand operand has been translated. Pass each simple operand through without delay.*

This action is illustrated in Figure 8.5.

The major problem we must resolve is to find what token will terminate the right-hand operand of a given operator. We must take both parentheses and priorities of operators into account. The first problem is easy. If a left parenthesis is in the

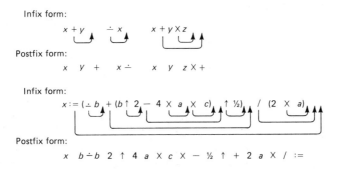

Figure 8.5. Delaying operators in postfix form

operand, then everything through the matching right parenthesis must also be. For the second problem, let us consider the first non-bracketed operator to the right of the given operator. If its priority is higher than that of the given one, then it must be done first; hence its result is part of the operand of the given operator. If its priority is lower, then it will not be a part of the right operand, but everything that comes before it will be. Because of the convention of left-to-right evaluation for operators of equal priority, an operator of the same priority will not be part of the operand. If the first non-bracketed operator is part of the operand (i.e., has strictly higher priority), then we can continue through the expression until we find an operator of equal or lower priority than that of the given operator; this operator will then terminate the right-hand operand. There are two more ways in which the right operand can terminate: the expression can end, or the given operator may itself be within a bracketed sub-expression, in which case its right operand will end when an unmatched right parenthesis ')' is encountered. In summary, we have the rules:

> *If op is an operator in an infix expression, then its right-hand operand contains all tokens on its right until one of the following is encountered:*
>
> *(a)   the end of the expression.*
> *(b)   an unmatched right parenthesis ')'.*
> *(c)   an operator of priority less than or equal to that of op, and not within a bracketed sub-expression.*

From these rules we can see that the appropriate way to remember the operators being delayed is to keep them on a stack. If operator op_2 comes on the right of operator op_1 but has higher priority, then op_2 will be output before op_1 is. Thus the operators are output in the order first in, last out.

The key to writing a non-recursive algorithm for the translation is to make a slight change in our point of view by asking, as each token appears in the input, which of the operators previously delayed (that is, on the stack) now have their right operands terminated because of the new token, so that it is time to move them into the output. The preceding three conditions then become:

(a)   At the end of the expression, all operators are output.

(b)   A right parenthesis causes all operators found since the corresponding left parenthesis to be output.

(c)   An operator causes all other operators of greater or equal priority to be output.

To implement rule *(b)*, we shall put each left parenthesis on the stack when it is encountered. Then when the matching right parenthesis appears, and the operators have been popped from the stack, the pair can both be discarded.

We can now incorporate these rules into a procedure. To do so, we shall use the same auxiliary types and procedures as in the last section, except that now the function Kind(···) can return two additional values:

leftparen rightparen

that denote, respectively, left and right parentheses. The procedures Push and Pop will now process tokens (operators) rather than values. In addition to the procedure GetToken( ) that obtains the next token from the input (infix expression), we use an auxiliary procedure

PutToken (t: token)

that puts the given token into the postfix expression. Thus these two procedures might read and write with files, or might only refer to arrays already set up, depending on the desired application. Finally, we shall use a function Priority(op) that will return the priority of an operator op.

With these conventions we can write the procedure.

```
procedure Translate;
const
  maxstack = 100;              {maximum allowable size of stack};
var
  Stack:      array[1 .. maxstack] of token;
  nstack:     0 .. maxstack;   {number of operators on the stack}
  t,                           {token currently being processed}
  x:          token;           {operator popped from stack}
  endright:   Boolean;         {End of right operand been reached?}

begin
  nstack := 0;                 {Initialize stack to be empty}
  repeat
    GetToken( t );
    case Kind( t ) of
      operand:    PutToken( t );
      leftparen:  Push( t );
```

```
rightparen:   begin
                 Pop( t );
                 while Kind( t ) <> leftparen do
                 begin
                   PutToken( t );
                   Pop( t )              {Discard the left parenthesis}
                 end
              end;
unaryop,      {no distinction needed between kinds of operators}
binaryop:     begin
                 repeat
                   if nstack = 0 then
                      endright := true
                   else if Kind( stack[nstack] ) = leftparen then
                      endright := true
                   else if Priority(stack[nstack]) < Priority(t) then
                      endright := true
                   else begin
                      endright := false;
                      Pop( x );
                      PutToken( x )
                   end
                 until endright;
                 Push( t )
              end;                        {processing operator}
endexpression:
                 while nstack > 0 do        {empty the stack}
                 begin
                   Pop( x );
                   PutToken( x )
                 end
       end                                 {case statement}
    until Kind( t ) = endexpression;
    PutToken( t );                         {Put endexpression into postfix.}
 end;                                       {procedure}
```

Figure 8.6 shows the steps performed to translate the quadratic formula

$$x: = (-b+(b\uparrow2-4\times a\times c)\uparrow\frac{1}{2})/(2\times a)$$

into postfix form, as an illustration of this algorithm. (Recall that we are using '$-$' to denote unary negation.)

Input Token	Contents of Stack (rightmost token is on top)	Output Token(s)
x		x
:=	:=	
(	:= (	
÷	:= (÷	
b	:= (÷	b
+	:= (+	÷
(	:= (+ (	
b	:= (+ (	b
↑	:= (+ (↑	
2	:= (+ (↑	2
−	:= (+ (−	↑
4	:= (+ (−	4
×	:= (+ (− ×	
a	:= (+ (− ×	a
×	:= (+ (− ×	×
c	:= (+ (− ×	c
)	:= (+	× −
↑	:= (+ ↑	
½	:= (+ ↑	½
)	:=	↑ +
/	/	
(	/ (	
2	/ (	2
×	/ (×	
a	/ (×	a
)	/	×
endexpression		/ :=

Figure 8.6. Translation of quadratic formula into postfix form

This completes the discussion of translation into postfix form. There will clearly be similarities in describing the translation into prefix form, but some difficulties arise because of the seemingly irrelevant fact that, in European languages, we read from left to right. If we were to translate an expression into prefix form working from left to right, then not only would the operators need to be rearranged but operands would need to be delayed until after their operators were output. But the relative order of operands is not changed in the translation, so the appropriate storage structure to keep the operands would not be a stack (it would in fact be a queue). Since stacks would not do the job, neither would recursive programs with no explicit arrays, since these two kinds of programs can do equivalent tasks. Thus a left-to-right translation into prefix form would need a different approach. The trick is to translate into prefix form by working from right to left through the expression, using methods quite similar to the left-to-right postfix translation that we have developed. The details are left as an exercise.

Exercises

1. Note that in procedure **Translate** the action taken at the end of the input is much the same as when a right parenthesis is encountered. Suppose that the entire expression is enclosed in a pair of parentheses to serve as sentinels for the beginning and end. Write a simplified version of procedure **Translate** that no longer needs to check explicitly for the end of input.

2. Procedure **Translate** is sadly deficient in error checking. Unmatched parentheses, for example, may send it off into a non-existent part of the expression. Add error checking to the procedure so that it will detect syntax errors in its input (infix) expression.

3. Modify procedure **Translate** so that it will accommodate unary operators that are written to the right of their operands. You should assume that the function Kind($\cdots$) returns the answer **rightunary** when such an operator appears.

4. Rewrite procedure **Translate** as a recursive procedure that uses no stack or other array.

5. Unary operators and exponentiation are normally performed from right to left in ordinary algebraic notation, but (without bracketing) our procedure **Translate** will do them in the reverse order. This difficulty can be resolved by introducing two kinds of priority functions for operators. Each operator is assigned both an *incoming priority* and an *in-stack priority*. Procedure **Translate** is then modified so that the **while** loop that pops operators from the stack proceeds while the in-stack priority of the operator on top of the stack is greater than or equal to the incoming priority of the new operator. Except for unary operators and exponentiation, the incoming and in-stack priorities will both equal the previously assigned priority, so that the modification will make no change. For unary operators and exponentiation the in-stack priority remains 7, but the incoming priority is defined to be 8. Verify that these modifications will produce the desired right-to-left evaluation of unary operators and exponentiation, and will not otherwise affect the correct functioning of procedure **Translate**.

8.5 An interactive expression evaluator.

There are many applications for a program that can evaluate a function that is typed in interactively while the program is running. One such application is a program that will draw the graph of a mathematical function (either on a plotter or on a graphics video terminal). Suppose that you are writing such a program to be used to help first-year calculus students graph functions. Most of these students will not know how to write or compile programs, so you wish to include in your program some way that the user can put in an expression for a function such as

$$x * \log(x) - x \uparrow 1.25$$

while the program is running. The program can then graph the function for appropriate values of x.

The goal of this section is to describe such a program, and especially to complete the writing of two subprograms to help with this problem. The first subprogram will take as input an expression involving constants, variable(s), arithmetic operators, and standard functions, with bracketing allowed, as typed in from the terminal. It will then translate the expression into postfix form and keep it in an appropriate array. The second subprogram will evaluate the expression for values of the variable(s) given as its calling parameter(s), and return the answer.

We undertake this project for several reasons. It shows how to take the ideas already developed for working with Polish notation, and build these ideas into a complete, concrete, and functioning program. In this way, the project illustrates a problem-solving approach to program design, in which we begin with solutions to the key questions, and complete the structure with auxiliary procedures as needed. Finally, since this project is intended for use by people with little computer experience, it provides opportunity to test *robustness*, that is, the ability of the program to withstand unexpected or incorrect input without catastrophic failure.

8.5.1 The main program.

The main program outlines how the work is divided into procedures; hence we look at it first.

```
program GraphFunction;
{Reads an expression from the terminal; converts it into postfix form;
evaluates postfix expression and graphs it over a specified range}

{Declarations of constants, types, variables, procedures and functions
will be inserted here.}

begin                                              {main program}
  Writeln('Welcome to the function-graphing program.');
  Write('Do you wish instructions');
  if Yes then Instruct;
  DefineTokens;
  repeat                                           {new expression}
    StartExpression;
```

```
repeat                                          {new graph}
  ReadGraphLimits;
  ReadParameters;
  x := xlow;
  repeat
    L[firstoperand].val := x;        {by convention, x is always the
                                      first entry in the list of operands.}
    EvaluatePostfix( y );
    Graph( x, y );
    x := x + increment
  until x > xhigh;
  Write('Repeat for new graphing limits')
until not Yes;
Write('Repeat for a new expression')
until not Yes;
Writeln('Graphing program has finished.')
end.                                            {main program}
```

1. Instructions.

As with most programs written for casual users, the first step is to determine if instructions should be given. To save space, however, we shall not include a text for procedure Instruct here. The response to questions to the user is obtained through the function Yes below.

```
function Yes: Boolean;
var
  ch: char;
begin
  repeat
    Write(' (y,n)?');
    Read(ch);
    Writeln;
  until ch in ['N', 'n', 'Y', 'y'];
  Yes := ch in ['Y', 'y']
end;
```

2. UCSD Pascal.

This function, and all parts of the program in this section, follow the requirements of the dialect UCSD Pascal*. This dialect is commonly implemented on micro-computers, where it is reasonable to expect that this program may be run. UCSD

---

* UCSD Pascal is a trademark of the Regents of the University of California.

Pascal has several non-standard features that we shall use. First, reading from the terminal is character by character; hence the Writeln after the Read. Second, **set of** char is legal, and will be used whenever convenient. Third, UCSD Pascal provides a predefined type string that is essentially **packed array of** char, but with a dynamically varying length attribute up to a bound shown in brackets in the type declaration. We shall both use indices to refer to locations within a string, and use the following predefined functions :

> Length(s: string): integer   {gives the length of string s.}
> Copy(s: string, i, j: integer): string {copies j characters from s starting
> at position i}.
> Concat(s, t: string): string   {concatenates strings s and t.}

Strings may be assigned, compared, and used as calling parameters. Constant strings, surrounded by apostrophes, may be used wherever strings are allowed.

3. Error processing.

In several procedures we shall use a procedure

procedure Error(s: string)

that will print the string and terminate the program. That is, for simplicity, we shall make all errors that the program detects be fatal to its execution.

4. Further procedures.

The second task of the main program is to establish the definitions of the predefined tokens (such as the operators $+$, $-$, $*$ amongst others, the operand x that will be used in the graphing, and perhaps some constants). We shall write procedure Define-Tokens after we have decided on the data structures.

Procedure StartExpression reads in an expression, splits it into tokens, and translates it into postfix form. Here arise several design problems, and the greatest need to check the input for possible errors that the user might make.

Procedure ReadGraphLimits sets up any initialization required to draw the graph, obtains the bounds and scale for drawing, and determines the range of values for x and the increment to be used. These requirements, unfortunately, differ greatly from one system to another, so we cannot hope to write a procedure that is widely applicable. For testing the program, therefore, we must be content with a small stub that only obtains the bounds and increment for x. Similarly, procedure Graph(x,y) that actually graphs the point (x,y) is also system dependent, and so is not included here. For testing our program, a stub that writes out the values of x and y will suffice.

It may be that the expression as typed in contains variables other than x, the one used for graphing. If so, our program will treat these other variables as parameters that will keep the same value while one graph is drawn, but whose values can be changed from one graph to the next, without other change in the expression. Procedure ReadParameters obtains values for these variables.

The innermost loop of the main program moves through the range of values for x, sets them into the place where they can be found by procedure EvaluatePostfix, and graphs the results.

8.5.2 Representation of the data.

Our data-structure decisions concern how to store and retrieve the tokens used in Polish expressions and their evaluation. For each different token we must remember (1) its name (as a string of characters), so that we can recognize it in the input expression; (2) its kind (unaryop, binaryop, operand, leftparen, rightparen, or endexpression); (3) for operators, its priority; for operands, its value. It is reasonable to think of representing each token as a record containing this information. One small difficulty arises: The same token may appear several times in an expression. If it is an operand, then we must be certain that it is given the same value each time. If we put the records themselves into the expressions, then when a value is assigned to an operand we must be sure that it is updated in all the records corresponding to that operand. We can avoid having to keep chains of references to a given variable by associating an integer code with each token, and placing this code in the expression, rather than the full record. We shall then set up a *lexicon* for the tokens, which will be an array indexed by the integer codes, and which will hold the full records for the tokens. In this way, if k is the code for a variable, then every appearance of k in the expression will cause us to look in position k of the lexicon for the corresponding value, and we are automatically assured of getting the same value each time.

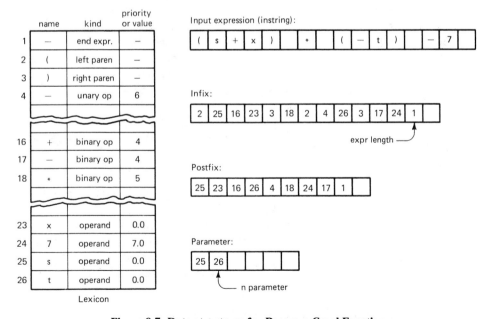

Figure 8.7. Data structures for Program GraphFunction

Placing integer codes rather than records in the expressions also has the advantage of saving some space, but space for tokens is unlikely to be a critical restraint for this project. The time required to evaluate the postfix expression at many different values of the argument x is more likely to prove expensive.

As the input expression is decoded, the program may find constants and new variables (parameters), which it will then add to the lexicon. These will all be classed as operands, but recall that in the case of parameters, the user will be asked to give values before the expression is evaluated. Hence it is necessary to keep one more list, a list of the codes that correspond to parameters.

All these data structures are illustrated in Figure 8.7, along with some of the data structures used in the principal procedures.

Let us summarize the data representation by giving the declarations to be inserted into the main program.

```
const
    maxexpression = 100;   {maximum number of tokens in an expression}
    maxstack      = 100;
    maxtoken      = 100;   {maximum number of distinct kinds of tokens}
    maxpriority   = 6;                     {largest priority of any operator}
    maxparam      = 50;              {largest number of variables allowed}
    namelength    = 7;                  {number of characters in an identifier}
    firstunary    = 4;       {where among tokens is first unary operator?}
    lastunary     = 15;                    {last code of a unary operator}
    firstbinary   = 16;          {what is code of first binary operator?}
    lastbinary    = 22;          {what is code of last binary operator?}
    firstoperand  = 23;                   {where do the operands start?}
            {By convention, firstoperand is the code for the variable x.}
    lastoperand   = 25;
                         {last predefined operand; other operands may be
                             introduced by the user within the expression}

type
    value         = real;
                {for simplicity, keep all the variables having the same type}
    priorrange    = 1 .. maxpriority;
    name          = string[ namelength ];    {feature of UCSD Pascal}
    token         = 0 .. maxtoken;    {codes; 0 denotes undefined}
    tokenkind     =                       (operand, unaryop, binaryop,
                                endexpression, leftparen, rightparen);
```

```
deftoken              = record
                          nm:      name;
                          case k:  tokenkind of
                          operand:  (val: value);
                          unaryop,
                          binaryop:  (pri: priorrange);
                          endexpression,
                          leftparen,
                          rightparen: ()                          {empty}
                          end;
expression            = array[ 1 .. maxexpression ] of token;
exprindex             = 0..maxexpression;
param                 = 0..maxparam;

var
  postfix:            expression;
  Lexicon:            array[ token ] of deftoken; {information on all tokens}
  nparameter:         param;              {count of number of parameters}
  parameter:          array[ param ] of token;    {list of operands whose
                                          values must be read in before graphing}
  x, y,                                   {y is expression evaluated at x}
  xlow, xhigh,                                   {bounds on x for plotting}
  ylow, yhigh,                                   {bounds on y for plotting}
  increment:          value;                     {increment for plotting}
```

8.5.3 Predefined tokens.

The only task to be done by procedure DefineTokens is to place the names, kinds, priorities (for operators) and values (for operands) of all the predefined tokens into the lexicon. Hence the procedure consists only of a long series of assignment statements, which we omit to save space.

The complete list of predefined tokens used in this implementation is shown in Figure 8.8. Note that we can add operators that are not a standard part of a computer language (such as the base 2 logarithm lg), and constants such as e and π. The expressions in which we are interested in this section begin and end with real numbers. Hence we do not include any Boolean or set-valued operations. Several integer-valued operations are included, since integers can sensibly be regarded as real numbers.

8.5.4 Translation of the expression.

In this section of the program, we must read an expression in ordinary (infix) form, check that it is syntactically correct, split it apart into tokens, and find their codes. As a sequence of tokens, the expression can then be converted to postfix form by the algorithm written earlier in the chapter.

Token	Name	Kind	Priority/Value
1		endexpression	
2	(	leftparen	
3	)	rightparen	
4	∸	unaryop	6 {negation}
5	abs	unaryop	6
6	sqr	unaryop	6
7	sqrt	unaryop	6
8	exp	unaryop	6
9	ln	unaryop	6
10	lg	unaryop	6 {base 2 log}
11	sin	unaryop	6
12	cos	unaryop	6
13	arctan	unaryop	6
14	round	unaryop	6
15	trunc	unaryop	6
16	+	binaryop	4
17	−	binaryop	4
18	*	binaryop	5
19	/	binaryop	5
20	div	binaryop	5
21	mod	binaryop	5
22	↑	binaryop	6
23	x	operand	0.00000
24	pi	operand	3.14159
25	e	operand	2.71828

Figure 8.8. Predefined tokens for GraphFunction program

1. Finding the definitions of tokens.

As each token is split from the input string, we must find its code. This is an information retrieval problem: the name of the token is the key, and the integer code must be retrieved. In the expression there will usually be no more than a few dozen tokens, and it is quite arguable that the best way to retrieve the code is by sequential search through the lexicon. Sequential search would be easy to program, would require no further data structures, and the cost in time over more sophisticated methods would be negligible. One object of this project, however, is to illustrate larger applications, where the expense of sequential search may no longer be negligible. In a compiler, for example, there may be many hundreds of distinct symbols that must be recognized, and more sophisticated symbol tables must be used. A good choice is to use a hash table together with the lexicon. In the hash table we shall store only codes, and use these to look in the lexicon to locate the token with a given name.

In this way, we obtain the following procedures.

2. The main procedure.

```
procedure      StartExpression;
const
  hashsize      = 101;
  maxstring     = 200;              {maximum length of input string}
type
  address       = 0 .. hashsize;
  indexname     = 0 .. namelength;  {used to loop through a name}
  indexstring   = 0 .. maxstring;   {used to traverse input string}
var
  infix:        expression;
                    {output from ReadExpression; input to Translate}
  H:            array[address] of token;          {hash table}
  tokencount:   token;        {count of number of distinct tokens}

begin                                     {Procedure StartExpression}
  MakeHashTable;
  ReadExpression;
  Translate
end;                                      {Procedure StartExpression}
```

3. Processing the hash table.

```
function Hash(x: name): address;
var
  a:   integer;
  ch: char;
  found: Boolean;
begin
  if length(x) <= 0 then
    Error('Hash attempted with empty name')
  else begin
    ch := x[1];
    a   := abs( ord(ch) ) mod hashsize;
    repeat
      if H[a] = 0 then
        found := true
      else if Lexicon[H[a]].nm = x then
        found := true
```

```
      else begin
        if length(x) > 1 then
          begin ch := x[2]; a := a + abs(ord(ch)) end
          else a := a + 29;
          if a > hashsize then a := a mod hashsize;
          found := false
      end
    until found;
    Hash := a
  end
end;
```

Since many of the tokens have names only one character long, we have written the hash function to give special emphasis to this possibility. The spread achieved by this function appears fairly good, although other functions may do better.

It is also necessary to initialize the hash table with entries corresponding to the predefined tokens. The first such token, however, is endexpression, which is determined by reaching the end of the input, and not by looking in the hash table. Hence token 1 is not placed in H.

```
procedure MakeHashTable;
var
  a:           address;
  t:           token;
begin
  for a   := 0 to hashsize do              {Initialize hash table.}
    H[a]   := 0;
  for t   := 2 to lastoperand do
    H[ Hash( Lexicon[t].nm ) ] := t;
end;
```

4. Decoding the expression.

Figure 8.8 includes both some tokens whose names are single special characters, and some tokens whose names are words beginning with a letter. These latter may be any of unary or binary operators or operands. It is also possible to have tokens that are numbers, that is, which are made up of digits (and possibly a decimal point). Hence in splitting the input expression into tokens, we shall consider three cases, using three procedures in the main loop,

FindWord   FindNumber   FindSymbol,

that will determine the name of the token and put its code into the output expression (still in infix at this stage).

We must now establish conventions regarding the input format. Let us assume that the input expression is typed as one line, so that when we reach the end of the line, we have also reached the end of the input string. Let us use the conventions of Pascal concerning spaces: blanks are ignored between tokens, but the occurrence of a blank terminates a token. If a token is a word, then it begins with a letter, which can be followed by letters or digits. Let us translate all lower-case letters to upper case, and use only upper case in comparisons (be sure that the predefined tokens are hashed as upper case only). Let us truncate names to namelength characters, where the constant namelength is defined in the main program.

It is in reading the input string that the greatest amount of error checking is needed to make sure that the syntax of the input expression is correct, and to make our program as robust as possible. Most of this error checking will be done in the subsidiary procedures, but in the main procedure we keep a counter to make sure that parentheses are nested correctly; that is, that more right than left parentheses never appear, and at the end the parentheses are balanced.

With these provisions, we obtain the following procedure.

```
procedure       ReadExpression;
var
  instring:      string[maxstring];          {expression as typed in}
  exprlength:    exprindex;                  {count of tokens in output}
  position:      indexstring;                {moves through input string}
  parencount:    integer;                    {checks for balanced parentheses}
  digit,
  alphabet,
  lower:         set of char;

begin                                        {Procedure ReadExpression}
  tokencount      := lastoperand;
  Writeln('Type in the expression to graph on the following line:');
  Readln(instring);
  instring := Concat(instring,' ');  {The blank is a sentinel for searches}
  exprlength      := 0;
  nparameter      := 0;
  parencount      := 0;
  position        := 1;
  lower           := ['a' .. 'z'];  {Assumes letters are contiguous, as in}
  alphabet        := lower + ['A' .. 'Z'];  { ASCII. Wrong for EBCDIC.}
  digit           := ['0' .. '9'];
  while position <= length(instring) do
    if instring[position] = ' ' then
      position    := position + 1   {Skip all blanks between tokens}
    else if instring[position] in alphabet then
      FindWord
```

```
        else if instring[position] in (digit + ['.']) then
          FindNumber
        else
          FindSymbol;
        {At this point, position has moved to the end of the input string.}
        if parencount <> 0 then
          Error('Numbers of left and right parentheses are not equal');
        if Leading then
          Error('Input expression is incomplete.');
        PutToken(1)                     {Put endexpression into the output.}
      end;                              {Procedure ReadExpression}
```

5. Error checking for correct syntax.

The most important aspect of error checking that makes its first appearance in this procedure is the Boolean-valued function **Leading**. To motivate the inclusion of this function, let us first consider a special case. Suppose that an expression is made up only from simple operands and binary operators, with no parentheses or unary operators. Then the only syntactically correct expressions are of the form

$$operand \ binaryop \ operand \ binaryop \ \cdots \ operand$$

where the first and last tokens are operands, and the two kinds alternate. It is illegal for two operands to be adjacent, or for two binary operators to be adjacent. In the leading position there must be an operand, as there must be after each operator, so we can consider these positions also as "leading", since the preceding operator must lead to an operand.

Now suppose that unary operators are to be inserted into this expression. Any number of unary operators can be placed before any operand (recall that we are allowing only unary operators that go to the left of their operands), but it is illegal to place a unary operator immediately before a binary operator. That is, unary operators can appear exactly where operands are allowed, in leading positions but only there. On the other hand, the appearance of a unary operator leaves the position still as a "leading" position, since an operand must still appear before a binary operator becomes legal.

Let us now, finally, also allow parentheses in the expression. A bracketed subexpression is treated as an operand, and therefore can appear exactly where operands are legal. Hence left parentheses can appear exactly in leading positions, and leave the position as leading, and right parentheses can appear only in non-leading positions, and leave the position as non-leading.

All the possibilities are summarized in Figure 8.9.

	Previous token *any one of:*	Legal tokens *any one of:*
Leading position:	start of expression binary operator unary operator left parenthesis	operand unary operator left parenthesis
Non-leading position:	operand right parenthesis	binary operator right parenthesis end of expression

Figure 8.9 Tokens legal in leading and non-leading positions

These requirements are built into the following function, that will be used in the subsidiary procedures to check the syntax of the input.

```
function Leading: Boolean;
var k: tokenkind;
begin
   if exprlength = 0 then                  {This is start of expression.}
      Leading := true
   else begin
      k := Kind(infix[exprlength]);             {Look at preceding token.}
      Leading := (k = leftparen) or (k = unaryop) or (k = binaryop)
   end
end;
```

6. Auxiliary subprograms.

Amongst the other auxiliary subprograms needed are the procedure

PutToken(t: token);

that adds a token to the list in the array infix, and the function

Kind(t: token): tokenkind;

that returns the kind of a token. PutToken is straightforward, and we leave it as an exercise. Kind could just as easily be written in line each time it is used, since we employ a record structure for tokens, but to remain consistent with earlier sections of this chapter (where Kind was used but not yet programmed), we instead use a separate function whose body consists of the single statement

Kind :=Lexicon[t].k

7. Case: Token is a word.

We now turn to the three subsidiary procedures for processing words, numbers and special symbols. The first of these must implement the decisions about the structure of words that we made in part 4 of this section. From Figure 8.8 we see that a word token can be any one of an operand, unary operator or binary operator. The error checking must be adjusted accordingly. Or it may be that the word token does not yet appear in the lexicon, in which case it represents the first appearance of a new variable, which must be entered accordingly into the lexicon and into the list of parameters. These requirements translate into the following procedure.

```
procedure FindWord;
var
    word:          name;
    t:             token;
    i:             indexname;
    newposition:   indexstring;
    ch:            char;

begin
    newposition := position + 1;
    while instring[newposition] in (alphabet + digit) do {find end of word}
        newposition := newposition + 1;
    if newposition − position <= namelength then
        word := copy(instring, position, newposition − position)
    else begin                              {truncate to namelength characters}
        word := copy(instring, position, namelength);
        Writeln('Warning: the name ', word, ' has been truncated.')
    end;
    for i := 1 to length(word) do                    {translate to upper case}
        if word[i] in lower then
            begin ch := word[i]; word[i] := chr(ord(ch) − 32) end;
    {Above statement changes to capital letters. Assumes ASCII ordering}

    t := H[ Hash(word) ];                    {Look for token in hash table.}
    if t <> 0 then                           {Token is one already defined.}
        if Leading then
            if Kind(t) = binaryop then
                Error('Binary operator in illegal position')
            else PutToken(t)       {Other kinds are legal in leading position.}
```

```
        else                          {Case: not in leading position}
          if Kind(t) <> binaryop then
            Error('Binary operator expected')
          else
            PutToken(t)
      else                    {new name for token; must set up definition}
        if tokencount >= maxtoken then
          Error('Too many distinct variables and constants')
        else if not Leading then
          Error('Operand immediately follows ) or another operand')
        else begin
          tokencount := tokencount + 1;
          H[ Hash(word) ] := tokencount;
          Lexicon[tokencount].nm := word;
          Lexicon[tokencount].k := operand;
          if nparameter >= maxparam then
            Error('Too many parameters');
          else begin
            nparameter := nparameter + 1;
            parameter[nparameter] := tokencount;
            PutToken(tokencount)
          end
        end;
      position := newposition
    end;
```

8. Case: Token is a number.

The treatment of numbers is generally similar to that of variables, but with two differences. One is that we must convert the number to binary so that we can use its value directly from the lexicon, rather than reading its value into a list of parameters. The other difference is that there is not necessarily a unique name for a number. If namelength is large enough so that a string can hold as many digits as the precision of the machine, then unique names can be assigned, but if not, two different numbers might get the same name. To guard against this possibility, we shall regard every occurrence of a number as a newly defined token, and act accordingly. We do assign the number a name, but only for debugging purposes, and we do not even enter the name into the hash table.

In converting the number into binary, for simplicity we exclude the scientific notation , and consider the integer and fractional parts separately. We use an auxiliary function to convert a string of digits into an integer (stored as a real). This function, which appears after the procedure, accepts an empty string and returns 0. Therefore our program will correctly interpret real numbers such as 7. or .5 that are not legal syntax in Pascal.

```
procedure FindNumber;
var
  numbername,
  x:          string;
  decpoint,                           {position of decimal point, if any}
  newposition: indexstring;
  fraction,
  r:          value;        {value of number, converted to binary}
  i:          integer;


begin                                 {Procedure FindNumber}
  if not Leading then
    Error('Constant in illegal position')
  else if tokencount > = maxtoken then
    Error('Too many constants and variables')
  else begin                          {legal case: make a new token}
    newposition   := position;
    while instring[newposition] in digit do
     newposition  := newposition + 1;
    x := copy(instring, position, newposition − position);
    if length(x) < = namelength then {name is made for debugging only}
        numbername  := x
    else numbername  := copy(x, 1, namelength);


    r  := ConvertReal(x);
    if instring[newposition] = '.' then
    begin                                      {fractional part}
      decpoint := newposition;
      repeat
        newposition := newposition + 1
      until not (instring[newposition] in digit);
      x := copy(instring, decpoint + 1, newposition − decpoint − 1);
      fraction := ConvertReal(x);
      for i := 1 to length(x) do
        fraction := fraction / 10.0;
      r := r + fraction
    end;                                       {fractional part}
```

```
     if instring[newposition] in ['E', 'e'] then
        Error('Sorry, scientific notation is not allowed');
     else begin
        tokencount := tokencount + 1;
        Lexicon[tokencount].nm := numbername;
        Lexicon[tokencount].k := operand;
        Lexicon[tokencount].val := r;
        PutToken(tokencount);
        position := newposition
     end
   end                                          {legal case}
 end;                                    {Procedure FindNumber}


 function ConvertReal(x: string): value;
 {Converts a string of digits into an integer; the result is stored as a real
                                             to avoid overflow}
 var
   ch: char;
   i: integer;
   sum: value;
 begin
   sum := 0.0;
   for i := 1 to length(x) do
   begin
    ch := x[i];
    sum := (10.0 * sum) + (ord(ch) − ord('0'))
      {Assumes that the ten digits have contiguous codes, as in ASCII}
   end;
   ConvertReal := sum
 end;
```

9. Case: Token is a special symbol.

The third subsidiary procedure treats the special symbols. Most of its work is simpler than the previous cases; it need create no new tokens: if it fails to recognize a symbol then an error occurs. The special symbols are all one character long, so counting positions in instring is easier.

The only complication concerns the two symbols '+' and '−', which can be either unary or binary operators. Fortunately, the function Leading will tell us which case occurs, since only a unary operator is legal in a leading position. We shall take no action for a unary '+', since it has no effect, and we replace a unary '−' by our private notation '÷'. Note, however, that this change is local to our program. The user is not required—or even allowed—to use the symbol '÷' for unary negation.

```
procedure FindSymbol;
var
 x: name;
 t: token;
begin
 x              := copy(instring, position, 1);
 t              := H[ Hash(x) ];
 if t           = 0 then
   Error('Unrecognized symbol in expression')
 else if Leading then
   if Kind(t) = rightparen then
     Error('Illegal place for closing parenthesis')
   else if Kind(t) = binaryop then
     {A binary operator is illegal here; it must be a unary operator.}
     if x = '+' then                {do nothing; forget a unary +}
       begin end
     else if x = '−' then
       begin                                    {unary negation}
         x := '±'
         t := H[ Hash(x) ];
         PutToken(t)
       end
     else
       Error('Binary operator in illegal position')
   else
     PutToken(t)         {other kinds are legal in leading position}

 else                                   {Case: not in leading position}
   if (Kind(t) = rightparen) or (Kind(t) = binaryop) then
     PutToken(t)
   else
     Error('Binary operator or ) expected');

 if Kind(t) = leftparen then
   parencount := parencount + 1
 else if Kind(t) = rightparen then
 begin
   parencount := parencount − 1;
   if parencount < 0 then Error('More right than left parentheses')
 end;
 position := position + 1
end;
```

10. Translation into postfix form.

At the conclusion of procedure ReadExpression, the input expression has been converted into an infix sequence of tokens, in exactly the form needed by procedure Translate as derived in Section 8.4. In fact, we now arrive at the key step of our algorithm and can apply the previous work without essential change; the only modifications needed in procedure Translate are the addition of two variables used to index the input and output expressions, and even this indexing is done only in the straightforward subsidiary procedures GetToken and PutToken, which we leave as exercises.

We also omit the auxiliary subprograms Push, Pop, and Priority, since they involve no new problems or ideas.

When procedure Translate has finished, the expression is a sequence of tokens in postfix form, and can be evaluated efficiently in the next stage. This efficiency, in fact, is important so that a graph can be drawn without undue delay, even though it requires evaluation of the expression for a great many different values.

8.5.5 Evaluating the expression.

1. Reading the parameters.

The first step in evaluating the expression is to establish values for the parameters, if any. This is done only once for each graph, in the straightforward procedure:

```
procedure ReadParameters;
var
  i: param;
begin
  if nparameter > 0 then
  begin
    Writeln('Type in values for each of the following parameters.');
    for i := 1 to nparameter do
      with Lexicon[parameter[i]] do
      begin
        Write('   ', nm:namelength, ' ? ');
        Readln(val)
      end
  end
end;
```

2. Postfix evaluation.

To evaluate the postfix expression, we again use a procedure developed in the first part of this chapter. Either the recursive or the non-recursive version of procedure EvaluatePostfix can be used, again with no significant change (the non-recursive version requires Push and Pop procedures for values). There will likely be no significant difference in running time between the two versions, so it is a matter of taste which to use. Both versions, however, require subsidiary functions GetValue, DoUnary, and DoBinary, to which we now turn.

3. Evaluation of operands.

The first function need only look in the lexicon:

```
function GetValue(t: token): value;
begin
  if Kind(t) <> operand then
    Error('Attempt to get value for non-operand')
  else
    GetValue := Lexicon[t].val
end;
```

4. Operators.

Since we have integer codes for all the tokens, the application of operators can be done within a simple but long **case** statement. We leave the one for unary operators as an exercise. For binary operators, we have the following function.

```
function DoBinary(t: token; x, y: value): value;
begin
  if (t < firstbinary) or (t > lastbinary) then
    Error(' Binary operator code out of range')
  else case t of
    16: DoBinary := x + y;
    17: DoBinary := x − y;
    18: DoBinary := x * y;
    19: if y = 0 then Error('Division by 0.0') else DoBinary := x / y;
    20: if round(y) = 0 then Error('Integer division by 0') else
          DoBinary := round(x) div round(y);
    21: if round(y) = 0 then Error('Attempt to use 0 modulus') else
          DoBinary := round(x) mod round(y);
    22: DoBinary     := Exponent(x, y)
  end
end;
```

Note that we can easily use the structure of this function to improve the error checking usually provided to the user by the operating system. The messages given for division by 0 will likely prove more helpful than something like

Floating point error,

which may be all that the system normally provides.

Since Pascal does not provide an exponentiation operator, we can also take this opportunity to write an exponentiation function. We use two different methods as appropriate: If the power is an integer (or very close to one), then we use a loop and multiplication or division to evaluate the exponent; otherwise, we use logarithms.

```
function Exponent(x, y: value): value;
const
  epsilon = 0.000001;              {tolerance to regard a number as an integer}
var
  i: integer;
  p: value;
begin
  if abs(y − round(y)) < epsilon then
  begin                                              {Treat y like an integer.}
    p := 1.0;
    if y >= 0.0 then
      for i := 1 to round(y) do
        p := p * x
    else if x = 0.0 then Error('Negative power of 0.0')
    else
      for i := −1 downto round(y) do
        p := p / x;
    Exponent := p
  end
  else if x > 0.0 then                         {Use logarithms and exponents}
    Exponent := exp(y * ln(x))
  else if abs(x) < epsilon then
    Exponent := 0.0
  else
    Error('Attempt to take negative number to non-integer power')
end;
```

8.5.6 Summary.

At this point, we have surveyed the entire project. Figure 8.10 lists all the subprograms required for this project, arranged in their proper hierarchy of declaration. Most of these appear in the text, but several have been left as exercises for the programmer to supply. These are marked with an asterisk (*) in the right margin.

```
program GraphFunction;
    function Kind( t: token ): tokenkind;
    function Yes: Boolean;
    procedure Error( message: string );                              *
    procedure Instruct;                                              *
    procedure DefineTokens;                                          *

    procedure StartExpression;
        function Hash(x: name): address;
        procedure MakeHashTable;

        procedure ReadExpression;
            procedure    PutToken( t : token ); {into infix expression} *
            function     Leading: Boolean;
            procedure    FindWord;
            procedure    FindNumber;
                function ConvertReal(x: string): value;
            procedure    FindSymbol;

        procedure Translate;
            procedure Push( t: token);                    {token} *
            procedure Pop( var t: token);                 {token} *
            procedure GetToken( var t: token); {from infix expression} *
            procedure PutToken( t: token);       {into postfix expr.} *
            function Priority( t: token): integer;             *

    procedure ReadParameters;

    procedure ReadGraphLimits;                                       *

    procedure Graph( x, y: value);                                   *

    procedure  EvaluatePostfix(var result: value);  { recursive or not}
        procedure Push( v: value);        {value, for non-recursive only}
        procedure Pop( var v: value);    {value, for non-recursive only}
        procedure P( var result: value);    {for recursive version only}
        procedure GetToken( var t: token); {from postfix expression} *
        function    GetValue(t: token): value;
        function    DoUnary(t: token; x: value): value;           *
        function    DoBinary(t: token; x, y: value): value;
            function Exponent(x, y: value): value;
```

Figure 8.10. Summary of subprograms for GraphFunction

Exercises

1. Provide the missing subprograms (marked with asterisks in Figure 8.10) and implement program GraphFunction on your computer. Most of the subprograms are straightforward, although several involve graphics and will be system dependent. If your system does not provide good string processing, and set types of adequate size, then you will need more extensive modifications in procedure ReadExpression and its subprograms.

2. State precisely what changes in the program are needed to add the base 10 logarithm function log( ) as an additional unary operator.

3. Naive users of this program might (if graphing a function involving money) write a dollar sign '$' within the expression. What will the present program do if this happens? What changes are needed so that the program will ignore a '$'?

4. Pascal or PL/1 programmers might accidentally type a semicolon ';' at the end of the expression. What changes are needed so that a semicolon will be ignored at the end of the expression, but will be an error elsewhere?

5. Explain what changes are needed to allow the program to accept either square brackets [···] or curly brackets {···} as well as round brackets (···). The nesting must be done with the same kind of brackets; that is, an expression of the form (···[···)···] is illegal, but forms like [···(···)···{···}···] are permissible.

6. Modify the program so that it will accept unary operators that are written on the right of the operand. Two examples of such operators that might be included are the factorial operator '!' and the percentage operator '%' that divides its operand by 100.0.

8.6 References for further study.

The Polish notation is so natural and useful that one might expect its discovery to be hundreds of years ago. It may be surprising to note that it is a discovery of this century:

JAN ŁUKASIEWICZ, *Elementy Logiki Matematyczny*, Warsaw, 1929; English translation: *Elements of Mathematical Logic*, Pergamon Press, Oxford, 1963.

The development of iterative algorithms to form and evaluate Polish expressions (usually postfix form) can be found in several data structures books, as well as more advanced books on compiler theory. The iterative algorithm for translating an expression from infix to postfix form appears to be due independently to E. W. DIJKSTRA and to C. L. HAMBLIN, and appears in:

E. W. DIJKSTRA, "Making a Translator for ALGOL 60, "*Automatic Programming Information*, number 7 (May 1961); reprinted in *Annual Rev. Automatic Programming 3* (1963), 347–356.

C. L. HAMBLIN, "Translation to and from Polish notation," *Computer Journal* 5 (1962), 210–213.

The recursive algorithm (Section 8.3.6) for evaluation of postfix expressions is derived, albeit from a rather different point of view, and for binary operators only, in:

EDWARD M. REINGOLD, "A comment on the evaluation of Polish postfix expressions, " *Computer Journal*, 24 (1981), 288.

The algorithm for translation from infix to postfix form that defines different priorities for incoming operators and stacked operators, so as to improve the treatment of unary operators and exponentiation, (see exercises in Section 8.4) is developed in both:

E. HOROWITZ and S. SAHNI, *Fundamentals of Data Structures,* Computer Science Press, Rockville, MD 1976.

J. P. TREMBLAY and P. G. SORENSON, *An Introduction to Data Structures and Applications,* McGraw-Hill, New York, 1976.

Chapter 9

Further Topics on Trees

This chapter continues the study of trees as data structures. Each section of this chapter is independent of the others, and can be studied separately. Chapter 5 provides all necessary prerequisites. Section 1 continues the study of balancing methods for binary search trees begun in Chapter 5. Section 2 introduces a sequential representation of binary trees that leads to an efficient sorting method for contiguous lists. Sections 3 and 4 examine multiway trees applied, respectively, as search trees and as file indices.

9.1 Height-balance: AVL trees.

The algorithm of Section 5.6 can be used to build a nearly balanced binary search tree, or to restore balance when it is feasible to restructure the tree completely. In many applications, however, insertions and deletions occur continually, with no predictable order. In some of these applications it is important to optimize search times by keeping the tree very nearly balanced at all times. The method of this section for achieving this goal was described in 1962 by two Russian mathematicians, G. M. ADEL'SON-VEL'SKIĬ and E. M. LANDIS, and the resulting binary search trees are called *AVL trees* in their honor.

AVL trees achieve the goal that searches, insertions and deletions in a tree with n nodes can all be achieved in time that is $O(\log n)$, even in the worst case. The height of an AVL tree with n nodes, as we shall establish, can never exceed $1.44 \lg n$, and thus even in the worst case the behavior of an AVL tree could not be much below that of a random binary search tree. In almost all cases, however, the actual length of a search is very nearly $\lg n$, and thus the behavior of AVL trees closely approximates that of the ideal, completely balanced binary search tree.

9.1.1 Definition.

In a completely balanced tree, the left and right subtrees of any node would have the same height. Although we cannot always achieve this goal, by building a search tree carefully we can always ensure that the heights of every left and right subtree never differ by more than 1. We accordingly make the following:

DEFINITION.   An *AVL tree* is a binary search tree in which the heights of the left and right subtrees of the root differ by at most 1, and in which the left and right subtrees are again AVL trees.

With each node of an AVL tree is associated a *balance factor* which is *left high*, *equal* or *right high* according, respectively, as the left subtree has height greater than, equal to, or less than that of the right subtree.

In drawing diagrams, we shall show a left-high node by '/', a node whose balance factor is equal by '‐', and a right-high node by '\'. Figure 9.1 shows several small AVL trees, as well as some binary trees that fail to satisfy the definition.

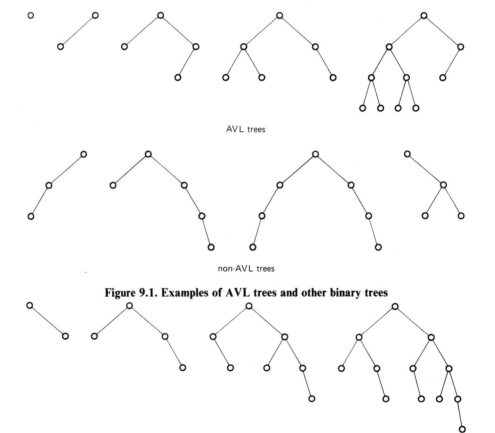

AVL trees

non-AVL trees

Figure 9.1. Examples of AVL trees and other binary trees

Figure 9.2. AVL trees skewed to the right

Note that the definition does not require that all leaves be on the same or adjacent levels. Figure 9.2 shows several AVL trees that are quite skewed, with right subtrees having greater height than left subtrees.

9.1.2 Insertion of a node.

1. Introduction.

We can insert a new node into an AVL tree by using the usual binary tree algorithm, comparing the key of the new node with that in the root, and inserting the new node into the left or right subtree as appropriate. It often turns out that the new node can be inserted without changing the height of the subtree, in which case neither the height nor the balance of the root will be changed. Even when the height of a subtree does increase, it may be the shorter subtree that has grown, so that only the balance factor of the root will change. The only case that can cause difficulty occurs when the new node is added to a subtree that is strictly taller than the other subtree, and the height is increased. This would cause one subtree to have height 2 more than the other, whereas the AVL condition is that the height difference is never more than 1. Before we consider this situation more carefully, let us illustrate in Figure 9.3 the growth of an AVL tree through several insertions, and then tie down the ideas by outlining our algorithm in Pascal.

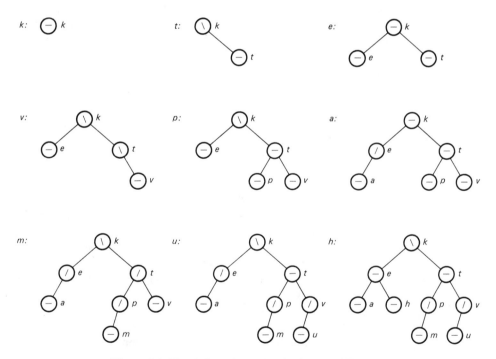

Figure 9.3. Simple insertions of nodes into an AVL tree

2. Pascal conventions.

The basic structure of our algorithm will be the same as the ordinary binary tree insertion algorithm of Section 5.4.1, but with certain additions to accommodate the structure of AVL trees. First, each record corresponding to a node will have an additional field (along with its key, information fields, and left and right pointers), defined as

bf: balancefactor;

where we employ the enumerated type

type balancefactor = (LH, EH, RH);

which symbols denote *left high, equal height,* and *right high,* respectively. Second, we must keep track of whether an insertion has increased the height or not, so that the balance factors can be changed appropriately. This we do by including an additional calling parameter **taller** of type Boolean.

```
procedure Insert(var root: pointer; newitem: pointer;
var taller: Boolean);
var
  tallersubtree: Boolean;        {Has the height of a subtree increased?}
begin
  if root = nil then
  begin
    root           := newitem;
    root↑.left     := nil;
    root↑.right    := nil;
    root↑.bf       := EH;
    taller         := true
  end
  else with root↑ do
  if newitem↑.key = key then
    Error                    {Duplicate key is not allowed in search tree}
  else if newitem↑.key < key then
  begin                                          {Insert in left subtree}
    Insert(left, newitem, tallersubtree);
    if tallersubtree then                   {Change balance factors}
      case bf of
        LH: LeftBalance;
        EH: begin bf := LH; taller := true end;
        RH: begin bf := EH; taller := false end
      end
    else taller := false
  end
```

```
else begin                                        {Insert in right subtree}
  Insert(right, newitem, tallersubtree);
  if tallersubtree then
    case bf of
      LH: begin bf := EH; taller := false end;
      EH: begin bf := RH; taller := true  end;
      RH: RightBalance
    end
  else taller := false
  end
end;
```

3. Rotations.

Let us now consider the case when a new node has been inserted into the taller subtree of the root, and its height has increased, so that now one subtree has height 2 more than the other, and the tree no longer satisfies the AVL requirements. We must now rebuild part of the tree to restore its balance. To be definite, let us assume that we have inserted the new node into the right subtree, its height has increased, and the original tree was right high. That is, we wish to consider the case covered by the procedure RightBalance. Let r be the root of the tree, and x the root of its right subtree. There are three cases to consider, depending on the balance factor of x.

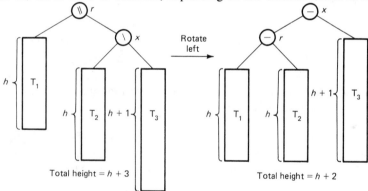

Figure 9.4. First case: Restoring balance by a left rotation

4. Case 1: right high.

The first case, when x is right high, is illustrated in Figure 9.4. The action needed in this case is called a *left rotation;* we have rotated the node x upward to the root, dropping r down into the left subtree of x; the subtree T_2 of nodes with keys between those of r and x now becomes the right subtree of r rather than the left subtree of x. A left rotation is succinctly described in the following Pascal procedure. Note especially that, when done in the appropriate order, the steps constitute a rotation of the values in three pointer variables. Note also that, after the rotation, the height of the rotated tree has decreased by 1; it had previously increased because of the insertion; hence the height finishes where it began.

```
procedure RotateLeft( var p: pointer);
var
  temp: pointer;
begin
  if p = nil then
    Error                               {impossible to rotate an empty tree}
  else if p↑.right = nil then
    Error                  {impossible to make an empty subtree the root}
  else begin
    temp      := p↑.right;
    p↑.right  := temp↑.left;  {Move the subtree of intermediate nodes}
    temp↑.left := p;                    {Drop the root into the left subtree}
    p         := temp   {Change the root to the former right subtree}
  end
end;
```

5. Case 2: left high.

The second case, when the balance factor of x is left high, is slightly more complicated. It is necessary to move two levels, to the node w that roots the left subtree of x, to find the new root. This process is shown in Figure 9.5 and is called a **double rotation**, because the transformation can be obtained in two steps by first rotating the subtree with root x to the right (so that w becomes its root), and then rotating the tree with root r to the left (moving w up to become the new root).

In this second case, the new balance factors for r and x depend on the previous balance factor for w. The diagram shows the subtrees of w as having equal heights, but it is possible that w may be either left or right high. The resulting balance factors are:

old w	new r	new x
—	—	—
/	—	\
\	/	—

6. Case 3: equal height.

It would appear, finally, that we must consider a third case, when the two subtrees of x have equal heights, but this case, in fact, can never happen. To see why, let us recall that we have just inserted a new node into the subtree rooted at x, and this subtree now has height 2 more than the left subtree of the root. The new node went

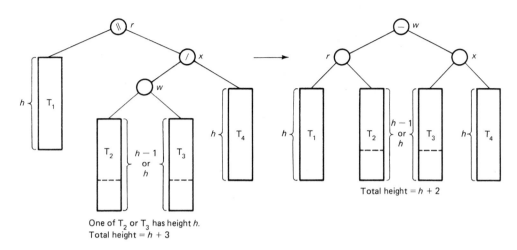

Figure 9.5. Second case: Restoring balance by double rotation

either into the left or right subtree of x. Hence its insertion increased the height of only one subtree of x. If these subtrees had equal heights after the insertion, then the height of the full subtree rooted at x was not changed by the insertion, contrary to what we already know.

7. Pascal procedure for balancing.

It is now straightforward to incorporate these transformations into a Pascal procedure. The forms of procedures RotateRight and LeftBalance are clearly similar to those of RotateLeft and RightBalance, respectively, and are left as exercises.

```
procedure RightBalance;            {to be written into Procedure Insert}
var
  x,                                 {pointer to right subtree of root}
  w: pointer;                                     {left subtree of x↑}
        {Also uses variables root and taller from procedure Insert}
begin
  x := root↑.right;
  case x↑.bf of
    RH: begin                                    {single rotation left}
          root↑.bf := EH;
          x↑.bf    := EH;
          RotateLeft(root);
          taller   := false
        end;
    EH: Error;                                    {impossible case}
```

```
LH: begin                                    {double rotation left}
        w := x↑.left;
        case w↑.bf of
          EH: begin root↑.bf := EH; x↑.bf := EH  end;
          LH: begin root↑.bf := EH; x↑.bf := RH  end;
          RH: begin root↑.bf := LH; x↑.bf := EH  end
        end;
        w↑.bf    := EH;
        RotateRight(x);
        root↑.right := x;
        RotateLeft(root);
        taller      := false
     end
  end
end;
```

Examples of insertions requiring single and double rotations are shown in Figure 9.6.

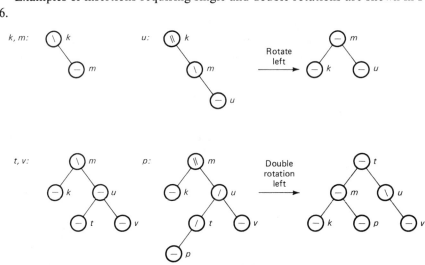

Figure 9.6. AVL insertions requiring rotations

8. Behavior of the algorithm.

The number of times that procedure Insert calls itself recursively to insert a new node can be as large as the height of the tree. At first glance it may appear that each one of these calls might induce either a single or double rotation of the appropriate subtree, but, in fact, at most only one (single or double) rotation will ever be done. To see this, let us recall that rotations are done only in procedures RightBalance and LeftBalance, and these procedures are called only when the height of a subtree has increased. When these procedures return, however, the rotations have removed the increase in height, so for the remaining (outer) recursive calls the height has not increased, and no further rotations or changes of balance factors are done.

Most of the insertions into an AVL tree will induce no rotations. Even when rotations are needed, they will usually occur near the leaf that has just been inserted. Even though the algorithm to insert into an AVL tree is complicated, it is reasonable to expect that its running time will differ little from insertion into an ordinary search tree of the same height. Later we shall see that we can expect the height of AVL trees to be much less than that of random search trees, and therefore both insertion and retrieval will be significantly more efficient in AVL trees than in random binary search trees.

9.1.3 Deletion of a node.

Deletion of a node x from an AVL tree requires the same basic ideas, including single and double rotations, that are used for insertion. We shall give only the steps of an informal outline of the method, leaving the writing of complete algorithms as a programming project.

1. Reduce the problem to the case when the node x to be deleted has at most one child. For suppose that x has two children. Find the immediate predecessor y of x under inorder traversal (the immediate successor would be just as good), by first taking the left child of x, and then moving right as far as possible to obtain y. The node y is guaranteed to have no right child, because of the way it was found. Place y (or a copy of y) into the position in the tree occupied by x (with the same parent, left and right children, and balance factor that x had). Now delete y from its former position, by proceeding as follows, using y in place of x in each of the following steps.

2. Delete the node x from the tree. Since we know (by step 1) that x has at most one child, we delete x simply by linking the parent of x to the single child of x (or to **nil**, if no child). The height of the subtree formerly rooted at x has been reduced by 1, and we must now trace the effects of this change on height through all the nodes on the path from x back to the root of the tree. We use a Boolean variable **shorter** to show if the height of a subtree has been shortened. The action to be taken at each node depends on the value of **shorter**, on the balance factor of the node, and sometimes on the balance factor of a child of the node.

3. The Boolean variable **shorter** is initially true. The following steps are to be done for each node p on the path from the parent of x to the root of the tree, provided **shorter** remains true. When **shorter** becomes false, then no further changes are needed, and the algorithm terminates.

4. Case 1: The current node p has balance factor equal. The balance factor of p is changed according as its left or right subtree has been shortened, and **shorter** becomes false.

5. Case 2: The balance factor of p is not equal, and the taller subtree was shortened. Change the balance factor of p to equal, and leave **shorter** as true.

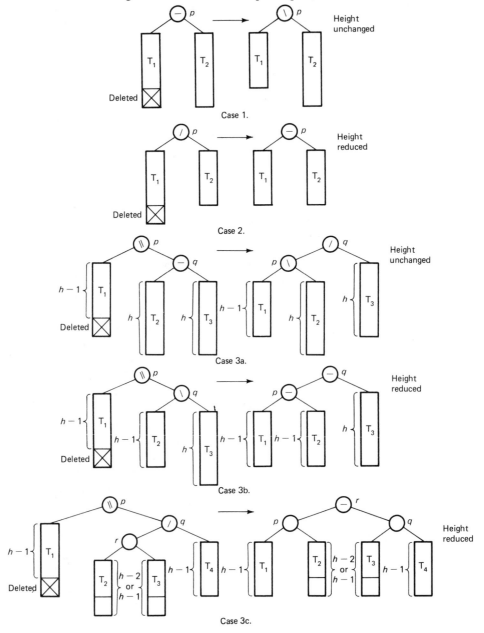

Figure 9.7. Sample cases, deletion from an AVL tree

6. Case 3: The balance factor of *p* is not equal, and the shorter subtree was shortened. The height requirement for an AVL tree is now violated at *p*, so we apply a rotation as follows to restore balance. Let *q* be the root of the taller subtree of *p* (the one not shortened). We have three cases according to the balance factor of *q*.

7. Case 3a: The balance factor of *q* is equal. A single rotation (with changes to the balance factors of *p* and *q*) restores balance, and **shorter** becomes false.

8. Case 3b: The balance factor of *q* is the same as that of *p*. Apply a single rotation, set the balance factors of *p* and *q* to equal, and leave **shorter** as true.

9. Case 3c: The balance factors of *p* and *q* are opposite. Apply a double rotation (first around *q*, then around *p*), set the balance factor of the new root to equal and the other balance factors as appropriate, and leave **shorter** as true.

In cases 3a, b, and c, the direction of the rotations depends on whether a left or right subtree was shortened. Some of the possibilities are illustrated in Figure 9.7, and an example of the deletion of a node appears in Figure 9.8.

9.1.4 The height of an AVL tree.

It turns out to be very difficult to find the height of the average AVL tree, and thereby to determine how many steps are done, on average, by the algorithms of this section. It is much easier, however, to find what happens in the worst case, and these results show that the worst-case behavior of AVL trees is essentially no worse than the average behavior of random trees. Empirical evidence suggests that the average behavior of AVL trees is much better than that of random trees, almost as good as that which could be obtained from a perfectly balanced tree.

To determine the maximum height that an AVL tree with *n* nodes can have, we can instead ask what is the minimum number of nodes that an AVL tree of height *h* can have. If F_h is such a tree, and the left and right subtrees of its root are F_l and F_r, then one of F_l and F_r must have height $h-1$, say F_l, and the other has height either $h-1$ or $h-2$. Since F_h has the minimum number of nodes among AVL trees of height *h*, it follows that F_l must have the minimum number of nodes among AVL trees of height $h-1$ (that is, F_l is of the form F_{h-1}), and F_r must have height $h-2$ with minimum number of nodes (so that F_r is of the form F_{h-2}).

The trees built by this rule, which are therefore as sparse as possible for AVL trees, are called ***Fibonacci trees***. The first few are shown in Figure 9.9.

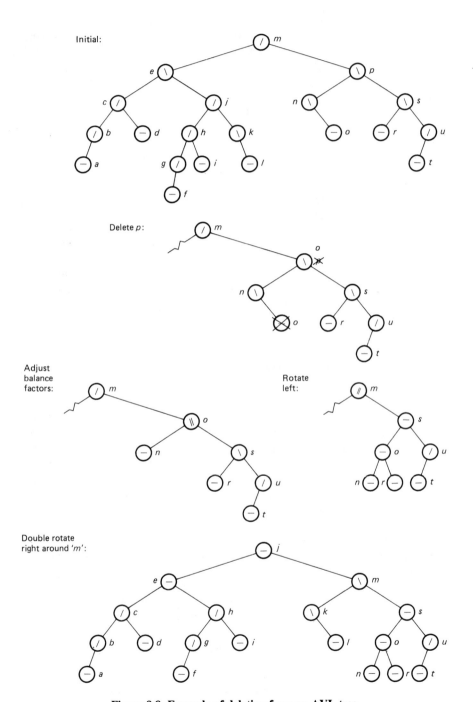

Figure 9.8. Example of deletion from an AVL tree

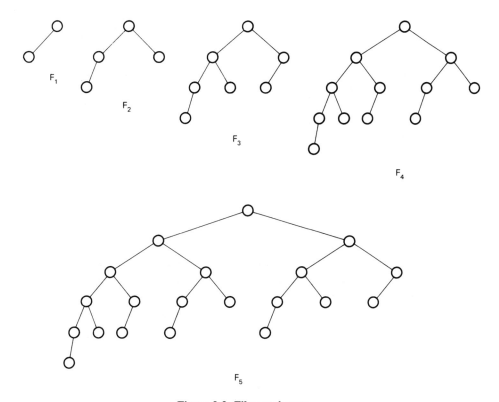

Figure 9.9. Fibonacci trees

If we write $|T|$ for the number of nodes in a tree T, we then have (counting the root as well as the subtrees) the recurrence relation

$$|F_h| \quad = \quad |F_{h-1}| + |F_{h-2}| + 1,$$

where $|F_0| = 1$, and $|F_1| = 2$. By adding 1 to both sides, we see that the numbers $|F_h| + 1$ satisfy the definition of the Fibonacci numbers (see Appendix A.4), with the subscripts changed by 3. By the evaluation of Fibonacci numbers in Appendix A.4 we therefore see that

$$|F_h| + 1 \quad \approx \quad \frac{1}{\sqrt{5}} \left[\frac{1 + \sqrt{5}}{2} \right]^{h+3}.$$

Next, we solve this relation for h by taking the logarithms of both sides, discarding all except the largest terms. The approximate result is that

$$h \quad \approx \quad 1.44 \lg |F_h|.$$

This means that the sparsest possible AVL tree with n nodes has height approximately 1.44 lg n. A perfectly balanced binary tree with n nodes has height about lg n, and a degenerate tree has height as large as n. Hence the algorithms for manipulating AVL trees are guaranteed to take no more than about 44% more time than the optimum. In practice, AVL trees do much better than this. It can be shown that, even for Fibonacci trees, which are the worst case for AVL trees, the average search time is only 4% more than the optimum. Most AVL trees are not nearly as sparse as Fibonacci trees, and therefore it is reasonable to expect that average search times for average AVL trees are very close indeed to the optimum. Empirical studies, in fact, show that the average number of comparisons seems to be about

$$\lg n + 0.25$$

when n is large.

Exercises

1. Determine which of the following binary search trees are AVL trees. For those that are not, find all nodes at which the requirements are violated.

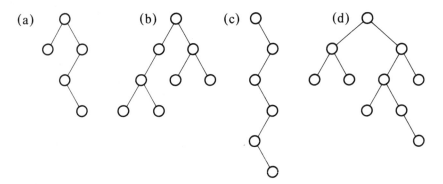

2. In each of the following, insert the keys, in the order shown, in order to build them into an AVL tree.

   (a) A, Z, B, Y, C, X   (d) A, Z, B, Y, C, X, D, W, E, V, F
   (b) A, B, C, D, E, F   (e) A, B, C, D, E, F, G, H, I, J, K, L
   (c) M, T, E, A, Z, G, P   (f) A, V, L, T, R, E, I, S, O, K

3. Delete each of the keys inserted in the above exercise from the AVL tree, in LIFO order (last key inserted is first deleted).

4. Delete each of the keys inserted in the above exercise from the AVL tree, in FIFO order (first key inserted is first deleted).

5. Prove that the number of (single or double) rotations done in deleting a key from an AVL tree cannot exceed half the height of the tree.

6. Write a Pascal program that will accept keys from the user one at a time, build them into an AVL tree, and write out the tree at each stage. You will need a procedure to print a tree, perhaps in the bracketed form defined in Exercise 9 of Section 5.4.

7. Write Pascal procedures to delete a node from an AVL tree, following the steps in the text.

8. [*Major project*] Conduct empirical studies to estimate, on average, how many rotations are needed to insert an item and to delete an item from an AVL tree.

9.2 Contiguous representation of binary trees: Heapsort.

There are several ways other than the usual linked structures to represent binary trees, and some of these ways lead to interesting applications. This section presents one such example: a contiguous representation of binary trees that is employed in a sorting algorithm for contiguous lists called **heapsort**. This algorithm sorts a contiguous list of length n with $O(n \log n)$ comparisons and movements of items, even in the worst case. Hence it achieves worst-case bounds better than those of quicksort, and for contiguous lists is even better than mergesort, since it needs only a small and constant amount of space apart from the array being sorted.

9.2.1 Binary trees in contiguous storage.

Let us begin with a complete binary tree such as the one shown in Figure 9.10, and number the vertices, beginning with the root, from left to right on each level.

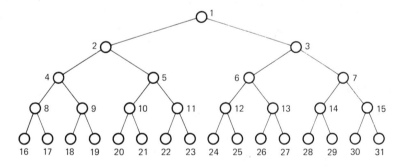

Figure 9.10. Complete binary tree with 31 vertices

We can now put the binary tree into a contiguous array by storing each node in the position shown by its label. We conclude that:

The left and right children of the node with index k are in positions 2k and 2k + 1, respectively. If these positions are beyond the bounds of the array, then these children do not exist.

This sequential representation can, in fact, be extended to arbitrary binary trees, provided that we can flag locations in the array to show that the corresponding nodes do not exist. The results for several binary trees are shown in Figure 9.11.

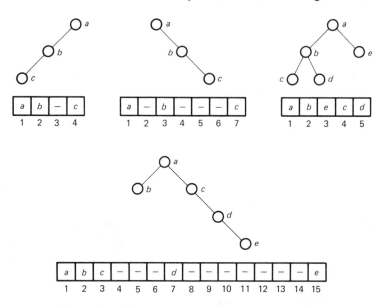

Figure 9.11. Binary trees in contiguous representation

It is clear from the diagram that, if a binary tree is far from a complete tree, then the contiguous representation wastes a great deal of space. When, however, all the leaves are on the same level, and all are as far to the left as possible, then no space at all is wasted. It is this last case that we shall now apply.

9.2.2 Heaps and heapsort.

1. Definition.

DEFINITION.   A *heap* is defined to be a binary tree with a key in each node, such that

1. All the leaves of the tree are on two adjacent levels;
2. All leaves on the lower level occur to the left; and
3. The key in the root is at least as large as the keys in its children (if any), and the left and right children (if they exist) are again heaps.

The first two conditions ensure that the contiguous representation of the tree will be space efficient. The third condition determines the ordering. Note that a heap is definitely *not* a search tree. The root, in fact, must have the largest key in the heap. Figure 9.12 shows four trees, the first of which is a heap, with the others violating one of the three properties.

REMARK. Some implementations of Pascal refer to the area used for dynamic memory as the "heap"; this use of the word "heap" has nothing to do with the present definition.

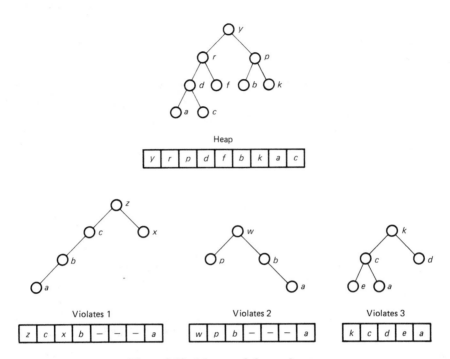

Figure 9.12. A heap and three other trees

2. Outline of heapsort.

Heapsort proceeds in two phases. The entries in the array being sorted are interpreted as a binary tree in contiguous representation. The first two properties of a heap are automatically satisfied, but the keys will not generally satisfy the third property. Hence the first phase of heapsort is to convert the tree into a heap.

For the second phase, we recall that the root (which is the first entry of the array as well as the top of the heap) has the largest key. This key belongs at the end of the list. We therefore move the first entry to the last position, replacing an entry x. We then decrease a counter k that keeps track of the size of the list, thereby excluding the largest entry from further sorting. The entry x that has been moved from the last position, however, may not belong on the top of the heap, and therefore we must insert x into the proper position to restore the heap property before continuing to loop in the same way.

Let us summarize this outline by rewriting it in Pascal. We use the same notation and conventions used for all the contiguous sorting algorithms of Chapter 4.

```
procedure HeapSort(var L: list; n: index);
var
   x: item;                        {temporary storage for moving items}
   k: index;                       {entries beyond k have been sorted}
begin
   BuildHeap;                                                    {first phase}
   for k := n downto 2 do
   begin
      x    := L[k];                {Extract the last element from the list}
      L[k] := L[1];                {Move top of the heap to end of the list}
      InsertHeap(x,1,k−1){Restore the heap properties for shortened list}
   end
end;
```

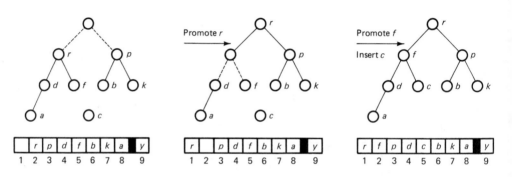

Figure 9.13. First stage of HeapSort

3. An example.

Before we begin work on the two procedures **BuildHeap** and **InsertHeap**, let us see what happens in the first few stages of sorting the heap shown as the first diagram in Figure 9.12. These stages are shown in Figure 9.13. In the first step, the largest key, 'y', is moved from the first to the last entry of the list. The first diagram shows the resulting tree, with 'y' removed from further consideration, and the last entry, 'c', put aside as the temporary variable x. To find how to rearrange the heap and insert 'c', we look at the two children of the root. Each of these is guaranteed to have a larger key than any other entry in its subtree, and hence the largest of these two entries or the new entry x = 'c' belongs in the root. We therefore promote 'r' to the top of the heap, and repeat the process on the subtree whose root has just been removed. Hence the largest of 'd', 'f' and 'c' is now inserted where 'r' was formerly. At the next step, we would compare 'c' with the two children of 'f', but these do not exist, so the promotion of entries through the tree ceases, and 'c' is inserted in the empty position formerly occupied by 'f'.

At this point we are ready to repeat the algorithm, again moving the top of the heap to the end of the list and restoring the heap property. The sequence of actions that occurs in the complete sort of the list is shown in Figure 9.14.

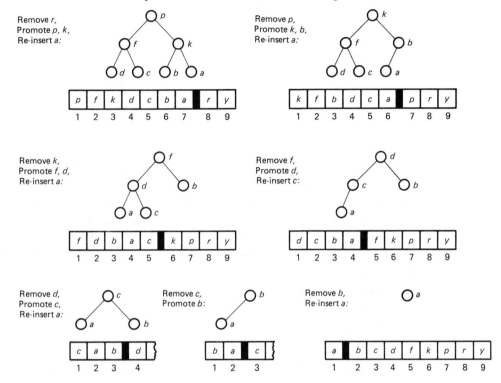

Figure 9.14. Trace of HeapSort

4. The procedure InsertHeap.

It is only a short step from this example to a formal procedure for inserting the entry x into the heap.

```
procedure InsertHeap( x: item; a, b: index);
{Inserts item x into the partial heap with empty root in index a.  The heap
occupies locations a through b of the array L.}
var
    m: integer;              {index of the child of L[a] with the larger key}
begin
    m := 2 * a;                          {m is now the left child of a}
    while m <= b do
    begin
        if m < b then if L[m].key < L[m + 1].key then
            m := m + 1;      {m is now the child of a with the larger key}
```

```
        if x.key >= L[m].key then           {If so, x belongs in position a}
          m := b + 1                         {Set m as a flag to terminate the loop.}
        else begin                           {Promote L[m] and move down the tree}
          L[a] := L[m];
          a := m;
          m := 2 * a
        end
      end;
      L[a] := x
    end;
```

5. Building the initial heap.

The remaining task that we must specify is to build the initial heap from a list in arbitrary order. To do so, we first note that a binary tree with only one node automatically satisfies the properties of a heap, and therefore we need not worry about any of the leaves of the tree, that is, about any of the entries in the second half of the list. If we begin at the midpoint of the list and work our way back toward the start, we can use the procedure InsertHeap to insert each entry into the partial heap consisting of all later entries, and thereby build the complete heap. The desired procedure is therefore simply:

```
procedure BuildHeap;
begin
  for k := (n div 2) downto 1 do
  begin
    x := L[k];
    InsertHeap(x, k, n)
  end
end;
```

9.2.3 Analysis of heapsort.

From the example we have worked it is not at all clear that heapsort is efficient, and in fact heapsort is not a good choice for short lists. It seems quite strange that we can sort by moving large keys slowly toward the beginning of the list before finally putting them away at the end. When n becomes large, however, such small quirks become unimportant, and heapsort proves its worth as one of very few sorting algorithms for contiguous lists that is guaranteed to finish in time $O(n \log n)$ with minimal space requirements.

First let us determine how much work InsertHeap does in its worst case. At each pass through the loop, the index a is doubled; hence the number of passes cannot exceed lg(b **div** a); this is also the height of the subtree rooted at L[a]. Each pass through the loop does two comparisons of keys (usually) and one assignment of items. Therefore, the number of comparisons done in InsertHeap is at most 2 lg(b **div** a) and the number of assignments lg(b **div** a).

Let $m = \lfloor \tfrac{1}{2}n \rfloor$. In **BuildHeap** we make m calls to **InsertHeap**, for values of $k = $ a ranging from m down to 1. Hence the total number of comparisons is about

$$2 \sum_{k=1}^{m} \lg(n/k) \;=\; 2(m \lg n - \lg m!) \;\approx\; 5m \;\approx\; 2.5n,$$

since, by Stirling's approximation (Corollary A.6) and $\lg m = \lg n - 1$, we have

$$\lg m! \;\approx\; m \lg m - 1.5m \;\approx\; m \lg n - 2.5m.$$

Similarly, in the sorting and insertion phase, we have about

$$2 \sum_{k=2}^{n} \lg k \;=\; 2 \lg k! \;\approx\; 2n \lg n - 3n$$

comparisons. This term dominates that of the initial phase, and hence we conclude that the number of comparisons is $2n \lg n + O(n)$.

One assignment of items is done in **InsertHeap** for each two comparisons (approximately). Therefore the total number of assignments is $n \lg n + O(n)$.

From Section 4.8.4 we can see that the corresponding numbers for quicksort in the average case are $1.39n \lg n + O(n)$ and $0.23n \lg n + O(n)$, respectively. Hence the worst case for heapsort is somewhat poorer than the average case for quicksort. Quicksort's worst case, however, is $O(n^2)$, which is far worse than the worst case of heapsort for large n. An average-case analysis of heapsort appears to be very complicated, but empirical studies show that (as for selection sort) there is relatively little difference between the average and worst cases, and heapsort usually takes about twice as long as quicksort. Heapsort, therefore, should be regarded as something of an insurance policy: On average heapsort costs about twice as much as quicksort, but avoids the slight possibility of a catastrophic degradation of performance.

9.2.4 Priority queues.

To conclude this section, we briefly mention another application of heaps. A *priority queue* is a data structure with only two operations:

1. Insert an item;
2. Remove the item having the largest (or smallest) key.

If items have equal keys, then the usual rule is that the first item inserted should be removed first.

In a time-sharing computer system, for example, a large number of tasks may be waiting for the CPU. Some of these tasks have higher priority than others. Hence the set of tasks waiting for the CPU forms a priority queue. Other applications of priority queues include simulations of time-dependent events, and solution of sparse systems of linear equations by row reduction.

We could represent a priority queue as a sorted contiguous list, in which case removal of an item is immediate, but insertion would take time proportional to n, the number of items in the queue. Or we could represent it as an unsorted list, in which case insertion is rapid but removal is slow. If we used an ordinary binary search tree (sorted by the size of the key) then, on average, insertion and removal could both be done in time $O(\log n)$, but the tree could degenerate and require time $O(n)$. Extra time and space may be needed, as well, to accommodate the linked representation of the binary search tree.

Now consider the properties of a heap. The item with largest key is on the top, and can be removed immediately. It will, however, take time $O(\log n)$ to restore the heap property for the remaining keys. If, however, another item is to be inserted immediately, then some of this time may be combined with the $O(\log n)$ time needed to insert the new item. Thus the representation of a priority queue as a heap proves advantageous for large n, since it is represented efficiently in contiguous storage and is guaranteed to require only logarithmic time for both insertions and deletions.

Exercises

1. Determine the contiguous representation of each of the following binary trees. Which of these trees are heaps? For those that are not, state which rule(s) is (are) violated at which node(s).

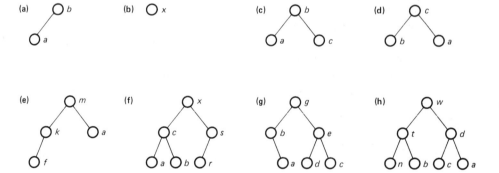

2. By hand, trace the action of **HeapSort** on each of the following lists. Draw the initial tree to which the list corresponds; show how it is converted into a heap; and show the resulting heap as each item is removed from the top and the new item inserted.

   (a) The list of five playing cards used in Chapter 4:

$$S\,Q \quad S\,A \quad C\,7 \quad H\,8 \quad D\,K$$

   (b) The list of seven numbers:

$$26 \quad 33 \quad 35 \quad 29 \quad 19 \quad 12 \quad 22$$

(c) The list of fourteen names:

     Tim Dot Eva Roy Tom Kim Guy Amy Jon Ann Jim Kay Ron Jan

3. Conduct empirical studies to compare the performance of HeapSort with Quick-Sort.

4. Design a procedure that will insert a new item into a heap, obtaining a new heap. (The procedure InsertHeap in the text requires that the root be unoccupied, whereas for this exercise the root will already contain the item with largest key, which must remain in the heap. Your procedure will increase the count n of items in the list.) Analyze the time and space requirements of your procedure.

5. Design a procedure that will delete the item with largest key (the root) from the top of the heap, and restore the heap properties of the resulting, smaller list. Analyze the time and space requirements of your procedure.

6. Design a procedure that will delete the item with index i from a heap, and restore the heap properties of the resulting, smaller list. Analyze the time and space requirements of your procedure.

7. Consider a heap of n keys, with x_k being the key in position k (in the contiguous representation) for $1 \leq k \leq n$. Prove that the height of the subtree rooted at x_k is $\lfloor \lg(n/k) \rfloor$, for $1 \leq k \leq n$. (*Hint*: Use "backward" induction on k, starting with the leaves and working back toward the root, that is x_1.)

8. Define the notion of a "ternary heap", analogous to an ordinary heap except that each node of the tree except the leaves has three children. Devise a sorting method based on ternary heaps, and analyze the properties of the sorting method.

9.3 Lexicographic search trees: tries.

Instead of searching by comparison of entire keys, we can consider a key as a sequence of characters (letters or digits, for example), and use these characters to determine a multi-way branch at each step. If our keys are alphabetic names, then we make a 26-way branch according to the first letter of the name, followed by another branch according to the second letter, and so on. This multi-way branching is the idea of a thumb index in a dictionary. A thumb index, however, is generally used only to find the words with a given initial letter; some other search method is then used to continue. In a computer we can proceed two or three levels by multiway branching, but then the tree will become too large, and we shall need to resort to some other device to continue.

9.3.1 Tries.

One method is to prune from the tree all the branches that do not lead to any key. In English, for example, there are no words that begin with the letters 'bb', 'bc', 'bd', 'bf', $\cdots$. Hence all the corresponding branches and nodes can be removed from the tree. The resulting tree is called a *trie.* (This term originated as letters extracted from the word *retrieval,* but is usually pronounced like the word 'try'.)

A trie of order *m* can be defined formally as being either empty, or consisting of an ordered sequence of exactly *m* tries of order *m*.

9.3.2 Searching for a key.

A trie describing the words (as listed in the *Oxford English Dictionary*) made up only from the letters 'a', 'b', and 'c' is shown in Figure 9.15. Along with the branches to the next level of the trie, each node contains a pointer to a record of information about the key, if any, that has been found when the node is reached. The search for a particular key begins at the root. The first letter of the key is used as an index to

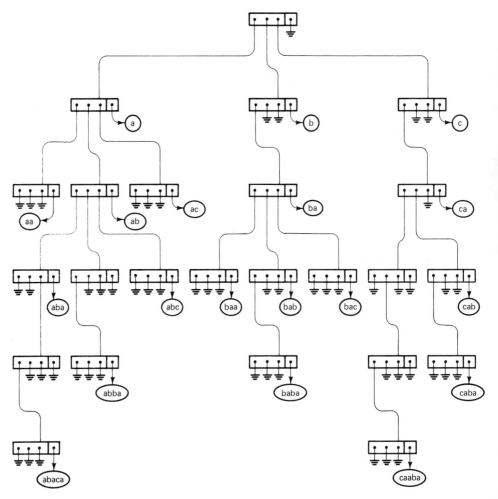

Figure 9.15. Trie of words constructed from 'a', 'b', 'c'

determine which branch to take. An empty branch means that the key being sought is
not in the tree. Otherwise, we use the second letter of the key to determine the branch
at the next level, and so continue. When we reach the end of the word, the information
pointer directs us to the desired information. A **nil** information pointer shows that the
string is not a word in the trie. Note, therefore, that the word 'a' is a prefix of the word
'aba', which is a prefix of the word 'abaca'. On the other hand, the string 'abac' is not
an English word, and therefore has a **nil** information pointer.

9.3.3 Pascal algorithm.

The search process just described translates easily into a procedure. First we need
some declarations.

```
type
  letter  = 'a'..'z';
  key     = array[1..maxlength] of char;  {contains only ' ' and 'a'..'z'}
  pointer = ↑node;
  node    = record
                branch: array[letter] of pointer;
                info:  keyinfo
            end;
```

The constant maxlength giving the maximum length of a key and the pointer type
keyinfo bound to some type that contains the desired information for each key are
assumed to be declared elsewhere. We shall assume that all keys contain only lower
case letters and blanks, and that a key is terminated by the first blank it contains. The
searching method then becomes the following procedure.

```
procedure TrieSearch(root: pointer; target: key; var p: pointer);
{root points to the root of a trie; at conclusion, p will point to the trie
record that points to the information record for the target if the search
is successful; p will be nil if the search is unsuccessful.}
var
  i: integer;
begin
  p := root;
  i := 1;
  while (i <= maxlength) and (p <> nil) do
    if target[i] = ' ' then
      i := maxlength + 1     {terminates search for a blank in target}
              {p is left pointing to the node with information for target}
    else begin
      p := p↑.branch[target[i]]; {move down appropriate branch of trie}
      i := i + 1                    {move to next character of target}
    end;
  if p <> nil then if p↑.info = nil then p := nil
end;
```

The termination condition for the loop is made more complicated to avoid an index error after an iteration with i $=$ maxlength. At the conclusion, **p** (if not **nil**) points to the node in the trie corresponding to the target. The information field can then be obtained from p↑.info.

9.3.4 Insertion into a trie.

Adding a new key to a trie is quite similar to searching for the key: we must trace our way down the trie to the appropriate point, and set the info pointer to the information record for the new key. If, on the way, we hit a **nil** branch in the trie, we must now not terminate the search, but instead we must add new nodes to the trie so as to complete the path corresponding to the new key. We thereby obtain the following procedure.

```
procedure InsertTrie(var root: pointer; k: key; info: keyinfo);
var
  i: integer;
  p: pointer;
  ch: letter;
begin
  if root = nil then          {create a new trie with all empty subtries}
  begin
    new(root);
    for ch := 'a' to 'z' do
      root↑.branch[ch] := nil;
    root↑.info := nil
  end;
  p := root;
  i := 1;
  while i <= maxlength do
    if k[i] = ' ' then
      i := maxlength + 1
    else begin
      if p↑.branch[k[i]] <> nil then
        p := p↑.branch[k[i]]
      else begin
        new(p↑.branch[k[i]]);
        p := p↑.branch[k[i]];
        for ch := 'a' to 'z' do
          p↑.branch[ch] := nil;
        p↑.info := nil
      end;
      i := i + 1
    end;
```

{At this point, we have tested for all non-blank characters of k}
if p↑.info $<>$ **nil then**
    Error   {k duplicates a key already in the trie}
else
    p↑.info := info
end;

9.3.5 Deletion from a trie.

The same general plan used for searching and insertion also works for deletion from a trie. We trace down the path corresponding to the key being deleted, and when we reach the appropriate node, we set the corresponding info field to **nil.** If now, however, this node has all its fields **nil** (all branches and the info field), then we should dispose of this node. To do so, we can set up a stack of pointers to the nodes on the path from the root to the last node reached. Alternatively, we can use recursion in the deletion algorithm, and avoid the need for an explicit stack. In either case, we shall leave the programming as an exercise.

9.3.6 Assessment of tries.

The number of steps required to search a trie (or insert into it) is proportional to the number of characters making up a key, not to a logarithm of the number of keys, as in other tree-based searches. If this number of characters is small relative to the (base 2) logarithm of the number of keys, then a trie may prove superior to a binary tree. If, for example, the keys consist of all possible sequences of five letters, then the trie can locate any of $n = 26^5 = 11,881,376$ keys in 5 iterations, whereas the best that binary search can do is $\lg n \approx 23.5$ key comparisons.

In many applications, however, the number of characters in a key is larger, and the set of keys that actually occur is sparse in the set of all possible keys. In these applications the number of iterations required to search a trie may very well exceed the number of key comparisons needed for a binary search.

The best solution, finally, may be to combine the methods. A trie can be used for the first few characters of the key, and then another method can be employed for the remainder of the key. If we return to the example of the thumb index in a dictionary, we see that, in fact, we use a multiway tree to locate the first letter of the word, but we then use some other search method to locate the desired word among those with the same first letter.

Exercises

1. Draw the tries constructed from each of the following sets of keys.

    (a) All three-digit integers containing only '1', '2', '3' (in decimal representation).
    (b) All three-letter sequences built from 'a', 'b', 'c', 'd' where the first letter is 'a'.
    (c) All four-digit binary integers (built from '0' and '1').

(d) The words

pal   lap   a   papa   al   papal   all   ball   lab

built from the letters 'a', 'b', 'l', 'p'.

2. Write a procedure that will traverse a trie and print out all its words in alphabetical order.

3. Write a procedure that will traverse a trie and print out all its words, with the order determined first by the length of the word, with shorter words first, and, second, by alphabetical order for words of the same length.

4. Write a procedure that will delete a word from a trie.

5. Run the insertion, search, and deletion procedures for appropriate test data, and compare the results with similar experiments for binary search trees.

9.4 External searching: B-trees.

In our work throughout this book we have assumed that all our data structures are kept in high-speed memory; that is, we have considered only *internal* information retrieval. For many applications this assumption is reasonable, but for many other important applications, it is not. Let us now turn briefly to the problem of *external* information retrieval, where we wish to locate and retrieve records stored in a disk file.

9.4.1 Access time.

The time required to access and retrieve a word from high-speed memory is a few microseconds at most. The time required to locate a particular record on a disk is measured in milliseconds, and for floppy disks can exceed a second. Hence the time required for a single access is thousands of times greater for external retrieval than for internal retrieval. On the other hand, when a record is located on a disk, the normal practice is not to read only one word, but to read in a large *page* or *block* of information at once. Typical sizes for blocks range from 256 to 1024 characters or words.

Our goal in external searching must be to minimize the number of disk accesses, since each access takes so long compared to internal computation. With each access, however, we obtain a block that may have room for several records. Using these records, we may be able to make a multiway decision concerning which block to access next. Hence multiway trees are especially appropriate for external searching.

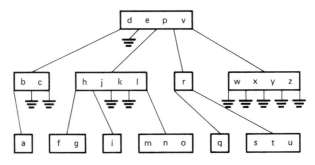

Figure 9.16. A 5-way search tree

9.4.2 Multiway search trees.

Binary search trees generalize directly to multiway search trees in which, for some integer m called the **order** of the tree, each node has at most m children. If $k \leq m$ is the number of children, then the node contains exactly $k-1$ keys, which partition all the keys into k subsets. If some of these subsets are empty, then the corresponding children in the tree are empty. Figure 9.16 shows a 5-way search tree in which some of the children of some nodes are empty.

9.4.3 Balanced multiway trees.

Our goal is to devise a multiway search tree that will minimize file accesses; hence we wish to make height of the tree as small as possible. We can accomplish this by insisting, first, that no empty subtrees appear above the leaves (so that the division of keys into subsets is as efficient as possible); second, that all leaves be on the same level (so that searches will all be guaranteed to terminate with about the same number of accesses); and, third, that every node (except the leaves) have at least some minimal number of children. We shall require that each node (except the leaves) have at least half as many children as the maximum possible. These conditions lead to the following formal definition.

DEFINITION. A **B-tree of order** m is an m-way tree in which

1. All leaves are on the same level.
2. All internal nodes except the root have at most m (non-empty) children, and at least $\lceil m/2 \rceil$ (non-empty) children.
3. The number of keys in each internal node is one less than the number of its children, and these keys partition the keys in the children in the fashion of a search tree.
4. The root has at most m children, but may have as few as 2 if it is not a leaf, or none if the tree consists of the root alone.

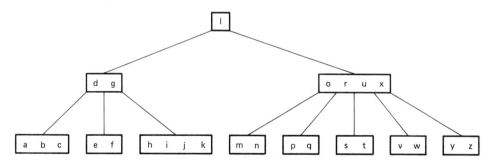

Figure 9.17. A B-tree of order 5

The tree in Figure 9.16 is not a B-tree, since some nodes have empty children, and the leaves are not all on the same level. Figure 9.17 shows a B-tree of order 5 whose keys are the 26 letters of the alphabet.

9.4.4 Insertion into a B-tree.

The condition that all leaves be on the same level forces a characteristic behavior of B-trees: In contrast to binary search trees, B-trees are not allowed to grow at their

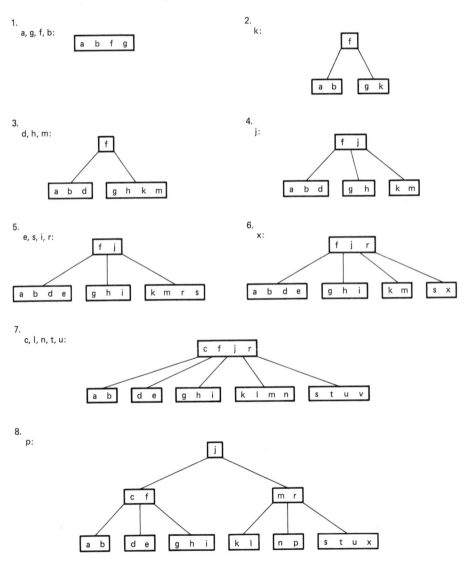

Figure 9.18. Growth of a B-tree

leaves; instead they are forced to grow at the root. The general method of insertion is as follows. First a search is made to see if the new key is in the tree. This search (if the key is truly new) will terminate in failure at a leaf. The new key is then added to the leaf node. If the node was not previously full, then the insertion is finished. When a key is added to a full node, then the node splits into two nodes on the same level, except that the median key is not put into either of the two new nodes, but is instead sent up the tree to be inserted into the parent node. When a search is later made through the tree, therefore, a comparison with the median key will serve to direct the search into the proper subtree. When a key is added to a full root, then the root splits in two and the median key sent upward becomes a new root.

This process is greatly elucidated by studying an example such as the growth of the B-tree of order 5 shown in Figure 9.18. We shall insert the keys

$$a \ g \ f \ b \ k \ d \ h \ m \ j \ e \ s \ i \ r \ x \ c \ l \ n \ t \ u \ p$$

into an initially empty tree, in the order given.

The first four keys will be inserted into one node, as shown in the first diagram of Figure 9.18. They are sorted into the proper order as they are inserted. There is no room, however, for the fifth key, 'k', so its insertion causes the node to split into two, and the median key, 'f' moves up to enter a new node, which is a new root. Since the split nodes are now only half full, the next three keys can be inserted without difficulty. Note, however, that these simple insertions can require rearrangement of the keys within a node. The next insertion, 'j', again splits a node, and this time it is 'j' itself that is the median key, and therefore moves up to join 'f' in the root.

The next several insertions proceed similarly. The final insertion, that of 'p', is more interesting. This insertion first splits the node originally containing 'k l m n', sending the median key 'm' upward into the node containing 'c f j r', which is, however, already full. Hence this node in turn splits, and a new root containing 'j' is created.

Two comments regarding the growth of B-trees are in order. First, when a node splits, it produces two nodes that are now only half full. Later insertions, therefore, can more likely be made without need to split nodes again. Hence one splitting prepares the way for several simple insertions. Second, it is always a median key that is sent upward, not necessarily the key being inserted. Hence repeated insertions tend to improve the balance of the tree, no matter in what order the keys happen to arrive.

9.4.5 Pascal algorithms: searching and insertion.

To develop Pascal algorithms for searching and insertion in a B-tree, let us begin with the declarations needed to set up a B-tree. For simplicity we shall construct our B-tree entirely in high-speed memory, using Pascal pointers to describe its structure. In most applications, these pointers would be replaced by the addresses of various blocks or pages on a disk, and taking a pointer reference would become making a disk access. We shall also construct our tree from keys alone; in any practical application each key would be associated with other information.

1. Declarations.

We assume that keytype is defined already. Within one node there will be a list of keys, and a list of pointers to the children of the node. Since these lists are short, we shall, for simplicity, use contiguous arrays and a separate variable count for their representation.

```
const
  max = 4;     {maximum number of keys in a node; max = m−1}
  min = 2;     {minimum number of keys in a node; min = ⌈½m⌉−1}
type
  pointer = ↑node;
  position = 0..max;
  node = record
    count: 0..max;          {except for the root, the lower limit is min}
    key: array[1..max] of keytype;
    branch: array[position] of pointer
  end;
```

The way in which the indices are arranged implies that in some of our algorithms we shall need to investigate branch[0] separately; and then consider each key in association with the branch on its right.

2. Searching.

As a simple first example we write down a procedure to search through a B-tree for a target key. The input parameters for the procedure are the target key and a pointer to the root of the B-tree. The first output parameter is a Boolean variable found that indicates if the target was found in the tree. If the target is found, then the second output parameter points to the node where the target was found, and the third parameter is the position of the target within that node. The general method of searching by working our way down through the tree is similar to a search through a binary search tree. In a multiway tree, however, we must examine each node more extensively to find which branch to take at the next step. This examination is done by the auxiliary procedure SearchNode, that returns output parameters found and targetpos, which is the position of the target if found, and otherwise is the number of the branch on which to continue the search.

```
procedure Search(target: keytype; root: pointer;
  var found: Boolean; var targetnode: pointer; var targetpos: position);
begin
  if root = nil then
    found := false
  else begin
    SearchNode(target, root, found, targetpos);
```

```
    if found then
      targetnode := root
    else
      Search(target, root↑.branch[targetpos], found, targetnode,
                                                        targetpos)
  end
end;
```

This procedure has been written recursively to exhibit the similarity of its structure to that of the insertion procedure to be developed shortly. The recursion is tail-end, however, and can easily be replaced by iteration if desired.

3. Searching a node.

This procedure determines if the target is in the current node, and, if not, finds which of the count + 1 branches will contain the target key. For convenience, the possibility of taking branch 0 is considered separately, and then a sequential search is made through the remaining possibilities.

```
    procedure SearchNode(target: keytype; p: pointer;
                    var found: Boolean; var k: position);
    {searches keys in node p↑ for target; returns location k of target, or
                          branch on which to continue search}
  begin
    with p↑ do
      if target < key[1] then
      begin
        found := false;
        k := 0
      end
      else begin                    {Start a sequential search through keys}
        k := count;
        while (target < key[k]) and (k > 1) do
          k := k - 1;
        found := (target = key[k])
      end
  end;
```

4. Insertion: the main procedure.

Insertion can be most naturally formulated as a recursive procedure, since after insertion in a subtree has been completed, a (median) key may remain that must be reinserted higher in the tree. Recursion allows us to keep track of the position within the tree, and work our way back up the tree without need for explicit auxiliary arrays.

We shall assume that the key being inserted is not already in the tree. The insertion procedure then needs only two parameters: **newkey**, the key being inserted, and **root**, the root of the B-tree. For the recursion, however, we need three additional output parameters. The first of these is the Boolean variable **pushup**, that indicates whether the root of the subtree has split into two, also producing a (median) key to be reinserted higher in the tree. When this happens, we shall adopt the convention that the old root node contains the left half of the keys, and a new node contains the right half of the keys. When a split occurs, the second output parameter x is the median key, and the third parameter xr is a pointer to the new node, the right half of the former root p↑ of the subtree.

To keep all these parameters straight, we shall do the recursion in a procedure called **PushDown**. This situation is illustrated in Figure 9.19.

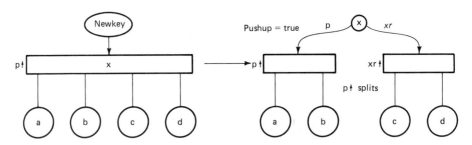

Figure 9.19. Action of PushDown procedure

The recursion is started by the main procedure **Insert**. If the outermost call to procedure PushDown should return with **pushup** true, then there is a key to be placed in a new root, and the height of the entire tree will increase. The main procedure appears as follows.

```
procedure Insert(newkey: keytype; var root: pointer);
{Inserts newkey into the B-tree with given root.  Requires that newkey is
not already present in the tree.}

var
  pushup:      Boolean;      {Has the height of the tree increased?}
  x:           keytype;        {node to be re-inserted as new root}
  xr,                               {subtree on right of x}
  p:           pointer;         {pointer for temporary use}
begin
  PushDown(newkey, root, pushup, x, xr);
  if pushup then                        {Tree grows in height.}
  begin                                    {Make a new root.}
    new(p);
    with p↑ do
```

```
      begin
        count        := 1;
        key[1]       := x;
        branch[0]    := root;
        branch[1]    := xr;
        root         := p
      end
    end
  end;
```

5. Recursive insertion into a subtree.

Next we turn to the recursive procedure **PushDown**. In a B-tree, a new key is first inserted into a leaf. We shall thus use the condition p=**nil** to terminate the recursion; that is, we shall continue to move down the tree searching for **newkey** until we hit an empty subtree. Since the B-tree does not grow by adding new leaves, we do not then immediately insert **target**, but instead set **pushup** true and send the key back up (now called x) for insertion.

When a recursive call returns and **pushup** is true, then we attempt to insert the key x in the current node. If there is room, then we are finished. Otherwise, the current node p↑ splits into p↑ and xr↑ and a (possibly different) median key x is sent up the tree. The procedure uses three auxiliary procedures: **SearchNode** (same as before); **PushIn** puts the key x into node p↑ provided that there is room; and **Split** chops a full node p↑ into two.

```
    procedure PushDown(newkey: keytype; p: pointer;
                   var pushup: Boolean; var x: keytype; var xr: pointer);
      var
        k:     position;            {branch on which to continue the search}
        found: Boolean;            {Is newkey already in the tree (error)?}
      begin
        if p = nil then
        begin            {cannot insert into empty tree; recursion terminates}
          pushup := true;
          x        := newkey;
          xr       := nil
        end
        else begin                            {search current node}
          SearchNode(newkey, p, found, k);
          if found then
            writeln('Error: inserting duplicate key');
          PushDown(newkey, p↑.branch[k], pushup, x, xr);
          if pushup then                        {reinsert median key x}
```

```
with p↑ do
  if count < max then
  begin
    pushup := false;
    PushIn(x, xr, p, k)
  end
  else begin
    pushup := true;
    Split(x, xr, p, k, x, xr)
  end
end
end;
```

6. Insert key into node.

The next procedure inserts the key x and its right-hand pointer xr into the node p↑. The procedure is called only when there is room for the insertion.

```
procedure PushIn(x: keytype; xr, p: pointer; k: position);
{inserts key x and pointer xr into node p↑ at position k}

var
  i: 0..max;                    {index to move keys to make room for x}
begin
  with p↑ do begin
    for i := count downto k+1 do     {shift all keys and branches to
                                                              right}
    begin
      key[i+1]    := key[i];
      branch[i+1] := branch[i]
    end;
    key[k + 1]    := x;
    branch[k + 1] := xr;
    count         := count + 1
  end
end;
```

7. Splitting a full node.

The next procedure inserts the key x with subtree pointer xr into the full node p↑; splits the right half off as new node yr↑; and sends the median key y upward for reinsertion later. It is, of course, not possible to insert key x directly into the full node: we must instead first determine whether x will go into the left or right half, divide the node (at position median) accordingly, and then insert x into the appropriate half. While this work proceeds, we shall leave the median key y in the left half.

```
procedure Split(x: keytype; xr, p: pointer; k: position;
                              var y: keytype; var yr: pointer);
{splits node p↑ with key x and pointer xr at position k into nodes p↑ and
                               yr↑ with median key y}

var
  i: 0..max;                      {used for copying from p↑ to new node}
  median: position;
begin
  if k <= min then                          {new key x goes to left half}
    median := min
  else
    median := min + 1;
  new(yr);                        {get new node and put it on the right}
  with p↑ do begin
    for i := median + 1 to max do
    begin
      yr↑.key[i − median] := key[i];
      yr↑.branch[i − median] := branch[i]
    end;
    yr↑.count := max − median;
    count := median;
    if k <= min then
      PushIn(x, xr, p, k)
    else
      PushIn(x, xr, yr, k − median);
    y := key[count];
    yr↑.branch[0] := branch[count];
    count := count − 1
  end
end;
```

9.4.6 Deletion from a B-tree.

1. Method.

During insertion, the new key always goes first into a leaf. For deletion we shall also wish to remove a key from a leaf. If the key that is to be deleted is not in a leaf, then its immediate predecessor (or successor) under the natural order of keys is guaranteed to be in a leaf (prove it!). Hence we can promote the immediate predecessor (or successor) into the position occupied by the deleted key, and delete the key from the leaf.

If the leaf contains more than the minimum number of keys, then one can be deleted with no further action. If the leaf contains the minimum number, then we first look at the two leaves (or, in the case of a node on the outside, one leaf) that are

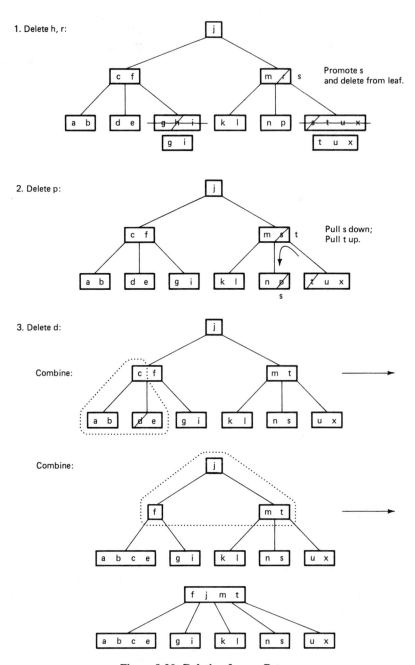

Figure 9.20. Deletion from a B-tree

immediately adjacent and children of the same node. If one of these has more than the minimum number of keys, then one of them can be moved into the parent node, and the key from the parent moved into the leaf where the deletion is occurring. If, finally, the adjacent leaf has only the minimum number of keys, then the two leaves and the median key from the parent can all be combined as one new leaf, that will contain no more than the maximum number of keys allowed. If this step leaves the parent node with too few keys, then the process propagates upward. In the limiting case, the last key is removed from the root, and then the height of the tree decreases.

2. Example.

The process of deletion in our previous B-tree of order 5 is shown in Figure 9.20. The first deletion, 'h', is from a leaf with more than the minimum number of keys, and hence causes no problem. The second deletion, 'r', is not from a leaf, and therefore the immediate successor of 'r', which is 's', is promoted into the position of 'r', and then 's' is deleted from its leaf. The third deletion, 'p', leaves its node with too few keys. The key 's' from the parent node is therefore brought down, and replaced by the key 't'.

Deletion of 'd' has more extensive consequences. This deletion leaves the node with too few keys, and neither of its sibling nodes can spare a key. The node is therefore combined with one of the siblings and with the median key from the parent node, as shown by the dotted line in the first diagram and the combined node 'a b c e' in the second diagram. This process, however, leaves the parent node with only the one key 'f'. The top three nodes of the tree must therefore be combined, yielding the tree shown in the final diagram of Figure 9.20.

3. Pascal procedures.

We can write a deletion algorithm with overall structure similar to that used for insertion. Again we shall use recursion, with a separate main procedure to start the recursion. Rather than attempting to pull a key down from a parent node during an inner recursive call, we shall allow the recursive procedure to return even though there are too few keys in its root node. The outer procedure will then detect this occurrence and move keys as required.

The main procedure is as follows.

```
procedure Delete(target: keytype; var root: pointer);
{Deletes the key target from the B-tree with the given root.}

var
  found: Boolean;            {has target been found in a subtree?}
  p: pointer;                {used to dispose of empty root}
begin
  RecDelete(target, root, found);
  if not found then
    Error                    {target was not in the B-tree}
```

```
      else if root↑.count = 0 then              {root is now empty}
      begin
        p := root;
        root := root↑.branch[0];
        dispose(p)
      end
    end;
```

4. Recursive deletion.

Most of the work is done in the recursive procedure. It first searches the current
node for the target. If it is found and the node is not a leaf, then the immediate
successor of the key is found and placed in the current node, and the successor is
deleted. Deletion from a leaf is straightforward, and otherwise the process continues
by recursion. When a recursive call returns, the procedure checks to see if enough keys
remain in the appropriate node, and, if not, moves keys as required. Auxiliary procedures are used in several of these steps.

```
        procedure RecDelete(target: keytype; p: pointer; var found: Boolean);
        var
          k: position;       {location of target, or of branch on which to search}
        begin
          if p = nil then
            found := false                  {hitting an empty tree is an error}
          else with p↑ do begin
            SearchNode(target, p, found, k);
            if found then
              if branch[k − 1] = nil then                    {case: p↑ is a leaf}
                Remove(p, k)               {removes key from position k of p↑}
              else begin
                Successor(p, k);           {replaces key[k] by its successor}
                RecDelete(key[k], branch[k], found);
                if not found then
                  Error                 {We know that new key[k] is in the leaf}
              end
            else                         {target was not found in current node}
              RecDelete(target, branch[k], found);

                  {At this point, procedure has returned from recursive call.}

            if branch[k] <> nil then
              if branch[k]↑.count < min then
                Restore(p, k)
          end
        end;
```

5. Auxiliary procedures.

The procedures Remove and Successor are straightforward.

```
procedure Remove(p: pointer; k: position);
{removes key[k] and branch[k] from p↑}

var
  i: position;                              {index to move entries}
begin
  with p↑ do begin
    for i := k+1 to count do
    begin
      key[i− 1] := key[i];
      branch[i− 1] := branch[i]
    end;
    count := count − 1
  end
end;

procedure Successor(p: pointer; k: position);
{replaces p↑.key[k] by its immediate successor under natural order}

var
  q: pointer;                    {used to move down the tree to a leaf}
begin
  q := p↑.branch[k];
  while q↑.branch[0] <> nil do
    q := q↑.branch[0];
  p↑.key[k] := q↑.key[1]
end;
```

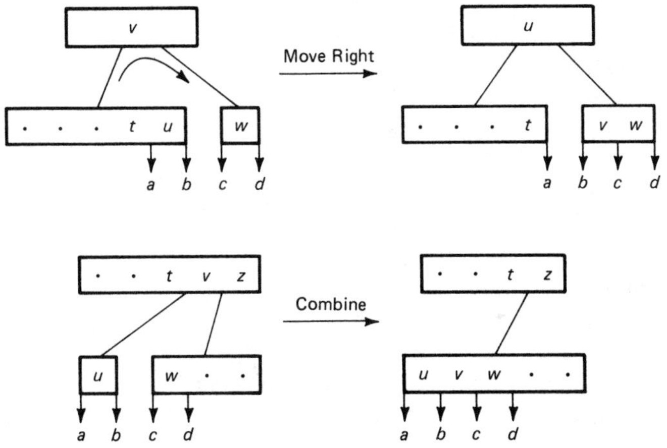

Figure 9.21. Restoration of minimum number of keys

Finally, we must show how to restore p↑.**branch[k]** to the minimum number of keys if a recursive call has reduced its count below the minimum. The procedure we write is somewhat biased to the left; that is, if k $>$ 0 it looks to the sibling on the left, and uses the right sibling only when there is none on the left. The steps that are needed are illustrated in Figure 9.21.

```
procedure Restore(p: pointer; k: position);
{finds a key and inserts it into p↑.branch[k]↑ so as to restore minimum}

begin
  if k > 0 then
    if p↑.branch[k − 1]↑.count > min then          {Move key to right}
      MoveRight(p, k)
    else
      Combine(p, k)
  else                                             {Case: k = 0}
    if p↑.branch[1]↑.count > min then
      MoveLeft(p, 1)
    else
      Combine(p, 1)
end;
```

The actions of the remaining three procedures MoveRight, MoveLeft and Combine are clear from Figure 9.21, but for completeness they are written in full below.

```
procedure MoveRight(p: pointer; k: position);
var
  c: position;
begin
  with p↑.branch[k]↑ do begin
    for c := count downto 1 do
    begin
      key[c + 1]    := key[c];
      branch[c + 1] := branch[c]
    end;
    branch[1]       := branch[0];
    count           := count + 1;
    key[1]          := p↑.key[k]
  end;
  with p↑.branch[k − 1]↑ do begin
    p↑.key[k]                := key[count];
    p↑.branch[k]↑.branch[0] := branch[count];
    count                    := count − 1
  end
end;
```

```
procedure MoveLeft(p: pointer; k: position);
var
  c: position;
begin
  with p↑.branch[k − 1]↑ do begin
    count            := count + 1;
    key[count]       := p↑.key[k];
    branch[count]    := p↑.branch[k]↑.branch[0]
  end;
  with p↑.branch[k]↑ do begin
    p↑.key[k]        := key[1];
    branch[0]        := branch[1];
    count            := count − 1;
    for c            := 1 to count do
    begin
      key[c]         := key[c + 1];
      branch[c]      := branch[c + 1]
    end;
  end
end;



procedure Combine(p: pointer; k: position);
var
  c: position;
  q: pointer;
begin
  q                  := p↑.branch[k];
  with p↑.branch[k − 1]↑ do begin
    count            := count + 1;
    key[count]       := p↑.key[k];
    branch[count]    := q↑.branch[0];
    for c            := 1 to q↑.count do
    begin
      count          := count + 1;
      key[count]     := q↑.key[c];
      branch[count]  := q↑.branch[c]
    end
  end;
```

```
with p↑ do begin
    for c              := k to count−1 do
    begin
        key[c]         := key[c+1];
        branch[c]      := branch[c+1]
    end;
    count              := count − 1
end;
dispose(q)
end;
```

Exercises

1. Insert the six remaining letters of the alphabet in the order

$$z, v, o, q, w, y$$

   into the final B-tree of Figure 9.18.

2. Insert the keys below, in the order stated, into an initially empty B-tree of order (a) 3, (b) 4, (c) 7.

   $$a \quad g \quad f \quad b \quad k \quad d \quad h \quad m \quad j \quad e \quad s \quad i \quad r \quad x \quad c \quad l \quad n \quad t \quad u \quad p$$

3. What is the smallest number of keys that, when inserted in an appropriate order, will force a B-tree of order 5 to have height 2 (that is, 3 levels)?

4. If a key in a B-tree is not in a leaf, prove that both its immediate predecessor and immediate successor (under the natural order) are in leaves.

5. Remove the tail-end recursion from the procedure Search.

6. Rewrite the procedure SearchNode to use binary search.

7. Combine all the procedures of this section into a complete program for manipulating B-trees. You will need to add procedures to input keys to be inserted or deleted, to traverse a B-tree, and to print its keys.

8. A *B*-tree* is a B-tree in which every node, except possibly the root, is at least two-thirds full, rather than half full. Insertion into a B*-tree moves keys between sibling nodes (as done during deletion) as needed, thereby delaying splitting a node until two sibling nodes are completely full. These two nodes can then be split into three, each of which will be at least two-thirds full.

   (a) Specify the changes needed to the insertion algorithm so that it will maintain the properties of a B*-tree.
   (b) Specify the changes needed to the deletion algorithm so that it will maintain the properties of a B*-tree.

(c) Discuss the relative advantages and disadvantages of B*-trees compared to ordinary B-trees.

9.5 Generalizations.

Linked data structures constitute powerful tools, especially when a node can contain multiple links, as we have seen in this chapter. We could, of course, allow even more links and intricate connections between different nodes in the data structure. Doing so would produce powerful tools. Such tools are, of course, meant to be used whenever necessary, but must always be used with great care, else their great power may be turned to confusion.

Perhaps the best safeguard in the use of powerful tools is to insist on regularity, that is, to use the powerful tools only in carefully defined and well understood ways. Thus we have never allowed links to be inserted or removed in data structures at random.

In this world, nonetheless, irregularities will always creep in, no matter how hard we try to avoid them. It is the bane of the systems analyst and programmer to accommodate these irregularities while trying to maintain the integrity of the underlying system design. Irregularity even occurs in the very systems that we use as models for the data structures we devise, models such as the family trees whose terminology we have always used. It is impossible to close this chapter save by reproducing a classic story, as quoted by N. WIRTH from a Zurich newspaper of July, 1922.

> I married a widow who had a grown-up daughter. My father, who visited us quite often, fell in love with my step-daughter and married her. Hence, my father became my son-in-law, and my step-daughter became my mother. Some months later, my wife gave birth to a son, who became the brother-in-law of my father as well as my uncle. The wife of my father, that is my step-daughter, also had a son. Thereby, I got a brother and at the same time a grandson. My wife is my grandmother, since she is my mother's mother. Hence, I am my wife's husband and at the same time her step-grandson; in other words, I am my own grandfather.

9.6 References for further study.

One of the most thorough available studies of trees is in the series of books by KNUTH. Volume 3, pages 422–480, discusses binary search trees, balance, AVL trees, and related topics. Heapsort is discussed in pages 145–149 of Volume 3.

The quotation at the end of the chapter is taken from

N. WIRTH, *Algorithms + Data Structures = Programs*, Prentice-Hall, Englewood Cliffs, N.J.,1976, page 170.

This book also contains (pages 189–264) an excellent exposition, with Pascal algorithms, of binary trees, balancing methods, and generalizations, including (pages 215–226) algorithms for insertion and deletion in AVL trees, and (pages 242–264) algorithms for processing B-trees.

A good mathematical analysis of the behavior of AVL trees appears in

> E. M. REINGOLD, J. NIEVERGELT, N. DEO, *Combinatorial Algorithms: Theory and Practice,* Prentice-Hall, Englewood Cliffs, N.J., 1977.

The original reference for AVL trees is:

> G. M. ADEL'SON-VEL'SKII and E. M. LANDIS, *Dokl. Akad. Nauk SSSR* 146 (1962), 263–266; English translation: *Soviet Math. (Dokl.)* 3 (1962), 1259–1263.

Heapsort was discovered and so named by

> J. W. J. WILLIAMS, *Communications of the ACM* 7 (1964), 347–348.

Tries were first studied in

> EDWARD FREDKIN, "Trie memory ," *Communications of the ACM* 3 (1960), 490–499.

The original reference for B-trees is

> R. BAYER and E. MCCREIGHT, "Organization and maintenance of large ordered indexes ," *Acta Informatica* 1 (1972), 173–189.

An interesting survey of applications and variations of B-trees is

> D. COMER, "The ubiquitous B-tree ," *Computing Surveys* 11 (1979), 121–137.

Appendices

Appendix A

Mathematical Methods

The first part of this appendix supplies several mathematical results used in algorithm analysis. The final two sections (Fibonacci and Catalan numbers) are optional topics for the mathematically inclined reader.

A.1 Sums of powers of integers.

The following two formulas are useful in counting the steps executed by an algorithm.

THEOREM A.1.

$$1 + 2 + \cdots + n \; = \; \frac{n(n+1)}{2}.$$

$$1^2 + 2^2 + \cdots + n^2 \; = \; \frac{n(n+1)(2n+1)}{6}.$$

PROOF. The first identity has a simple and elegant proof. We let S equal the sum on the left side, write it down twice (once in each direction), and add vertically:

$$
\begin{array}{ccccccccccccc}
1 & + & 2 & + & 3 & + & \cdots & + & n-1 & + & n & = & S \\
n & + & n-1 & + & n-2 & + & \cdots & + & 2 & + & 1 & = & S \\
\hline
n+1 & + & n+1 & + & n+1 & + & \cdots & + & n+1 & + & n+1 & = & 2S
\end{array}
$$

There are n columns on the left; hence $n(n+1) = 2S$ and the identity follows.

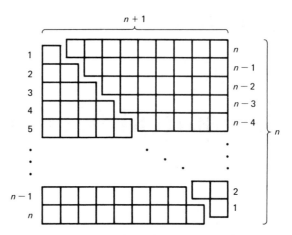

Figure A.1. Geometrical proof of sums of integers

We shall use the method of ***mathematical induction*** to prove the second identity. This method requires that we start by establishing an initial case, called the ***induction base,*** which for our formula is the case $n = 1$. In this case the formula becomes

$$1^2 = \frac{1(1+1)(2+1)}{6},$$

which is true, so the induction base is established. Next, using the formula for the case $n-1$, we must establish it for case n. For case $n-1$ we thus shall assume:

$$1^2 + 2^2 + \cdots + (n-1)^2 = \frac{(n-1)n(2(n-1)+1)}{6}.$$

It follows that

$$1^2 + 2^2 + \cdots + (n-1)^2 + n^2 = \frac{(n-1)n(2(n-1)+1)}{6} + n^2$$

$$= \frac{2n^3 - 3n^2 + n + 6n^2}{6}$$

$$= \frac{n(n+1)(2n+1)}{6},$$

which is the desired result, and the proof by induction is complete.

A convenient shorthand for a sum of the sort appearing in these identities is to use the capital Greek letter sigma

$$\Sigma$$

in front of the typical summand, with the initial value of the index controlling the summation written below the sign, and the final value above. Thus the preceding identities can be written:

$$\sum_{k=1}^{n} k = \frac{n(n+1)}{2}$$

$$\sum_{k=1}^{n} k^2 = \frac{n(n+1)(2n+1)}{6}.$$

Two other formulas are also useful, particularly in working with trees.

THEOREM A.2.

$$1 + 2 + 4 + \cdots + 2^{m-1} = 2^m - 1.$$

$$1\times 1 + 2\times 2 + 3\times 4 + \cdots + m\times 2^{m-1} = (m-1)\times 2^m + 1.$$

In summation notation these equations are:

$$\sum_{k=0}^{m-1} 2^k = 2^m - 1.$$

$$\sum_{k=1}^{m} k\times 2^{k-1} = (m-1)\times 2^m + 1.$$

PROOF.   The first formula will be proved in a more general form. We start with the following identity, which, for any value of $x \neq 1$, can be verified simply by multiplying both sides by $x - 1$:

$$\frac{x^m - 1}{x - 1} = 1 + x + x^2 + \cdots + x^{m-1}$$

for any $x \neq 1$. With $x = 2$ this expression becomes the first formula.

To establish the second formula we take the same expression in the case of $m+1$ instead of m:

$$\frac{x^{m+1} - 1}{x - 1} = 1 + x + x^2 + \cdots + x^m$$

for any $x \neq 1$, and differentiate with respect to x:

$$\frac{(x-1)(m+1)x^m - (x^{m+1}-1)}{(x-1)^2} = 1 + 2x + 3x^2 + \cdots + mx^{m-1}$$

for any $x \neq 1$. Setting $x = 2$ now gives the second formula.

Suppose that $|x| < 1$ in the preceding formulas. As m becomes large, it follows that x^m becomes small, that is

$$\lim_{m\to\infty} x^m = 0.$$

Taking the limit as $m\to\infty$ in the preceding equations gives:

THEOREM A.3.   *If $|x| < 1$ then*

$$\sum_{k=0}^{\infty} x^k = \frac{1}{1-x}.$$

$$\sum_{k=1}^{\infty} kx^{k-1} = \frac{1}{(1-x)^2}.$$

A.2 Logarithms.

The primary reason for using logarithms is to turn multiplication and division into addition and subtraction, and exponentiation into multiplication. Before the advent of pocket calculators, logarithms were an indispensable tool for hand calculation: witness the large tables of logarithms, and the once ubiquitous slide rule. Even though we now have other methods for numerical calculation, the fundamental properties of logarithms give them importance that extends far beyond their use as computational tools.

The behavior of many phenomena, first of all, reflects an intrinsically logarithmic structure; that is, by using logarithms we find important relationships that are not otherwise obvious. Measuring the loudness of sound, for example, is logarithmic: if one sound is 10 db. (decibels) louder than another, then the actual acoustic energy is 10 times as much. If the sound level in one room is 40 db. and it is 60 db. in another, then the human perception may be that the second room is half again as noisy as the first, but there is actually 100 times more sound energy in the second room. This phenomenon is why a single violin soloist can be heard above a full orchestra (when playing a different line), and yet the orchestra requires so many violins to maintain a proper balance of sound.

Logarithms, secondly, provide a convenient way to handle very large numbers. The scientific notation, where a number is written as a small real number (often in the range from 1 to 10) times a power of 10, is really based on logarithms, since the power of 10 is essentially the logarithm of the number. Scientists who need to use very large numbers (like astronomers, nuclear physicists and geologists) frequently speak of orders of magnitude, and thereby concentrate on the logarithm of the number.

A logarithmic graph, thirdly, is a very useful device for displaying the properties of a function over a much broader range than a linear graph. With a logarithmic graph we can arrange to display detailed information on the function for small values of the argument, and at the same time give an overall view for much larger values. Logarithmic graphs are especially appropriate when we wish to show percentage changes in a function.

A.2.1 Definition of logarithms.

Logarithms are defined in terms of a real number $a > 1$, which is called the **base** of the logarithms. (It is also possible to define logarithms with base a in the range $0 < a < 1$, but doing so would introduce needless complications into our discussion.) For any number $x > 0$ we define $\log_a x = y$ where y is the real number such that $a^y = x$. The logarithm of a negative number, and the logarithm of 0, are not defined.

A.2.2 Simple properties.

From the definition and from the properties of exponents we obtain:

$$\log_a 1 = 0.$$
$$\log_a a = 1.$$
$$\log_a x < 0$$

for all x such that $0 < x < 1$.

$$0 < \log_a x < 1$$

for all x such that $1 < x < a$.

$$\log_a x > 1$$

for all x such that $a < x$.

The logarithm function has a graph like the one in Figure A.2. We also obtain the identities:

$$\log_a(xy) = (\log_a x) + (\log_a y)$$
$$\log_a(x/y) = (\log_a x) - (\log_a y)$$
$$\log_a x^z = z \log_a x$$
$$\log_a a^z = z$$
$$a^{\log_a x} = x$$

that hold for any positive real numbers x and y, and for any real number z.

From the graph in Figure A.2 you will observe that the logarithm grows more and more slowly as x increases. The graphs of positive powers of x less than 1, such as the square root of x or the cube root of x, also grow progressively more slowly, but never become as flat as the graph of the logarithm. In fact:

As x grows large, $\log x$ grows more slowly than x^c, for any $c > 0$.

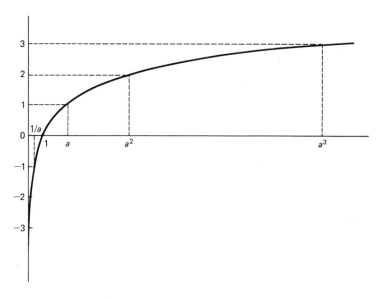

Figure A.2. Graph of the logarithm function

A.2.3 Choice of base

Any real number $a > 1$ can be chosen as the base of logarithms, but certain special choices appear much more frequently than others. For computation and for graphing the base $a = 10$ is often used, and logarithms with base 10 are called *common* logarithms. In studying computer algorithms, however, base 10 appears very infrequently, and we do not often use common logarithms. Instead, logarithms with base 2 appear the most frequently, and we therefore reserve the special symbol

$$\lg x$$

to denote a logarithm with base 2.

A.2.4 Natural logarithms.

In studying mathematical properties of logarithms, and in many problems where logarithms appear as part of the answer, the number that appears as the base is

$$e = 2.718281828459\cdots.$$

Logarithms with base e are called *natural* logarithms. In this book we always denote the natural logarithm of x by

$$\ln x.$$

In many mathematics books, however, other bases than e are rarely used, in which case the unqualified symbol $\log x$ usually denotes a natural logarithm.

The properties of logarithms that make e the natural choice for the base are thoroughly developed as part of the calculus, but we can mention a few of these properties without proof. First, the graph of $\ln x$ has the property that its slope at each point x is $1/x$; that is, the derivative of $\ln x$ is $1/x$ for all real numbers $x > 0$. Second, the natural logarithm satisfies the infinite series

$$\ln(x+1) \;=\; x - \frac{x^2}{2} + \frac{x^3}{3} - \frac{x^4}{4} + \cdots$$

for $-1 < x < 1$, but this series requires a great many terms to give a good approximation, and therefore is not useful directly for computation. It is much better to consider instead the exponential function that "undoes" the logarithm, and that satisfies the series

$$e^x \;=\; 1 + x + \frac{x^2}{2!} + \frac{x^3}{3!} + \cdots$$

for all real numbers x. This exponential function e^x also has the important property that it is its own derivative.

A.2.5 Change of base.

Logarithms with respect to one base are closely related to logarithms with respect to any other base. To find this relation we start with the following relation that is essentially the definition:

$$x \;=\; a^{\log_a x}$$

for any $x > 0$. Then

$$\log_b x \;=\; \log_b a^{\log_a x} \;=\; (\log_a x)(\log_b a).$$

The factor $\log_b a$ does not depend on x, but only on the two bases. Therefore:

Logarithms can be converted from one base to another simply by multiplying by a constant factor, the logarithm of the first base with respect to the second.

The most useful numbers for us in this connection are

$$\lg e \;\approx\; 1.442695041$$
$$\ln 2 \;\approx\; 0.693147181$$
$$\ln 10 \;\approx\; 2.302585093$$

A.2.6 Logarithmic graphs.

In a logarithmic scale the numbers are arranged as on a slide rule, with larger numbers closer together than smaller numbers. In this way, equal distances along the scale represent equal *ratios*, rather than the equal *differences* represented on an ordinary linear scale. A logarithmic scale should be used when percentage change is

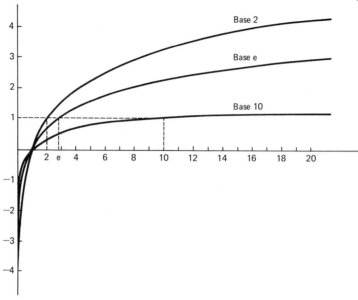

Figure A.3. Logarithms with three bases

important to measure, or when perception is logarithmic. Human perception of time, for example, would seem to be nearly linear in the short term—what happened two days ago is twice as distant as what happened yesterday—but is more nearly logarithmic in the long term: we draw less distinction between one million years ago and two million years ago than we do between ten years ago and one hundred years ago. Figure A.4 graphs the consumer price index over a short period, so a linear scale is used for the time. The linear scale on the vertical axis gives a more dramatic impression that inflation is running wild, but the logarithmic scale reflects the percentage change in the index, which is the important factor to measure.

Graphs in which both the vertical and horizontal scales are logarithmic are called *log-log graphs.* In addition to phenomena where the perception is naturally logarithmic in both scales, log-log graphs are useful to display the behavior of a function over a very wide range. For small values the graph records a detailed view of the function, and for large values a broad view of the function appears on the same graph. For searching and sorting algorithms, we wish to compare methods both for small problems and large problems; hence log-log graphs are appropriate. See Figure A.5.

One observation is worth noting: Any power of x graphs as a straight line with a log-log scale. To prove this, we start with an arbitrary power function $y = x^n$, and take logarithms on both sides, obtaining

$$\log y \ = \ n \log x.$$

A log-log graph in x and y becomes a linear graph in $u = \log x$ and $v = \log y$, and the equation becomes $v = nu$ in terms of u and v, which indeed graphs as a straight line.

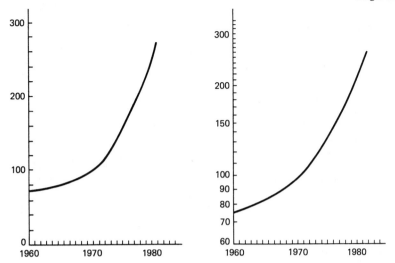

Figure A.4. Consumer Price Index, Canada

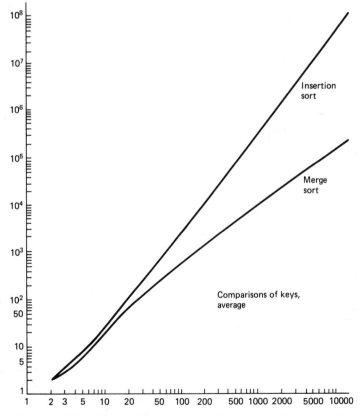

Figure A. 5. Log-log graph, comparisons, insertion and merge sorts

A.2.7 Harmonic numbers.

As a final application of logarithms, we obtain an approximation to a sum that appears frequently in the analysis of algorithms, especially that of sorting methods. The nth **harmonic number** is defined to be the sum

$$H_n = 1 + \frac{1}{2} + \frac{1}{3} + \cdots + \frac{1}{n}$$

of the reciprocals of the integers from 1 to n.

To evaluate H_n we consider the function $1/x$, and the relationship shown in Figure A.6. The area under the step function is clearly H_n, since the width of each step is 1, and the height of step k is $1/k$, for each integer k from 1 to n. This area is approximated by the area under the curve $1/x$ from ½ to $n+$½. The area under the curve is

$$\int_{½}^{n+½} \frac{1}{x} dx = \ln(n+½) - \ln ½ \approx \ln(n) + 0.7.$$

When n is large, the fractional term 0.7 is insignificant, and we obtain $\ln n$ as a good approximation to H_n.

By refining this method of approximation by an integral, it is possible to obtain a very much closer approximation to H_n, if such is desired. Specifically,

THEOREM A.4.   *The harmonic number* H_n, $n \geq 1$, *satisfies*

$$H_n = \ln n + \gamma + \frac{1}{2n} - \frac{1}{12n^2} + \frac{1}{120n^4} - \epsilon,$$

where $0 < \epsilon < 1/(252n^6)$, *and* $\gamma \approx 0.577215665$ *is known as* **Euler's constant.**

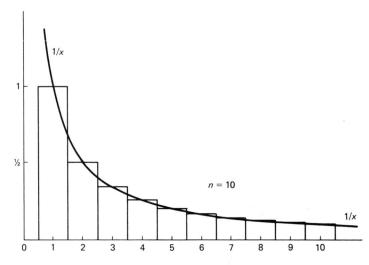

Figure A.6. Approximation of Harmonic Numbers

A.3 Permutations, Combinations, Factorials.

A.3.1 Permutations.

A *permutation* of objects is an ordering or arrangement of the objects in a row. If we begin with n different objects, then we can choose any of the n objects to be the first one in the arrangement. There are then $n-1$ choices for the second object, and since these choices can be combined in all possible ways, the number of choices multiplies. Hence the first two objects may be chosen in $n(n-1)$ ways. There remain $n-2$ objects, any one of which may be chosen as the third in the arrangement. Continuing in this way, we see that the number of permutations of n distinct objects is

$$n! \ = \ n\times(n-1)\times(n-2) \times \cdots \times 2 \times 1.$$

objects to permute: a b c d

choose a *first:*	a b c d	a b d c	a c b d	a c d b	a d b c	a d c b
choose b *first:*	b a c d	b a d c	b c a d	b c d a	b d a c	b d c a
choose c *first:*	c a b d	c a d b	c b a d	c b d a	c d a b	c d b a
choose d *first:*	d a b c	d a c b	d b a c	d b c a	d c a b	d c b a

Figure A.7. Constructing permutations

Note that we have assumed that the objects are all distinct, that is, that we can tell each object from every other one. It is often easier to count configurations of distinct objects than when some are indistinguishable. The latter problem can sometimes be solved by temporarily labeling the objects so they are all distinct, then counting the configurations, and finally dividing by the number of ways in which the labeling could have been done. The special case in the next section is especially important.

A.3.2 Combinations.

A *combination* of n objects taken k at a time is a choice of k objects out of the n, without regard for the order of selection. The number of such combinations is denoted either by

$$C(n, \ k) \text{ or by } \binom{n}{k}.$$

We can calculate $C(n, \ k)$ by starting with the $n!$ permutations of n objects, and form a combination simply by selecting the first k objects in the permutation. The order, however, in which these k objects appear is ignored in determining a combination, so we must divide by the number $k!$ of ways to order the k objects chosen. The order of the $n-k$ objects not chosen is also ignored, so we must also divide by $(n-k)!$. Hence:

$$C(n, \ k) \ = \ \frac{n!}{k!(n-k)!}.$$

Objects from which to choose: a b c d e f

a b c	a c d	a d f	b c f	c d e
a b d	a c e	a e f	b d e	c d f
a b e	a c f	b c d	b d f	c e f
a b f	a d e	b c e	b e f	d e f

Figure A.8. Combinations of 6 objects, taken 3 at a time

The number of combinations $C(n , k)$ is called a **binomial coefficient,** since it appears as the coefficient of $x^k y^{n-k}$ in the expansion of $(x+y)^n$. There are hundreds of different relationships and identities about various sums and products of binomial coefficients. The most important of these can be found in textbooks on elementary algebra and on combinatorics.

A.3.3 Factorials.

We frequently use permutations and combinations in analyzing algorithms, and for these applications we must estimate the size of $n!$ for various values of n. An excellent approximation to $n!$ was obtained by JAMES STIRLING in the eighteenth century:

THEOREM A.5.

$$n! \approx \sqrt{2\pi n}\left(\frac{n}{e}\right)^n\left[1 + \frac{1}{12n} + o\left(\frac{1}{n^2}\right)\right].$$

We usually use this approximation in logarithmic form instead:

COROLLARY A.6.

$$\ln n! \approx (n+\tfrac{1}{2})\ln n - n + \tfrac{1}{2}\ln(2\pi) + \frac{1}{12n} + O\left(\frac{1}{n^2}\right).$$

Note that, as n increases, the approximation to the logarithm becomes more and more accurate, that is, the difference approaches 0. The difference between the direct approximation to the factorial and $n!$ itself will not necessarily become small (that is, the difference need not go to 0), but the percentage error becomes arbitrarily small (the ratio goes to 1). KNUTH (Volume 1, page 111) gives refinements of Stirling's approximation that are even closer.

The complete proof of Stirling's approximation requires techniques from advanced calculus that would take us too far afield here. We can, however, use a bit of elementary calculus to illustrate the first step of the approximation. First, we take the natural logarithm of a factorial, noting that the logarithm of a product is the sum of the logarithms:

$$\ln n! = \sum_{x=1}^{n}\ln x.$$

Next, we approximate the sum by an integral, as shown in Figure A.9. It is clear from the diagram that the area under the step function, which is exactly $\ln n!$, is approximately the same as the area under the curve, which is

$$\int_{½}^{n+½} \ln x \, dx \;=\; (x \ln x - x)\Big|_{½}^{n+½}$$

$$=\; (n+½) \ln (n+½) - n + ½ \ln 2.$$

For large values of n, the difference between $\ln n$ and $\ln(n+½)$ is insignificant, and hence this approximation differs from Stirling's only by the constant difference between $½\ln 2$ (about 0.35) and $½\ln(2\pi)$ (about 0.919).

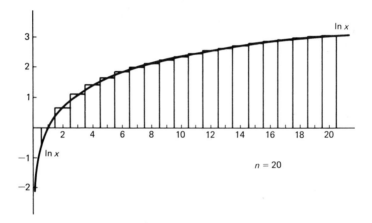

Figure A.9. Approximation of $\ln n!$ by an integral

A.4 Fibonacci numbers.

The Fibonacci numbers originated as an exercise in arithmetic proposed by Leonardo Fibonacci in 1202:

> *How many pairs of rabbits can be produced from a single pair in a year? We start with a single newly born pair; it takes one month for a pair to mature, after which they produce a new pair each month, and the rabbits never die.*

In month 1, we have only one pair. In month 2, we still have only one pair, but they are now mature. In month 3, they have reproduced, so we now have two pairs. And so it goes. The number F_n of pairs of rabbits that we have in month n satisfies

$$F_0 = 0, \quad F_1 = 1, \quad \text{and} \quad F_n = F_{n-1} + F_{n-2} \text{ for } n \geq 2.$$

This same sequence of numbers, called the **Fibonacci sequence,** appears in many other problems. In Section 9.1.4, for example, F_n appears as the minimum number of nodes in an AVL tree of height n. Our object in this section is to find a formula for F_n.

We shall use the method of **generating functions,** which is important for many other applications. The generating function is a formal infinite series in a symbol x, with the Fibonacci numbers as coefficients:

$$F(x) = F_0 + F_1 x + F_2 x^2 + \cdots + F_n x^n + \cdots .$$

We do not worry about whether this series converges, or what the value of x might be, since we are not going to set x to any particular value. Instead, we shall only perform formal algebraic manipulations on the generating function.

Next, we multiply by powers of x:

$$F(x) = F_0 + F_1 x + F_2 x^2 + \cdots + F_n x^n + \cdots$$

$$xF(x) = F_0 x + F_1 x^2 + \cdots + F_{n-1} x^n + \cdots$$

$$x^2 F(x) = F_0 x^2 + \cdots + F_{n-2} x^n + \cdots$$

and subtract the second two equations from the first:

$$(1 - x - x^2) F(x) = F_0 + (F_1 - F_0) x = x$$

since $F_0 = 0$, $F_1 = 1$, and $F_n = F_{n-1} + F_{n-2}$ for all $n \geq 2$. We therefore obtain

$$F(x) = \frac{x}{1 - x - x^2}.$$

The roots of $1 - x - x^2$ are $\frac{1}{2}(-1 \pm \sqrt{5})$. By the method of partial fractions we can thus rearrange the formula for $F(x)$ as:

$$F(x) = \frac{1}{\sqrt{5}} \left(\frac{1}{1 - \phi x} - \frac{1}{1 - \psi x} \right)$$

where

$$\phi = \frac{1}{2}(1 + \sqrt{5}) \quad \text{and} \quad \psi = 1 - \phi = \frac{1}{2}(1 - \sqrt{5}).$$

(Check this equation by putting the two fractions on the right over a common denominator.) The next step is to expand the fractions on the right side by dividing their denominators into 1:

$$F(x) = \frac{1}{\sqrt{5}} (1 + \phi x + \phi^2 x^2 + \cdots - 1 - \psi x - \psi^2 x^2 - \cdots).$$

The final step is to recall that the coefficients of $F(x)$ are the Fibonacci numbers, and therefore to equate the coefficients of each power of x on both sides of this equation. We thus obtain

$$F_n = \frac{1}{\sqrt{5}} (\phi^n - \psi^n).$$

Approximate values for ϕ and ψ are

$$\phi \approx 1.618034 \quad \text{and} \quad \psi \approx -0.618034.$$

This surprisingly simple answer to the values of the Fibonacci numbers is interesting in several ways. It is not even immediately obvious why the right side should always be an integer. Secondly, ψ is a negative number of sufficiently small absolute value that we always have $F_n = \phi^n/\sqrt{5}$ rounded to the nearest integer. Thirdly, the number ϕ is itself interesting. It has been studied since the times of the ancient Greeks, is often called the **golden mean,** and the ratio of ϕ to 1 is said to give the most pleasing shape of a rectangle.

A.5 Catalan numbers.

The purpose of this section is to count the binary trees with n vertices. We shall accomplish this result via a slightly circuitous route, discovering along the way several other problems that have the same answer. The resulting numbers, called the **Catalan numbers,** are of considerable interest in that they appear in the answers to many apparently unrelated problems.

A.5.1 The main result.

DEFINITION. For $n \geq 0$, the nth **Catalan number** is defined to be

$$\text{Cat}(n) = \frac{C(2n, n)}{n+1} = \frac{(2n)!}{(n+1)!\,n!}$$

THEOREM A.7. *The number of distinct binary trees with n vertices, $n \geq 0$, is the nth Catalan number $\text{Cat}(n)$.*

A.5.2 The proof by one-to-one correspondences.

1. Orchards.

Let us first recall the one-to-one correspondence (Theorem 5.2) between the binary trees with n vertices and the orchards with n vertices. Hence to count binary trees, we may just as well count orchards.

2. Well-formed sequences of parentheses.

Second, let us consider the set of all well-formed sequences of n left parentheses '(' and n right parentheses ')'. Such a sequence is **well-formed** means that, when scanned from left to right, the number of right parentheses encountered never exceeds the number of left parentheses. Thus '((()))' and '()()()' are well-formed, but '())(()' is not, nor is '(()', since the total numbers of left and right parentheses in the expression must be equal.

LEMMA A.8.   *There is a one-to-one correspondence between the orchards with n vertices and the well-formed sequences of n left parentheses and n right parentheses, n ≥ 0.*

To define this correspondence, we first recall that an orchard is either empty, or is an ordered sequence of ordered trees. We define the ***bracketed form*** of an orchard to be the sequence of bracketed forms of its trees, written one after the next in the same order as the trees in the orchard. The bracketed form of the empty orchard is empty. We recall also that an ordered tree is defined to consist of its root vertex, together with an orchard of subtrees. We thus define the ***bracketed form*** of an ordered tree to consist of a left parenthesis '(' followed by the (name of the) root, followed by the bracketed form of the orchard of subtrees, and finally a right parenthesis ')'.

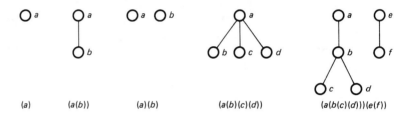

Figure A.10. Bracketed form of orchards

The bracketed forms of several ordered trees and orchards appear in Figure A.10. It should be clear that the mutually recursive definitions above produce a unique bracketed form for any orchard, and that the resulting sequence of parentheses is well-formed. If, on the other hand, we begin with a well-formed sequence of parentheses, then the outermost pair(s) of parentheses correspond to the tree(s) of an orchard, and within such a pair of parentheses is the description of the corresponding tree in terms of its root and its orchard of subtrees. In this way, we have now obtained a one-to-one correspondence between the orchards with n vertices and the well-formed sequences of n left and n right parentheses.

In counting orchards we are not concerned with the labels attached to the vertices, and hence we shall omit the labels, and, with the correspondence just outlined , shall now count well-formed sequences of n left and n right parentheses, with nothing else inside the parentheses.

3. Stack permutations.

Let us note that, by replacing each left parenthesis by $+1$ and each right parenthesis by -1, the well-formed sequences of parentheses correspond to sequences of $+1$ and -1 such that the partial sums from the left are always non-negative, and the total sum is 0. If we think of each $+1$ as pushing an item onto a stack, and -1 as popping the stack, then the partial sums count the items on the stack at a given time. From this it can be shown that the number of stack permutations of n objects (see exercises in

Section 2.2) is yet another problem for which the Catalan numbers provide the answer. Even more, if we start with an orchard and perform a complete traversal (walking around each branch and vertex in the orchard as though it were a decorative wall), counting $+1$ each time we go down a branch and -1 each time we go up a branch (with $+1$ -1 for each leaf), then we thereby essentially obtain the correspondence with well-formed sequences over again.

4. Arbitrary sequences of parentheses.

Our final step is to count well-formed sequences of parentheses, but to do this we shall instead count the sequences that are *not* well-formed, and subtract from the number of all possible sequences. We need a final one-to-one correspondence:

> LEMMA A.9.   *The sequences of n left and n right parentheses that are not well-formed correspond exactly to all sequences of $n-1$ left parentheses and $n+1$ right parentheses (in all possible orders).*

To prove this correspondence, let us start with a sequence of n left and n right parentheses that is not well-formed. Let k be the first position in which the sequence goes wrong, so the entry at position k is a right parenthesis, and there is one more right parenthesis than left up through this position. Hence strictly to the right of position k there is one fewer right parenthesis than left. Strictly to the right of position k, then, let us replace all left parentheses by right and all right parentheses by left. The resulting sequence will have $n-1$ left parentheses and $n+1$ right parentheses altogether.

Conversely, let us start with a sequence of $n-1$ left parentheses and $n+1$ right parentheses, and let k be the first position where the number of right parentheses exceeds the number of left (such a position must exist, since there are more right than left parentheses altogether). Again let us exchange left for right and right for left parentheses in the remainder of the sequence (positions after k). We thereby obtain a sequence of n left and n right parentheses that is not well formed, and have constructed the one-to-one correspondence as desired.

5. End of the proof.

With all these preliminary correspondences, our counting problem reduces to simple combinations. The number of sequences of $n-1$ left and $n+1$ right parentheses is the number of ways to choose the $n-1$ positions occupied by left parentheses from the $2n$ positions in the sequence, that is, the number is $C(2n, n-1)$. By Lemma A.9, this number is also the number of sequences of n left and n right parentheses that are not well formed. The number of all sequences of n left and n right parentheses is similarly $C(2n, n)$, so the number of well formed sequences is

$$C(2n, n) \; - \; C(2n, n-1)$$

which is precisely the nth Catalan number.

Because of all the one-to-one correspondences, we also have:

> COROLLARY A.10.   *The number of well-formed sequences of n left and n right parentheses, the number of permutations of n objects obtainable by a stack, the number of orchards with n vertices, and the number of binary trees with n vertices are all equal to the nth Catalan number* Cat(n).

A.5.3 History.

It is, surprisingly, for none of the above questions that Catalan numbers were first discovered, but rather for questions in geometry. Specifically, Cat(n) provides the number of ways to divide a convex polygon with $n+2$ sides into triangles by drawing $n-1$ non-intersecting diagonals. See Figure A.11. This problem seems to have been proposed by L. EULER and solved by J. A. V. SEGNER in 1759. It was then solved again by E. CATALAN in 1838. Sometimes, therefore, the resulting numbers are called the *Segner numbers,* but more often they are called *Catalan numbers.*

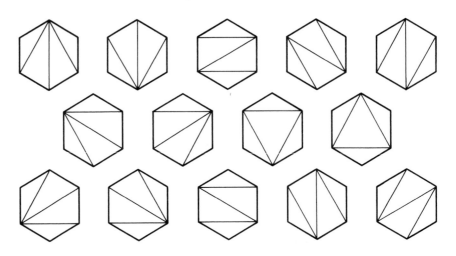

Figure A.11. Triangulations of a hexagon by diagonals

A.5.4 Numerical results.

We conclude this section with some indications of the sizes of Catalan numbers. The first twenty values are given in Figure A.12.

n	$\text{Cat}(n)$	n	$\text{Cat}(n)$
0	1	10	16,796
1	1	11	58,786
2	2	12	208,012
3	5	13	742,900
4	14	14	2,674,440
5	42	15	9,694,845
6	132	16	35,357,670
7	429	17	129,644,790
8	1,430	18	477,638,700
9	4,862	19	1,767,263,190

Figure A.12.   The first twenty Catalan numbers

For larger values of n, we can obtain an estimate on the size of the Catalan numbers by using Stirling's approximation. When it is applied to each of the three factorials, and the result is simplified, we obtain

$$\text{Cat}(n) \approx \frac{4^n}{(n+1)\sqrt{\pi n}}.$$

When compared with the exact values in Figure A.12, this estimate gives a good idea of the accuracy of Stirling's approximation. When $n = 10$, for example, the estimated value for the Catalan number is 17,007, compared to the exact value of 16,796.

A.6 References for further study.

More extensive discussions of proof by induction, the summation notation, sums of powers of integers, and logarithms appear in many algebra textbooks. These books will also provide examples and exercises on these topics. An excellent discussion of the importance of logarithms and of the subtle art of approximate calculation is

> N. DAVID MERMIN, "Logarithms!", *American Mathematical Monthly* 87 (1980), 1–7.

Several interesting examples of estimating large numbers and thinking of them logarithmically are discussed in

> DOUGLAS R. HOFSTADTER, "Metamagical themas" (Regular column), *Scientific American* 246, no. 5 (May 1982), 20–34.

Several surprising and amusing applications of harmonic numbers are given in the non-technical article

> RALPH BOAS, "Snowfalls and elephants, pop bottles and π", *Two-Year College Math. J.* 11 (1980), 82–89.

The detailed estimates for both harmonic numbers and factorials (Stirling's Approximation) are quoted from KNUTH, Volume 1, pp. 108–111, where detailed proofs may be found. KNUTH, Volume 1, is also an excellent source for further information regarding permutations, combinations, and related topics. The original reference for Stirling's approximation is

> JAMES STIRLING, *Methodus Differentialis* (1730), p. 137.

The branch of mathematics concerned with the enumeration of various sets or classes of objects is called ***combinatorics.*** This science of counting can be introduced on a very simple level, or studied with great sophistication. Two elementary textbooks containing many further developments of the ideas introduced here are:

> GERALD BERMAN and K. D. FRYER, *Introduction to Combinatorics,* Academic Press, New York, 1972.

> ALAN TUCKER, *Applied Combinatorics,* John Wiley and Sons, New York, 1980.

The derivation of the Fibonacci numbers will appear in almost any book on combinatorics, as well as in KNUTH, Volume 1, pp. 78–86, who includes some interesting history as well as many related exercises.

A derivation of the Catalan numbers   (applied to triangulations of convex polygons) appears in the first of the above books on combinatorics (pp. 230–232). KNUTH, Volume 1, pp. 385–406, enumerates several classes of trees, including the Catalan numbers applied to binary trees. A list of forty-six references providing both history and applications of the Catalan numbers appears in

> W. G. BROWN, "Historical note on a recurrent combinatorial problem, " *American Mathematical Monthly* 72 (1965), 973–977.

The original references for the derivation of the Catalan numbers are:

> J. A. V. SEGNER, "Enumeratio modorum, quibus figuræ planæ rectilinæ per diagonales dividuntur·in triangula ," *Novi Commentarii Academiae Scientiarum Imperialis Petropolitanae,*7 (1758–1759), 203–209.

> E. CATALAN, "Solution nouvelle de cette question: un polygone étant donné, de combien de manieres peut-on le partager en triangles au moyen de diagonales?," *Journal de Mathématiques Pures et Appliquées,*4 (1839), 91–94.

Appendix B

Removal of Recursion

In some contexts (like FORTRAN and COBOL) it is not possible to use recursion. This appendix discusses methods for reformulating algorithms to remove recursion. First comes a general method that can always be used, but is quite complicated and yields a program whose structure may be obscure. Next is a simpler transformation that, although not universally applicable, covers many important applications. This transformation yields, as an example, an efficient non-recursive version of quicksort. Finally this appendix studies threaded binary trees, which provide all the capabilities of ordinary binary trees without reference to recursion or stacks.

Although the methods developed in this appendix can be used with any higher-level algorithmic language, they are most appropriate in contexts that do not allow recursion. When recursion is available, the techniques described here are unlikely to save enough computer time or space to prove worthwhile, or to compensate for the additional programming effort that they demand. To emphasize this distinction, we shall not use Pascal for most of the sample programs, but shall instead write them in a dialect of FORTRAN (structured WATFOR®). Section 7.5 should be studied before consulting this appendix.

B.1 General methods for removing recursion.

Recall from Section 7.5.2 that each call to a subprogram (recursive or not) requires that the subprogram have a storage area where it can keep its local variables, its calling parameters, and its return address (that is, the location of the statement following the one that made the call). In a recursive implementation, the storage areas for subprograms are kept in a stack. Without recursion, one permanent storage area is often reserved for each subprogram, so that an attempt to make a recursive call would change the values in the storage area, thereby destroying the ability of the outer call to complete its work and return properly.

WATFOR® is a trademark of the Waterloo Foundation for the Advancement of Computing.

To simulate recursion we must therefore eschew use of the local storage area reserved for the subprogram, and instead set up a stack, in which we shall keep all the local variables, calling parameters, and the return address for the procedure.

B.1.1 Preliminary assumptions.

It is frequently true that stating a set of rules in the most general possible form requires so many complicated special cases that it obscures the principal ideas. Such is indeed true for recursion removal, so we shall instead develop the methods only for a special case, and separately explain how the methods can be applied to all other categories of subprograms.

Recursion is said to be **direct** if a subprogram calls itself; it is **indirect** if there is a sequence of more than one subprogram call that eventually calls the first subprogram, such as when procedure A calls procedure B, which in turn calls A. We shall first assume that the recursion is direct, that is, we deal only with a single subprogram that calls itself.

For simplicity we shall, second, assume that we are dealing with a procedure rather than a function. This is no real restriction, since any function can be turned into a procedure by including one extra calling parameter that will be used to hold the output value. This output parameter is then used instead of the function name in the calling program.

We have used two kinds of parameters for procedures: those called by value and those called by address (reference). Parameters called by value are copied into local variables within the procedure that are discarded when the procedure returns; parameters called by address exist in the calling program, so that the procedure refers to them there. The same observations are true of all other variables used by the procedure: they are either declared locally within the procedure, or exist outside, globally to the procedure. Parameters and variables in the first category are created anew every time the procedure is started; hence before recursion they must be pushed onto a stack so that they can be restored after the procedure returns. Parameters and variables of the second category must not be stacked, since every time the procedure changes them it is assumed that the global variables have been changed, and if they were restored to previous values the work of the procedure would be undone.

If the procedure has parameters called by address (those in Pascal declared with **var** in the procedure heading), then we shall assume that the actual parameters are exactly the same in every call to the procedure. This is again no real restriction, since we can introduce an additional global variable, say t, and instead of writing P(x) and P(y) for two different calls to the procedure, we can write

$$\textbf{begin } t := x; \; P(t); \; x := t \textbf{ end}$$

for one and

$$\textbf{begin } t := y; \; P(t); \; y := t \textbf{ end}$$

for the other.

B.1.2 General rules.

We now take P to satisfy these assumptions; that is, P is a directly recursive procedure for which the actual parameters called by address in P are the same in every call to P. We can translate P into a non-recursive procedure by including instructions in P to accomplish the following tasks. These steps involve insertion of statement labels and **goto** statements, as well as other constructions that will make the result appear messy. At the moment, however, we are proceeding mechanically, essentially playing compiler, and doing these steps is the easiest way to go, given that the original procedure works properly. Afterward, we can clean and polish the procedure, making it into a form that will be easier to follow and be more efficient.

1. Declare a stack (or stacks) that will hold all local variables, parameters called by value, and flags to specify whence P was called (if it calls itself from several places). As the first executed statement of P, initialize the stack(s) to be empty by setting the counter to 0. The stack(s) and the counter are to be treated as global variables, even though they are declared in P.

2. To enable each recursive call to start at the beginning of the original procedure P, the first executable statement of the original P should have a label (statement number) attached to it.

The following steps should be done at each place inside P where P calls itself.

3. Make a new statement label L_i (if this is the ith place where P is called recursively) and attach the label to the first statement after the call to P (so that a return can be made to this label).

4. Push the integer i onto the stack. (This will convey on return that P was called from the ith place.)

5. Push all local variables and parameters called by value onto the stack.

6. Set the dummy parameters called by value to the values given in the new call to P.

7. Replace the call to P with a **goto** to the statement label at the start of P.

At the end of P (or wherever P returns to its calling program), the following steps should be done.

8. If the stack is empty then the recursion has finished; make a normal return.

9. Otherwise, pop the stack to restore the values of all local variables and parameters called by value.

10. Pop an integer i from the stack and use this to go to the statement labeled L_i. In FORTRAN this can be done with a *computed go to* statement, in BASIC with an on $\cdots$ go to, and in Pascal with a **case** statement.

By mechanically following the preceding steps we can remove direct recursion from any procedure.

B.1.3 Indirect recursion.

The case of indirect recursion requires slightly more work, but follows the same idea. Perhaps the conceptually simplest way (which avoids **goto**'s from one procedure to another) is first to rename variables as needed to ensure that there are no conflicts of names of local variables or parameters between any of the mutually recursive procedures, and then write them one after another, not as separate procedures, but as sections of a longer one. The above steps can then be carried through for each of the former procedures, and the **goto**'s used according as which procedure is calling which. Separate stacks can be used for different procedures, or all the data can be kept on one stack, whichever is more convenient.

B.1.4 Towers of Hanoi.

As an illustration of this method, let us write out a non-recursive version of the program for the Towers of Hanoi, as it was developed in Section 7.1, to which you should compare the following program. This program is obtained as a straightforward application of the rules just formulated. First we translate the procedure **Move** from recursive Pascal into non-recursive FORTRAN. You should compare the result with the original version.

```
        Subroutine Move(n, a, b, c)
C       Moves n disks from needle a to b using c for temporary storage
C       flag gives place of recursive call, ns is stack counter,
C       Sflag, Sn, Sa, Sb, Sc are arrays holding the stacks

        Integer n, a, b, c
        Integer flag, ns, Sflag(64), Sn(64), Sa(64), Sb(64), Sc(64)

        ns = 0
C       Begin by setting stack empty. Next start original program.
100     if (n .eq. 0) goto 101
C       This is the if statement of original program in obverse form.
C       Simulate Call Move(n-1, a, c, b)
        ns = ns + 1
        Sflag(ns) = 1
        Sn(ns) = n
        Sa(ns) = a
        Sb(ns) = b
        Sc(ns) = c
        n = n - 1
        b = c
        c = Sb(ns)
C       Note trick: b is retrieved from stack since value of b has changed.
        goto 100
C       Above instructions replace Call Move(n-1, a, c, b)
```

```
C           Will eventually reach here after return from recursion.
1           Write(5, 10) a, b
10          Format(' Move a disk from' I2 ' to ' I2)
C           Next simulate Call Move(n−1, c, b, a)
                ns = ns + 1
                Sflag(ns) = 2
                Sn(ns) = n
                Sa(ns) = a
                Sb(ns) = b
                Sc(ns) = c
                n = n − 1
                a = c
                c = Sa(ns)
                goto 100
C           Above instructions replace Call Move(n−1, c, b, a)

C           Will reach here after return from second recursion
2           Continue
C           This point corresponds to innermost end of original program.
C           Next insert code to make a return from recursion.
101         if (ns .eq. 0) Return
                c = Sc(ns)
                b = Sb(ns)
                a = Sa(ns)
                n = Sn(ns)
                flag = Sflag(ns)
                ns = ns − 1
                goto (1, 2), flag
            end
```

As with the original version, the main program that calls this subroutine is almost trivial.

```
Program Hanoi2
call Move(64, 1, 3, 2)
stop
end
```

As you can see, a short and easy recursive program has turned into a complicated mess. The program even contains branches that jump from outside into the middle of the block controlled by an **if** statement, an occurrence that should always be regarded as very poor style, if not an actual error. Fortunately, much of the complication results only from the mechanical way in which the translation was done. We can now make several simplifications.

First, we might note that only one, non-recursive call to **Subroutine Move** remains, so there is no benefit in leaving **Move** as a separate subprogram. Second, and more important, note what happens when the subroutine recursively returns from a call at the second place (**flag** is 2). After the stack is popped it branches to statement 2, which does nothing except run down to pop the stack again. Thus what was popped off the stack the first time is lost, so that there was no need to push it on in the first place. In the original program, the second recursive call to **Move** occurs at the end of the procedure. At the end of any procedure its local variables are discarded; thus there was no need to preserve all the local variables before the second recursive call to **Move**, since they will be discarded when it returns in any case.

This situation is *tail-end recursion,* and from this example we see graphically the unnecessary work that tail-end recursion can induce. Before translating any program to non-recursive form, we should be careful to apply Theorem 7.2 and remove the tail-end recursion.

B.1.5 Further simplifications.

While we are considering simplifications, we can make a more general observation about local variables and parameters called by value. In a procedure being transformed to non-recursive form, these will need to be pushed onto the stack before a recursive call only when they have both been set up before the call, and will be used again after the call, with the assumption that they have unchanged values. Some variables may have been used only in sections of the procedure not involving recursive calls, so there is no need to preserve their values across a recursive call. For example, the index variable of a **for** loop might be used to control loops either before or after a recursive call or even both before and after, but if the index variable is initialized when a loop starts after the call, there is no need to preserve it on the stack. On the other hand, if the recursive call is in the middle of a **for** loop, then the index variable must be stacked. By applying these principles we can simplify the resulting program and conserve stack space, and thereby perform optimizations of the program that a recursive compiler would likely not do, since it would probably preserve all local variables on the stack.

B.2 Recursion removal by folding.

B.2.1 Program schemata.

We can now further simplify our method for removing recursion: a procedure that includes a recursive call from only one place will not need to include flags to show where to return, since there is only one possibility. In many cases, we can also rearrange parts of the program to clarify it by removing **goto**'s.

After removal of the tail-end recursion, the second recursive version of the procedure **Move** for the Towers of Hanoi, as given in Section 7.5.3, is a program of the general schema:

```
procedure P( {parameters} );                        {recursive version}

{local declarations to be inserted here}

begin
  while not termination do begin
    Block A;          {first part of program; empty for our example}
    P;                          {only recursive call to procedure itself}
    Block B;                                   {next part of program}
  end;
  Block C;            {final part of program; empty for our example}
end;                                                        {procedure}
```

Our general rules presented in the last section will translate this schema into the non-recursive form:

```
procedure P( {parameters} );        {preliminary non-recursive version}

label 100, 101;                   {used to simulate recursive returns}
{local declarations to be inserted here}
{declaration of stack goes here}

begin
  Set stack to be empty;
100:
  while not termination do
  begin
    Block A;                               {first part of program}
    Push data onto stack and change parameters;
    goto 100;
101:
    Block B;                                {next part of program}
  end;
  Block C;                                  {final part of program}
  if stack not empty then
  begin
    Pop data from stack;
    goto 101
  end
end;                                                    {procedure}
```

If we terminate the **while** loop after the line changing the parameters, then we can eliminate the **label** 100 and the **goto** 100. Doing this will require that, when Block B is complete, we go back to the **while** statement. By moving the part of the schema that pops the stack to the front of Block B, we no longer need the other **goto.** On the first time through, the stack will be empty, so the popping section will be skipped. These steps can all be accomplished by enclosing the procedure in a statement

repeat $\cdots$ **until** stack is empty.

We thus obtain:

```
procedure P( {parameters} );                    {non-recursive version}

   {local declarations to be inserted here}
   {declaration of stack goes here}
begin
   Set stack to be empty;
   repeat
      if stack is not empty then begin
         Pop data from stack;
         Block B;                                {next part of program}
      end;
      while not termination do begin
         Block A;                                {first part of program}
         Push data onto stack and change parameters;
      end;
      Block C;                                   {final part of program}
   until stack is empty
end;
```

This rearrangement is essentially *folding* the loop around the recursive call. Thus the part coming after the recursive call now appears at the top of the program instead of the bottom.

B.2.2 Proof of the transformation.

Since deriving this rearrangement has required several steps, let us now pause to provide a formal verification that the changes we have made are correct.

> THEOREM B.1.   *The recursive procedure P of the form given previously, and the folded, non-recursive version of P both accomplish exactly the same steps.*

To prove the theorem, we shall trace through the recursive and the folded non-recursive versions of *P*, and show that they perform exactly the same sequence of blocks *A, B* and *C*. The remaining parts of both versions do only bookkeeping, so that if the same sequence of the blocks is done, then the same task will be accomplished. In tracing through the programs, it will help to note that there are two ways to call a recursive procedure: either from outside, or from within itself. We refer to these as *external* and *internal* calls, respectively. These two forms of call are indistinguishable for the recursive version, but are quite different for the non-recursive form. An external call starts at the beginning of the procedure and finishes at the end. An internal call starts after the data are pushed onto the stack and the parameters are changed, and finishes when the line is reached that pops the stack.

We shall prove the theorem by using mathematical induction on the height of the recursion tree corresponding to a given call to P. The starting point is the case when P is called with the termination condition already true, so that no recursion takes place (the height of the tree is 0). In this case the recursive version performs Block C once, and nothing else is done. For the non-recursive version we consider the two kinds of calls separately. If the call is external, then the stack is empty, so that the **if** statement does nothing, and the **while** statement also does nothing since the termination condition is assumed to be true. Thus only Block C is done, and since the stack is empty, the procedure terminates. Now suppose that the call to P is internal. Then P has arrived at the line that pushes the stack (so it is not empty). Since the termination condition is true, the **while** loop now terminates, and Block C is done. Since the stack is not empty, the **repeat** loop next proceeds to the line that pops the stack, and this line corresponds to returning from the internal call. Thus in every case when the recursion tree has height 0, only Block C is done once.

For the induction step we consider a call to P where the recursion tree has height $k > 0$, and by induction we assume that all calls whose trees have height less than k will translate correctly into non-recursive form. Let r be the number of times that the **while** loop iterates in the call to P under consideration.

This situation is illustrated in the sample recursion tree shown in Figure B.1. Each node in this tree should be considered as expanded to show the sequence of

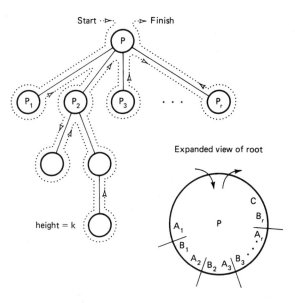

Figure B.1. Traversal of a recursion tree

blocks being performed at each stage. The tree also, of course, shows when the stack will be pushed and popped: Consider traversing the tree by walking around it in a counterclockwise direction following each edge both down and up and going around each node. It is precisely as a branch is traversed going downward that the stack is pushed, and as we return up a branch the stack is popped.

The recursive version thus performs a sequence of blocks and calls:

$$A_1 \quad P_1 \quad B_1 \quad A_2 \quad P_2 \quad B_2 \ldots A_r \quad P_r \quad B_r \quad C$$

where the subscipts specify only the iteration at which the block or call is done. The calls to P denoted P_1, P_2, $\cdots$, P_r all have recursion trees of heights strictly less than k (at least one has height exactly $k-1$), so by induction hypothesis the sequence of blocks embedded in these calls will be the same for the recursive and non-recursive versions (provided that we can show that the sequence of outer blocks is the same, so that the calling parameters will be the same). In tracing through the non-recursive procedure, we again consider the two kinds of calls separately.

If the call is external, then the stack is initially empty, so the **while** loop begins iterating. First Block A is done, and then an internal call to P is started by pushing the stack. The corresponding return occurs when the stack is eventually popped and becomes empty again. The sequence of blocks and calls occurring in the meantime all correspond to the recursive call P_1, and by induction hypothesis correspond correctly to the recursive version. When the stack is popped and empty, then Block B is done and we reach the **while** statement to begin the second iteration. The program thus continues, with each iteration starting with Block A, then an internal call, then Block B. After r iterations the total sequence of blocks will have been the same as in the recursive version, and therefore the termination condition will become true for the first time, and so the **while** loop will be skipped. Block C is then done, and since the stack is empty, the procedure terminates. Hence the total sequence of blocks is the same as in the recursive version.

Finally, consider that the call (with tree of height k) is internal. The call then begins where the stack is pushed, so it then has $s > 0$ sets of data. Next Block A is done, and another internal call instituted, that includes all steps until the stack is popped and again has exactly s sets of data. Next Block B is done, and the iterations continue as in the previous case, except that now the returns from internal calls that interest us are those leaving s sets of data on the stack. After r iterations the termination condition becomes true, so the **while** loop terminates, and Block C is done. The stack has $s > 0$ entries, so the procedure now moves to the line that pops the stack, which constitutes the return from the internal call that we have been tracing. Thus in every case the sequence of blocks done is the same, and the proof of the theorem is complete.

B.2.3 Towers of Hanoi: the final version.

With the method of folding that we have now developed, we can now write our final non-recursive version of the program for the Towers of Hanoi, a version that is much clearer than the first non-recursive one, although still not as natural as the recursive program. With the restrictions of a non-recursive language like FORTRAN, however, we cannot expect too much further improvement.

```
      program Hanoi3
      Integer n, a, b, c, t
C     n is number of disks to move at this pass, a is source needle,
C     b is destination, c is intermediate, and t is for temporary storage.
C     ns is count, and Sn, Sa, Sb, Sc are the arrays holding the stacks
      Integer ns, Sn(64), Sa(64), Sb(64), Sc(64)
          ns = 0
          n = 64
          a = 1
          b = 2
          c = 3
C     The repeat loop begins here.
    1     if (ns .eq. 0) goto 2
C         First pop the stack.
              c = Sc(ns)
              b = Sb(ns)
              a = Sa(ns)
              n = Sn(ns)
              ns = ns − 1
C         Start Block B of schema.
              Write(5, 10) a, b
   10         Format(' Move a disk from' I2 ' to' I2)
C         Next change parameters to Move(n − 1, c, b, a)
              n = n − 1
              t = a
              a = c
              c = t
C     End of block under control of if statement
C         while n > 0 do begin
    2         if (n .eq. 0) goto 3
C             Simulate Call Move(n − 1, a, c, b)
                  ns = ns + 1
                  Sn(ns) = n
                  Sa(ns) = a
                  Sb(ns) = b
                  Sc(ns) = c
                  n = n − 1
                  b = c
                  c = Sb(ns)
```

```
C     Trick: b is retrieved from stack since value of b has changed.
      goto 2
C     End of while loop
C     This marks the end of a repeat loop.
3     if (ns .gt. 0) goto 1
      Stop
      end
```

Exercises

1. Show that the program **Queen** from Section 7.2.2 has the schema needed for Theorem B.1, and apply folding to remove the recursion. Run both the recursive and non-recursive versions to see which is faster. (To ensure a fair comparison, both versions should be in the same language.)

2. Remove the tail-end recursion from the algorithm for preorder traversal of a linked binary tree (Section 5.3). Show that the resulting program fits the schema of Theorem B.1, and thereby devise a non-recursive algorithm, using a stack, that will traverse a binary tree in preorder.

3. Repeat the above exercise for inorder traversal.

4. Devise a non-recursive algorithm, using one or more stacks, that will traverse a linked binary tree in postorder. Why is this project more complicated than the preceding two exercises?

5. Consider a pair of mutually recursive procedures P and Q that have the following schemata.

```
procedure P;                          procedure Q;
{local declarations for P}            {local declarations for Q}
begin                                 begin
  while not termP do                    while not termQ do
  begin                                 begin
    Block A;                              Block X;
    Q;                                    P;
    Block B;                              Block Y;
  end;                                  end;
  Block C;                              Block Z;
end;                                  end;
```

Assume that there are no conflicts of names between local variables or dummy parameters in P and in Q.

(a) Write a non-recursive procedure made up from the blocks in P and Q that will perform the same action as a call to P.

(b) Prove that your translation is correct in a way similar to the proof of Theorem B.1.

B.3 Non-recursive quicksort.

Because of its importance as an efficient sorting algorithm for contiguous lists, we shall devise a non-recursive version of quicksort, as an application of the methods of the last section. We shall write this version in Pascal to facilitate its comparison with the recursive version. Before proceeding, you should briefly review Section 4.8, to which we refer constantly, and from which we take all the notation.

The first observation to make about the original recursive procedure Quick-Sort(low, high) is that its second call is tail-end recursion, which can easily be removed. We thus obtain the following intermediate form.

```
procedure QuickSort(head, tail: index);
var
  lowhead, lowtail,                          {bounds of lower sublist}
  highhead, hightail: index;                 {bounds of upper sublist}
begin
  while head < tail do
  begin
    Partition( head, tail, lowhead, lowtail, highhead, hightail );
    QuickSort(lowhead, lowtail);
    head := highhead; {Prepare to sort interval (highhead, hightail).}
    tail := hightail
  end
end;
```

This procedure is in precisely the form covered by Theorem B.1, so it can be folded to remove the recursive call. The only variables needed after the recursive call are highhead and hightail, so only these two variables need to be stacked.

Before we proceed with the program transformation, let us note that, in doing the sorting, it really makes no difference which half of the list is sorted first. The calling parameters to be stacked mark the bounds of sublists yet to be sorted. It turns out that it is better to put the longer sublist on the stack and immediately sort the shorter one. The longer sublist will account for at least half of the items. Hence at each level of recursion, the number of items remaining to be sorted is reduced by half or more, and therefore the number of items on the stack is guaranteed to be no more than lg n. In this way, even though quicksort has a worst-case running time that is $O(n^2)$, the extra space needed for its stack can be guaranteed not to exceed $O(\log n)$.

This decision to stack the larger sublist at each stage does not affect the application of folding, but only introduces an **if** statement at the appropriate point. We thus arrive at the following non-recursive version of quicksort.

```
procedure NRQuickSort(var L: list; n: index);
const
  maxstack      = 20;       {allows sorting up to 1,000,000 items}
```

```
var
  head, tail,                              {bounds of list being sorted}
  lowhead, lowtail,                        {bounds of lower sublist}
  highhead, hightail: index;               {bounds of upper sublist}
  {Declare two arrays for the stack, as required by most non-recursive
                                                              languages.}
  headstack,
  tailstack:      array[1 .. maxstack] of index;
  nstack:         0 .. maxstack;
begin
  nstack := 0;
  head := 1;
  tail := n;
  repeat
    if nstack > 0 then
    begin                                                {Pop the stack.}
      head := headstack[nstack];
      tail := tailstack[nstack];
      nstack := nstack − 1
    end;
    while head < tail do
    begin
      Partition(head, tail, lowhead, lowtail, highhead, hightail);
      {Push larger sublist onto stack, and do smaller.}
      if lowtail − lowhead < hightail − highhead then
      begin                            {Stack right sublist and do left.}
        if nstack >= maxstack then overflow; {separate procedure}
        nstack := nstack + 1;
        headstack[nstack] := highhead;
        tailstack[nstack] := hightail;
        head := lowhead;
        tail := lowtail
      end
      else begin                       {Stack left sublist and do right.}
        if nstack >= maxstack then overflow; {separate procedure}
        nstack := nstack + 1;
        headstack[nstack] := lowhead;
        tailstack[nstack] := lowtail;
        head := highhead;
        tail := hightail
      end
    end
  until nstack = 0
end;
```

B.4 Threaded binary trees.

Because of the importance of linked binary trees, it is worthwhile to develop non-recursive algorithms to manipulate them, and to study the time and space requirements of these algorithms. We shall find that, by changing the **nil** links in a binary tree to special links called *threads*, it is possible to perform traversals, insertions and deletions without using either a stack or recursion.

B.4.1 Introduction.

First let us note that the second recursive call in the ordinary recursive versions of both preorder and inorder traversal of a linked binary tree is tail-end recursion, and so can be removed easily, with no need to set up a stack. From now on we shall assume that this has been done, so that preorder and inorder traversal each involve only one recursive call.

The situation with postorder traversal is more complicated, so we shall postpone its study to the end of the section.

Removal of the remaining recursive call in preorder or inorder traversal does appear to require a stack. Let us see how many entries can possibly be on the stack. Since the procedures use no local variables, the only value to be stacked is the calling parameter, which is a (simple, one-word) pointer variable, a pointer to the current position in the tree. After the pointer has been stacked the algorithm moves to the left subtree as it calls itself. (Note that when the algorithm later moves to the right subtree it need only change the pointer, not push it onto the stack, since the tail-end recursion has been removed). The pointers stop being stacked and the recursion terminates when a leaf is reached. Thus the total number of pointers that may appear on the stack is the number of left branches taken in a path from the root to a leaf of the tree, plus one more since a pointer to the leaf itself is stacked. The algorithms could easily be rewritten to avoid stacking this last pointer.

Since most binary trees are fairly bushy, the number of pointers on the stack is likely to be $O(\log n)$ if the tree has n nodes. Since $\lg n$ is generally small in comparison to n, the space taken by the stack is usually small in comparison to the space needed for the nodes themselves. Thus, if it is reasonable to assume that the tree is quite bushy, then it is probably not worth the effort to pursue sophisticated methods to save space, and either the recursive algorithms or their straightforward translation to non-recursive form with a stack will likely be satisfactory.

It is, on the other hand, certainly possible that a binary tree will have few right branches and many left branches. In fact, the tree that is a straight chain moving to the left will put pointers to every one of its nodes onto the stack before working out of the recursion. Hence, if we wish to ensure that the traversal algorithms will never fail for want of space, we must be careful to reserve stack space for $n+1$ pointers if there are n nodes in the binary tree. (Keeping the recursion for the system to handle will, of course, not help at all, since the system must still find space for the stack, and will likely also use space for stacking return addresses, etc., and so will need more than $n+1$ words of memory.) If we are working with a large binary tree that takes almost all the memory, then finding extra stack space can be a problem.

Whenever you run out of some resource, a good question to ask yourself is whether some of that same resource is being left unused elsewhere. In the current problem, the answer is *yes*. For all the leaves of any binary tree, both the left and right pointers are **nil,** and often for some of the other nodes one of the pointers is **nil**. In fact, the following easy observation shows that there are exactly enough **nil** pointers in the tree to take care of the stack.

LEMMA B.2. *A linked binary tree with n nodes, n ≥ 0, has exactly n+1 **nil** links.*

PROOF.   We first note that each node of the tree contains two pointers, so there are $2n$ pointers altogether in a tree with n nodes, plus one more in the header. There is exactly one pointer to each of the n nodes of the tree (coming from the parent of each node except the root, and from the header to the root). Thus the number of **nil** pointers is exactly

$$(2n+1)-n \quad = \quad n+1.$$

With this result, we could devise an algorithm to use the space occupied by **nil** pointers and traverse the tree with no need for auxiliary space for a stack.

We shall not solve the problem this way, however, because of one danger in such a method. If the program should happen to crash in the middle of traversing the binary tree, having changed various pointers within the tree to reflect a (now-forgotten) current situation, it may later be difficult or impossible to recover the structure of the original tree. We might thereby lose all our data, with far more serious consequences than the original crash.

What we want, then, is a way to set up the pointers within the binary tree permanently so that the **nil** pointers will be replaced with information that will make it easy to traverse the tree (in either preorder or inorder) without setting up a stack or using recursion.

Let us see how far ordinary inorder traversal can go before it must pop the stack. It begins by moving left as many times as it can, while the left subtree is not empty. Then it visits the node and moves to the right subtree (if non-empty) and repeats the process, moving to the left again. Only when it has just visited a node and finds that its right subtree is empty must it pop the stack to see where to go next. In Pascal we could write:

```
p := root;                      {pointer that moves through the tree}
while p <> nil do
begin
  while p↑.left <> nil do p := p↑.left;
  Visit(p);
  p := p↑.right
end;
```

When this sequence of instructions is complete, we have **p** = **nil,** and we must find some way to locate the next node under inorder traversal.

B.4.2 Threads.

In a ***right-threaded binary tree*** each **nil** right link is replaced by a special link to the successor of that node under inorder traversal, called a ***right thread.*** Using right threads we shall find it easy to do an inorder traversal of the tree, since we need only follow either an ordinary link or a thread to find the next node to visit. For later applications, we shall also find it useful to put ***left threads*** into the tree, which means to replace each **nil** left link by a special link to the predecessor of the node under inorder traversal. The result is called a ***fully threaded binary tree.*** The word *fully* is omitted if there is no danger of confusion. Figure B.2 shows a threaded binary tree, where the threads are shown as dotted lines.

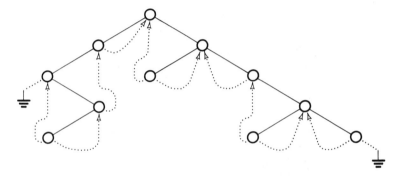

Figure B.2. A fully threaded binary tree

Note that two threads have been left as **nil** in the diagram, the left thread from the first node under inorder traversal, and the right thread from the last node. We shall leave these two pointers as **nil.** Another convention that is sometimes useful is to let these two nodes have threads pointing back to the root of the tree. This convention sometimes makes termination conditions slightly more complicated, but sometimes allows easier repetition of the full traversal of the tree, if that is desired.

In implementing threads in a programming language, we must have some way to determine whether each link is a true pointer to a non-empty subtree, or a thread to some node higher in the tree. In Pascal, the usual way to do this would be to add to each node a Boolean variable (that need only take one bit) that specifies if the pointer is a link or a thread.

In some environments, however, we can represent threads even more compactly. Non-recursive traversal is most commonly used in non-recursive languages, and in this case the nodes are usually represented as entries of arrays, and the pointers are indices within the arrays. Thus true links are represented as positive integers, and the **nil** link is usually represented as 0. We can then easily represent threads as negative integers, so that if a pointer variable p is less than 0, then it is a thread to the node at $-p$.

For the remainder of this section we shall adopt this positive-negative convention, and write our procedures in FORTRAN. We shall need to make some assumptions regarding the use of arrays. To be definite, we take all arrays to contain 100 entries. This bound would be changed as appropriate for the desired application. To emphasize the similarity of our underlying data structures with those of Chapter 5, we assign names to our arrays (which we assume to be in a Common block) as follows:

Common Key(100), Info(100), left(100), right(100)

where the array Key contains the keys, arrays left and right hold the links, and Info will be replaced by whatever other arrays are desired to hold information for each node of the tree.

B.4.3 Inorder and Preorder traversal.

First, let us see how easy it now is to traverse a threaded binary tree in inorder.

```
      Subroutine Inorder (root)
C     Do Inorder traversal of threaded binary tree.
      Common Key(100), Info(100), left(100), right(100)
      Integer Key, left, right, p, root
C
C     Find the first (leftmost) node for inorder traversal.
      p = root
      While (left(p) .gt. 0) do
         p = left(p)
      Endwhile
C     Now visit node, and go to its successor.
      While (p .ne. 0) do
         Call Visit(p)
         p = right(p)
C     If thread link, then it gives successor.
         If (p .lt. 0) then do
            p = -p
C     Otherwise, move as far left as possible.
         Else if (p .gt. 0) then do
            While (left(p) .gt. 0) do
               p = left(p)
            Endwhile
C     If neither section is done, then p = 0 and traversal done.
         Endif
      Endwhile
      Return
      End
```

As you can see, this algorithm is longer than the original algorithm for inorder traversal, but much of the length is in meeting the syntactical requirements of FORTRAN. A direct translation of the original algorithm into non-recursive form would be of comparable length, and would require additional space for a stack that is not needed when we use threaded trees.

It is a surprising fact that preorder traversal of an inorder threaded tree is just as easy to write.

```
        Subroutine Preorder (root)
C       Preorder traversal of binary tree with (inorder) threads.
        Common Key(100), Info(100), left(100), right(100)
        Integer Key, left, right, p, root
C
C       In preorder, we first visit node, then move left, then right.
        p = root
        While (p .gt. 0) do
          Call Visit (p)
          If (left(p) .gt. 0) then do
            p = left(p)
          Else if (right(p) .gt. 0) then do
            p = right(p)
C         Otherwise, p is a leaf. We must take its right thread,
C         which will return to a node already visited, and then
C         move to the right again.
          Else do
            While (right(p) .lt. 0) do
              p = - right(p)
            Endwhile
            p = right(p)
          Endif
        Endwhile
        Return
        End
```

B.4.4 Insertion in a threaded tree.

To use threaded trees, we must be able to set them up. Thus we need an algorithm to add a node to the tree. We consider only the case where a node is added to the left of a node that previously had an empty left subtree. The other side is similar. Since the node we are considering has empty left subtree, its left link is a thread to its predecessor under inorder traversal, which will now become the predecessor of the new node being added. The successor of the new node will be the node to which it is attached on the left. This situation is illustrated in Figure B.3.

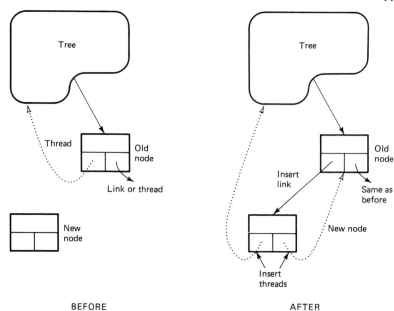

Figure B.3. Adding a node to a threaded binary tree

This process translates directly into the following algorithm.

```
        Subroutine LeftInsert (q, p)
C           Inserts the node at index q as left subtree of node at p.
        Common Key(100), Info(100), left(100), right(100)
        Integer Key, left, right, p, q
C
        If (left(p) .gt. 0) Call error
        left(q) = left(p)
        right(q) = −p
        left(p) = q
        Return
        End
```

As you can see, this algorithm is hardly more complicated than that required to add a node to an unthreaded tree. Similarly, an algorithm to delete a node (which is left as an exercise) is also no more difficult than before. It is only in the traversal algorithms where the additional cases lengthen the programs. Whether the saving of stack space is worth the programming time needed to use threads depends, as usual, on the circumstances. The differences in running time will usually be insignificant; it is only the saving in stack space that need be considered. Even this is lessened if the device of using negative indices to represent threads is not available (as it is not, for example, with Pascal pointer types).

Finally, we should mention the possibility of shared subtrees. In some applications a subtree of a binary tree is sometimes processed separately from other actions taken on the entire tree. With ordinary binary trees this can be done easily by setting the root of the subtree to the appropriate node of the larger tree. With threads, however, traversal of the smaller tree will fail to terminate properly, since after all nodes of the subtree have been traversed, there may still be a thread pointing to some successor node in the larger tree. Hence threads are often better avoided when processing really complicated data structures with shared substructures.

B.4.5 Postorder traversal.

Traversal of a threaded binary tree in postorder, using neither recursion nor stacks, is somewhat more complicated than the other traversal orders. The reason is that postorder traversal investigates each node several times. When a node is first reached, its left subtree is traversed. The traversal then returns to the node in order to traverse its right subtree. Only when it returns to the node the third time does it actually visit the node.

We can obtain an initial outline of an algorithm by following these steps. We shall use an integer code of 1, 2, or 3 to indicate the stage of processing the node.

```
Procedure PostOrder;
While not all nodes have been visited do
   If code = 1 then
      Begin Traverse left subtree; return to node; set code := 2 end
   Else if code = 2 then
      Begin Traverse right subtree; return to node; set code := 3 end
   Else
      Begin Visit the node; move to next node and set its code end;
```

Note that this algorithm is written so that it performs three iterations for each node. In this way, at every point we need only know the code to determine at what stage of the traversal we are. Had we written the three stages sequentially within a single iteration of the loop, then we would need to use recursion or a stack to determine our status upon completion of traversal of a subtree.

Closer consideration, however, will show that even our outline above does not yet succeed in avoiding the need for a stack. As we traverse a subtree, we shall continually change the code as we process each node of the subtree. Hence we must use some method to determine the previous value as we return to the original node. We shall first postpone this problem, however, by assuming the existence of an auxiliary procedure **Parent**, which will determine the parent of a node and the new value of the code.

Given the parent and the proper code of each node at all three stages of the traversal, we can arrive at the following subroutine.

```
      Subroutine PostOrder(root)
C     Performs postorder traversal of binary tree with (inorder) threads.
      Common Key(100), Info(100), left(100), right(100)
      Integer Key, left, right, p, q, root, code
C
      p = root
      code = 1
      While (p .ne. 0) do
        If (code .eq. 1) then do
C         Traverse left subtree if non-empty.
          If (left(p) .gt. 0) then do
            p = left(p)
          Else do
            code = 2
          Endif
        Else if (code .eq. 2) then do
C         Traverse right subtree if non-empty.
          If (right(p) .gt. 0) then do
            p = right(p)
            code = 1
          Else do
            code = 3
          Endif
        Else do
C         Case: code = 3. Visit node and move to next node.
          Call Visit(p)
          Call Parent(p, q, code)
          p = q
        Endif
      Endwhile
      Return
      End
```

Finally, we must solve the problem of locating the parent of a node and determining the proper value of the code, without resorting to stacks or recursion. The solution to this problem, fortunately, already appears in the outline obtained earlier. If we have just finished traversing a left subtree, then we should now set the code to 2; if we have traversed a right subtree, then the code becomes 3. We can determine which of these cases has occurred by using the threads, and at the same time we can find the node that is the parent node of the last one visited. If we are in a left subtree, then we find the parent by moving right as far as possible in the subtree, and then take a right thread. If the left child of this node is the original node, we know that we have found the parent and are in a left subtree. Otherwise, we must do the similar steps through left branches to find the parent. This process is illustrated in Figure B.4.

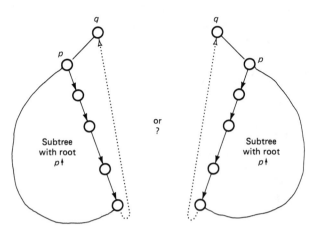

Figure B.4. Finding the parent of a node in a threaded tree

The translation of this method into a formal subroutine is straightforward.

```
          Subroutine Parent(p, q, code)
C         Finds the parent of node p, and sets q to the parent.
C         Returns code = 2 if p is the left child of q, and code = 3
C         if p is the right child of q. If p is the root, returns q = 0.
C

          Common Key(100, Info(100), left(100), right(100)
          Integer Key, left, right, p, q, code
C
C         Locate inorder successor of p; set to q.
          q = p
          While (q .gt. 0) do
             q = right(q)
          Endwhile
          If (q .eq. 0) then do
C            no successor: p cannot be a left child.
             code = 3
          Else if (left(−q) .eq. p) then do
C            Case: p is the left child of −q.
             code = 2
             q = −q
          Else do
             code = 3
          Endif
```

```
C       If code = 2, then finished. If code = 3, find parent as
C       the inorder predecessor of subtree of p.
        If (code .eq. 3) then do
          q = p
          While (q .gt. 0) do
            q = left(q)
          Endwhile
          q = −q
          If (q .gt. 0) then do
            If (right(q) .ne. p) Call error
          Endif
        Endif
        Return
        End
```

Exercises

1. Write the threaded-tree algorithms in Pascal for (a) insertion of a new node on the left, (b) inorder traversal, and (c) preorder traversal, using Boolean flags to determine whether links are threads or real branches.

2. What changes must be made in the algorithm of Section 5.2 in order to search for a key in a threaded binary search tree?

3. Write a FORTRAN subroutine to insert a new node on the right of a node in a threaded binary tree.

4. Write a FORTRAN subroutine that will search a threaded binary search tree for a given key, and, if it is not present, will insert it in the proper place.

5. Write a FORTRAN subroutine to delete a node from a threaded binary tree.

6. Write a FORTRAN subroutine that will insert threads into an unthreaded binary tree by traversing it once in inorder, using a stack.

7. Modify the subroutine of Exercise 6, so that it uses no extra space for a stack, but the unused link space and threads already constructed instead.

8. Write an algorithm (FORTRAN or Pascal) to insert a new node between two others in a threaded binary tree. That is, if p is a link to a node in the threaded tree, and p has non-empty left subtree, insert the new node (with q the pointer to it) as the left subtree of the one at p, with the left subtree of q being the former left subtree of p, and the right subtree of q being empty. Be sure to adjust all threads properly.

B.5 References for further study.

Techniques and procedures for the removal of recursion are a topic of current research. Some good ideas appear in

> D. E. KNUTH, "Structured programming with goto statements," *Computing Surveys,* 6 (1974), 261–302.
>
> R. S. BIRD, "Notes on recursion elimination," *Communications of the ACM,* 20 (1977), 434–439.
>
> R. S. BIRD, "Improving programs by the introduction of recursion," *Communications of the ACM,* 20 (1977), 856–863.

KNUTH (*op. cit.,* page 281) writes:

> There has been a good deal published about recursion elimination . . .; but I'm amazed that very little of this is about "down to earth" problems. I have always felt that the transformation from recursion to iteration is one of the most fundamental concepts of computer science, and that a student should learn it at about the same time he is studying data structures.

Presentation of non-recursive versions of quicksort is a common topic, but so many slight variations are possible that few of the resulting programs are exactly the same. More extensive analysis is given in:

> ROBERT SEDGEWICK, "The analysis of quicksort programs," *Acta Informatica,* 7 (1976/77), 327–355.

Threaded binary trees constitute a standard topic in data structures, and some discussion will appear in most textbooks on data structures. Many of these books, however, leave the more complicated algorithms (such as postorder traversal) as exercises. The original reference for right-threaded binary trees is:

> A. J. PERLIS and C. THORNTON, "Symbol manipulation by threaded lists," *Communications of the ACM,* 3 (1960), 195–204.

Fully threaded trees were independently discovered by:

> A. W. HOLT, "A mathematical and applied investigation of tree structures for syntactic analysis," Ph.D. Dissertation (mathematics), University of Pennsylvania, 1963.

Appendix C

Pascal Notes

This appendix supplies several tables and lists of guidelines and rules, to serve as a reference for the writing of Pascal programs.

C.1 Syntax diagrams.

The syntax of Pascal is determined by tracing through the diagrams in the direction shown by arrows. Symbols or words within circles or ovals must be included exactly as given. These Pascal keywords are shown in all capital letters. Rectangular boxes refer to other syntax diagrams. The syntax of all classes such as {function} identifier, {variable} identifier, or {type} identifier all have the same syntax as identifier: the qualifying words in braces are only intended to clarify the meanings of the diagrams.

These diagrams are based on the ISO draft international standard DIS 7185 for Pascal, and include some features, such as conformant array schemata, that may not be available on all compilers. These features are marked with asterisks (*) in the diagrams.

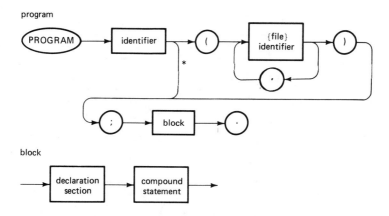

declaration section

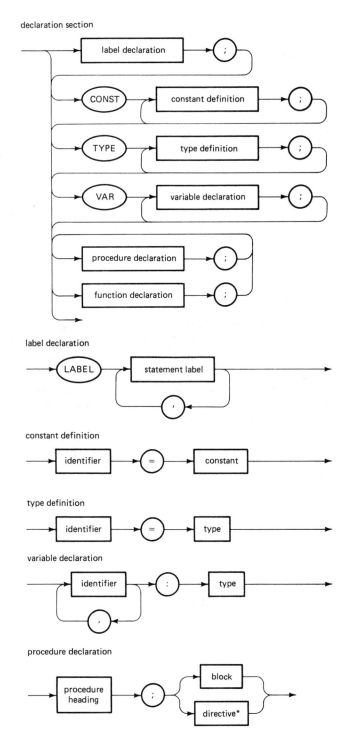

label declaration

constant definition

type definition

variable declaration

procedure declaration

function declaration

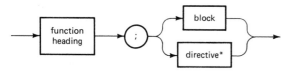

procedure heading

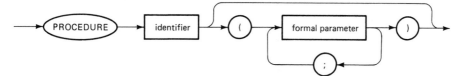

function heading

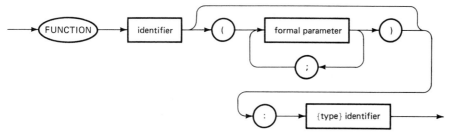

formal parameter

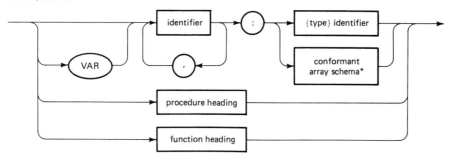

conformant array schema*

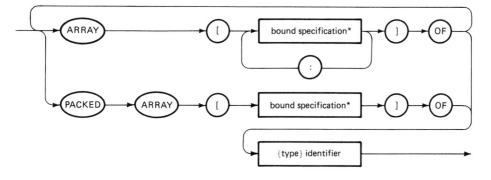

bound specification*

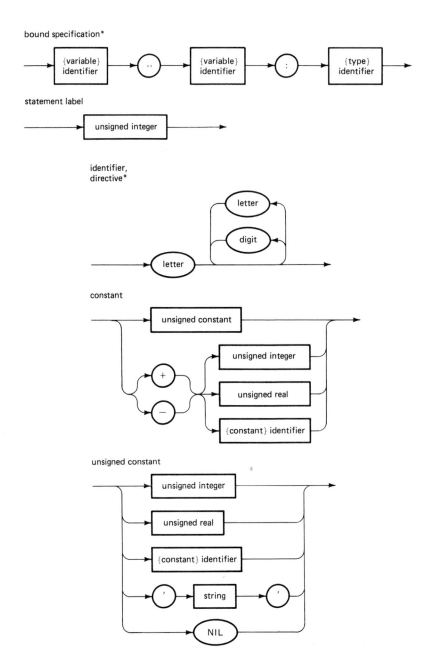

statement label

identifier,
directive*

constant

unsigned constant

string

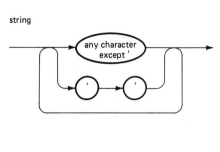

unsigned integer

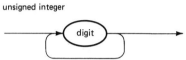

unsigned real

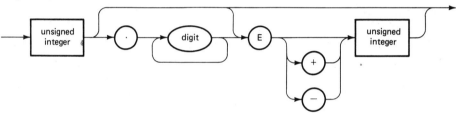

type

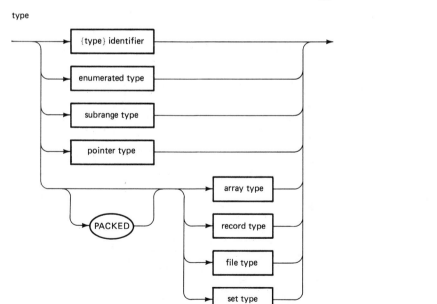

enumerated type

subrange type

pointer type

array type

record type

field list

variant

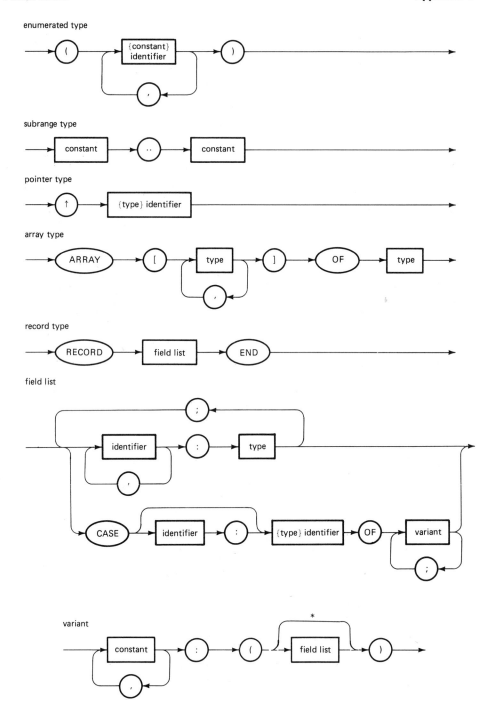

file type

set type

compound statement

statement

assignment statement

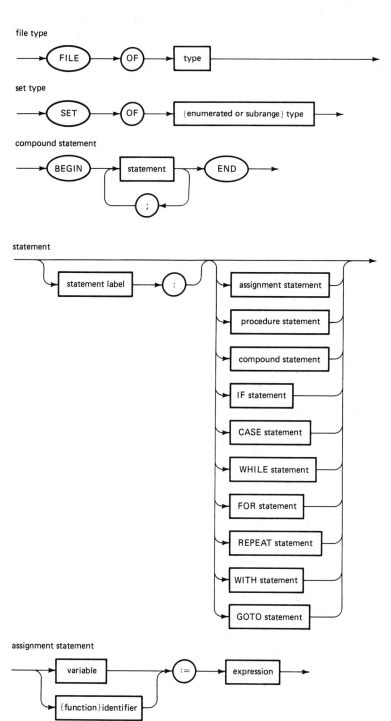

procedure statement

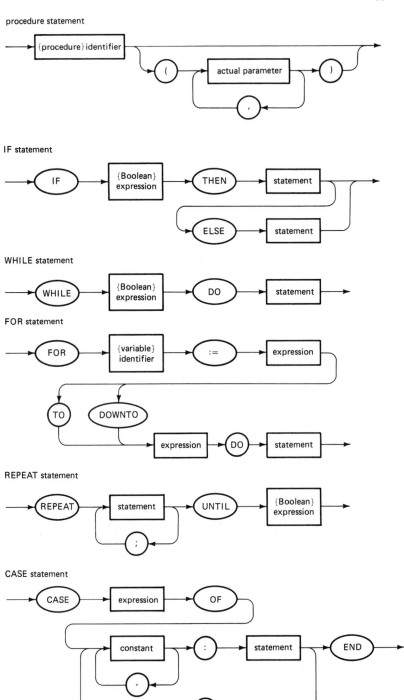

IF statement

WHILE statement

FOR statement

REPEAT statement

CASE statement

WITH statement

GOTO statement

actual parameter

expression

simple expression

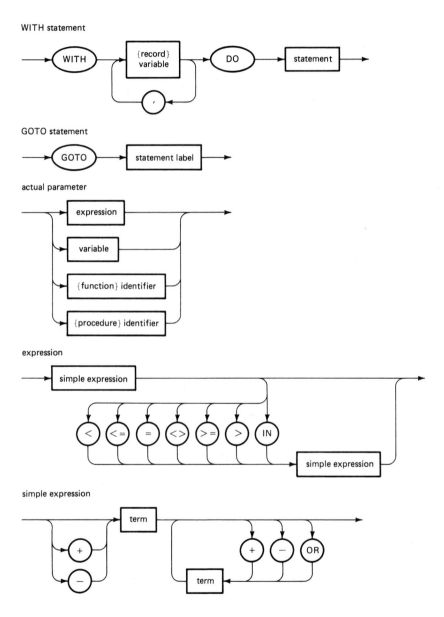

term

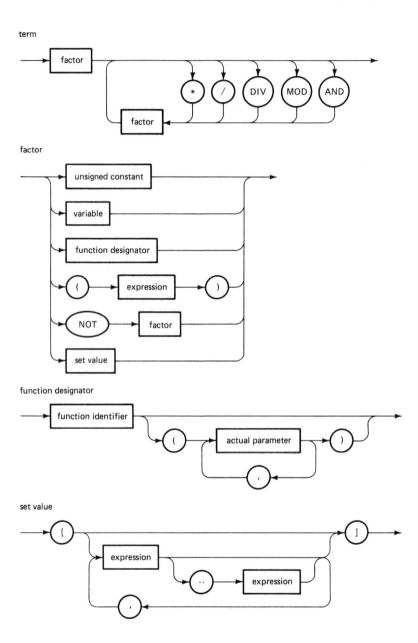

factor

function designator

set value

variable

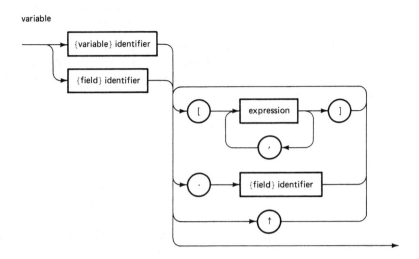

C.2 General rules.

C.2.1 Identifiers.

An identifier can be as long as desired, subject to the following rules.

1. No blanks (spaces) can be inside an identifier (this is one difference from FORTRAN).

2. An identifier cannot be divided between two lines (thus its maximum length is the length of a line, usually 80 characters).

3. Standard Pascal requires that, to be regarded as different, identifiers must differ somewhere in the first eight characters. (Many Pascal compilers relax this rule to recognize differences in any position.)

4. Small letters and capital letters can be used as desired (if both are available). Most, but not all, compilers treat small and capital letters as the same.

5. The following *reserved words* may not be used as identifiers, or for any purpose other than the uses specified for them in appropriate syntax diagrams:

and	downto	if	or	then
array	else	in	packed	to
begin	end	label	procedure	type
case	file	mod	program	until
const	for	nil	record	var
div	function	not	repeat	while
do	goto	of	set	with

6. Although it is not standard Pascal, some compilers allow the underscore character '_' within identifiers. How this symbol is treated depends on the compiler: it may be ignored, treated like a letter, or like a numeral.

7. The following **standard identifiers** are pre-defined as part of the Pascal language. It is legal for the programmer to use these identifiers for purposes other than the usual ones, but it is generally unwise to do so, since by declaring a different use the original use is lost. You can, for example, declare the word write to be a variable if you so desire, but if you do so you will be unable to use the standard procedure that writes to a file or the terminal. The complete list of standard identifiers follows.

abs	eoln	new	read	sqrt
arctan	exp	odd	readln	succ
Boolean	false	ord	real	text
char	get	output	reset	true
chr	input	pack	rewrite	trunc
cos	integer	page	round	unpack
dispose	ln	pred	sin	write
eof	maxint	put	sqr	writeln

8. See Section 1.3.1 for guidelines on choosing identifiers.

C.2.2 Rules for Spaces.

1. Spaces are never allowed inside identifiers, reserved words, numbers or the special symbols made up of more than one character (e.g. <=, <>, >=, :=).

2. At least one space must be included when needed to prevent one identifier, reserved word, or number from running into another (For example,

ForX:=AtoBdo

would be a syntactically correct assignment statement in Pascal if the variables were declared, not the beginning of a **for** loop).

3. Inside of apostrophes '···' (i.e., in a string constant) spaces are treated like any other character.

4. Except in the preceding cases, all spaces are ignored and may be inserted where desired.

5. The end of a line is treated in exactly the same way as a space, and therefore a statement can be continued from one line to the next at any place where a space is allowed.

6. A comment is treated in exactly the same way as a space, can be inserted wherever a space is allowed, and can be continued from one line to the next.

C.2.3 Guidelines used in book for program format.

The following guidelines for indenting are used in most, but not all, programs in this book.

1. The words **const, type, var,** and **record** appear alone on a line, unless the complete declaration easily fits on one line.

2. Only one item is declared per line, except when several logically related items share exactly the same declaration.

3. The lines containing items being declared are each indented slightly.

4. The word **begin** appears on a line by itself, except in the phrase **else begin**, which usually appears on one line.

5. The word **end** appears on a line by itself, and is lined up with the corresponding word or phrase **begin, else begin, case,** or **record.**

6. Statements or declarations between one of these words or phrases and its corresponding **end** are indented slightly.

7. A single statement immediately following one of the words **then, do, repeat,** or **else** is indented slightly, but the word **begin** is not indented after any of these words.

8. Normally only one assignment statement appears per line.

9. Each alternative of a **case** statement appears on a new line, indented slightly beyond the word **case.**

10. Blank lines are inserted in longer programs wherever needed to separate logical sections of the program.

11. In the text the declarations of functions and procedures are generally separated from that of the main program. When the declarations are inserted in their proper place, however, they are surrounded by enough blank space to show clearly where one subprogram stops and the next starts.

C.2.4 Punctuation.

The syntax diagrams provide precise rules for the punctuation of a Pascal program, and when difficulties arise, you should check the syntax diagrams to locate the errors. Even so, there remain several errors common for programmers new to Pascal, for which some guidelines and hints may help.

1. Items that Pascal is to treat in the same way are generally separated by commas, and items that may be treated differently by semicolons. Thus variables with exactly the same declaration are separated by commas, as are the indices in a (multidimensional) array, the actual parameters for a subprogram, and the alternatives sharing the same action in a **case** statement. On the other hand, semicolons separate declarations of variables of (possibly) different types, separate

different statements, separate formal parameters (which may be declared differently) of subprograms, and different alternatives in a **case** statement.

2. Semicolons are used to *separate* items or statements, not to *terminate* statements, as in PL/1. Hence Pascal uses fewer semicolons than PL/1.

3. The illegal inclusion or omission of a semicolon will usually not produce an error diagnostic for the line on which the error occurs, but will usually produce a strange and irrelevant diagnostic for the line *after* the error.

4. A semicolon is always illegal immediately before (or at the end of the line immediately preceding) one of the words

and	**downto**	**mod**	**or**	**set**
array	**else**	**nil**	**packed**	**then**
div	**file**	**not**	**program**	**to**
do	**in**	**of**	**record**	

Of all these reserved words, the only one likely to cause trouble is **else.**

5. A semicolon is almost never needed immediately after **begin** or immediately before **end** or **until,** but its redundant inclusion is not an error.

C.2.5 Alternative symbols.

On systems where certain standard symbols are not available, the following substitutions are made:

For ↑ or ∧ substitute @
For { and } substitute (* and *)
For [and] substitute (. and .)

C.3 Standard declarations.

C.3.1 Constants.

The predefined constants are false, true, and maxint.

1. Common values for maxint.

Most 8 and 16 bit machines: maxint = 32,767
Most 32 bit machines: maxint = 2,147,483,647
Most 60 bit machines: maxint = 281,474,976,710,655

2. ASCII codes for characters, with ordinals.

0 NUL	16 DLE	32 SP	48 0	64 @	80 P	96 `	112 p
1 SOH	17 DC1	33 !	49 1	65 A	81 Q	97 a	113 q
2 STX	18 DC2	34 "	50 2	66 B	82 R	98 b	114 r
3 ETX	19 DC3	35 #	51 3	67 C	83 S	99 c	115 s
4 EOT	20 DC4	36 $	52 4	68 D	84 T	100 d	116 t
5 ENQ	21 NAK	37 %	53 5	69 E	85 U	101 e ·	117 u
6 ACK	22 SYN	38 &	54 6	70 F	86 V	102 f	118 v
7 BEL	23 ETB	39 '	55 7	71 G	87 W	103 g	119 w
8 BS	24 CAN	40 (	56 8	72 H	88 X	104 h	120 x
9 HT	25 EM	41)	57 9	73 I	89 Y	105 i	121 y
10 LF	26 SUB	42 *	58 :	74 J	90 Z	106 j	122 z
11 VT	27 ESC	43 +	59 ;	75 K	91 [	107 k	123 {
12 FF	28 FS	44 ,	60 <	76 L	92 \	108 l	124	
13 CR	29 GS	45 −	61 =	77 M	93]	109 m	125 }
14 SO	30 RS	46 .	62 >	78 N	94 ↑	110 n	126 ~
15 SI	31 US	47 /	63 ?	79 O	95 _	111 o	127 DEL

Alternative symbols are:

Code 94 may print as ∧
Code 126 may print as ¬

3. EBCDIC codes for characters, with ordinals.

0 NUL	21 NL	43 CU2	79		124 @	150 o	195 C	227 T
1 SOH	22 BS	45 ENQ	80 &	125 '	151 p	196 D	228 U
2 STX	23 IL	46 ACK	90 !	126 =	152 q	197 E	229 V
3 ETX	24 CAN	47 BEL	91 $	127 "	153 r	198 F	230 W
4 PF	25 EM	50 SYN	92 *	129 a	155 }	199 G	231 X
5 HT	26 CC	52 PN	93)	130 b	161 ~	200 H	232 Y
6 LC	27 CU1	53 RS	94 ;	131 c	162 s	201 I	233 Z
7 DEL	28 IFS	54 UC	95 ¬	132 d	163 t	208 }	240 0
10 SMM	29 IGS	55 EOT	96 −	133 e	164 u	209 J	241 1
11 VT	30 IRS	59 CU3	97 /	134 f	165 v	210 K	242 2
12 FF	31 IUS	60 DC4	106 ⁞	135 g	166 w	211 L	243 3
13 CR	32 DS	61 NAK	107 ,	136 h	167 x	212 M	244 4
14 SO	33 SOS	63 SUB	108 %	137 i	168 y	213 N	245 5
15 SI	34 FS	64 SP	109 _	139 {	169 z	214 O	246 6
16 DLE	36 BYP	74 ¢	110 >	145 j	173 [	215 P	247 7
17 DC1	37 LF	75 .	111 ?	146 k	189]	216 Q	248 8
18 DC2	38 ETB	76 <	121 `	147 l	192 {	217 R	249 9
19 DC3	39 ESC	77 (	122 :	148 m	193 A	224 \	250	
20 RES	42 SM	78 +	123 #	149 n	194 B	226 S	

4. Mnemonic meanings of common control codes.

The *control codes* are the characters with ASCII ordinals of 32 or less, together with 127, or the EBCDIC characters with ordinals of 64 or less. These characters do not produce a visible printed output, but may produce special effects. The meanings of some of the common control codes are below.

NUL null (ignored)	HT horizontal tab	CR carriage return
ETX end of text	LF line feed	ESC escape
BEL rings a bell	VT vertical tab	SP space (blank)
BS back space	FF form feed	DEL delete

C.3.2 Types.

The predeclared types are:

```
integer
real
Boolean = (false, true)
char
text = packed file of char
```

The terms used to display various categories of types are shown in Figure C.1.

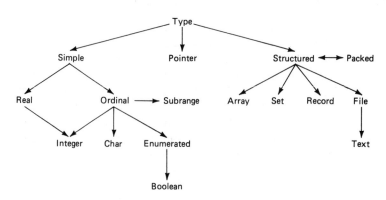

Figure C.1. Categories of types

C.3.3 Variables.

The only predeclared variables are the files, with type text,

Input   Output.

C.3.4 Procedures.

The predeclared procedures are:

For input and output:
    Reset,   Rewrite,   Get,   Put,   Read,   Write,   Readln,   Writeln,   Page

For pointer types:
    New,   Dispose

For packed data:
    Pack,   Unpack

C.3.5 Functions.

Name	Argument	Result	Action
Arithmetic functions			
Abs	integer, real	*same as arg.*	*Absolute value*
Sqr	integer, real	*same as arg.*	*Square of argument*
Sqrt	integer, real	*real*	*Square root of argument*
Exp	integer, real	*real*	*Exponential*
Ln	integer, real	*real*	*Natural logarithm*
Sin	integer, real	*real*	*Sine*
Cos	integer, real	*real*	*Cosine*
Arctan	integer, real	*real*	*Angle with given tangent*
Type conversion:			
Chr	integer	char	*Character with given code*
Ord	*ordinal type*	integer	*Ordinal code of argument*
Round	real	integer	*Rounds to closest integer*
Trunc	real	integer	*Truncates to integer part*
File processing:			
Eof	*file type*	Boolean	*Checks end of file*
Eoln	text	Boolean	*Checks end of line*
Miscellaneous:			
Odd	integer	Boolean	*Is integer odd?*
Succ	*ordinal type*	*same type*	*Next value in order*
Pred	*ordinal type*	*same type*	*Preceding value in order*

C.4 Operators.

Operator	*operand type(s)*	*result type*	*action*
Assignment:			
:=	*any type but file*	*same type*	*copies right operand to left*
Arithmetic:			
+	integer, real	*same type*	*addition or unary positive*
−	integer, real	*same type*	*subtraction or unary negative*
*	integer, real	*same type*	*multiplication*
div	integer	integer	*division with truncation*
mod	integer	integer	*remainder after* **div**
/	integer, real	real	*division*
Comparison:			
=	*any type but file*	Boolean	*equality*
<>	*any type but file*	Boolean	*not equals*
<	*any simple type*	Boolean	*less than, precedes*
>	*any simple type*	Boolean	*greater than, follows*
<=	*any simple type*	Boolean	*less than or equal to*
>=	*any simple type*	Boolean	*greater than or equal to*
Logical:			
not	Boolean	Boolean	*logical negation*
and	Boolean	Boolean	*conjunction*
or	Boolean	Boolean	*disjunction*
Set operations:			
+	*any set type*	*same type*	*set union*
*	*any set type*	*same type*	*set intersection*
−	*any set type*	*same type*	*set difference*
<=	*any set type*	Boolean	*set inclusion*
>=	*any set type*	Boolean	*set containment*
in	*left: ordinal type* *right: set of type of left operand*	Boolean	*set membership*
[ ]	*ordinal type*	**set of** *type*	*constructs set of operand(s)*

Priorities of operators.

Highest: 1. * / **div** **mod** **and**
            2. + − **or**
            3. = < <= > >= <> **in**
Lowest: 4. :=

Index

DATE DUE